John Dewey and Chinese Education

Beijing Normal University International Education Series

Series Editors

Xudong Zhu (*Beijing Normal University, PR China*)
Michael A. Peters (*Beijing Normal University, PR China*)
Tina Besley (*Beijing Normal University, PR China*)

Editorial Board

Ronald Barnet
Gert Biesta
James Conroy
Trevor Gale
Mingyuan Gu
David T. Hansen
Ruth Hayhoe
Kekang He
Ruyu Hung
Liz Jackson
Duck-Joo Kwak
Wing-on Lee
Zeus Leonardo
Jian Li
Jun Li
Mang Li
Ke Lin
Dian Liu
Yongcan Liu
Jeffrey Ayala Milligan
Greg William Misiaszek
Lauren Misiaszek

Lijuan Pang
Marianna Papstepanou
Klas Roth
Paul Standish
Hugh Starkey
Lynda Stone
Rob Tierney
Sharon Todd
Kwok Kuen Tsang
Jan Vermunt
Yusef Wahid
Chengbing Wang
Yingjie Wang
Liao Wei
E. Jayne White
Cora Lingling Xu
Binxian Zhang
Heyi Zhang
Huajun Zhang
Xinrong Zheng
Binglin Zhong

VOLUME 1

The titles published in this series are listed at *brill.com/bnie*

John Dewey and Chinese Education

A Centennial Reflection

Edited by

ZHANG Huajun and Jim GARRISON

BRILL

LEIDEN | BOSTON

All chapters in this book have undergone peer review.

The Library of Congress Cataloging-in-Publication Data is available online at https://catalog.loc.gov

Typeface for the Latin, Greek, and Cyrillic scripts: "Brill". See and download: brill.com/brill-typeface.

ISSN 2667-0704
ISBN 978-90-04-51145-3 (paperback)
ISBN 978-90-04-51146-0 (hardback)
ISBN 978-90-04-51147-7 (e-book)

Copyright 2022 by Koninklijke Brill NV, Leiden, The Netherlands, except where stated otherwise. Koninklijke Brill NV incorporates the imprints Brill, Brill Nijhoff, Brill Hotei, Brill Schöningh, Brill Fink, Brill mentis, Vandenhoeck & Ruprecht, Böhlau Verlag and V&R Unipress.
All rights reserved. No part of this publication may be reproduced, translated, stored in a retrieval system, or transmitted in any form or by any means, electronic, mechanical, photocopying, recording or otherwise, without prior written permission from the publisher. Requests for re-use and/or translations must be addressed to Koninklijke Brill NV via brill.com or copyright.com.

This book is printed on acid-free paper and produced in a sustainable manner.

Advance Praise for
John Dewey and Chinese Education: A Centennial Reflection

"A hundred years ago, Dewey came to China. His visit brought provocative ideas to Chinese academia then and made significant contribution to China's intellectual enlightenment. However, it was true that Chinese people in radical change were attracted by a more revolutionary program of social change, rather than the ameliorate pragmatism. Therefore, Deweyan fever soon vanished. Until the period of the 1980s and the 1990s, Chinese academia showed new interests in Dewey. Then, Chinese scholars realized that Dewey was not only a world-class philosopher and educator, but also Dewey's pragmatism shared many commonalities with Chinese traditional thoughts. More studies emerged on the dialogues between Deweyan philosophy, his philosophy of education and Chinese traditional thoughts. This book is a most updated and outstanding collection responding to this recent trend of Deweyan study. It includes works of the most excellent scholars in the related fields. The themes are about Dewey and China, Deweyan philosophy and its relation to education, etc. This is a must-read scholarly book with great value for readers who are concerned with these topics."
– CHEN Yajun, Director of Dewey Center at Fudan University, Professor of Philosophy at Zhejiang University, China

"In recent decades, an increasing amount and depth of dialogues between Western and Eastern traditions and perspectives has immensely enriched and advanced the field of international Dewey and pragmatism studies. As the director of the Dewey Center at the University of Cologne, Germany, I have had the pleasure of participating in numerous such conversations through cooperation with the Chinese Dewey Center at Fudan University in Shanghai, the US-American Center for Dewey Studies at Southern Illinois University in Carbondale and many others. The scope of how productive and challenging these dialogues are and how much they invite to a mutual reconsideration, reinterpretation and reconstruction of one's own philosophical and educational perspectives and backgrounds has deeply impressed me. The present book is a perfect example for the inspiring results of such intellectual exchanges. One hundred years after John Dewey's two years long stay in China, the contributions gathered here explore his historical impact on Chinese thought and education as well as the immense potentialities of dialogues between Western and Eastern traditions like pragmatism, Confucianism and Buddhism. They thereby highlight many important philosophical, educational, social, cultural, political, technological and ecological implications for more sustainable ways into a common global future."

– **Stefan NEUBERT, Professor of Education, Director of the Dewey Center, University of Cologne, Germany**

"This volume constitutes an absorbing study of the synergies, and differences, between John Dewey's philosophical outlook and Chinese philosophical traditions, particularly as they bear on contemporary educational thought and practice. The contributors are leading scholars of Dewey and of Chinese philosophy of education. They provide an enlightening comparative perspective that is informed by wide-ranging historical and philosophical analysis. They show why the interaction between Deweyan and Chinese ideas can become a transaction in which all such ideas are transformed in a truly generative manner. The book is a goldmine of insights and the contributors raise numerous questions for further research. It is a timely text in the scholarly world's promising efforts to bring Chinese and Western educational thought into a deeper dialogue."

– **David T. HANSEN, Past-President of the John Dewey Society and Weinberg Professor of Philosophy and Education, Teachers College, Columbia University, USA**

"This book on John Dewey's contribution to education in China embodies significant works by scholars in multiple disciplines from both China and the United States. Its publication on the centennial anniversary of his departure from China is to be celebrated for its timeliness. It surely marks a huge milestone in the research on this topic."

– **ZHANG Binxian, Professor of History of Education at Beijing Normal University, China**

Contents

Foreword IX
    Larry A. HICKMAN
Series Editors' Foreword XII
    ZHU Xudong, Michael A. PETERS and Tina BESLEY
Acknowledgements XIV
Notes on Contributors XV
Note on Original Publications XVIII

Introduction: A Centennial Reflection on Dewey's Visit of China: A
Renewed Dialogue on Becoming Persons 1
    ZHANG Huajun and Jim GARRISON

PART 1
Historical Reflections

1   John Dewey and Chinese Education: Comparative Perspectives and
Contemporary Interpretations 9
    SU Zhixin

2   Recent Studies in Mainland China on John Dewey's Visit to China
(1919–1921) 41
    ZHOU Hongyu and LI Yong

3   The Chinese Reception of Dewey: Three Enduring Errors 51
    Lei WANG

4   Why Did Hu Shi Introduce Deweyan Pragmatism to China as Only a
Method? 78
    ZHAO Kang

5   New Confucian Liang Shuming's Transformation of John Dewey's
Philosophy in Chinese Rural Education 93
    James Zhixiang YANG

6   A Seed Found Its Ground: John Dewey and the Construction of the
Department of Education at Beijing Normal University 114
    LIU Xing

VIII   CONTENTS

7   100 Years of Dewey in China, 1919–1921: A Reassessment   131
     Michael A. PETERS

PART 2
Philosophical Reflections

8   Mahayana Buddhism and Deweyan Philosophy   151
     Jim GARRISON

9   Confucianism and Deweyan Pragmatism: A Dialogue   168
     Roger T. AMES

10   Democratic Self-Cultivation   193
     Leonard J. WAKS

11   John Dewey and Early Confucianism on the Idea of
     Self-Cultivation   212
     ZHANG Huajun

12   Humanities Education in the Age of AI: Reflections from Deweyan and
     Confucian Perspectives   234
     Sor-hoon TAN

13   Education and the Reconstruction of a Democratic Society: Two Main
     Themes in Dewey's Philosophy of Education   254
     WANG Chengbing and DONG Ming

     Index   267

Foreword

It was with great delight that I received an advance copy of the essays, reviews, and other materials selected for inclusion in this book. The year of 2021 marks the 100th anniversary of Dewey's departure from China after 27 momentous months during which he lectured in most of China's provinces as they were then configured.

John and Alice Dewey arrived at Shanghai on April 30, 1919, just days before the May 4th student demonstrations which, when joined by workers' protests, precipitated an inflection point in Chinese political and cultural thought. As James Zhixiang Yang's essay in this volume argues, "the May Fourth movement provided scholars of a New Confucianism with an unparalleled opportunity to reform Confucianism." Very much in the vein of Dewey's pragmatic pluralism, the new Confucianism would be dedicated to synthesizing Confucianism, Buddhism, and Taoism and supporting the introduction of Western philosophy into China. As an internationally known advocate for progressive education, Dewey was in the right place at the right time. His lectures in Beijing, Nanjing, and elsewhere played an important supporting role in these political and cultural events, including the introduction of American-style school systems.

Readers wishing access to an expansive account of the relation of Neo-Confucianism to Deweyan pragmatism, as both continue to develop, can do no better than turn to Roger T. Ames' essay in this volume. Dewey's rejection of structural/analytic philosophical approaches in favor of genetic/functional models, for example, corresponds nicely to Neo-Confucianism "as a continuing cultural narrative [that] presents us with a rolling, continuous, and always contingent tradition out of which emerges its own values and its own logic."

Most of the contributions to this volume continue the conversation regarding the relation between Deweyan pragmatism and Confucianism. The papers by Zhang Huajun and Len Waks discuss Confucian self-cultivation. Waks suggests ways the Confucian emphasis on the reverential study of classics and ritual performance can enhance Dewey's democratic educational project. Zhang identifies many similarities between Dewey and Confucian thinking about individual self-cultivation to suggest ways education can create transactionally inclusive relationships in the context of global conflict.

Zhang's paper builds on Zhao Kang's contribution showing that Dewey's pragmatism was initially presented to China as merely a method. Meanwhile, Lei Wang identifies other problems with Dewey's initial reception in China. All three papers discuss and correct errors in Dewey's original reception that still persist, thereby clearing the way for more fruitful conversations in the future.

Su Zhixin examines important differences between Chinese and American views on Dewey's influence on Chinese education during three different periods of China's history (the first 30-years, 1949–1979, and post 1979). Michael Peters offers some provocative criticisms of Dewey especially in the Chinese context. Zhou Hongyu and Li Yong provide a valuable review of the most recent studies on Dewey's visit to China while offering useful suggestions for future research. Also looking toward the future, Sor-hoon Tan intersects Confucianism and Deweyan thinking regarding the role humanities in response to the global transformations brought on by Artificial Intelligence (AI). By revisiting the idea of "home education" Wang Chengbing and Dong Ming provide an original response to critics that underestimate Dewey's claims regarding the educational and democratic value of working from local communities toward what Dewey called "the Great Community."

Jim Garrison enriches the conversation further with his discussion of the relation of Dewey's process philosophy to central ideas of Nichiren Buddhism. Both approaches avoid the pitfalls of perfectionism, that is, the idea that we are progressing to some ideal end. Both are nevertheless committed to meliorism, that is, the idea creative intelligence can improve existing conditions as we find them. As Daisaku Ikeda, the world's leading practitioner of Nichiren educational thought has said, "religion is important, but education is equally important."

Although there are many institutional players in the growing interest in Dewey's educational philosophy among Chinese educators, three stand out. The role of East China Normal University Press in the continuing revival of interest in Dewey's educational philosophy has been enormous. Their publication of translations of the 37 volumes of Dewey's *Collected Works* under the editorship of Liu Fangtong has altered the landscape of Dewey studies in China. Beijing Normal University's Department of Education, founded in 1919 shortly after Dewey's arrival (see Liu Xing's contribution to this volume), has also played an important role in dissemination of his ideas. Fudan University's Center for Dewey Studies was instrumental in the translation of Dewey's *Collected Works* and has for some two decades sponsored international conferences focused on East-West interpretations of his work.

In this brief Foreword it has been possible only to scratch the surface of the delights that await the readers of the essays in this volume. Together, they testify to Dewey's idea that education is the cornerstone of philosophy, and not merely one of its sub-disciplines. For Dewey, Nichiren Buddhism, and Neo-Confucianism alike, education is the warp on which the tapestry of a culture, including its philosophy, is woven. Local cultures, with their histories, rituals, and ideals provide one educational reference point. Another is provided by goals and aspirations of a common humanity. Without education, as the growth of individuals and communities, including global communities, the cultural tapestries would be threadbare and slack.

On August 8, 1921, John and Alice Dewey departed China, sailing from Tsingtao on the first leg of their journey back to their home in New York. But as his correspondence reveals, China and its people remained in his heart. Now, 100 years later, it is important to recognize that despite some intervals of interruption and eclipse, there is an important sense in which Dewey never left China.

Larry A. HICKMAN
Director Emeritus, Center for Dewey Studies
Southern Illinois University Carbondale

Series Editors' Foreword

The *Beijing Normal University International Education Series* (BNIE) is mainly based on the special issues of the *Beijing International Review of Education* (BIRE), the official English journal of Beijing Normal University, as an occasional volume in international educational theory and empirical education science. The series is a means for reaching a wider audience especially for journal issue-based themes that are enduring.

Since being established in 2019 and having published 8 issues up until the end of 2020 (4 issues per year), the journal *Beijing International Review of Education* is focused on the critical issues in the field of education and includes issues such as "The Future of Teaching," "John Dewey and Chinese Education: A Centennial Reflection," "Visual Inquiry in Educational Research," "Play in Childhood," and "Digital Youth." In these issues, well-established scholars and emerging younger scholars around the world have contributed with their recent research. In the future, we will have more policy-oriented issues to emphasize the important international themes in education with also a specific section of the journal devoted to "China Watch," alerting readers to major new initiatives in Chinese education. It is a broadly conceived review of educational issues. We consider the journal, and this book series (BNIE), as significant platforms to exchange the pioneering research in educational studies. We want to provide high quality research of educational study on society, culture, and economy and to develop cutting-edge new research of interest to academics, policy makers, teachers and postgraduate students. The series also has the capacity to published books that expand on journal themes and also to adopt new themes and issues.

Both the book series and the journal BIRE is published by Brill. We are very happy that we have this opportunity to collaborate with Brill, which is both very professional and very open to the ideas we proposed.

In today's world, the trajectory of globalization has become more uncertain and faces many serious challenges. It is even more important to have a global vision and make the continuous international exchange of ideas possible. We wish that the *Beijing Normal University International Education Series* will play its role on exchanging ideas and we invite more scholars around the world to join us by contributing to this series.

ZHU Xudong
Dean, the Faculty of Education, Beijing Normal University

SERIES EDITORS' FOREWORD

Michael A. PETERS
Distinguished Professor, the Faculty of Education, Beijing Normal University

Tina BESLEY
Distinguished Professor, the Faculty of Education, Beijing Normal University

Acknowledgements

This book is the fruit of a multilateral collaboration. First, we would like to thank the Faculty of Education at Beijing Normal University for their support in preparing this book. Second, we would like to thank the book series editors Zhu Xudong, Michael Peters, and Tina Besley for their trust and support. We are very honored to edit this book as the first in the Beijing Normal University International Series. Also, we would like to thank all the authors for their contributions to this study of Dewey's visit to China. To some extent, this internationally collaborative book project historically echoes Dewey's dialogue with his Chinese friends a hundred years ago. By deliberate efforts like this one, we hope to establish an organic connection and continuity with that historical episode. Thanks also go to Brill for allowing us to reprint selected articles as well as to the publisher, John Bennett, for his professional and timely guidance. We would like to thank John Wiley and Sons Company for permission to reprint Roger Ames's chapter "Confucianism and Deweyan Pragmatism: A Dialogue". Finally, we would like to thank Carrie Wilson for her help proofreading and editing.

Notes on Contributors

Roger T. AMES

is Humanities Chair Professor of Philosophy at Peking University, and Professor of Philosophy Emeritus at the University of Hawai'i. He has translated a number of the Chinese philosophical canons and has also authored several interpretative studies of Chinese philosophy and culture.

DONG Ming

is a Ph.D. candidate in the School of Philosophy at Beijing Normal University. His research field is American pragmatism.

Jim GARRISON

is Professor of Philosophy of Education at Virginia Tech University. Although he is widely published in many fields, his specialty is pragmatism, especially the pragmatism of John Dewey. Jim has books and papers in 11 languages.

Larry A. HICKMAN

is the Director Emeritus of the Center for Dewey Studies and emeritus professor of philosophy at Southern Illinois University, Carbondale. He is a past president of the John Dewey Society and an internationally recognized authority on the philosophy of John Dewey.

LI Yong

(Ph.D., 2012) is Associate Professor of Modern Chinese Education History and American Chinese Education History at South-Central University for Nationalities (China). He published books on the history of Chinese modern education, including *Exclusion and Acceptance: A Historical Review of Chinese Education in San Francisco (1848–1943)* (Wuhan: Huazhong University of Science and Technology Press, 2015).

LIU Xing

(Ph.D., 2018, Hiroshima University) is International Research Fellow at Hiroshima University, and a Lecturer at Faculty of Education, Beijing Normal University. He is currently studying the history of Chinese education from a global perspective, based upon archives in China, Japan and U.S.A. He has published more than 20 articles in academic journals of China, England, America and Japan.

Michael A. PETERS

is Distinguished Professor of Education at Faculty of Education, Beijing Normal University and Emeritus Professor at the University of Illinois at Urbana–Champaign. He is the executive editor of the journals, *Educational Philosophy and Theory* and *The Beijing International Review of Education*.

SU Zhixin

(Ph.D., 1989) is Professor of Education at California State University, Northridge. She was selected as the Dewey Lecturer for the 2019 Annual Conference of the American John Dewey Society, and has published numerous research articles in American, European and Chinese journals and books, including *American Journal of Education, Oxford Review of Education, Teachers College Record*, and *International Review of Education*.

Sor-hoon TAN

(Ph.D., 2000, University of Hawaii) is Professor of Philosophy at Singapore Management University. She has published monographs and articles on comparisons of Pragmatism and Confucianism.

Leonard J. WAKS

is Distinguished Professor of Educational Studies at Hangzhou Normal University. He has earned doctorates in philosophy and psychology and has taught at Purdue, Stanford, Penn State and Temple universities. He is a past president of the John Dewey Society and has been awarded the Society's lifetime achievement award.

WANG Chengbing

is Professor of philosophy at the School of Philosophy and Sociology, Shanxi University (China). He is Associate Editor in Chief of the English journal *Frontiers of Philosophy* in China. His interests include pragmatism, postmodern philosophy, and the theory of identity.

Lei WANG

(Ph.D., 2019) teaches Educational Science at University of Cologne, Germany. She published on Studies in Deweyan Education as well as intercultural understanding. Her thesis *John Dewey's Democratic Education and Its Influence on Pedagogy in China 1917–1937* (Springer, 2019) is published in English and German.

NOTES ON CONTRIBUTORS

James Zhixiang YANG
(Ph.D., 2016, University of Oklahoma) is Assistant Professor of the Chinese Language and Culture Centre and the Program of Chinese Culture and Global Communication at BNU-HKBU United International College. Dr. Yang has published some articles on Dewey and Confucius.

ZHANG Huajun
is Associate Professor at the Faculty of Education, Beijing Normal University. She has published books and articles on philosophy of education and teacher education, both in English and Chinese, including *John Dewey, Liang Shuming and China's Education Reform: Cultivating Individuality* (Lexington, 2013).

ZHAO Kang
(Ph.D., 2009, University of Exeter) is Associate Professor of History and Theory of Education at Zhejiang University, China. He has published monographs, translations and many articles on educational history and theory, including *Learning, Identity and Narrative in the Late Modern Age* (ZJU Press, 2014).

ZHOU Hongyu
(Ph.D., 1991) is Professor of Educational History and Educational Policy Research at Central China Normal University. He published books on Chinese education history and Chinese education policy, especially study on Tao Xingzhi, including *Research on Tao Xingzhi from a Global Perspective* (Beijing Normal University Press, 2015).

Note on Original Publications

The following chapters are reprints and were originally published as:

Chapter 1: SU, Zhixin. (2019). John Dewey and Chinese education: Comparative perspectives and contemporary interpretations. *Beijing International Review of Education, 1*(4), 714–745.

Chapter 4: ZHAO, Kang. (2019). Why did Hu Shi introduce Deweyan pragmatism to China as only a method? *Beijing International Review of Education, 1*(4), 658–672.

Chapter 5: YANG, James Zhixiang. (2019). New Confucian Liang Shuming's transformation of John Dewey's philosophy in Chinese rural education. *Beijing International Review of Education, 1*(4), 673–694.

Chapter 6: LIU, Xing. (2019). A seed found its ground: John Dewey and the construction of the Department of Education at Beijing Normal University. *Beijing International Review of Education, 1*(4), 695–713.

Chapter 7: PETERS, Michael A. (2019), 100 years of Dewey in China, 1919–1921: A reassessment. *Beijing International Review of Education, 1*(1), 9–26.

Chapter 8: GARRISON, Jim. (2019). Mahayana Buddhism and Deweyan philosophy. *Beijing International Review of Education, 1*(4), 609–625.

Chapter 9: AMES, Roger. (2003). Confucianism and Deweyan pragmatism: A dialogue. *Journal of Chinese Philosophy, 30*(3–4), 403–417.

Chapter 10: WAKS, Leonard J. (2019). Democratic self-cultivation. *Beijing International Review of Education, 1*(4), 626–644.

Chapter 13: WANG, Chengbing, & DONG, Ming. (2019). Education and the reconstruction of a democratic society: Two main themes in Dewey's philosophy of education. *Beijing International Review of Education, 1*(4), 645–657.

INTRODUCTION

A Centennial Reflection on Dewey's Visit of China

A Renewed Dialogue on Becoming Persons

ZHANG Huajun and Jim GARRISON

In *Analects*, Confucius once said, "Is it not delightful to have friends coming from distant quarters?" This quotation could perfectly apply to John Dewey's visit of China from 1919 to 1921. Dewey and his wife Alice Dewey received enthusiastic welcome when they arrived in Shanghai on April 30th just a few days before the start of the historical event of the May Fourth Movement that began on May 4th, 1919. In recent decades, there has been a steady spate of publications relating to Deweyan studies on China written by both Chinese and international scholars in the fields of education and other disciplines, primarily philosophy. However, in light of the turbulent history of such scholarship in China over the last 100 years, the recent burgeoning of Deweyan studies in China and on China should not be taken for granted. Instead, it should be viewed in the context of China's developmental trajectory that has entailed highly complex social and political conditions.

Here is a brief summary of the reception of Dewey's thought in the past hundred years. Before and after Dewey's visit of China, Dewey's thought was enthusiastically explored by intellectuals and youth, mainly in the latter part of the 1910s and in the early 1920s. Many of Dewey's works were translated into Chinese, and his pragmatic philosophy was seriously considered a potential approach for promoting China's social development. However, it was soon replaced by Marxism. Later, during the period of 1949–1976, Dewey's philosophy was completely rejected in mainland China as he was perceived to be a capitalist enemy. However, after China initiated the open-and-reform policy after 1978, he was once again acclaimed and recognized as an important Western thinker. Dewey's philosophy acquired renewed value among scholars from different disciplines and was re-introduced to Chinese audiences. It is conceivable that scholars and students in the field of education may be the most appreciative members of Dewey's readership.

On the other hand, in recent decades, there has been a resurgence of interest in Dewey's philosophy in the West that began with Richard Rorty. Following Rorty (1979), an increasing number of intellectuals has acknowledged the

© KONINKLIJKE BRILL NV, LEIDEN, 2022 | DOI:10.1163/9789004511477_001

problems associated with liberal atomistic individualism and the crisis of individual-centered democracy (e.g., Rockefeller, 1991). Many western scholars have proposed exploring different resources for democracy and have sought to acquire intellectual resources from other schools of thought, such as Confucianism and Buddhism (e.g., Nevillie, 1985; Ames & Hall, 1999; Grange, 2004; Garrison, 2019). Regarding the comparative study of Confucianism and pragmatism, scholars have suggested that the cultivation of relational beings holds promise for renewing and strengthening democracy. Thus, the legacy of Confucianism, which highlights the harmony of a communitarian living and considers self-cultivation to be the key to education, is appealing.

Dewey's emphasis on the intellectual, ethical, and aesthetic experiences of the individual resonates with the idea of self-cultivation in such Eastern philosophies as Confucianism and Buddhism. The commonalities between Deweyan pragmatism and the Eastern philosophies are also indicative of a possible vision for a new humanism in the contemporary world where clashes and violence are prevalent. The western critiques of humanism have been devastating; however, they leave Eastern humanism untouched. It is interesting that Dewey is entirely compatible with Eastern humanism, which integrates the human being into nature and recognizes the social nature of the self. Also, we hold that to illuminate Dewey's legacy for Chinese education in the global context, it is necessary to consider his philosophy as a whole as opposed to extracting the part focusing on education from the wider body of his pragmatic thought. This exercise requires in-depth dialogue among scholars from different disciplines as well as from different societies, which is the primary objective of this book.

By discussing Dewey's philosophy in historical context as well as with the comparative perspective, we try to highlight the view of Dewey's philosophy that shares commonalities with Eastern philosophies. That is, humanness of the person could be learned and could be ameliorated. This humanism is based on the continuous efforts of self-cultivation so that the transformation of daily experience from "the ordinary into the extraordinary" is possible (Ames, 2019: 557). In Confucian language, learning to become a person is conducted through the practice of self-cultivation. It is exactly on this point of "person-becoming" through the practice of self-cultivation in daily life that the meaning of Dewey's encounter with China in the 21st century is renewed. Also, it is on this point that the discussion of Dewey's philosophy in the context of Chinese modern history inspires new value in the idea of philosophy as "the general theory of education" if we consider the adventure of "person-becoming" as a synonym of education.

1 Structure of the Book

In the first part of the book (Chapters 1 to 7), we aim to assess the historical value of Dewey's visit of China and to examine how and to what extent his legacy holds lessons for contemporary development in China. The authors review the studies on Dewey's visit of China and examine the historical and social values of this event. Also, some chapters pose new questions on this historical episode and clarify some popular misunderstandings. In the second part of the book (Chapters 8 to 13), the authors explore the commonalities between Dewey's philosophy and Eastern philosophies, mainly Buddhism and Confucianism. Dialogues are proposed between Dewey and Eastern philosophies on the themes of self-cultivation, person becoming, humanistic education and constructing democratic communities.

Now, we will briefly introduce the content of each chapter. Su Zhixin's chapter titled "John Dewey and Chinese Education: Comparative Perspectives and Contemporary Interpretations" provides a literature review of Chinese education over the past century that addresses the concern regarding the historical value of Deweyan scholarship. The author examines the major differences between Chinese and American critics' views on Dewey's influence on Chinese education in different historical periods. Zhou Hongyu and Li Yong's chapter titled "Recent Studies in Mainland China on John Dewey's Visit to China (1919–1921)" focuses on the recent studies on this topic by Chinese scholars in mainland China. Through the review, the authors provide a detailed historical landscape of this event. They also provide several directions for future studies on the historical event of Dewey's visit of China. Lei Wang's chapter titled "The Chinese Reception of Dewey: Three Enduring Errors" discusses three misunderstandings in the Chinese reception of Dewey's basic ideas of democratic education and their enduring philosophical, educational and political consequences. Through analyzing historical materials, the author points out the misinterpretation of Dewey's conception of inquiry and experience as the first error, the misinterpretation of the tension between individual and society as the second error, and the misinterpretation of the "child-centered" method as the third error in the reception of Dewey in China. The author concludes that the correction of these errors would help us to learn from Dewey better in today's context. Zhao Kang's chapter titled "Why Did Hu Shi Introduce Deweyan Pragmatism to China as Only a Method?" discusses how Dewey's Chinese disciple Hu Shi transformed Dewey's thoughts in Chinese context during the May Fourth Movement period. Zhao argues that Hu Shi's deliberate introduction of Dewey's pragmatism to China as only a method was influenced by Hu's worldview of materialistic naturalism, which was very different from Dewey's radical empiricism. Also, Zhao examines the particular sociopolitical context in Hu's time and the impact of Hu's academic inclination on Chinese traditional textual research. James Zhixiang Yang's chapter titled "New Confucian Liang Shuming's Transformation of John Dewey's Philosophy in Chinese Rural Education" describes the efforts of Liang Shuming, a modern Confucian and a contemporary of Dewey, towards the objective of reforming Confucianism in a modern society. Interestingly, while Liang Shuming was considered a conservative by such liberal intellectuals as Hu Shi, Liang found Dewey's pragmatic philosophy compatible with his Confucian program of modernization. Yang's study provides a complex and subtle landscape of thoughts in that period. Liu Xing's chapter titled "A Seed Found its Ground: John Dewey and the Construction of the Department of Education at Beijing Normal University" examines the historical event of Dewey's influence on the construction of the department of education at Beijing Normal University during Dewey's visit of China from 1919 to 1921. He uses archival sources available at Beijing Normal University to examine Dewey's role in the construction of China's first department of education. This study provides a detailed example of Dewey's impact on China's modern education.

Michael Peters' chapter titled "100 Years of Dewey in China, 1919–1921: A Reassessment" serves as a transitional chapter in this book from the historical review to philosophical study. This chapter mainly uses Dewey's *Letters* and his *Lectures in Social and Political Philosophy, 1919–21* given on invitation at the University of Peking. The author poses some criticisms of Dewey's pragmatism for the lack of contextualism. The book then turns to the second part on the philosophical dialogues between Deweyan pragmatism and Eastern philosophies. Jim Garrison's chapter titled "Mahayana Buddhism and Deweyan Philosophy" identifies several dimensions of congruence between Mahayana Buddhism and Deweyan pragmatism, including the nature of knowledge, the nature of humans, and the relationship between life and the environment. This perspective was rarely discussed in Deweyan scholarship. It indicates a potential direction for more dialogues between Deweyan philosophy and Chinese traditional thoughts, with Buddhism obviously being an influential one. Roger Ames's chapter titled "Confucianism and Deweyan Pragmatism: A Dialogue" highlights the common vocabulary of Deweyan pragmatism and Confucianism. For example, he juxtaposes Dewey's social concept of individuality with the Confucian notion of person-becoming as well as Dewey's idea of religious humanism and Confucian human-centered religiousness. By doing this dialogical analysis, he highlights the potentiality of ordinary life experience to achieve a religious sensibility that contributes to human flourishing. Leonard Waks' chapter titled "Democratic Self-Cultivation" draws on Confucian self-cultivation education with the aim of enhancing Dewey's democratic education project, raising up interesting but controversial issues, such as classical study and ritual practice in contemporary Western Schools. The author suggests that we can invent new rituals to replace customary rituals in school life so that new rituals can help build democratic social relationships for a better world. Zhang Huajun's chapter titled "John Dewey and Early Confucianism on the Idea of Self-cultivation" echoes the same themes of individuality and self-cultivation as Ames' and Waks' chapters. She examines the philosophy of experience in Dewey's later works and relates it to Dewey's conception of individuality. She argues that the new understanding of Dewey's philosophy of experience can be connected to the tradition of early Confucianism on the idea of self-cultivation, which is a creative and dynamic process of transaction between the individual and the world. Sor-hoon Tan's chapter titled "Humanities Education in the Age of AI: Reflections from Deweyan and Confucian Perspectives" critically examines the role of humanities in education in response to the opportunities and challenges of the widespread use of artificial intelligence (AI). She suggests that both Confucianism and Dewey's pragmatism provide insights on the humanistic purpose of education in the age of AI. She highlights the shared vision of Dewey and Confucianism on personal cultivation and growth, which is still relevant in today's world. Finally, the book concludes with Wang Chengbing and Dong Ming's chapter titled "Education and the Reconstruction of Democratic Society: Two Main Themes in Dewey's Philosophy of Education." It considers "the growth of the individual" to be the key to understanding Dewey's philosophy of democracy. Even though they do not connect this idea of "the growth of the individual" with the Chinese tradition of "becoming persons," their connection to Dewey's idea of democracy and growth helps clarify some main misunderstandings of Dewey's thoughts, such as Dewey's method of intelligence, the so-called purposelessness of education, and the idea of growth, which were often misinterpreted in Chinese academia. The authors defend Dewey's call to develop the local community for the sake of the Great Community. This call is more important now than ever before.

2   Additional Notes

This book originated in a special issue, "John Dewey and Chinese Education: A Centennial Reflection," published in the journal *Beijing International Review of Education* (Vol. 1, No. 4, 2019). We included seven research articles from the special issue and invited six more authors to join this book project.

Readers may notice that there are many Chinese names and references in this issue. We adopted the pinyin (拼音) romanization system to denote

Chinese names. However, because the pinyin system was adopted after 1958 in the mainland of China, Chinese names used before that time, or those used outside of the mainland, were based on the earlier Wade-Giles romanization system. For example, Hu Shi is the spelling based on the pinyin system, whereas Hu Shih is the spelling based on the Wade-Giles system. In some chapters, we have retained the spelling based on the older system used in some of the references while also providing the pinyin romanization and the Chinese characters; for example, Hu Shih (Hu Shi, 胡适) is used to enhance readability. Another source of confusion relating to Chinese names concerns the order of the appearance of the family and first names. Articles written in English generally follow a convention in which the first name appears before the family name. However, for the Chinese names appearing in this issue, we have applied the Chinese convention in which the family name appears first, followed by the first name; for example, Tao Xingzhi (陶行知) is used to respect the traditional style and integrity of the names.

References

Ames, R. (2019). Dewey and Confucian philosophy: A dialogue on becoming persons. In S. Fesmire (Ed.), *The Oxford handbook of Dewey*. Oxford University Press.

Ames, R., & Hall, D. (1999). *The democracy of the dead: Dewey, Confucius, and the hope for democracy in China*. Open Court.

Dewey, J. (1916/1944). *Democracy and education*. The Free Press.

Garrison, J. (2019). Nichiren Buddhism and Deweyan pragmatism: An eastern-western integration of thought. *Educational Studies*, *5*(1), 12–27.

Grange, J. (2004). *John Dewey, Confucius, and global philosophy*. SUNY Press.

Nevillie, R. C. (1985). Wang Yangming and John Dewey on the ontological question. *Journal of Chinese Philosophy*, *12*, 283–295.

Rockefeller, S. (1991). *John Dewey: Religious faith and democratic humanism*. Columbia University Press.

Rorty, R. (1979). *Philosophy and the mirror of nature*. Oxford University Press.

PART 1

Historical Reflections

CHAPTER 1

John Dewey and Chinese Education

Comparative Perspectives and Contemporary Interpretations

SU Zhixin

Abstract

It has been widely claimed that no Western scholar has exerted greater influence on Chinese education than the American education philosopher John Dewey, who visited and lectured in China for more than two years between 1919 and 1921. A comparison of Chinese and American scholars' evaluations of Dewey's impact on Chinese education reveals many contradictions and controversies, especially in China during different historical periods. This paper examines the major differences between Chinese and American critics' views on Dewey's influence on Chinese education, with a focus on the dramatic changes in Chinese scholars' perspectives in three distinct stages: from early praise and positive acceptance during the first 30 years after Dewey's visit to China (1919–1949), to severe criticism and rejection over the next 30 years (1949–1979), and then to new interpretations since China's opening up to the outside world in 1979. Although Dewey and his education theories were first extolled and then abandoned in China, they have received open and warm reappraisals from Chinese educators in recent decades and have emerged from rejection to renewed appreciation in Chinese education. To fully understand the significance and implications of Dewey's visit to and lectures in China, both Chinese and American Dewey scholars need to create and sustain continued dialogue on this most fascinating episode in the intellectual histories of China and the US.

Keywords

John Dewey – Chinese education – comparison and evaluation – US–China relations

1 Introduction

The year 2019 marks the 100th anniversary of John Dewey's historic visit to China in 1919. Although the American Philosophical Society (APS) has been silent about Dewey's impact on China, the John Dewey Society (JDS), an influential

© KONINKLIJKE BRILL NV, LEIDEN, 2019 | DOI:10.1163/9789004511477_002

educational philosophy research association affiliated with the American Educational Research Association (AERA), decided to establish "Dewey in/and China: Cultural Transformation & Progressive Education in International Settings Today" as the major theme for its 2019 annual conference. The author was invited to deliver the keynote speech at this annual event on the topic of "John Dewey and Chinese Education" because of her earlier studies on Dewey and China and her significant publications in the US on the comparative analysis and critical evaluation of Dewey's influence on Chinese education (Su, 1995, 1996). She became the first Chinese scholar to be honored as a Dewey Lecturer in the history of the JDS. Former JDS Dewey Lecturers have included John Goodlad, Lee Shulman, Lawrence Cremin, Larry Hickman, Nel Noddings, Jeannie Oakes, Diane Ravitch, Eliott Eisner, Herbert M. Kleibard, Philip Jackson, Maxine Greene, and other prominent American education scholars.

The 2019 JDS annual conference was well attended by both American and international researchers, including a large number of Chinese scholars. This was in striking contrast to the 1994 Dewey Symposium, where the author was the only Chinese scholar in attendance and likely the first researcher to present on the topic of Dewey's influence on Chinese education at a JDS conference. Her work was immediately recognized by Philip Jackson, JDS president at the time, as the "most exciting Dewey scholarship" and subsequently published in the *American Journal of Education* (Su, 1995) and *Teachers College Record* (Su, 1996). Unfortunately, only a small cadre of scholars in the US has made an effort to inquire into this topic. In fact, most Americans, including educators and philosophers, seem to be unaware of this important historical episode in Dewey's life and in US–China relations. Meanwhile, since his visit to China commencing in 1919, Dewey has become the most controversial Western philosopher in China. His education theories have been widely studied but also heavily criticized by Chinese educational scholars in their efforts to learn from the West in relation to China's educational development and reform.

In this paper, the author reviews the historical background of Dewey's visit to China, examines major differences between Chinese and American critics' views on Dewey's influence on Chinese education, and evaluates the dramatic changes in Chinese scholars' perspectives on Dewey and his theories during several distinct historical periods: from acceptance of and eager experimentation using his ideas in the first 30 years following Dewey's visit to China (1919–1949), to severe criticism and total abandonment of Dewey's theories in Chinese education over the next 30 years (1949–1979), and then to new understandings of Dewey's philosophy in the era of opening up and modernization since the normalization of US–China relations in 1979, with a focus on contemporary interpretations of Dewey's influence on Chinese education over the last decade.

2 Historical Background

While traveling extensively in China from 1919 to 1921, John Dewey lectured to large audiences on social and political philosophy, the philosophy of education, ethics, and the main trends in modern education. Although he visited many nations and regions during his lifetime, Dewey spent more time and exercised more influence on education in China than in any other foreign country (Hu, 1962; Clopton & Ou, 1973). China had become, according to Dewey's daughter, the country nearest to his heart, after his own (Jane Dewey, 1939). Dewey visited China at a very significant moment in Chinese history. When the First Opium War (1840–1842) revealed the decay and decline of the feudal dynasty and heightened the social crisis in China, many Chinese intellectuals recognized the need to learn Western science and technology to reform the old system of education, which was characterized by Confucian learning and imperial examination that emphasized memorization rather than reasoning. Once they rejected the past models, they were eager to search for Western ideas that might be relevant to China.

By the turn of the century, the more Westernized elements in China had seized control, and the moment of transition from the old to the new arrived with the outbreak of the famous May Fourth Movement in 1919, a nationwide student movement opposing Japanese imperialism and domestic Chinese corruption (Chow, 1960; Keenan, 1977). In every sphere of social activity the old order was challenged, attacked, undermined, or overwhelmed by a complex series of processes – political economic, social, ideological, and cultural – that were set in motion in China as a result of the penetration of the dominant, expanding, and powerful Western Europe and America (Teng & Fairbank, 1954). Because many of the leaders of the May Fourth Movement had studied abroad, they turned to philosophers of education in other countries for ideas and models to rebuild China. Dewey, then an established scholar in American educational philosophy and a professor at Columbia University, was called upon by his former students in China to address the professors and students of the new Chinese universities, to offer suggestions concerning the best intellectual approach to reality, and to indicate just what adaptations China should make to survive both nationally and internationally in the new world order. As Smith (1985) observes, Dewey clearly saw his own capacities and the orientation of his thoughts as both appropriate and adequate for the task. He also saw himself, as his lectures in China amply demonstrate, as well-prepared to teach his audiences ways to live and to think in an age of science and technology, and how to understand the possibilities and problems attendant on the development of a democratic form of government (Hughes, 1938; Su, 1995).

Dewey's lectures in China were largely based on three of his books, *The School and Society* (1899), *Democracy and Education* (1916), and *Reconstruction in Philosophy* (1920), a part of which contained the substance of the lectures he had recently given in Japan. A number of Dewey's former students interpreted his lectures into Chinese. For several of his major series of lectures, his Chinese hosts selected competent journalists to report every lecture in full for the daily newspapers and periodicals. What came to be known as "Dewey's Five Major Series of Lectures" in Beijing, totaling 58 lectures, were recorded and reported in full and later published in book form, with ten large reprints even before Dewey left China in 1921, and continued to be reprinted for three decades until the founding of the People's Republic of China. Later, most of Dewey's written works were translated into Chinese in mainland China, Taiwan, and Hong Kong, and have been used as key textbooks in Chinese teacher-training institutions. His lectures in China were also republished by major Chinese education presses.

In addition to giving lectures, Dewey took part in educational conferences and met with educational and political leaders, including Dr. Sun Yat-sen, leader of the Chinese revolution that overthrew the last feudal dynasty. Bankers and editors frequented his residences, teachers and students flocked to his classrooms, clubs competed to entertain him and to hear him speak, and newspapers vied with each other to translate his latest utterances. His speeches and lectures were eagerly read, and his biography had been elaborately written. Serious-minded scholars commented on his philosophy, while common audiences grew familiar with his name. A group of his Chinese disciples followed him from city to city and regarded him as a sort of modern-day sage, a source of explanation of modernity in the West (Keenan, 1977). At one point, Dewey was even likened to Confucius, especially after his Chinese friends learned that his sixtieth birthday in 1919 fell on the day that the rotating lunar calendar indicated was the birth date of Confucius. Chinese and American critics who have commented on Dewey's visit to China all agree that Dewey enjoyed the warmest welcome of all the foreign scholars who have visited China, both past and present. There is no dispute in this regard.

3   American Evaluation of Dewey's Influence on Chinese Education

In evaluating Dewey's influence on Chinese education, American and Chinese scholars differ in several fundamental ways (Su, 1995). In the United States, the central point of contention is whether the Dewey experiment in China – the legacy of his ideas – is in large part a success or a failure. Clopton and Ou (1973), in their introduction to the English translation of *John Dewey, Lectures in China, 1919–1920*, claimed that Dewey's influence on Chinese education was profound. They argued that of all the Western educators, Dewey most influenced the course of Chinese education, both in theory and in practice, and observed that Dewey's philosophy of education dominated the teaching of educational theory in all Chinese teachers' colleges and in university education departments for many years. His *Democracy and Education* was used everywhere, and most of his major works were translated into Chinese. In addition, both during and after his visit to China, numerous articles, books, and pamphlets were published to introduce and interpret Dewey's philosophy of education. Some of his most widely used phrases – "education is life," "school is society," and "learning by doing" – were familiar at all levels of the Chinese educational world. Thus, "Dewey became the highest educational authority in China, and there were many more converts to his views in Chinese educational circles than among professional philosophers" (Clopton & Ou, 1973: 22).

The success of Dewey's experiment in China can also be seen in practice in earlier years, according to Clopton and Ou (1973). First, Chinese educational aims were reconsidered in the light of Dewey's thoughts in the 1920s. While the old educational aims emphasized military education modeled on the Japanese pattern, the new goals embraced the aim and spirit of American education: "the cultivation of perfect personality and the development of democratic spirit." Second, the national school system was reformed according to the American pattern – the 6-3-3 plan – and governed by a set of principles advocated by Dewey that aimed "to promote the spirit of democracy," "to develop individuality," "to promote education for life," and "to facilitate the spread of universal education." Third, child-centered education predominated in the revision of the curriculum. Fourth, new methods of teaching in accord with Dewey's theory of pragmatism were initiated. Fifth, experimental schools multiplied. Sixth, student government was widely extended as a mode of school discipline. Seventh, literary reform was encouraged, and elementary school textbooks written in the vernacular were adopted. Finally, and most importantly, Dewey's essential ideas were advanced and adapted in practice by his former students and disciples in China, most notably Hu Shih, Tao Xingzhi, and Chen Heqin, who became famous educators in China. On the basis of these examples, Clopton and Ou concluded that Dewey's influence on Chinese education was both profound and extensive.

While not disagreeing with Clopton and Ou on their observations regarding the various changes in Chinese education that resulted from Dewey's visit, Berry (1960), Sizer (1966), Pavela (1970), and Keenan (1977) maintained that Dewey's experimentalism in China was, ultimately, largely a failure. They seemed to believe that although Dewey greatly impressed his Chinese audiences, he did not leave a lasting message. The opportunity to build a strong belief in the humanitarian ideals of the West and in democracy as a system of values was not fully exploited. As a distinct political party, the democratic movement envisaged by Dewey was never successful in China. They observed that although Dewey's influence was considered to be original and decisive in relation to education, opposition to his influence was also very strong. First came the opposition from Confucian scholars who objected to the iconoclastic attitude adopted toward the cultural traditions of the past. Second, the Marxist challenge to Dewey was even more effective than that of the Confucians. Marxism began to awaken in the Chinese a response of great depth and enthusiasm, and in the 1920s, it was already winning the allegiance of many professors and students throughout the country. In comparison, the liberal bourgeois democracy and American pragmatism represented and advocated for by Dewey offered a less dynamic political and educational program than that of Marxist proletarian Communism and dialectical materialism. Eventually, the majority of Chinese intellectuals saw a valid picture of the modern world in the Chinese Communist Party, while the order supposed by Dewey's liberalism simply failed to develop in a chaotic Old China (Berry, 1960). As Billings (1981–82) insightfully pointed out, Dewey's problem was that he could not provide the necessary bridge between old Chinese tradition and modern Western liberalism. The October Revolution taught the young Chinese intellectuals that Western liberalism could be bypassed and Communism could be adopted directly. Grieder (1970, 1972) in his discussion of Hu Shih (Hu Shi, 胡适) and the Chinese renaissance – the May Fourth experience – also concluded that the Chinese liberals failed because they were overwhelmed by the confluence of two great historical movements, one traditional, the other modern, both of which equated politics with the totality of human experience and obscured the distinction between public and private, thus denying the importance of individual liberty. Dewey and the Chinese liberals considered this to be a key condition without which a true political order could neither come into being nor survive.

What is clear is that it was the political arena that ultimately mattered to China at that time. Deweyan experimentalism – as a way of thinking, as a way of acting politically, and as a component of democratic education – offered no strategy that Dewey's followers could use to affect political power in China. Without such a strategy, failure was the main consequence of his followers' pragmatic reform efforts. Their reformism was paralyzed by dilemma. Dewey himself recognized this failure after his visit to China, writing: "The difficulties in the way of a practical extension and regeneration of Chinese education are all but insuperable. Discussion often ends in an impasse: no political reform

JOHN DEWEY AND CHINESE EDUCATION

of China without education; but no development of schools as long as military men and corrupt officials divert funds and oppose schools from motives of self-interest. Here are the materials of a tragedy of the first magnitude" (Dewey, 1983: 231). The experimentalist philosophy, conceived in a rich, literate, industrial, and relatively serene America and propagated by well-intentioned but somewhat sheltered Chinese intellectuals, was in many ways not appropriate for a huge, varied, agricultural, particularistic country like China.

The American evaluation of Dewey's influence on Chinese education has taken some new turns in recent decades. While studying as a doctoral student at Indiana University, Jessica C. S. Wang conducted in-depth research on Dewey's experiences in China as a learner (Wang, 2007). This was a new and thought-provoking appraisal of the significance of Dewey's visit to China. Her main goal was to redress the imbalance of previous studies in the US that had neglected to consider the ways in which Dewey himself might have been influenced by his Chinese experience. She concluded that Dewey had learned as much as he taught during his stay in China. Viewed from this perspective, Dewey's visit to China was a great success in terms of his personal growth and learning, providing a fine example of the value of educational exchange visits and cross-cultural learning for other educators and their students.

Indeed, many American scholars and students have followed in Dewey's footsteps by visiting and learning from China in the four decades since China's opening up. Most recently, to celebrate the 100th anniversary of Dewey's seminal visit to China, a group of high school students from the University of Chicago Laboratory Schools, the Chicago Charter Schools, and the Laboratory School's Beijing partner high school retraced Dewey's steps in China. Moderated by Larry Hickman, former Director of the Center for Dewey Studies at the University of Southern Illinois, the American and Chinese students who participated in this historical journey shared their unique experiences at the 2019 Centennial Colloquium on "Dewey, Then and Now," held at the University of Chicago Laboratory Schools, which was founded by Dewey more than 100 years ago. The students observed that even though they could learn about China from newspapers and academic texts, the conversations they had with peers in China around Dewey's ideas and his ideals for the Laboratory Schools on this trip taught them so much more. American Dewey scholars can now claim that Dewey's trip to China 100 years ago is successfully influencing a new generation, although it has only impacted a limited number of young people thus far (Braendel, 2019). Dewey himself would have loved seeing students in his Laboratory Schools having this kind of learning experience – learning by doing and traveling the routes that he took, reflecting on real-life experiences, and discussing and debating ideas with peers and educators in China.

4 Chinese Evaluation and Reception of Dewey in the First 30 Years (1919–1949)

In China, studies of the Deweyan influence and experiment in China have not focused on its success or failure, unlike American studies, but have concentrated on the positive and negative aspects of Dewey's ideas and influence as measured by Chinese political ideology and educational needs during different historical periods. While American scholars do not question Dewey's sincerity in promoting the development of a democratic society or the worthiness of Dewey's educational philosophy, the Chinese have been involved in constant debates over the intentions and worthiness of Dewey's ideas for Chinese schools and society; some praise him as a saint, while others condemn him as an enemy. In many ways, it has been an ideological struggle between Dewey's pragmatism and experimentalism and Marxist–Leninist Communism, which began soon after Dewey's visit to China (Su, 1995).

During the first 30 years after Dewey's historic visit to China, Dewey's pragmatic educational theory dominated the Chinese educational field. Nearly all of his educational works were translated into Chinese, and his influence was apparent in major Chinese educational publications (Zhou, 1991). The Chinese education system underwent a significant transformation based on the American model and Dewey's ideas (Ou, 1970; Clopton & Ou, 1973). The most successful of Dewey's experiments in relation to Chinese education was the establishment and operation of the Morning Village Normal School (1927–1930) by Tao Xingzhi, a former student of Dewey, who creatively transformed Dewey's theories of "life as education," "school as society," and "learning by doing" to "education as life," "society as school," and "unity of teaching, learning, and reflective acting," respectively, in his tireless efforts to improve China's rural education and society (Su, 1996; Chu, 2019). Tao was the first of Dewey's Chinese followers to develop his own system of educational theory and practice, and the first to seek to extend Dewey's influence from the city to rural areas. Forced to close by the Nationalist Army in 1930, the Morning Village Normal School was re-opened in 1949, and has since evolved into Nanjing Xiaozhuang (Morning Village) University and become a national model for training elementary and rural school teachers. Tao continued to apply Dewey's theories in his practices in other educational institutions and communities in China up until his death in 1946. His creative adaption of Dewey's ideas into the Chinese education context from the 1920s to the 1940s is still considered a shining example for modern Chinese educators (Su, 2018; Zhang, 2019).

Another famous Dewey-inspired experiment during this period was the creation of child-centered and experience-based preschools in China by Chen

Heqin, also a former student at Columbia University, although he did not study directly under Dewey. As a faculty member at the Nanjing Higher Teacher Education Institute when Dewey visited China, Chen was an active participant in Dewey's lectures and served as his translator on several occasions. He and Tao Xingzhi shared Dewey's thoughts on the nature of education and educators' roles in education. Based on Dewey's theory of "education as life," Chen developed a theory of "live education" with more than 30 principles and established experimental preschools that emphasized learning by doing and participation in real-life experiences in nature and the wider society. Chen had great admiration for Dewey's Laboratory Schools in Chicago, and closely followed the Laboratory Schools model when developing preschools in China. Chen's preschools were widely regarded as a successful product of the fusion of Chinese and Western educational thoughts (Ke & Peng, 2019).

While Dewey's disciples and their liberal journals extolled Dewey's theories on education and democracy as a very positive force and the greatest hope for building a new China, a large number of intellectuals had been won over by the Communist cause, and the remaking of China along Marxist lines had begun in the universities of China and in the publications that appeared during these decisive years. In fact, the Chinese Communist Party was founded during the two-year period that Dewey spent in China (Passow, 1982). Eventually, the Communists obtained superior standing among the intellectuals, particularly the professors and students, who found it difficult to accept the West as a teacher, but saw in socialism a practical philosophy through which they could reject both the traditions of the Chinese past and the Western domination of the present (Hsu, 1970). To them, Western ideas as presented by Dewey were more negative than positive for China. Such a psychological climate did not work to the advantage of Dewey's teaching (Ching, 1985), although Tao Xingzhi and Chen Heqin's experiments based on Dewey's ideas were still considered relevant to China, and continued to operate in the New China.

It should be noted that as a young activist in the May Fourth Movement, the Chinese revolutionary leader Mao Zedong attended Dewey's lectures in the spring of 1920. Mao not only was familiar with Dewey's theories, but also highly recommended Dewey's *Five Major Lectures*, and included it in his initial stock when he opened a revolutionary bookstore in Hunan later that year (Yu, 1991). Clearly, Dewey's ideas exerted considerable influence on the young Mao's mind. Later, however, Mao chose Marxist–Leninist Communism over Dewey's pragmatism and experimentalism, as did many other young Chinese intellectuals at that time. Dewey lived to see the establishment of the New China – the People's Republic of China – in 1949, and watched as his closest followers, including Hu Shih, left mainland China.

5   Chinese Evaluation and Rejection of Dewey in the Closed-door Period (1949–1979)

At the founding of New China in 1949, Mao Zedong (1949) officially denounced Dewey's intellectual followers and the form of cultural influence the United States had exerted in China as "imperialist spiritual aggression." Mao identified Dewey's students with the United States, an association that implied support of the defeated Nationalists.

In the new republic, the ideological struggle intensified in the 1950s, characterized by severe criticism and total denial of Dewey's experimentalism and his followers in China. The movement began with two articles by Cao Fu (1950, 1951), "Introduction to the Criticism of John Dewey, Parts 1 and 2," in the official education journal, *People's Education* (《人民教育》). Ironically, Cao was a graduate of the University of Colorado, having done his doctoral dissertation on the topic of "The Individual and the Society in John Dewey's Educational Philosophy," thereby establishing himself as a promising Dewey scholar before he returned to work in Chinese educational institutions. Cao urged that criticism of Dewey should begin with a critique of his anti-Marxist, reactionary position, both in his lectures in China and in his writings on political and social philosophy. Cao analyzed the fundamental differences in the political and philosophical positions of Marx and Dewey, and labeled Dewey as the "biggest obstacle to the cause of building the people's education" (Cao, 1950). Following his lead, other Chinese scholars launched unrelenting attacks on Dewey and accused him of being "a sly enemy disguised under a progressive mask" (Teng, 1957), "a supporter of American imperialism" (Wang, 1954), and "a guardian of modern imperialist forces," "a defender of criminal acts of Wall Street bosses," "a speaker for reactionary forces all over the world," and "an enemy of the Chinese people and all people in the world who love peace and freedom" (Chen, 1957). Dewey was portrayed as a deliberate supporter of the capitalist system and a vicious enemy who tried to use education as a means of reproducing the evils of Western society (T. Zhang, 1955; J. Zhang, 1955; Zhu, 1956).

Ching (1985) was correct in her observation that the Chinese reactions to Dewey in the 1950s were entirely negative. There was no longer any discussion of pros and cons, nor any impartial analysis of Dewey's thoughts and influence. It is interesting to note here that in the United States, as early as the 1930s some scholars had argued that there were striking similarities between Dewey and Marx in their methodological commitment, and Dewey himself admitted that his experimentalism was most closely aligned to some form of democratic socialism (Hook, 1976; Gavin, 1988). In addition, while Dewey was attacked in socialist China as anti-Marxist and a defender of imperialism, he has been criticized for his leftist, socialist Marxist tendencies in Taiwan (Liu, 1990) and the United States (Tanner, 1994). Nevertheless, in the 1950s, Dewey's pragmatic educational philosophy was considered to be totally incompatible with the prevailing educational philosophy in China. The words "malicious," "ridiculous," "reactionary," "fallacy," "sly," "dirty," and "ugly" were constantly used to describe Dewey and his ideas (Su, 1995). Such descriptions were not limited to Dewey, but rather were typical of critiques of every intellectual of any influence, Chinese or Western, during this period.

The most severe attack on Dewey was launched by his former disciple, Chen Heqin, who actively promoted Dewey's theories and practices in moderniz-ing China's preschool system in the first 30 years following his visit to China. In the 1950s, Chen was forced to denounce Dewey during the course of his public "confession of error": "As one who has been most deeply poisoned by his reactionary educational ideas, as one who has worked hard and longest to help spread his educational ideas, I now publicly accuse that great fraud and deceiver in the modern history of education, John Dewey!" (Chen, 1955: 2–3). Thus, Dewey's educational theories were thoroughly criticized in China during the 1950s. The first target was his opposition to education with an external end and his claim that "education is all one with growing; it has no end beyond itself" (Dewey, 1916: 53). When this was translated into Chinese, it was often referred to as "Dewey's notorious theory of education without a purpose," which is quite different in meaning from Dewey's original intention. Never-theless, Chinese critics argued that Dewey was using this claim as a disguise for his real position, that is, education should only have individual, temporary, small goals and not social, future, larger purposes. Dewey's real intention, the Chinese critics said, was to cheat the working-class people and prevent them from demanding the establishment of new educational goals based on their interests (Cao, 1955; Li, 1956).

In addition to the so-called theory of education without a purpose, Dewey was condemned by his Chinese critics in the 1950s for his emphasis on chil-dren's interests and experiences in the educational process (Su, 1995). He was blamed for the lack of discipline, lack of teacher authority, and therefore the lack of rigorous teaching and learning in schools. Furthermore, Dewey's argu-ment that "education is life" and "school is society," which was literally imple-mented in some Chinese schools from the 1920s to the 1940s, was interpreted as an attempt to eliminate a formal curriculum, systematic knowledge, and formal schooling, which were considered essential elements for a good educa-tion in China (Li, 1956). By the end of the 1950s, Dewey's educational theories had been rendered totally worthless, and were considered to be poisonous and harmful in China. Deliberate efforts were made to eliminate his influence from all spheres of Chinese society. In the 1960s and 1970s, Chinese intellectuals, including the most severe Dewey critics, were heavily involved in the chaotic Great Cultural Revolution (1966–1976), and many became targets for criticism and punishment, having been labeled "capitalist roaders" and "bourgeois intellectuals." Dewey and his theories were largely ignored, if not totally abandoned during these decades (Su, 1995, 2019).

6 Chinese Reevaluation and Reception of Dewey in the Open-door Era (1979–2009)

With the normalization of relations between the US and China in 1979, China began to open up to the outside world and embarked on a speedy path to modernization and globalization. Dramatic changes have taken place since then in China's social and political climates and in its relationship with the outside world. Since 1980, more than six million Chinese students and scholars have gone abroad to study, most of whom have landed in the United States. By 2018, more than 360,000 Chinese students were studying in various educational institutions in the US (IIE, 2018). Many American scholars and students have also traveled to China to study, although the number of American students studying in China (less than 12,000 in 2017) is much smaller than the number of Chinese students studying in America. By the mid-1980s, Chinese colleges and universities had already established extensive educational exchange and cooperation programs with the Western world (Hayhoe & Bastid, 1987). Deng Xiaoping's political and economic pragmatism paved the way for Chinese intellectuals to turn once again to Western pragmatism.

Under these circumstances, a serious reevaluation of Dewey's influence on Chinese education began to emerge among Dewey scholars in China in the 1980s. Some critics suggested that the worthiness of certain elements of Dewey's educational philosophy and its status in the history of philosophy should be revisited. They recommended that instead of totally rejecting Dewey, China should selectively borrow Dewey's ideas and make use of them in Chinese educational practices (see, for example, Zhao, 1980; Wang, 1982; Meng, 1985; Wu, 1985; Xia, 1985a; Zheng, 1985; Wang, 1986; Li, 1987; Liu, 1987). In 1982, the second annual meeting of the Chinese Society for the Study of Educational History included special panels on Dewey that received enthusiastic responses from many scholars. They proposed that the study of Dewey's educational theories should be conducted with an open mind and result in an honest, matter-of-fact evaluation (Xia, 1985b). Some even quoted Lenin in support of their efforts to reevaluate Dewey: "We should transform the most rich cultural tradition, knowledge, and skills accumulated in the capitalist society from a means for capitalism into a means for socialism" (Chen, 1982: 86). A Chinese scholar studying in the United States went so far as to note the striking similarities between Dewey and Mao (Xu, 1992) in terms of their educational theories and practices. He observed that "although Dewey and Mao emerged from completely different cultures, times, and contexts, their theories had amazing similarities. Their logs, 'learning by doing' (Dewey) and 'learning by practicing' (Mao), ring a similar note. Moreover, their views on the significant connections between school and society, the social role of education, the role of experience in learning, and their stress on moral education overlap a great deal" (Xu, 1992: 3).

Within such a positive political atmosphere, the Chinese evaluation and reception of Dewey was in many ways drastically different from the observations on Dewey made by Chinese scholars in the 1950s. The focus was no longer on whether Dewey's educational theories were positive or negative influences politically, but on the contributions that Dewey had made to world education, the similarities between Dewey and Chinese educators and politicians, and the usefulness of his ideas for the improvement of China's educational practices in modern times. For example, Chen Jingpan, who had used the most derogatory terms in his harsh criticism of Dewey in the 1950s, barely mentioned any of those terms in his new essays on Dewey in the 1980s (Chen, 1957, 1982, 1985). The much-criticized theory of "education without a purpose" was subject to reappraisal and a more accurate interpretation of Dewey's original meaning. Shi (1985) pointed out that the conclusion drawn in the 1950s in relation to Dewey's theory of educational purpose was too simplistic and subjective, and thus unfair. He cited different arguments from Dewey's works to demonstrate that as a pragmatist, Dewey firmly believed in the role of education as a means of social reform for a democracy; thus, he had a very clear social goal for education. Zhang (1989) also observed that Dewey had a strong focus on society in his discussion on creating a balance between individual growth and social development in the educational process. Zhang further quoted from Dewey's lectures in China, which offered explicit warnings to Chinese educators against pursuing education without a purpose.

Dewey's theories on the curriculum and instruction also received a positive reevaluation in China in the new era (Yuan, 1983). A major area of contention in the 1950s was Dewey's emphasis on organizing class activities around the children's experiences, needs, and interests (Chen, 1952), his delegation of a facilitator's role to classroom teachers (Liu, 1955; Fu, 1957), and his promotion of "learning by doing" (Chen, 1956; Liu, 1955). In reassessing Dewey, many Chinese scholars seemed to agree that his ideas represented a forceful and revolutionary criticism of the empty formalism in the old education system, although they were not sufficiently constructive to replace the traditional, teacher-centered, discipline-oriented education model (Wu & Zhao, 1988). These scholars maintained that child-centered activities with teachers as facilitators could serve as a supplement to, rather than a replacement of, the existing teacher-centered curriculum. However, some Chinese critics, such as Zhao (1982), Wu (1985), Meng (1985), Ren (1985), Wang (1986), and Zhang (1989), provided a different perspective on this issue. They pointed out that while emphasizing children's interests, needs, and activities, Dewey also attached great importance to the role of the teacher, who continued to have both the authority and the obligation to help students in their studies. The teacher's role was even more difficult than it had been before. They recognized that Dewey had sharply criticized those schools that misunderstood his theory on independent thinking and neglected the role of the teacher and other adults in the schools. Furthermore, they now understood that Dewey dialectically and appropriately handled the relationship between the child, the teaching materials, and the curriculum, and that this was a significant contribution to education (Zhang, 1989).

Also emerging in China in the 1980s was a new interpretation of Dewey's theory of "learning by doing." In the 1950s, the critics argued that Dewey overemphasized the process of knowing and neglected the consequences of this process knowledge, which was best represented by systematically organized academic subjects, as in a traditional education model. They concluded that students in Deweyan schools, both in the United States and in China, "know how to think, but have no knowledge" (Cao, 1950). In reevaluating Dewey's ideas on this issue, Zhao (1980, 1982) argued that Dewey did not oppose learning organized by subject matter, but was merely against spoon-feeding students with prepackaged knowledge that was disconnected from students' experiences and therefore could not be understood by them. By advocating "learning by doing," Dewey encouraged students to acquire useful knowledge by solving problems in their own everyday activities organized around different types of knowledge. Meng (1985) also had a high regard for Dewey's "learning by doing," and observed that Dewey's method built an excellent connection between theory and practice and motivated students to make the necessary effort to learn. In between these contrasting interpretations, Wu (1985: 76) offered an eclectic position: "We do not want children to learn by doing, but we do not oppose children's participation in practice. We can experiment with different structures of curriculum to create conditions for children to apply what they learn in practice". Essentially, this position wanted to maintain the traditional teacher-centered, discipline-oriented classrooms, but at the same time create extra "learning by doing" activities for the students. Thus, in this view, Dewey's ideas were of limited use in improving Chinese educational practices. Some Chinese educators had labeled these types of extra activities as "the second classroom," or "the second channel of learning" (Wang, 1984). In reality, most Chinese classrooms in the 1980s were still highly traditional, teacher-centered, and textbook-oriented, with very few hands-on activities for the students (Su, 1989). In a comparative study of science education in the United States and China that the author conducted in the early 1990s, the participating visiting Chinese scholars were impressed by the student-centered, real-life, experience-oriented science classrooms in American schools. They took a particular interest in the activity curriculum and the project method, which were the natural products of the Dewey theory (Ou, 1961). The Chinese scholars all expressed a desire to recommend these models to Chinese schools, although they also recognized the weakness of these methods, namely, the lack of emphasis on systematic knowledge and theoretical reasoning (Su, Z., Su, J. & Goldstein, 1994). In fact, this central concern continued to be a major deterrent to experiments based on Dewey's ideas and American models in Chinese educational practices even after Dewey's theories came to be viewed under a favorable light in the open-door era.

By the end of the twentieth century, Dewey's reputation in China had been effectively rehabilitated, with more objective and mostly positive evaluations by Dewey scholars in key positions, as Liu Fangtong (1996) claimed in his summary of the reevaluation of Dewey's pragmatism in China. He observed that Dewey was the most familiar Western philosopher to Chinese academics, but also the most misunderstood, and deserved to be reevaluated. Liu alleged that the severe criticism of Dewey in the 1950s was politically motivated and mostly delivered by critics who did not fully understand Dewey's philosophy. He invited Chinese educators to reconsider Dewey's recommendations for progressive reform in China, and went on to establish the Center for Dewey and American Philosophy Studies at Fudan University in 2004, which was renamed the Dewey Center in 2014. The Center immediately took on the task of translating all 37 volumes of Dewey's Collected Works into Chinese, which took 11 years and involved nearly 100 experts and translators from all over China. Thus, by the beginning of the twenty-first century, Chinese educators, heavily influenced by what they had learned from the West, were once again eager to make changes in Chinese education, although they were not quite ready to totally abandon the established system. They saw the necessity of incorporating useful elements from Western education, including Dewey's ideas, into the Chinese system, but they also tried to avoid going to extremes, such as "traditional education" as represented by Confucius's and Herbart's educational theories or "modern education" as represented by the more radical reformers in society. In many ways, they were searching for a viable alternative, a "third way," or "the Chinese way," as Zhang (2019) termed it later, and Dewey's philosophy became a valuable guide at this point.

7 Contemporary Interpretations of Dewey's Influence (Since 2009)

In the decade since 2009, Chinese education scholars have developed more positive interpretations of Dewey's influence and offered a more enthusiastic welcome to Dewey's ideas, which marked the beginning of a new wave of interest in Dewey in the twenty-first century. First, Dewey's progressive philosophy and humanistic approach have been found to be highly relevant to the core spirit of and new emphasis on students as individuals and centers of attention in China's new plans for educational reform and development for 2010–2020 that were published by the Chinese National Ministry of Education in 2010 (MOE, 2010). New reform directions in Chinese education are focused on quality education and the holistic development of students, hands-on experience and problem-solving skills, the cultivation of creativity and critical thinking, attention to students as individuals with various potentials and interests, and moral education. Hence, Chinese scholars have found considerable support for these goals in Dewey's theories (Liu, 2011; Zhang, 2013, 2019; Su, 2019). For the first time in the history of Chinese education, the new national plans promote the goals of helping individuals to pursue freedom, happiness, and liberation, and these goals are exactly what Dewey wanted to achieve through his educational ideas. Second, Chinese scholars now believe that Dewey's theory on the importance of experience in education has special implications for reform of the curriculum and instruction in Chinese education (You, 2014). In addition, because China's new social reform places a heavy emphasis on creating a harmonious society, Chinese scholars are finding inspiration and commonality in Dewey's theories on building a democratic society with associated living, good communication and shared interests for all the people (Zhang, 2013).

A major manifestation of the remarkable acceptance of Dewey's ideas in China was the publication of *The Complete Works of John Dewey* in Chinese by East China Normal University (ECNU) Press in 2015. This publication contains 38 volumes, and was edited by Liu Fangtong, then Director of the Dewey Center at Fudan University. Fudan University and ECNU jointly held a "Complete Works of John Dewey (in Chinese) Release" press conference at Fudan University, with about 50 Chinese and American scholars in attendance, including

Larry Hickman, then Director of the Center for Dewey Studies at Southern Illinois University, Carbondale, and Roger Ames, a notable American Dewey scholar at the University of Hawaii. At the same time, the International Symposium on Dewey and Pragmatism Studies was convened by the Dewey Center at Fudan University. In addition to serving as the major organizer and coordinator of the translation and publication of the *Complete Works of John Dewey*, the Dewey Center has also initiated and hosted annual conferences on pragmatism studies in China and served as an important platform for communication between Chinese and international scholars (Su, 2019).

Another outstanding event in relation to the reevaluation and study of Dewey in China over the past decade was the 2016 Academic Forum on the "Continuing Transformation of Education, Democracy and Experiences" in celebration of the centenary of the publication of Dewey's book *Democracy and Education* at ECNU. Several leading education scholars from ECNU's International and Comparative Education Institute delivered speeches on the relevance of Dewey's theories to modern Chinese education development and reform. While Zhou Yong suggested that Chinese educational policy researchers should learn from Dewey in conducting comprehensive, in-depth investigations of the transformation of Chinese society over the past few decades to determine the best direction for China's "new education" and develop China's own educational theories, Cheng Liang expounded on Dewey's ideas regarding "experience and education" and compared Dewey's concepts with traditional concepts relating to experience. However, the most forceful presentation at this forum was delivered by Peng Zhengmei, a senior scholar affiliated with ECNU's International and Comparative Education Institute. He explored Dewey's educational theories from a critical perspective and observed that Dewey's goals in education were to cultivate active citizens with critical thinking skills, which has become a major goal in Chinese education today. Therefore, he regarded the new curriculum reform in China as a Deweyan reform, aimed at laying a solid basic educational foundation to enable China to cultivate a new generation with globally competitive competences, self-initiative, STEAM capabilities, foreign-language skills, and high-level thinking abilities. Peng argued that the Deweyan model contained the essential elements of internationalism and could provide sustained momentum for China's modernization and globalization efforts (Deng, 2016). This new recognition reflects Dewey's significant impact on current reforms in Chinese education.

Moreover, to commemorate the centenary of Dewey's arrival in China, the *Journal of ECNU* dedicated a full issue of "Educational Sciences" early in 2019 to publications on John Dewey and Chinese education. Several Dewey scholars, both Chinese and foreign, contributed articles to this issue, which provided more positive interpretations of Dewey's influence on Chinese education. Zhang Hua, a leading scholar in comparative education and curriculum studies, offered a comprehensive reevaluation of Dewey's influence on Chinese educational reform at different historical periods. Zhang recognized Dewey's important contribution to and personal involvement in the creation of the new education system and curriculum in the 1920s. He also observed that Dewey personally mentored and influenced several prominent liberal education thinkers and reformers in China including Hu Shi, Jiang Mengling, and Tao Xingzhi, who diligently and creatively implemented his ideas in relation to China's educational practices. In addition, Zhang credited Dewey with establishing important links between Chinese and American educators that resulted in more fruitful visits to China in the 1920s by American educators including Paul Monroe, William H. Kilpatric, and George R. Twiss. Together, they exerted significant influence on Chinese education reform, especially the curriculum reform in the 1920s. Although China's political conditions did not allow Dewey's ideas to flourish for several decades during the closed-door period, Zhang found a renewed interest in Dewey's theories among Chinese educators during the 1988 Basic Education Curriculum Reform in Shanghai, which placed a strong emphasis on developing students' individuality and freedom through more hands-on activities and inquiry methods. This renewed interest in Dewey and American schools' activity- and project-based methods was further enhanced by the national Basic Education Curriculum Reform in 2001 that promoted the all-round development of each student. Understanding the hesitation among some Chinese scholars in adapting Western educational theories to Chinese practices, Zhang praised Dewey for "thinking like the Chinese" and complimented him for his brilliant proposal of a "third philosophy" or a "third way" that could help Chinese educators to avoid the pitfalls of extreme conservatism and radicalism, to pursue Chinese liberalism, and to achieve an "Eastern-style" or "Chinese-style" democracy as part of China's unique path toward educational development and reform. Zhang concluded that Dewey is still very much "alive" in today's China, and encouraged scholars to continue to interpret Dewey's ideas creatively in the search for "Eastern democracy" in Chinese education (Zhang, 2019). Zhang's interpretation of Dewey's ideas initiated a new way of thinking and acting among Chinese education reformers.

The special issue of the *Journal of ECNU* in 2019 also included a fresh perspective on Dewey by James Yang (2019), continuing on from his research on Dewey and China (Yang, 2016). Yang followed the example of Wang (2007) in exploring how Dewey's views and world outlook were shaped by his extensive encounters with the Chinese people during his two-year visit to China. Yang observed that Dewey's Chinese experiences not only increased his understanding of and appreciation for diverse cultures but also broadened his vision for democracy and enabled him to see the danger in the narrow definition of patriotism or nationalism that led to the notion and promotion of "America first" among some American politicians. Like Yang, Shane Ralsto, a Dewey scholar from the UK and another contributor to the special issue, examined how Dewey's experiences in China had helped to change his views (Ralsto, 2019). After explaining how Dewey conceived experience and why he appreciated his own Chinese experiences, Ralsto observed that Dewey learned the importance of time in dealing with the Chinese people and understood that time and more time would help resolve important issues and yield valuable results in China (Dewey, 1996). Based on Dewey's revelation, Ralsto recommended that in dealing with the Chinese diplomat, the American diplomat must not hurry negotiations nor rush to reach agreement – a lesson worth revisiting now to improve current US–China relations.

One of the most interesting proposals contained in this special issue came from Leonard Waks, former President of the American JDS and now a distinguished professor at Hangzhou Normal University. After comparing Dewey to Confucius from both historical and philosophical points of view, he suggested placing Dewey and Confucius together for a dialogue. He argued that the time was now ripe to investigate how each can contribute to educational revitalization in China. He believed that the Confucian ideal of moral self-cultivation could supplement Dewey's educational program, while Dewey's active learning strategies could fill a gap in Confucian learning in science and technology, fields that occupied Dewey's thoughts in his lectures in China (Waks, 2019). This interpretation represents a sharp departure from the critics' views in the 1920s, when Chinese intellectuals extolled Dewey's educational philosophy as a much-needed alternative to China's feudal system of learning as represented by Confucius and his followers.

In addition to the increasingly active dialogue and discussion regarding Dewey's ideas among educators and scholars in China, the study of Dewey's works is now readily available and often required for students in Chinese teacher education and graduate education programs, either as a part of the basic or advanced education theory courses, in a guided-reading class, or as an elective. At major research universities such as ECNU, all graduate students in education are required to take a course on education classics, which usually includes Dewey's work. In the more practice-oriented teacher-training universities such as Shanghai Normal University (SHNU), there are four areas of study for future educators: required core courses, required elective courses, optional elective courses, and practicum. Dewey's theories, together with those of Tao Xingzhi, can be found in all four areas, especially in the required core courses, which cover topics on Chinese and foreign education histories, educational philosophy, sociology, moral education, and teaching methods. In addition, SHNU provides special training workshops for school principals to enable them to study Dewey's theories on topics related to cultivating individuality in students. At Nanjing Xiaozhuang University, which was founded by Dewey's former student Tao Xiangzhi as the Morning Village Normal School, as mentioned earlier, the faculty now offers a guided-reading course on *Democracy and Education* to students who aspire to become elementary and rural school teachers. The students interviewed by the author on her visits there in recent years wanted to have more guided-reading classes on Dewey and to receive more detailed explanation and guidance from their faculty. They believed that Dewey's ideas helped them to create a vision for education and build a shield against the increasing temptation of materialism in society when they began to teach in schools (Su, 2018).

In contrast to the active learning programs on Dewey's works in Chinese education institutions, American students today seem to have lost the opportunity for such learning. Stephen T. Asma (2014), a professor of philosophy at Columbia College Chicago and a Fulbright Scholar in China at the Beijing Foreign Language School, observed that "in China, enthusiasm for Dewey's philosophy in particular is growing rapidly, while back home interest in it languishes. My students in Beijing and Shanghai all know John Dewey's name, but most of my Chicago undergrads back home do not." Sadly, this situation is also true in American teacher education programs, as most of them have eliminated educational foundations courses (and the faculty members who teach them) that offered a study of Dewey's works. This is because the current teacher performance expectations in the US do not contain anything related to educational foundations (see, for example, California Commission on Teacher Credentialing, 2016). In the author's own teacher education courses in a major state university in California, none of the students she has taught in the past decade has studied any of Dewey's works, and many did not even know who John Dewey was when questioned (Su, 2019).

8 China Education Improvement Society and Dewey Forums in Beijing – A "New Platform"

The most exciting event in relation to Dewey and Chinese education in the past decade was the revival of the China Education Improvement Society in 2011. The Society was founded in 1921 in response to Dewey's visit to China and was led by Dewey's former student Tao Xingzhi as the Secretary-General.

Cai Yuanpei, Hu Shi, Guo Bingwen, Chen Heqin, and other prominent Chinese educators and educational leaders became the core members of the Society. More importantly, John Dewey and Paul Monroe served as honorary board members and made significant recommendations in relation to the Society's international activities. One of the Society's original missions and tasks was to advocate and promote Dewey's ideas and experiments in China. However, because of the turmoil in China at that time, the Society ceased to convene its annual meetings in 1926, and remained dormant for many years thereafter. Since its revival in 2011, it has become an increasingly important educational association in China, with Chu Zhaohui, a leading scholar on Tao Xingzhi and senior researcher at the Chinese Central Institute of Educational Sciences, as the Chairman of its Board of Directors.

To commemorate the centenary of John Dewey's arrival in China in 1919 and his distinguished lectures in China from 1919 to 1921, the Chinese Education Improvement Society, together with the Columbia University Global Center in Beijing, initiated and convened not just one but *three* consecutive Dewey Forums in Beijing in the Spring of 2019, which attracted hundreds of Dewey scholars from all over China. The theme for the First Dewey Forum was "Dewey and Famous Chinese Educators," with four keynote speakers and more than 100 Chinese scholars in attendance. The speakers recognized and honored the five most famous Chinese educators, Tao Xingzhi, Hu Shih, Chen Heqin, Jiang Menglin, and Guo Binwen, all of whom were Dewey's students in China. These notable figures successfully transformed and implemented Dewey's ideas in Chinese educational practices. The presenters summarized the major scholarship interests shared by Dewey and his Chinese students into seven areas: agreement on the importance of experimentalism in education; promotion of democratic and scientific education; emphasis on active East–West educational communication; belief in education as a means of social reform; emphasis on cultivating individuality; promotion of educational experiments; and emphasis on the connection between education and life. Tao Xingzhi was considered to be the best role model in terms of implementing Dewey's theories in Chinese education. In light of this knowledge, Chu Zhaohui, China's leading Tao scholar and chief organizer of the Forum, delivered a candid reevaluation of Dewey and Tao Xingzhi. He examined the close friendship and genuine trust between Dewey and Tao and praised Dewey's strong support of Tao's efforts in relation to political and educational reform in China. Chu observed that Dewey and Tao's relationship in the field of education was one of theory and application, because Tao's educational thoughts and practices represented the best application of Dewey's theories in the Chinese context. Chu explained that Tao never surpassed Dewey in terms of theory development, either in breadth or in depth, but his application of Dewey's ideas in Chinese educational practices was both creative and widespread, establishing a shining example for other educators in China (Chu, 2019). Following these positive interpretations, the First Dewey Forum participants called for continued dialogue and a deeper level of Dewey studies to provide strong theoretical underpinnings for the current educational reform in China (China Education Improvement Society, 2019).

The Second Dewey Forum in Beijing focused on "Dewey and Chinese School Education" as the major theme. Six keynote speeches by Chinese Dewey scholars were delivered to more than 120 educators from all over China at Capital Normal University. The scholars explored the current meanings of Dewey's educational theories and observed that Dewey's ideas were still relevant to Chinese education and society because there was great value in using his theories to identify, discuss, and resolve issues relating to Chinese education. Recognizing that the twenty-first century was not only an era of technology but also a special period for human development, the speakers maintained that humanism should be the guiding principle for the modernization of Chinese education and society. They observed that Dewey's theories were consistent with this principle, as he advocated the use of scientific methods, reflective thinking, cooperation and social responsibility, a new form of individualism, democracy, and humanism. Furthermore, these scholars believed that Chinese schools could draw useful lessons from Dewey's child-centered Laboratory Schools in Chicago, which implemented a non-graded, group-oriented, no-testing approach, and was facilitated by experts. The Second Dewey Forum participants advocated more extensive utilization of the rich resources provided by Dewey studies to improve Chinese education. As Chu Zhaohui concluded at the end of the Second Dewey Forum, the renewed warm embrace of Dewey's educational theories in China was no accident, but the result of the internal needs of modern China (Ding, 2019a).

The Third Dewey Forum, the final one in the 2019 series, was held on the campus of Beijing Normal University, and attracted more than 150 participants from 50 educational institutions and other walks of life in China. "Dewey and Chinese Education" was the major theme, and more than 30 scholars delivered keynote speeches and panel presentations at the Forum. A.G. Rud, then president of the American John Dewey Society, and Hope Leichter from Teachers College at Columbia University were unable to attend, but sent congratulatory video messages to the Forum. The presentations at this Forum demonstrated tremendous respect for Dewey and included highly positive evaluations of Dewey's influence on Chinese education by leading scholars in Dewey studies in China (Ding, 2019b). Shan Zhonghui, a senior Dewey scholar from ECNU, presented a new interpretation of Dewey's lectures in China, identifying four distinct characteristics of Dewey's lectures: the freshness of his educational ideas; multiple examples to explain and illustrate his theories; use of good humor and ordinary or oral language in his presentations; and connection of his theories to Chinese educational reality. Wang Wenling from Nanjing Xiaozhung University, which was founded by Tao Xingzhi based on Dewey's educational philosophy, as mentioned earlier, believed that Dewey's philosophy of pragmatism, despite having aged over time, remained a useful tool for scholars and students who had returned to China after studying in the West in breaking down barriers in both traditional education and Western education and creating a "Chinese-style education" that is most suitable for China's current educational conditions.

One of the most inspirational keynote speeches at the Third Dewey Forum was delivered by Liu Fangtong, a senior Dewey scholar and Founding Director of the Dewey Center at Fudan University. He has devoted considerable time during his academic career to studying Dewey's philosophy, and was the chief editor of *The Complete Works of John Dewey* (published in Chinese), as noted earlier. Liu reviewed the historical background to Dewey's visit to China, explained the political contexts underlying the initial warm reception and later rejection of Dewey during different periods in China's recent history, examined the important characteristics of Dewey's philosophy that were relevant to the harmonious development of the individual and society, and reconfirmed Dewey as an international educator who had exerted significant influence on Chinese education. Liu expressed his deep admiration of Dewey as a master of masters among Chinese educators, and regarded Dewey's ideas as important sources of thought regarding the development of educational theories and practices in China. In fact, Liu played a critical role in reevaluating and rehabilitating Dewey in the 1980s, and helped to reestablish Dewey's reputation in China as a great philosopher (Liu, 2019).

In summarizing the new interpretations and consensus that had been reached at the conclusion of the Third Dewey Forum, Chu Zhaohui removed any remaining doubts as to the importance of Dewey's role in China's educational modernization efforts, both in the past and today. He concluded that if Chinese educators intended to continue their long march on the path of educational modernization, they must not ignore Dewey's theories, and should consider Dewey's ideas as valuable resources and effective problem-solving tools for the modernization of Chinese education. Chu and the other Forum participants expressed their firm belief that Dewey was "the front-runner in solving difficult problems in the modernization process because he has the richest thoughts and theories and has prepared the most solid foundation, thinking methods and technical tools." Citing the newly published national plan, "Chinese Education

Modernization 2035" (Chinese State Council, 2019), Chu pointed out that the nature of educational modernization was the modernization of the human being, that is, the transformation of human thoughts, thinking abilities, and socialization competencies. He viewed Dewey's role as both fundamental and critical in reducing the resistance to change from both traditional and conservative forces, in stimulating human thinking, and in cultivating the modern being (Ding, 2019b). No other education conference in China has ever produced such bold statements and expressed such high hopes in relation to Dewey's work.

Therefore, the significance of the three Dewey Forums that were held in Beijing in 2019 cannot be overestimated. It was the first time in the history of Chinese education that a forum in Dewey's name had been convened in China. Further, no education association, either in China or anywhere else in the world, has organized three consecutive forums focused on one education scholar to gauge and celebrate his influence on education. As Shan Zhonghui enthusiastically announced in his keynote speech, the 2019 Dewey Forums in Beijing marked a "new period" in Dewey studies in China, reached a "new height," and created a "new platform" for Dewey scholars in China (Shan, 2019).

9 Conclusion

One hundred years after his significant visit in China in 1919, Dewey's lectures remain in print in Chinese, and his influence on Chinese education remains strong. The encounter between Dewey and China is one of the most fascinating episodes in the intellectual history of the twentieth century. Despite the difficulties and opposition he encountered, Dewey accomplished a lot during his visit to China, a fact recognized by both American and Chinese Dewey scholars. Among his greatest contributions, Dewey established a communication of minds between American and Chinese educators, encouraged the Chinese people to break away from the harmful elements of the old tradition, and helped pave the way for Chinese education to move toward modernization and globalization. This is Dewey's singular success, one that no other foreign visitor to China has ever achieved, although efforts to implement his ideas and develop an Eastern style of democracy in Chinese education were met with strong resistance and objections for long periods of time as a result of the drastic social and political changes that occurred in Chinese society in the decades following his visit. American scholars' evaluation of the Dewey experiment in China has been ambivalent at best, and most Americans, including educators, remain unaware of Dewey's connection with China. However, the centenary of Dewey's arrival in China has stimulated vital dialogue between American and

Chinese Dewey scholars, and Dewey's spirit is now inspiring some American youth to follow his path. Despite this, most higher education institutions in the US are still not offering Dewey's theories to students – including student teachers – in present-day courses.

In China, Dewey's ideas were widely studied and eagerly implemented in Chinese education during the first 30 years after his visit, but the following 30 years witnessed severe criticism and the total abandonment of Dewey in China. However, Dewey received an open and warm reappraisal from Chinese educators in the 1980s after China began to open up to the outside world. While some Chinese critics still consider his political and philosophical positions to be unacceptable, most education scholars in China have recognized Dewey's valuable contributions to the history of education and his significant influence on both Chinese and worldwide education. They have also recognized the worth of certain aspects of his educational philosophy, especially his ideas on child-centered and experience-based learning, his emphasis on reflective thinking and active communication, his advocacy for harmonious and associated living in a democratic society (and its manifestation in schools), and his focus on cultivating creativity, critical thinking, and problem-solving abilities in children, which are well-aligned with the current national education goals and recommendations for curriculum reform in China.

The revival of the China Education Improvement Society in 2011 marked the beginning of a new wave of enthusiasm in China for Dewey and his educational philosophy, as demonstrated by the publication of Dewey's complete works in Chinese, the institutionalization of learning about Dewey's works in Chinese education institutions, presentations and publications by leading education scholars on Dewey and China, and the recent Dewey Forums in Beijing, which have resulted in creative and positive interpretations of Dewey and his influence on Chinese education. However, traditional barriers and new challenges still exist for Dewey scholars in China as they strive to seek a third way – the Chinese way or the Eastern style of democracy. Further communication between Chinese and American Dewey scholars is needed to form friendships and establish trust, thereby creating new grounds for collaboration.

As the US–China trade war continues to intensify, it is increasingly important that Dewey scholars and educators, as well as politicians and diplomats, on both sides "spend time and more time" together to develop friendships and cultivate deep mutual understanding, as Dewey did with the Chinese people when he visited China 100 years ago. There is great potential and many more opportunities now than previously existed for Chinese and American scholars to collaborate in their research and reform efforts. Future developments in China and the US may lead to more definitive and diverse appraisals of the

Dewey experiment in Chinese education, but there is little doubt that Dewey and his ideas will continue to resonate in Chinese educational development and reform. As the scholars at the 2019 Dewey Forums in Beijing predicted, Dewey's philosophy will continue to serve as a bridge for deep exchanges in the humanities between the US and China (Ding, 2019b). Dewey's visit to China brought educators from both countries together in their pursuit of democratic aims in education, although they have clearly applied different methods and followed different paths over the last 100 years. Democracy cannot be achieved in one country alone, and will only flourish when it is established everywhere throughout the world, as Dewey sincerely expressed in his personal letter to Tao Xingzhi in 1944 (Su, 1996). Dewey's statement could not be more apt in today's world, even though there will always be new obstacles and challenges.

Acknowledgments

This paper is based on the author's Dewey Lecture at the annual conference of the John Dewey Society, Toronto, April 5, 2019 and her earlier historical study of John Dewey's influence on Chinese education. The author wishes to thank Vice President Huang Tao and Professor Chen Xian of Nanjing Normal University, President Wang Zenong and Dean Cao Huiying of Nanjing Xiaozhuang University, and Director Chi Tianliang of Nanjing Municipal Government Personnel Bureau for their support to the initial research for this study in Nanjing, China. Thanks also to Professor Philip W. Jackson and Professor A.G. Rud, former presidents of the John Dewey Society, for their encouragement to the presentations and publications of the study papers in the US. Special thanks to Lu Airong, Zhou Xiaohong and Ding Xiaona, visiting scholars at California State University, Northridge, for their assistance on references and translation, and to Dr. Zhang Huajun of Beijing Normal University for her useful suggestions of revision on the final draft of this manuscript.

This chapter is a reprint from: SU, Zhixin. (2019). John Dewey and Chinese education: Comparative perspectives and contemporary interpretations. *Beijing International Review of Education, 1*(4), 714–745.

References

Asma, S. T. (2014, June 8). From China, with pragmatism. *New York Times.*
　http://opinionator.blogs.nytimes.com/2014/06/08/from-china-with-pragmatism/
　?_r=1

Berry, T. (1960). Dewey's influence in China. In J. Blewett (Ed.), *John Dewey: His thought and influence*. Fordham University Press.

Billings, H. F. (1981–82, Winter). John Dewey in China: The limits of social reconstruction. *Educational Studies, 12*(4), 381–386.

Braendel, C. (2019, June 7). A century later, John Dewey's travels to China influence a new generation. *University of Chicago News*. https://news.uchicago.edu/story/century-later-john-deweys-travels-china-influence-new-generation.

California Commission on Teacher Credentialing. (2016). *California teaching performance expectations*. Sacramentor, California.

Cao, F. (1950). Introduction to criticism of Dewey [曹孚.杜威批判引论（上篇）.人民教育], *6*, 21–28.

Cao, F. (1950). Introduction to criticism of Dewey [曹孚.杜威批判引论（下篇）.人民教育], *7*, 22–29.

Cao, F. (1955). A critique of pragmatist educational theory on purposes of education [曹孚.批判实用主义教育学关于教育的作用和目的的谬论.人民教育], *9*, 43–46.

Chen, H. (1952). Self-criticism of living education. [陈鹤琴.关于生活教育的自我批评.人民教育], *4*, 8–10.

Chen, H. (1955). Critique of the philosophic bases of John Dewey's reactionary pedagogy. *Wenhui Bao, 2*, [陈鹤琴.批判杜威反动教育学的哲学基础.文汇报], 2–28（第2版）.

Chen, H. (1956). *A Critique of Dewey's Reactionary Educational Philosophy*. New Knowledge.

Chen, J. (1957). *Criticism of Dewey's moral education philosophy*. Hubei People's Press. [陈景磐，杜威的道德教育思想批判.武汉：湖北人民出版社].

Chen, J. (1982). A supplement to criticism of Dewey's aloral education philosophy. *Educational Studies, 2*, 80–86. [陈景磐.《杜威的道德教育思想批判》的补充.教育研究，2，80–86].

China Education Improvement Society. (2019). Dewey's Influence on Chinese Educators. *Beijing, China Education Improvement Society*. [中华教育改进社：杜威与中国教育家].

Chinese State Council. (2019). Chinese Education Modernization 2035 [《中国教育现代化2035》.北京：中央国务院].

Ching, J. (1985). China's responses to Dewey. *Journal of Chinese Philosophy, 12*(3), 261–81.

Chow, T. (1960). *The May Fourth Movement: Intellectual revolution in Modern China*. Harvard University Press.

Clopton, R. W., & Ou, T. (1973). Introduction. In J. Dewey (Ed.), *John Dewey lectures in China, 1919–1920*. University of Hawaii Press.

Chu, Z. H. (2019). *Dewey's Influence on Tao Xiangzhi*. China Education Improvement Society. [储朝晖.杜威对陶行知的影响.北京：中华教育改进社].

Deng, L. (2016). News on "The Scholarly Meeting to Celebrate the Centennial of the Publication of John Dewey's Democracy and Education". Organized by The Institute of International and Comparative Education Research at East China Normal University. [邓莉. 华东师范大学比较所主办纪念杜威《民主主义与教育》发表100周年学术报告会]. http://iice.ecnu.edu.cn/s/446/t/1051/3e/9b/info147099.htm.

Dewey, J. (1899). *The school and society*. The University of Chicago Press.

Dewey, J. (1916). *Democracy and education*. Macmillan.

Dewey, J. (1920). *Reconstruction in philosophy*. Dover Publications, Inc.

Dewey, J. (1937). *Experience and education*. Collier Books.

Dewey, J. (1939). *Freedom and culture*. Putnam.

Dewey, J. (1983). America and Chinese education. In J. Boydston (Ed.), *John Dewey, the Middle Works, 1899–1924* (Vol. 13). Southern Illinois University Press. (Original work published 1922)

Dewey, J. (1996). *The collected works of John Dewey: The electronic edition* (A. Hickman). Interlex Corporation.

Ding, Y. (2019a). *Do education and modernization in the Chinese society still need Dewey?* China Education Improvement Society. [丁永为. 中国教育与社会现代化还需要杜威吗？北京：中华教育改进社].

Ding, Y. (2019b). *Dewey's ideas are still important resources for Chinese Education Modernization*. China Education Improvement Society. [丁永为. 杜威思想仍然是中国教育现代化的重要资源。北京：中华教育改进社].

Fu, T. (1957). *A critique of the reactionary pragmatic educational theory*. Hubei People's Press. [傅统先. 反动的实用主义教育思想批判. 武汉：湖北人民出版社].

Fu, T., & Zhang, W. (1986). *Educational philosophy*. Shangdong Education Press. [傅统先，张文郁. 教育哲学. 济南：山东教育出版社].

Gavin, W. J. (1988). *Context over foundation: Dewey and Marx*. Reidel.

Grieder, J. B. (1970). *Hu Shih and the Chinese Renaissance*. Harvard University Press.

Grieder, J. B. (1972). The question of 'Politics' in the May Fourth era. In B. I. Schwartz (Ed.), *Reflections on the May Fourth Movement: A symposium*. East Asia Research Center, Harvard University.

Hayhoe, R., & Bastid, M. (Eds.). (1987). *China's education and the industrial world*. Sharpe.

Hook, S. (Ed.). (1976). *John Dewey: Philosopher of science and freedom*. Greenwood.

Hsu, I. C. Y. (1970). *The rise of Modem China*. Oxford University Press.

Hu, S. (1962). John Dewey in China. In C. A. Moore (Ed.), *Philosophy and culture-east and west*. University of Hawaii Press.

Hughes, E. R. (1938). *The invasion of China by the Western World*. Macmillan.

Institute of International Education (IIE). (2018). *Open door report*. IIE.

Ke, X., & Peng, H. (2019). The influence of John Dewey's educational thoughts to Chen Heqin's construction of Chinese early childhood education. *Journal of Shanxi Early Childhood Norma School, 35*(6), 84–89 [柯小卫，彭海蕾. 杜威教育思想对于陈鹤琴"中国化"幼教改造的影响.陕西学前师范学院学报].

Keenan, B. (1977). *The Dewey experiment in China: Educational reform and political Power in the Early Republic.* Harvard University Press.

Li, B. (1956). Eliminating the influence of pragmatic educational ideas in our country. *People's Education, 2,* 53–56. [李秉德. 清除实用主义教育思想在我國教育界的影响. 人民教育，2，53-56].

Li, Y. (1987). On Dewey's theory of developing students' thinking abilities. In D. Du (Ed.), *Foreign education references.* Institute for Educational Research, East China Teachers University.

Liu, S. (1990). "The Echo of Hu Shi." *World of Chinese Language and Literature, 6*(7), 23–31.

Liu, X. (1987). Dewey on the training of creative thinking attitude. *Foreign Education Trends, 5,* 11–13.

Liu, F. (1996). Re-evaluating Dewey's pragmatism. *Exploration and Debate, 8,* 46–48. [刘放桐. 重新认识杜威的实用主义. 探索与争鸣].

Liu, F. (2011). Dewey: the misunderstood "pragmatist". *Social Sciences News* [刘放桐.杜威：被误解的"实用主义者". 社会科学报]，04–07006.

Lui, F. (1955). What is the reactionary pragmatic educational theory? In *A critic of bourgeois educational theory* (Vol. 2). Cultural Education. [刘佛年. 什么是反动的实用主义.上海：文化教育出版社编.资产阶级教育思想批判（第二集）].

Mao, Z. (1949). Friendship or aggression. Selected Works of Mao Zedong (Vol. 4). People's Publishing. [《毛泽东全集》第四卷。北京：人民出版社].

Meng, X. (1985). On the significance of Dewey's educational philosophy in the history of education. In Chinese Society on the Study of Educational History (Ed.), *Study of Dewey and Herbart's educational ideas.* Shandong Education Press. [孟宪德. 论杜威教育哲学体系在教育史上的地位.中国教育史研究会编.《杜威、赫尔巴特教育思想研究》.济南：山东教育出版社].

Ministry of Education (MOE). (2010). *National mid-term and long-term plan for educational reform and development 2010–2020* [《国家中长期教育改革和发展规划纲要（2010–2020 年）》.北京：中国教育部].

Ou, T. (1961). A re-evaluation of the educational theory practice of John Dewey. *Educational Forum, 25,* 277–300.

Ou, T. (1970). Dewey's lectures and influence in China. In J. A. Boydston (Ed.), *Guide to the works of John Dewey.* Southern Illinois University Press.

Passow, A. H. (1982). John Dewey's influence on education around the world. *Teachers College Record, 83*(3), 401–417.

Pavela, G. (1970). *John Dewey, Hu Shih and the failure of experimentalism in China* [Master's thesis]. Connecticut Wesleyan University.

Ralston, S. (2019). John Dewey's experience in China (1919–1921): How China changed Dewey. *Journal of ECNU (Educational Sciences), 2,* 59–62. [尚恩.罗尔斯顿.杜威在华经验考述（1919–1921）：中国是如何改变杜威的？冯家渔译.华东师范大学学报（教育科学版）].

Ren, B. (1985). On Dewey's child-centered education. In Chinese Society on the Study of Educational History (Ed.), *Study of Dewey and Herbart's educational ideas.* Shandong Education Press. [任宝祥.杜威的儿童中心论述评.《杜威、赫尔巴特教育思想研究》（中国教育史研究会编）.济南：山东教育出版社].

Shi, W. (1985). A macro-analysis of Dewey's educational purpose. *Foreign Education References, 1,* 10–13. [石伟平. 杜威教育目的的宏观分析. 外国教育参考，1, 10–13].

Sizer, N. F. (1966). John Dewey's ideas in China, 1919 to 1921. *Comparative Education Review, 19,* 390–403.

Smith, J. E. (1985). Pragmatism at work: Dewey's lectures in China. *Journal of Chinese Philosophy, 12*(3), 231–259.

Su, Z. (1989). People's education in the people's Republic of China. *Phi Delta Kappan, 70*(8), 723–727.

Su, Z. (1995). A critical evaluation of John Dewey's influence on Chinese education. *American Journal of Education, 105*(3), 302–325.

Su, Z. (1996). Teaching, learning, and reflective acting: A Dewey experiment in Chinese teacher education. *Teachers College Record, 98*(1), 126–152.

Su, Z. (2018). Tao Xingzhi's creative implementation of Dewey's theories in Chinese teacher education. *Educational Research Monthly, 312*(7), 3–21. [苏智欣. 陶行知的创新实践：杜威理论在中国师范教育中的应用与发展.《教育学术月刊》312（7），3–21].

Su, Z. (2019). John Dewey and Chinese education: A comparative perspective, Dewey Lecture at the 2019 Annual Meeting of the American John Dewey Society, Toronto.

Su, Z., Su, J., & Goldstein, S. (1994). Teaching and learning science in American and Chinese high schools. *Comparative Education, 30,* 255–270.

Tanner, D. (1994). *The crisis of the American academic left.* Paper presented at the annual meeting of the American Educational Research Association, New Orleans.

Teng, D. (1957). Criticising Dewey's theory on ethics. *Philosophical Research, 4,* 58–70. [滕大春.批判杜威的道德论.《教育研究》.4, 58–70].

Teng, S., & Fairbank, J. K. (1954). *China's response to the west.* Harvard University Press.

Wang, J. (2007). *John Dewey in China: To teach and to learn* (SUNY Series in Chinese Philosophy and Culture). State University of New York Press.

Wang, P. (1986). *On Dewey's educational reform theory. Foreign education trends.* [王佩雄.杜威教育改革观.外国教育], 5, 44–49.

Wang, R. (1954, December 28). Hu Shih and Dewey in the May Fourth Movement. *People's Daily*. [王若水. 五四运动中的胡适和杜威. 人民日报（第3版）].

Wang, T. (1927). Exploring Dewey's educational ideas. *Social Sciences, Beijing Teachers University, 3*(1982), 461–480. [王天一. 杜威教育思想探究. 北京师范大学学报：社会科学版，（3）：461–480].

Waks, L. (2019). John Dewey and Confucius in dialogue: 1919–2019. *Journal of ECNU (Educational Sciences)*. 2, 45–52. 伦纳德.瓦克斯. 杜威与孔子的对话：1919–2019. 华东师范大学学报（教育科学版）. 年第2期：45–52.

Wu, S., Zhao, R., Huang, X., Li, M., Shan, Z., & Xu, R.(1988). *Brief history of education in foreign countries*. Educational Science. [吴式颖，赵荣昌等. 外国教育史简编. 北京：教育科学出版社].

Wu, Y. (1985). On Dewey's 'learning by doing.' In Chinese Society on the Study of Educational History (Ed.), *Study of Dewey and Herbart's educational ideas*. Shandong Education Press. [吴元训. 试评杜威的"从做中学". 中国教育史研究会会编.《杜威、赫尔巴特教育思想研究》. 济南：山东教育出版社].

Xia, Z. (1985a). Dewey's pragmatic educational theory. In T. Wang, Z. Xia, & M. Zhu (Eds.), *History of foreign education*. Beijing Teachers University. [夏之莲. 杜威的教育理论. 王天一，夏之莲编著. 外国教育史. 北京：北京师范大学出版社].

Xia, Z. (1985). Some of Dewey's educational theories should be studied seriously. In Chinese Society on the Study of Educational History (Ed.), *Study of Dewey and Herbart's educational ideas(b)*. Shandong Education Press [夏之莲. 杜威提出的一些教育、教学课题应认真研究. 中国教育史研究会编.《杜威、赫尔巴特教育思想研究》. 济南：山东教育出版社].

Xu, D. (1992). *A comparison of the educational ideas and practices of John Dewey and Mao Zedong in China*. Mellen Research University Press.

Yan, K. (1955, September 27). A critique of Dewey's child-centered education fallacy. *Wenhui Bao*.

Yang, J. Z. (2016). *When confucius encounters John Dewey: A historical and philosophical analysis of Dewey's visit to China* [Doctoral dissertation]. University of Oklahoma.

Yang, J. Z. (2019). How China shaped Dewey's ideas of cultural diversity and democracy. *Journal of ECNU* (Educational Sciences), 2, 53–58. [杨志祥. 论中国之行对杜威多元文化观念及民主思想的影响. 华东师范大学学报（教育科学版）. 年第2期：53–58].

Yu, X. (1991, November 19–22). *The encounter of Dewey and Mao Zedong*. Paper presented at the Conference of Chinese Education for the 21st Century, Honolulu, Hawaii.

Yuan, R. (1983). Influence of Dewey's 'child-centered education' on modern education. *Foreign Education Trends, 5*, 47–49.

Zhang, H. (2013). *John Dewey, Liang Shuming, and China's education reform: Cultivating individuality*. Lexington Books.

Zhang, J. (1955). Criticizing Dewey's pragmatism and its fallacy on school education. *People's Education, 6*, 23–25. [张健. 批判杜威实用主义教育学说中有关学校教育的谬论. 人民教育，6，23–25].

Zhang, T. (1955). What is the reactionary nature of the pragmatic education theory? *People's Education, 5*, 26–30. [张腾霄. 实用主义教育学的反动实质何在. 人民教育，5，26–30].

Zhang, Y. (1989). The dialectics in Dewey's educational theory. *Educational Studies, 2*, 63–67. [张勇. 杜威教育理论中辩证法之我见. 教育研究，2，63–67].

Zhang, H. (2019). On John Dewey and China's education reform. [张华. 杜威和中国教育改革. 华东师范大学学报（教育科学版）第2期：18–28].

Zhao, X. (1982). The design and theory of Dewey's Chicago Lab School. *Philosophical Sciences, East China Teachers' University, 6*, 60–68. [赵祥麟. 杜威芝加哥实验的设计和理论述评. 华东师范大学学报（哲学社会科学版），（6），60–68].

Zhao, X. (1980). Reevaluating Dewey's pragmatic educational ideas. *Social Sciences, East China Teachers University, 2*, 439–460. [赵祥麟. 重新评价杜威实用主义教育思想. 华东师范大学学报（哲学社会科学版），（2），439–460].

Zheng, D. (1985). An iInitial exploration of Dewey's pedagogy. In Chinese Society on the Study of Educational History (Ed.), *Study of Dewey and Herbart's educational ideas*. Shandong Education Press. [杜威、赫尔巴特教育思想研究（中国教育史研究会编）. 济南：山东教育出版社].

Zhou, G. (1991). The spread and influence of modern western education theories in China. *Educational Sciences, East China Teachers' University, 3*, 77–96. [周谷军. 近代西方教育学在中国的传播及其影响. 华东师范大学学报：教育科学版，（3），77–96].

Zhu, Z. (1956). *Criticism of the reactionary views in Pragmatist Dewey's psychology theory*. People's Education. [朱智贤. 批判实用主义者杜威在心理学方面的反动观点. 北京：人民教育出版社].

CHAPTER 2

Recent Studies in Mainland China on John Dewey's Visit to China (1919–1921)

ZHOU Hongyu and LI Yong

Abstract

John Dewey, an American philosopher and educator, was invited to visit the Republic of China on April 30, 1919. Attracted by the May 4th Movement and its consequent social changes in China, Dewey stayed until August 2, 1921, mainly delivered talks and lectures. During his visit, he promoted his pragmatism which was widely accepted and became popular in the new wave of educational thoughts and reforms during that time period in China. One hundred years later, Dewey's visit to China was studied again by researchers in China to continuously explore his influence on Chinese education. Given the insight and influence of pragmatist theory on educational issues, it can be said that Dewey's influence on China was significant and profound in the past, which is worthy of being examined today and can be used for reference in the future. This article reviews the latest studies mainly by scholars in mainland China on his visit to China.

Keywords

John Dewey – China – the May 4th Movement – educational exchange

•••

One hundred years ago (1919–1921), Dewey's visit to China had a great impact in the Chinese intellectual circle. Since then, the fate of Dewey's thoughts in China has seen ups and downs. It was not until the 1980s that Dewey and his thoughts regained their recognition. The year of 2019 is the 100th anniversary of Dr. John Dewey's visit to China. In order to commemorate this special historical event, the educational community in China has successively published research articles on his visit in multiple Chinese journals such as *Educational Research*, *Peking University Education Review*, *Journal of East China Normal University* (*Educational Science*), *Educational Science Research*, *University*

© KONINKLIJKE BRILL NV, LEIDEN, 2022 | DOI:10.1163/9789004511477_003

Education Science, Journal of Ningbo University (Educational Science Edition), etc. Moreover, Beijing Normal University, Capital Normal University, and the China Education Improvement Institute (*zhonghua jiaoyu gaijinshe* 中华教育改进社) have organized several academic events to honor Dewey's centennial trip to China and there have been pertinent publications like *Dewey's Educational Thoughts in China* (Zhang & Liu, 2019), *An Academic Chronicle of John Dewey in China* (Gu, 2019a) and *Dewey Picture Biography* (Dai, 2019). The above series of activities showcased the resounding response of Chinese scholars to Dewey's 100-year history of visiting China. In 2019, the academic database China National Knowledge Infrastructure (CNKI) encompassed more than 400 Dewey's related articles or reports. If we search the title with "Dewey" as a keyword, we can retrieve 170 research-based papers with a publication year of 2019. This chapter mainly selects and summarizes academic papers related to Dewey's visit to China written by Chinese scholars in 2019, marking a hundred years of Dewey's visit of China. We try to provide the new progress of the study on this event by Chinese scholars for the English readers.

Unlike Dewey's visit to Japan in February 1919, his visit to China was a kind of provisional plan. At first, Dewey's students at Columbia, including Guo Bingwen (郭秉文), Hu Shi (胡适), Jiang Menglin (蒋梦麟), and Tao Xingzhi (陶行知), invited him to China. The invitation was organized by three institutions, Peking University, Nanjing Higher Normal Institute and Education Society of Jiangsu Province. Since Dewey arrived in China, due to financial constraints, wide dissemination, and immense concerns regarding Dewey's visit within Chinese academia, many groups volunteered to participate in the arrangement of his visit. Four days after Dewey arrived in China, the May 4th Movement broke out. Although Dewey had no knowledge of the May 4th Movement in advance, he stayed in China for more than two years and can be said to be a witness and bystander of the May 4th Movement. Especially, staying with progressive scholars and young students deepened Dewey's understanding of the May 4th Movement. Dewey's support for the May 4th Movement can be seen from his attitude towards the participants of the movement (Liu, 2019). Although Dewey initially planned to stay in China only for a short time, he was so attracted by the spirit of the Chinese intellectuals' struggle to establish an independent, unified democratic nation state that he dramatically changed his trip plan in China. In order to witness the significance of this movement in promoting China's social and cultural progress, his original schedule of the visit was extended from two months to more than two years.

Dewey came to Shanghai on April 30, 1919, left from Qingdao to the United States on August 2, 1921. He stayed for 2 years, 3 months and 3 days. He visited twelve provinces of China, besides of the city of Beijing during this period.

Dewey's visit to China is a milestone of the history of educational exchange between China and the United States and is still viewed as a continued legacy. Not only with philosophy but also with dialogue, Dewey successfully established a dynamic relationship with China (Peng, 2019a). Dewey's series of lectures has profoundly influenced China's educational modernization, because they have involved the spirit of democracy and science (Guo, 2019) and resonated the patriotism advocated in the May 4th Movement. More importantly and deeply, Dewey's speeches to Chinese audience had its cultural appropriation. Therefore, the enthusiastic reception of Dewey's thought had its social and cultural foundations in that particular time period and it resonated with the liberal intellectuals' cultural identity and imagination they held for a modern nation state (Yang and Li, 2019).

Dewey's visit of China was the time when the Chinese New Culture Movement (1915–1927) was widely carried out. Although a major theme of the New Culture Movement is to criticize the value of Confucianism as the barrier of China's modernization, on October 19, 1919, Dewey's 60th birthday, Cai Yuanpei (蔡元培), then the President of Peking University and one of the leading figure of the New Culture Movement, delivered a birthday speech for Dewey and highly praised him as a Contemporary Confucius. The comparison of Dewey with Confucius is an excellent way of localizing Dewey's theory. It became the strategy of popularization and promotion of his theories (Dong, 2019). To some extent, the great success of Dewey's first year speeches promoted the spread of democratic thought and encouraged university students strikes. At that time, the Chinese academic circles had high expectation for Dewey, hoping that he could become the spokesperson of the "Mr. Democracy" (德先生), who could clean up the deep-rooted old culture and lead the reform and innovation of Chinese society (Feng, 2019). Dewey interprets democracy as a way of living together and he closely links democracy and education. The conventional concept of democracy has gained new connotations and a brand-new way of realizing it by practicing education as life itself (Peng, 2019b). As a matter of fact, since Dewey came to China, the voice of democracy has been rising day by day. In terms of the student movement, when students become more and more radical in the second year of the May Fourth Movement, they favored the trajectory towards extreme and comprehensive change of the society. Dewey harshly criticized the radical inclination of the movement and tried to guide the student movement to the road of positive construction.

Dewey's honorable popularity in China was predominantly decided by the efforts of Guo Bingwen, Hu Shi, Jiang Menglin, Zhang Bolin (张伯苓), Li Jianxun (李建勋), Deng Cuiying (邓萃英) and other overseas students returned from Columbia University (Wu, 2019). Benefiting from Dewey's visit, his Chinese students established the School of Deweyan Education (Wang, 2019) and hoped to apply Dewey's discourse of pragmatic education as an external force to promote educational reforms in China. The popularity of Dewey's theory had influenced Chinese higher education in pervasive way. Dewey had several visits to Nanjing Higher Normal Institute, one of the organizing institutions for his visit to China, and his multiple lectures and talks resulted in the long-term development of the Institute (Zhou & Li, 2019). For example, with Dewey's Chinese disciples at Nanjing Higher Normal Institute as the core members, they formed the Chinese Dewey School of Education (*zhongguo duwei jiaoyu xuepai* 中国杜威教育学派), which changed the direction of the development of Chinese modern pedagogy. They put Dewey's ideas into practice, established experimental schools, and led the education reform in modern China (Feng, 2019).

Dewey's visit to China also further deepened the understanding of Dewey's theory among Chinese students at Teachers College of Columbia University. As far as Tao Xingzhi was concerned, the in-depth contact with Dewey after Tao's return to China had also become an important starting point for him to propose a theory of life education that is different from Dewey (Chu, 2019). In addition, during his visit to China, Dewey believed that universities represent the torch of truth, and universities should undertake the task of educating leaders who are pillars of society (Zhu, 2019). While spreading his thoughts, Dewey's visit to China also boosted the establishment of many societies such as the China Education Improvement Society. And it contributed to the new school system in 1922 and new courses and textbooks that matched the new school system. Generally speaking, Dewey and Dewey's speeches are not only an organic part of the new education reform, but also an organic part of the new cultural movement.

The close relationship between Dewey and his Chinese students determined the "direct contact" between Dewey and his Chinese audience. For instance, the audience often understood Dewey's talks as translated by Hu Shi – sometimes interpreted by Hu's own thoughts (Zhao, 2019). Additionally, the Dewey Fever also caused dissatisfaction of returnees graduated from Harvard University against those from Columbia University. The former group founded the School of *Xueheng* (学衡派) and held the opposite view as of Dewey's (Shen, 2019). In the late 1920s, based on social and political struggles and academic practices, the academia's confidence and enthusiasm towards Dewey's theory decreased gradually (Zhong & Tu, 2019).

On the other hand, the visit to China from 1919 to 1921 also had a significant and long-term impact on Dewey. First of all, it improved Dewey's understanding of China. In the long-term sojourn life, Dewey learned about Chinese social psychology and philosophy of life. He learned to understand and respect China in his own way. Secondly, the sojourn in China for more than two years gave Dewey new inspiration for his academic work. Finally, to some extent, the trip to China became a turning point in Dewey's life as a public intellectual. Due to Dewey's visit to China and his efforts to help Chinese schools achieve modernization, they have been widely reported and recognized, which has caused many foreign governments to invite Dewey to inspect their education system. Dewey thus became an international renowned philosopher (Li & Zhou, 2020).

Considering the 100-year history of Dewey's visit to China, we must not only examine what was said by Dewey but also what kind of intellectual assets he has been left for us. Although Dewey was not responsible for transforming the old China with his theory of education, his talks and lectures are still relevant to today's China with considerable insight and wisdom. One of the lessons that we can learn from Dewey is that we must avoid radicalism toward the change of Chinese society and educational policy (Zhang, 2019). Also, the study of Dewey's visit of China reminds us to pay close attention to implementing new educational reforms in the Republic of China. Tao Xingzhi (陶行知) and other scholars have combined the educational wisdom of Chinese tradition with what they learned from Western philosophies to realize the creative transformation of the western theories. For example, addressing China's problem, Tao studied Dewey's educational thoughts with a developmental perspective and transformed the Dewey's concept of "Education as a Necessity of Life" to "Life as Education." This is Tao's innovation of Deweyan pragmatism in Chinese context (Gu, 2019b).

By reviewing the recent studies on Dewey's visit to China by scholars in mainland China, we suggest that researchers could further explore this field in the following five areas. First, Chinese scholars need to pay serious attention to the collection and editing of historical materials, both in English and in Chinese, on Dewey's visit to China. The historical materials can help to correct the omissions or fallacies in Dewey's visit to China. For example, on the basis of the existing data, the scholars have edited the Chinese historical documents on Dewey's visit to China from 1919 to 1921: *Democracy and Education: Dewey's Speeches in China* (Zhou & Chen, 2013a), and *An Academic Chronicle of John Dewey in China* (Gu, 2019). In addition, we could translate and sort out Dewey's comments published in magazines such as the *New Republic* and his letters with colleagues, family members and friends during his visit to China. Through the efforts in these two aspects, Dewey's visit to China will be better known and the data foundation for the follow-up studies will be laid.

Second, we can update the research ideas or research methods to achieve new perspectives and findings on Dewey's visit to China. Many researchers in educational history are working to explore new research fields. For example, the published book *Frontier Research of Educational History* (Zhou & Zhou, 2019) introduces the history of educational activities, the history of educational life, the history of bodies in education, the history of emotion in education, the history of memories in education, the history of images in education, etc. It analyzes the origin of the above-mentioned research, research theories and methods, the main progress of the research, and the development trend of the research. With the inspiration of the new methods and new fields conducted by the historians mentioned above, we can collect more documents on the life situation that Dewey and his family had during the time of Dewey's visit of China.

Third, the study can extend from Dewey's visit to China as a clue to the research on the interaction between scholars and their Chinese students at Teachers College of Columbia University in the first half of the 20th century. For example, besides Dewey, Paul Monroe, William Heard Kilpatrick and others have visited China continuously since 1913, the year of Monroe's first-time visit of China. The times of their visit, the length of their stay, the wide range of the areas they visited, the deep relationship they established with Chinese political and cultural circles, and the great influence they had on China are beyond the reach of scholars at any other foreign university organizations. All of them have such close interaction, which is rooted in the friendship between these scholars and their Chinese students in the earlier years of their study at Columbia. Dewey was the first scholar from Columbia that gained nationwide fame in China, followed by Monroe, and then by Kilpatrick. As for the other two heavyweights at Teachers College, the visits of Monroe and Kilpatrick can be found in *Differences between Old and New Education: Monroe's Speech in China* (Zhou & Chen, 2013b), *What Kind of Educational Principles Are Most Needed in China: Kilpatrick's Speech in China* (Zhou & Chen, 2013c), *Paul Monroe and China's Educational Modernization* (Zhou & Chen, 2021), and *Chronicle of Paul Monroe's Activities in China* (Zhou & Chen, 2021). These works focus on the cooperation and exchanges between the follow-up visiting scholars Monroe, Kilpatrick and the Chinese educational circles. These studies could help to extend the scope of Dewey's study in China, and also help to view or measure the modern transformation of Chinese education from the perspective of "outsiders."

Fourth, this chapter analyzes the learning, spreading and transformation of American educational theories of Dewey by Chinese scholars. It explores the process of realizing the localization of western educational knowledge. Also, the communication is mutual. The study of Dewey's visit of China could tell this historical story of Chinese modern educational reform to the West as well. For example, based on the following research of Tao Xingzhi, an outstanding student of Dewey and an innovator of Dewey's theories in China, the researchers explored Tao Xingzhi's creative transformation of Dewey's educational theory. These works include *A Pictorial Biography of Tao Xingzhi* (Zhou, 2011), *Research on Tao Xingzhi from a Global Perspective* (8 volumes) (Zhou, 2015), *An*

Extended Biography of Tao Xingzhi (Zhou, 2016), *The Overseas Studies on Tao Xingzhi (New Edition)* (Zhou, 2017a), *Tao Xingzhi's Theory Series* (Zhou, 2020), *A Complete Chronicle of Tao Xingzhi* (Zhou & Liu, 2021). In addition, we could continue to explore the research of Guo Bingwen, Hu Shi, Jiang Menglin, Chen Heqin (陈鹤琴), Zheng Xiaocang (郑晓沧), Zhuang Zexuan (庄泽宣) and other scholars of the Chinese Dewey School of Education in the period of the Republic of China. As historians of education, we've established the research plans. We will highlight the points of their echoing Dewey's spirit of experimentalism, devoting themselves to educational practice and taking root in Chinese soil to practice education.

Finally, the study of Dewey and his Columbia colleagues' visit of China, and the study of their communication and influence with their Chinese students could tell the western academia more critical details on the historical stories of Chinese modern education and its contemporary consequences. At present, some Chinese scholars have introduced Tao Xingzhi's educational thoughts and practice to the west. For example, one of the authors of this chapter Zhou Hongyu have published two works on this theme: *Changing the World through Education: The Life of Tao Xingzhi* (Zhou, 2017b) and *Life Education – Selected Readings of Tao Xingzhi's English Works* (Zhou, 2017c). However, on the whole, there are still lots of work to do on the academic translation and study of Chinese educators' works in the period of the Republic of China. It is also a long way to go for Chinese educational scholars to promote educational exchanges between China and foreign countries. But it is a promising direction to study the history of educational exchange between China and the West to explore the unique characteristics of China's educational modernization.

Acknowledgments

This is a revised and updated version of ZHOU, Hongyu, & LI, Yong. (2019). Recent studies on Dewey's visit to China (1919–1921), *Beijing International Review of Education*, 1(4), 749–754.

References

Chu, Z. H. (2019). On the influence of Dewey to Tao Xingzhi. *Peking University Education Review*, 17(2), 76–90. [储朝晖.杜威与陶行知:走出"投射效应". 北京大学教育评论.]

Dai, W. F. (2019). *A pictorial biography of John Dewey*. Shandong Education Press. [戴伟芬.杜威画传.济南:山东教育出版社.]

Dong, B. (2019). An analysis of the "Dewey effect": A perspective of academic history. *Educational Research*, *40*(4), 15–21. [董标.解析"杜威效应"：一种学术史考察.教育研究.]

Feng, J. J. (2019). Dewey's visit to China and the development of education science in Nanjing Higher Normal School. *Journal of Southeast University (Philosophy and Social Science)*, *21*(4), 5–13. [冯建军.杜威中国之行与南高师——东南大学教育学科的发展.东南大学学报(哲学社会科学版).]

Feng, J. Y. (2019). Faces of democracy: Chinese translation of Dewey's Democracy and education. *Journal of East China Normal University (Educational Sciences)*, *37*(2), 29–36. [冯加渔.民主的多重面向:杜威Democracy and education中文译名的世纪流变.华东师范大学学报(教育科学版).]

Gu, H. L. (2019a). *An academic chronicle of John Dewey in China*. East China Normal University Press. [顾红亮. 杜威在华学谱.上海: 华东师范大学出版社.]

Gu, H. L. (2019b). A Sinicized interpretation of Dewey's concept of "Education is life." *Educational Research*, *40*(4), 22–27. [顾红亮.杜威"教育即生活"观念的中国化诠释.教育研.]

Guo, F. Q. (2019). Dewey's trip to China: A hundred-year echo of educational thoughts. *Educational Research*, *40*(4), 28–33. [郭法奇.杜威的中国之行：教育思想的百年回响. 教育研究.]

Li, Y., & Zhou, H. Y. (2020). The mystery of an educational trip of a "wise man" – A clarification of some issues concerning Dewey's visit to China during the May 4th Movement. *Journal of Hainan Normal University (Social Sciences)*, *33*(4), 85–94. [李永,周洪宇."智者"教育之旅的"迷雾":"五四"时期杜威访华若干问题之厘清.海南师范大学学报(社会科学版).]

Liu, F. T. (2019). Marxist interpretation of Dewey's visit to China: A centennial commemoration. *Journal of China Executive Leadership Academy Pudong*, *13*(5), 52–60. [刘放桐.对杜威来华访问的马克思主义解读——纪念杜威访华百周年.中国浦东干部学院学报.]

Peng, S. S. (2019a). Dewey's interactive experience with China during the May Fourth Movement. *Modern Chinese History Studies*, *2*, 41–50. [彭姗姗.五四期间杜威与中国的一段"交互经验".近代史研究.]

Peng, S. S. (2019b). John Dewey and the May Fourth New Culture Movement. *Chinese Culture Research*, *2*, 18–25. [彭姗姗.杜威与五四新文化运动.中国文化研究.]

Shen, W. W. (2019). The controversy between Columbia and Harvard: The contribution of two groups of American students studying abroad to China's new education and new literature. *Exploration and Free Views*, *5*, 23–25. [沈卫威.哥大哈佛之争：两大留美学人群体对中国新教育及新文学的贡献.探索与争鸣.]

Wang, Y. (2019). The way of conformity: Dewey and Chinese Dewey school's development of traditional education. *Journal of Ningbo University (Educational Science Edition)*, *41*(4), 38–48. [王颖.契合的路径:杜威与中国杜威教育学派对传统教育的发展[J].宁波大学学报（教育科学版）.]

Wu, D. G. (2019). Trip to the University of Chicago: 100 years after Dewey's transformative trip to China. *Fudan Education Forum*, 17(3), 104–112. [邬大光.芝加哥大学之旅：纪念杜威访华100年. 复旦教育论坛.]

Yang, X., & Li, J. Q. (2019). Culture-appropriate: The deep reasons for the transmission and prevalence of Dewey's educational theory in China. *Educational Science Research*, 3, 82–87. [杨旭，李剑萍.文化契合性：杜威教育理论在中国传播流行的深层原因.教育科学研究.]

Zhang, B. X., & Liu, Y. S. (2019). *Dewey's educational thoughts in China*. Peking University Press. [张斌贤，刘云杉.杜威教育思想在中国.北京：北京大学出版社.]

Zhang, H. (2019). On John Dewey and China's educational reform. *Journal of East China Mortal University (Educational Science)*, 37(2), 18–28. [张华.论杜威与中国教育改革.华东师范大学学报（教育科学版）.]

Zhao, K. (2019). Hu Shi's reception and transformation of Dewey's educational ideas in the Early Republic of China: With a focus on the period of Dewey's visit to China. *Peking University Education Review*, 17(2), 91–108 & 189–190. [赵康.胡适对杜威教育思想的吸收和转化：以杜威访华时期为中心.北京大学教育评论.]

Zhong, J. W., & Tu, Y. (2019). A foreign lever: Dewey in China's education reform in the 1920s. *Journal of East China Normal University (Educational Science)*, 37(2), 37–44. [仲建维，涂悦.外来的杠杆：20世纪20年代中国教育改革中的杜威.华东师范大学学报（教育科学版）.]

Zhou, H. Y. (2011). *A pictorial biography of Tao Xingzhi*. Shandong Education Press. [周洪宇.陶行知画传.济南：山东教育出版社.]

Zhou, H. Y. (Ed.). (2015). *Research on Tao Xingzhi from a global perspective (8 volumes)*. Beijing Normal University Press. [周洪宇总主编.全球视野下的陶行知研究（8卷本）.北京：北京师范大学出版社.]

Zhou, H. Y. (2016). *An extended biography of Tao Xingzhi*. People's Education Press. [周洪宇.陶行知大传.北京：人民教育出版社.]

Zhou, H. Y. (2017a). *The overseas studies on Tao Xingzhi* (new ed.). People's Education Press. [陶行知研究在海外（新编本）.北京：人民教育出版社.]

Zhou, H. Y. (2017b). *Changing the world through education: The life of Tao Xingzhi*. CN Times Books, Inc.

Zhou, H. Y. (Ed.). (2017c). *Life education – Selected readings of Tao Xingzhi's English works*. CN Times Books, Inc.

Zhou, H. Y. (Ed.). (2021). *Tao Xingzhi's theory series*. Central China Normal University Press. [周洪宇总主编.陶行知学文库.武汉：华中师范大学出版社.]

Zhou, H. Y., & Chen, J. R. (2013a). *Democracy and education: Dewey's speech in China*. Anhui Education Press. [周洪宇，陈竞蓉.民主主义与教育：杜威在华演讲录.合肥：安徽教育出版社.]

Zhou, H. Y., & Chen, J. R. (2013b). *Differences between old and new education: Monroe's speech in China*. Anhui Education Press. [周洪宇，陈竞蓉.旧教育与新教育的差异：孟禄在华演讲录.合肥：安徽教育出版社.]

Zhou, H. Y., & Chen, J. R. (2013c). *What kind of educational principles are most needed in China: Kilpatrick's speech in China.* Anhui Education Press. [周洪宇，陈竞蓉.中国最需要何种教育原则：克伯屈在华演讲录.合肥：安徽教育出版社.]

Zhou, H. Y., & Chen, J. R. (2021a). *Paul Monroe and China's educational modernization.* Central China Normal University Press. [周洪宇，陈竞蓉.孟禄与中国教育现代化.武汉：华中师范大学出版社.]

Zhou, H. Y., & Chen, J. R. (2021b). *Chronicle of Paul Monroe's activities in China.* Central China Normal University Press. [周洪宇，陈竞蓉.孟禄在华活动年谱长编.武汉：华中师范大学出版社.]

Zhou, H. Y., & Li, Y. (2019). An investigation of the relations between Nanjing Teachers College and Dewey's visit to China during the May Fourth Period. *Journal of Nanjing Normal University (Social Science Edition)*, *3*, 16–30. [周洪宇，李永.五四时期杜威访华与南京高师的关系考察[J].南京师大学报（社会科学版）.]

Zhou, H. Y., & Liu, D. W. (2021). *A complete chronicle of Tao Xingzhi.* People's Education Press. [周洪宇，刘大伟.陶行知年谱长编.北京：人民教育出版社.]

Zhou, H. Y., & Zhou, C. (Eds.). (2019). *Frontier research of educational history.* Shandong Education Press. [周洪宇，周采主编.教育史学前沿研究.济南：山东教育出版社.]

Zhu, J. R. (2019). John Dewey's view on university education and its enlightenment. *University Education Science, 5,* 111–115. [朱镜人.杜威的大学教育观及启示.大学教育科学.]

CHAPTER 3

The Chinese Reception of Dewey

Three Enduring Errors

Lei WANG

Abstract

This paper is based on the results of my research on John Dewey's pedagogical influences in the historical context of China. The thesis was published by Springer in German and English (Wang, 2019). This paper expands further on three crucial and powerful misunderstandings in the Chinese reception of Dewey's basic ideas of democratic education and their enduring philosophical, educational, and political consequences. The results of my study will clarify and correct errors that continue to have an impact today.

Keywords

Dewey – democracy and education – Dewey and Chinese education – misunderstanding and translation errors – Dewey's lectures in China

1 Introduction

Dewey came to China in 1919 at the invitation of his former Columbia University students, who were pioneers of the New Culture Movement (新文化运动 1915–1927) as well as leaders of Chinese educational reform in the 1920s; among them were Hu Shi, Guo Bingwen, Jiang Menglin, and Tao Xingzhi. From the Chinese hosts' point of view, Dewey's pragmatic philosophy could have provided the way for their reform movement. Together, they formed core networks to spread pragmatic education in connection to Dewey's philosophy.

Evaluation of Dewey's influence in China was and continues to be controversial (Su, 2019). On the one hand, as Hu Shi has remarked, "no Western scholar had enjoyed such a large influence as Dewey" (cited in Yang, 2016: 3). Nowadays, there is a consensus among Chinese scholars "that Dewey exerted

© KONINKLIJKE BRILL NV, LEIDEN, 2022 | DOI:10.1163/9789004511477_004

an exceptional influence on China" (Schulte, 2011: 5). A number of studies have been conducted to provide support for this argument (e.g., Wang, 2007; Yuan, 2001; Yang, 2016). Meanwhile, many scholars find that the spread of Deweyan philosophy in China was accompanied by misunderstandings (e.g., Gu, 2000; Wang, 2007, 2015, 2019; Schulte, 2011; Zhao, 2019). Liu Fangtong noted that "Dewey was the most familiar Western philosopher to Chinese academics, but also the most misunderstood, and deserved to be reevaluated" (cited in Su, 2019: 728). Gu Hongliang's (2000) study reveals that Dewey's influence on modern Chinese philosophy is multifaceted and complex. Schulte (2011) was convinced that Dewey was intentionally misunderstood. This statement would be confirmed by Chiang Y.C. (2015).

Furthermore, researchers worldwide are faced with a dilemma in that the original manuscript of Dewey's China lectures is considered lost. The existing publications of the lectures are based on transcriptions made in Chinese while Dewey was delivering his lectures.[1] Numerous research results show that these transcripts partly showed discrepancies with Dewey's basic ideas. Ross found that the transcription he reviewed was "more than dubious" and that "[t]he possibility of error in this final text is beyond calculation" (Ross in MW12: XXIX). He thought the translation errors in Dewey's China lectures were caused by the language differences between Chinese and English (ibid.). Jessica Wang (2007) brings up the question, "Whose Teaching? Or Hu's Teaching?" to distinguish Dewey's thought from Hu Shi's translation. While Wang does not imply Hu Shi's intention to be manipulative, Chiang Y.C. (2015) believes that it was a faulty, imprecise translation. To put it another way, it was a deliberate manipulation to use Dewey's lectures to advance his own cultural and political agenda (95). Zhao Kang (2019: 658) noted that "Hu's reception and interpretation of Deweyan pragmatism was a highly complicated process"; social historical context should also be considered.

In *John Dewey's Democratic Education and its Influence on Pedagogy in China 1917–1937*, I explore Dewey's pedagogical influence exercised before, during, and after his stay (1919–1921) in the historical context of China. My research results show that the influence of Dewey's democratic ideal remained limited at that time, and this was overshadowed by false translations of his lectures. In my view, some crucial and powerful misunderstandings continue to have an impact. Today, Dewey's China lectures are actively being published. The misinterpretations remain unexplained. They continue to be quoted as Dewey's view in current literature, so it is necessary to engage in a historical examination to gain a deeper understanding of this problem and clarify the errors.

To sum up, an inquiry on the issues of misunderstanding of Dewey's basic ideas and translation errors in his China lectures can be considered with varied aspects: social, cultural, and historical background as well as political intentions, misunderstanding of the original author's ideas, and linguistic factors, as scholars worldwide have dealt with. This paper will concentrate on three crucial and powerful misunderstandings in the Chinese reception of Dewey's democratic education. I will underline the consequences of the misinterpretations and mistranslations from a democratic perspective because these consequences have an impact on our lives and our thoughts.

Firstly, for each issue, I am going to identify the misinterpretation of Dewey's basic ideas in his China lectures as well as in the works of Chinese scholars. Secondly, I will emphasize the discrepancy between Dewey's Chinese advocates and his basic ideas towards democracy and education. Furthermore, I am going to draw the philosophical, educational, and political consequences of the misinterpretations in the historical context. To conclude, I will highlight consequences of the misunderstanding in Chinese society today.

2 Misinterpretations of Dewey's Conception of Inquiry and Experience

2.1 *"To Know Is Difficult, to Act Is Easy" by Sun Yat-sen Is a Total Reversal of Dewey's Basic Ideas*

On May 12, 1919, just after his arrival in China, Dewey met Sun Yat-sen. Both were fascinated by this intellectual exchange, however, there was a great intercultural misunderstanding with consequences for political and social action that Dewey did not expect. This conversation took place with Hu Shi and Jiang Menglin, who translated orally.

Shortly after the meeting with Dewey, Sun published *On Psychological Reconstruction* (《心理建设建国方略之一》). In this book, he reflected on the failure of the early Republic after the Xinhai Revolution[2] (辛亥革命 1911). Sun was convinced that the behavior of his own comrades was impacted from the old saying "to know is easy, to act is difficult." That led them to regard Sun's plan for China's renewal as a kind of utopia and to renounce responsibility for the reconstruction of China. Sun undertook refuting this traditional way of thinking to remove the obstacles for a national revolution. He arrived at the conclusion with a new thesis: "To know is difficult, to act is easy" (Sun, 1994: 1–4 and 53–54). In chapter four, Sun Yat-sen referred to his meeting with the American philosopher and wrote:

> On the eve of the publication of the first edition of this book, Dr. Dewey happened to be in Shanghai. I confirmed my theory with him. He said, "We Westerners only think to know is difficult, but no one would think to act is a difficult matter." (Sun, 1994: 50; cited in Ou, 1978: 10)

Here, a fundamental misunderstanding between Sun and Dewey occurs, relating to Dewey's theory and Sun's slogan "to know is difficult, to act is easy" in which Sun's hierarchical-authoritarian understanding of politics is embedded.

While Sun used the encounter with Dewey as a justification for his ideology, he was not persuaded by the concept of inquiry or democracy and education that Dewey espoused. Sun held the view that China was not yet ready for democracy. In his opinion, the existing corrupt "warlordist" regime would not allow the fulfillment of such goals. For this reason, he firmly believed that the first step toward building a new China would have to be a political revolution in which the old bureaucrats, militarists, and politicians would be wiped out. Only after this destruction could reconstruction be achieved (cf. Chow, 1960: 247f.).

In Sun's view, scientific knowledge was a prerequisite for any action and, above all, for the revolution and the reconstruction of the state. At the same time, Sun thought that concrete knowledge wasn't necessary for each individual to participate in the social process. As knowledge was difficult to acquire, and there was a lack of time to acquire it, Sun believed that only a small group of political elites could acquire the necessary knowledge to work out plans for the reconstruction of China. This group of elites was able to take the leading role while the masses had to follow them (Sun, 1994, chapters 5–7).

Obviously, with his proverb "to know is difficult, but to act is easy," Sun attempted to justify a theory helping him persuade his supporters to recognize him as a leader and to follow him blindly in order to advance the political mobilization of the population (Hu, 1998d: 595–597; see also Grieder, 1970: 231–235; Ebertshäuser, 2001: 99–100; Klein, 2007: 82). This initiative was a total reversal of Dewey's basic ideas.

2.2 Hu Shi's Misinterpretation of Inquiry and Experience Concept

Dewey was not aware of the political misinterpretation of Sun Yat-sens' idea. In lectures and public speeches, Dewey quotes Sun Yat-sen, e.g., in the lecture *A Philosophy of Education* at the University of Peking, Dewey presented the scientific method and emphasized the role of action in the thinking process. Afterwards, the statement of Sun Yat-sen was quoted. Dewey's speech was translated as follows:

> I have been told that there is a Chinese proverb to the effect that, to know is easy, to act is difficult. This is just the opposite of the experimental method, for in this method it is only after we have acted upon a theory that we really understand it. There can be no true knowledge without doing. It is only doing that enables us to revise our outlook, to organize

THE CHINESE RECEPTION OF DEWEY   55

our facts in a systematic way, and to discover new facts. The conclusion is that we cannot expect to gain true knowledge without acting upon our ideas. (cited in Clopton & Ou, 1973: 246f.; cf. Yuan et al., 2004: 450)

In this translation, we see that action in the inquiry process was strongly emphasized. Hu Shi was the translator; in his introductory work to Dewey's theory, we can see this relationship presented in the same way and, as a result, see how it shows divergence from Dewey.

In Hu's *Experimentalism* (1998b), he reduced Dewey's theory of inquiry, the five-step thinking process, into two steps: "The scientific method means nothing more than 'courageously setting up hypotheses and carefully searching for evidence.'" This slogan emphasizes the active character of the experimental method but ignores the connection between experiment, experience, and inquiry (cf. Gu, 2000: 110) as well as the conditions and consequences of action.

Hu interprets the concept of experience in a similar way. He writes: "Experience is life, and life is the coherent behavior of man and his environment, the application of thought as a guide to all action" (Hu, 1998b: 231). Hu Shi here misappropriates the role of habits in Dewey's thinking, but apart from that the argument is still almost in line with Dewey's thinking. However, Hu Shi went further in the appeal to "use the environment, subdue it, dominate it, control it" (ibid.).

That was at least Hu Shi's understanding of experimentalism. From Dewey, he adopted first and foremost the formulation of intellectual methodology; it was the methodological aspect of experimentalism that he invariably emphasized in his later works. The philosophical and comprehensive democratic aspects of the pragmatic approach were not in his interest. Faced with the urgent tasks of reconstructing and overcoming challenges during transformation, Hu Shi was consciously looking for a method that promised to remove cultural and intellectual barriers that hindered China's modernization. However, in contrast to Dewey's idea of interaction with the environment, Hu Shi's method is of a narrow utilitarian nature: Firstly, it would practically benefit Chinese reality instead of follow theoretical logic and argumentation. This method even led to distortions of Dewey's original thoughts in some places.

2.3   Dewey's Concepts of Experience and Inquiry and His Proposal for a Spiritual Renewal of China

The concept of experience is of crucial importance for Dewey's philosophy. It opens a "pragmatist way to an antidualistic foundation of knowledge" (Garrison, Neubert & Reich, 2012: 10) in which human action becomes "rendered meaningful through overcoming difficulties and problems" (ibid.: 11).

For Dewey, experience comprises both perception and consciousness, which are not merely subjective phenomena but are always understood from the perspective of interaction and continuity. These two elements form the essential criteria of experience.

From Dewey's perspective, action means "first and foremost a form of inter-action between an organism and its environment that cannot be reduced to linear effects, but rather a reciprocal interplay of forces of change and adaptation" (Neubert, 1998: 149). Dewey believes that we can only make experiences in the full sense if we participate in an activity that involves an active phase of doing and a passive phase of undergoing. Only when both aspects are connected can we speak of a meaningful experience (see further explanation in chapter 4 of this article: "Dewey's experience-based approach"). In this context, he noted, "A separation of the active doing phase from the passive undergoing phase destroys the vital meaning of an experience" (MW9: 158). If these two are separated, experience loses its vitality and degenerates either into senseless routine or into arbitrary or impulsive activism (Garrison, Neubert & Reich, 2012: 12).

Moreover, Dewey considered intelligence "the only source and sole guarantee of a desirable and happy future" (LW2: 19). For him, intelligent thinking has the value of an increase in freedom of action, a liberation from chance and doom (cf. MW12: 163), and knowledge is "itself already action, active being in the world" (Neubert, 1998: 110); it cannot be "detached from the context of experience" (ibid.). Knowledge requires a process of reflective experience, which is characterized by this in Dewey's own words (in the following I refer to MW9: 157):

(i) perplexity, confusion, doubt, due to the fact that one is implicated in an incomplete situation whose full character is not yet determined;

(ii) a conjectural anticipation – a tentative interpretation of the given elements, attributing to them a tendency to effect certain consequences;

(iii) a careful survey (examination, inspection, exploration, analysis) of all attainable consideration which will define and clarify the problem in hand;

(iv) a consequent elaboration of the tentative hypothesis to make it more precise and more consistent, because squaring with a wider range of facts;

(v) taking one stand upon the projected hypothesis as a plan of action which is applied to the existing state of affairs: doing something overtly to bring about the anticipated result, and thereby testing the hypothesis.

This five-step inquiry method Dewey developed is considered not only a model for the teaching method of pragmatic education but also generally a basis for exploration in all situations of human life, including social and political institutions, in the reflection of habits, customs, conventions, and institutions where reflective thinking is required.

Dewey suggested Chinese reformers should develop a stance of inquiry and undertake a gradual transformation. This approach emphasized the importance of experiments, the study of concrete events, and the application of knowledge and intelligence towards social change. Social reformers were expected to pay more attention to identifying, investigating, and diagnosing concrete problems. All ideas and theories were to first be regarded as hypotheses and tested through practical application. The aim of the reform was to advance the common good and to achieve a continuous improvement of society. This pragmatic attitude called for the rejection of extreme idealism and radical revolution (Dewey, 2015: 11–15).

Likewise, Dewey was convinced that China would only be strengthened by a spiritual renewal from within and that cultivating an inquiring mind is essential. For instance, in the essay *What holds China back* (MW12: 53–59), Dewey mentions the conversation with Sun Yat-sen. Sun's assumption that the root of Chinese conservatism could be found in the old proverb "to know is easy, to act is difficult" seemed too superficial to Dewey. He came to a different conclusion: To cope with the drastic changes and challenges, China needs to experience a spiritual renewal from within that means consciously readjusting its own long-established customs and traditions to the new situation. With this new spirit, China would be able to cope with the problematic situations and to handle the lurking evils and dangers during the process of industrialization and transformation. In this context, Dewey spoke of "Transforming the Mind" with "changes of thought, of belief, of outlook on the world" (MW11: 205; MW13: 95); he also spoke of a "transformation of ideas" (MW13: 110), "a new mind and a new morale" (MW13: 95).

Notably, Dewey's of transforming the mind to rebuild China was based on his belief in pluralistic, participatory, deliberative, and communicative democracy. For Dewey, democracy was more than a specific form of government, constitution, or state: It was first and foremost a form of associated life and of common and shared experiences (cf. MW9: 93). Dewey considers education a foundation for building democracy. This not only refers to school education but also includes all spheres of social life. For him, the democratic process is an effective instrument of education. This spiritual renewal is not an individual possession nor a possession of a small group of elites but instead a cooperative intelligence for all Chinese regardless of social status, gender, ethnic origin, etc.

From this perspective, Dewey rejects the approach of setting up a centralized government through violent revolution by Sun Yat-sen or anyone else.

Dewey was convinced that the failure of the Xinhai Revolution was "because it was external, formal, touching the mechanism of social action but not affecting conceptions of life, which really control society" (MW13: 110). He advocates a bottom-up process for developing a democratic way of life. For this purpose, he recommended the dissemination of voluntary organizations as an excellent tool (cf. Yuan et al., 2004: 15; LW2: 351ff.). Through participation in associated processes, individual forces are activated and their full development made possible. This cultivates the ability to organize and cooperate and develops an interest in networking on the basis of common interests and goals. In this sense, Dewey is engaged in empowering individuals to think and judge independently and encouraging them to participate cooperatively. To ensure these goals are met, Dewey emphasizes equal opportunities and participation as guiding principles for social and political reconstruction, for economic and technological development, and for the structure of the educational system.

3   Misinterpretation of the Tension between Individual and Society

In his lectures in China, Dewey's view of the relationship between individual and society was completely misinterpreted. This was transferred to the educational goals so that the essence of his pragmatic approach, based on democratic education, was lost.

In the lecture series on educational philosophy, Dewey discussed this issue from the perspective of democratic education. His speech was translated as follows: "Individuals and society not only stand in different directions, they even seem to interlock directly" (Yuan et al., 2004: 480). Furthermore, in a democracy, "each person develops his/her personality, with the end result that they will be a useful member of society, making a contribution for the realization of a common aim. The common aim is supreme, and individuality is developed through the ability to take responsibility for the common good and the spirit of sacrifice" (ibid.). Regarding the goal of education, the text pointed out that the relationship between personality and society is of the most importance in moral education and concluded that the main problem of moral education is "how to cultivate the individuality for expanding the individual's social sympathy, to be loyal to society and willing to sacrifice" (ibid). Obviously, these are not Dewey's views.

Exploring the writings of Hu Shi and other Dewey supporters, the following tendency can be observed: emphasizing individual responsibility to the society but ignoring the cultural and social context while overemphasizing the social over the individual. The above translation is clearly influenced by this viewpoint.

Referring to a lecture on *True and False Individualism* that Dewey gave in January 1920 in Tianjin, Hu Shi wrote that true individualism means independent thought, that one is fully responsible for the results of one's own thoughts and beliefs. Moreover, he adds a third category that is not found in Dewey's lecture. For Hu Shi, individualism does not only mean autonomous self-realization. In Hu's opinion, self-realization depends on others and always includes a concrete responsibility for society. Under the situation at that time, this duty to social responsibility effects an opposition to traditional structures and a struggle for new framework conditions that enable free development of the personality. In order to reform traditional customs and social attitudes, every Chinese person was obliged to make an active contribution. A responsible participant in society should cultivate a conscientious self-critical habit of the mind, reflecting every action in everyday life (cf. Hu, 1998c: 564–572).

At the same time, Hu Shi sees the relationship between individual and society as hierarchical. Hu Shi interprets society as the "big-self" and the individual as the "small-self." In his writings, society—the "big-self," including the state—is immortal and requires the individual to have a high sense of responsibility for his or her own behavior (Hu, 1998a).

Hu Shi was not alone in this view. Jiang Menglin attaches absolute weight to the state over the individual; he writes:

> If you compare the individual with the state, the former is as light as a feather and the latter as heavy as the Taishan Mountain. Individuals are born for the country and they will die for the country. An individual should do the best for his country. If the country gets into trouble, the individual should be ready to sacrifice his own life. (Jiang, 2001: 113f.)

Some researchers believe that this view has a root in the Confucian ideal (Grieder, 1970; Gu, 2000); differing from those estimates, Zhang Huajun (2013) noted that Hu Shi's concept is a "deliberate abandonment of the Chinese tradition" (549). Exploring history, this hierarchical "big-self" and "small-self" model was first proposed by Liang Qichao, who was inspired by Yan Fu's work of *Tian Yan Lun* (Huang 2012: 211). It might be pointed out that in this book Yan Fu translated Huxley's *Evolution and Ethics*, but he made an important conceptual shift, thus turning it into Yan Fu's own theory of evolution. With the ideas of "natural selection" and "survival of the fittest," represented by Herbert Spencer, Yan Fu introduced Huxley's work to Chinese readers (cf. Schwartz, 1964: 98–113).

In the social Darwinian sense, "survival of the fittest" was usually interpreted as "survival of the strongest." Yan Fu gave an important commentary on this:

> Peoples and living things struggle for survival. At first, species struggle with species; then as [people] gradually progress, there is a struggle between one social group and another. The weak invariably become the prey of the strong, the stupid invariably become subservient to the clever. (cited in Spence, 2013: 280)

This commentary was understood as a guide to transforming and strengthening society for Chinese reformers (cf. Spence, 2013: 280). Drawing on this statement, Liang Qichao proposed the "big-self" and "small-self" concept to define the relationship between individual and society: For Liang, individual freedom meant "the limited liberty enjoyed by citizens, with the purpose of achieving this liberty being to enable the individual to contribute to the benefits of the collective, particularly the survival and strengthening of the Chinese nation" (Yan, 2010: 24).

This hierarchical "big-self" and "small-self" model reflects the philosophy and the expectation of Hu Shi and his contemporary liberal reformers to motivate their countrymen to transform traditional ways of life in order to build a new society. Nevertheless, their attitude contained a utilitarian tendency. In fact, the "big-self" and "small-self" concept causes a division between the individual and the society in which the individual lives and does not suggest a solution to overcome this split (Zhang, 2013: 548). Obviously, this approach promotes absolute submission of the individual to external authority. This is a major divergence from Dewey's thought.

3.1 Dewey's Ideas of a Dynamic Relationship between the Individual and Society

Dewey rejected Huxley's dualism between society and the individual, nature and mankind. Dewey believed that their relationship was not mutually exclusive but instead was in interaction and continuity. From the perspective of pragmatic philosophy, humans are a part of nature: Our source of life comes from the natural and social environment, and our life always interacts with these environments. Also, human thinking is a product of natural evolution that can be traced back to constant interaction with the environment in order to enable survival and reproduction (cf. Garrison, Neubert & Reich, 2016: 11). Human action influences the physical and biological natural world. Humanity has the potential to shape this world in "this way or that, according as men judge, prize, love and labor" (MW11: 50). From this point of view, one must never forget one's original participation and dependence and that one bears ecological responsibility. This world is therefore "our past and our future, our challenge and our means" (Campbell, 1995: x).

Dewey explicitly rejected the notion of progress as "natural," "automatic," or "the inevitable triumph of the strongest individual" that is enshrined in Spencer's social Darwinism. Dewey sees that social progress is not the result of natural selection but "depends upon human intent and aim and upon acceptance of responsibility for its production"; progress takes place gradually, and it is "a responsibility and not as an endowment" (MW10: 238). In Dewey's view, the term *progress* "indicates amelioration, or change toward a more desirable state of affairs" (Hickman, 1990: 178). Progress requires "trained intelligence and forceful character" and that "progressive societies depend for their very existence upon educational resources" (MW7: 333). For Dewey, the idea of social progress as a result of natural selection is precisely the opposite of progress because "[p]rogress is brought about by release of the strictures of outworn and irrelevant customs, conventions, and habits. But without education, the loosing of such bonds tends toward destructive and uncontrolled results" (Hickman, 1990: 178).

Dewey attaches particular importance to the individual in the reconstruction or renewal of existing customs and institutions. "[T]he role of the individual," he writes, is "the redirection, or reconstruction of accepted beliefs" (MW9: 305). He is convinced that "[e]very new idea, every conception of things differing from that authorized by current belief, must have its origin in an individual" (MW9: 305). Dewey notes that individual variations can contribute to the progress of society (cf. ibid). He points out that without encouraging individual participation in associated living processes, organizations, societies, and states, they become static, rigid, institutionalized, and unable to sustain themselves and handle new challenges (cf. MW12: 198). He suggests that "[t]he best guarantee of collective efficiency and power is liberation and use of the diversity of individual capacities in initiative, planning, foresight, vigor and endurance" (MW12: 199).

Above all, Dewey here refers to "an individual who evolves and develops in a natural and human environment, an individual who can be educated" (LW2: 20). He means neither an individual per se (i.e., the concept of individuality as proposed by empiricism and the classical school of western philosophy) nor individuals fixed in isolation and set up for themselves. Dewey rejects atomistic individualism. He considers the idea of an ahistorical, socially distanced individual born with a mind, free will, and reason pursuing only their own interests to be an empty abstraction (cf. Garrison, Neubert & Reich, 2016: 54). From his perspective, the individual does not naturally have a predestined absolute existence because "except in and through communication of experience from and to others, he remains dumb, merely sentient, a brute animal" (MW12: 198).

By this Dewey means that individuality is first and foremost a potential personality trait (Garrison, Neubert & Reich, 2016: 80), which is "created under the influences of associated life" (MW12: 193), and "[o]nly in association with fellows does he become a conscious center of experience" (MW12: 198). That means that humans are social beings and that the realization of individuality is only possible through active participation in an associated life.

In this sense, "Dewey thinks it is society's obligation to actualize the unique potential of each of its members so that they could make their unique contribution to the greater good of the society" (Garrison, Neubert & Reich, 2016: 88). This individual contribution to the welfare of society should not be misunderstood as a relatively narrow, unreflective adaptation to already existing social conditions, expectations, practices, routines, and institutions "but rather as a claim that in a democracy a citizen must receive an education sufficient to function as adequate critics of proposed values" in order to improve social conditions (Campbell, 1995: 214). The role of education is to promote real freedom, which means to promote intellect; i.e., encouraging individuals to think better, observe more clearly, and judge more appropriately (MW6: 232). In Dewey's view, "intelligence is the key to freedom in act" (MW14: 210) and freedom is "the ultimate product of intelligent, reconstructive inquiry, which often requires deconstruction of established habits and customs" (Garrison, Neubert & Reich, 2012: 55).

In this regard, Dewey does not approve of educational systems that aim to build "individuals with minds" (LW1: 169–170); by this he means "passively, obediently, and uncritically conform to the existing customs of a given culture" (Garrison, Neubert & Reich, 2016: 31). Dewey advocates democratic education whose primary aim is encouragement and empowerment for "individual minds" (LW1: 169–170); i.e., "more fully educated individuals as self-determined partakers in culture and society" (Garrison, Neubert & Reich, 2016: 31). Dewey believes that the individual mind, "the vehicle of experimental creation" (LW2: 20), is the only means of directing change and that "[t]hese individuals working alone, or more successfully in voluntary groups, are the initiating means of social reconstruction" (Campbell, 1995: 200). In this regard, Dewey advocates encouragement and empowerment for "full, active, competent, critical, creative and self-determined membership and participation in social processes" (Garrison, Neubert & Reich, 2016: 31).

4   Misinterpretation of the so-Called "Child-Centered" Method

A widespread misunderstanding of educational thought in China is the assumption that Dewey advocated a "child-centered approach." In Dewey's

THE CHINESE RECEPTION OF DEWEY

lectures in China, as well as in publications of educators at that time and in current publications, the "child-centered" method was equated with "Dewey's teaching method." For example, the "child-centered" method was considered to have a significant influence of Dewey on Chinese school education (cf. Zhou, 2005; Gu, 2000: 294; Yuan, 2001; Zhao & Wang, 1981: 11; Wang, 2010: 240). Zhou (2005) noted that the "child-centered" method was institutionalized in the 1922 Renxu education programme (壬戌学制) and that its influence was clearly felt until the new 1929 curriculum. Chen Heqin and Tao Xingzhi were regarded as representatives of this educational idea, and they adapted it to the Chinese situation (cf. Gu, 2000: 294–299).

While researching this issue, it struck my attention that Dewey's own formulation could lead to a misunderstanding. E.g., in *The School and Society* (1899), which was translated into Chinese and published in 1935, he writes:

> Now the change which is coming into our education is the shifting of the center of gravity. It is a change, a revolution, not unlike that introduced by Copernicus when the astronomical center shifted from the earth to the sun. In this case the child becomes the sun about which the appliances of education revolve; he is the center about which they are organized. (MW1: 23)

This quote became the argument that Dewey was in favor of the "child-centered" method (see e.g., Yuan, 2001: 47f.; Gu, 2000: 289; Teng, 1990: 18; Chen & Ren, 2017). In his China lectures, Dewey probably expressed himself in a similar way (cf. Yuan et al., 2004: 419).

Dewey indeed opposed an exaggerated "child-centered" method. We find his criticism in *The Child and the Curriculum*:

> The child is expected to "develop" this or that fact or truth out of his own mind. He is told to think things out, or work things out for himself, without being supplied any of the environing conditions which are requisite to start and guide thought. Nothing can be developed from nothing; nothing but the crude can be developed out of the crude – and this is what surely happens when we throw the child back upon his achieved self as a finality, and invite him to spin new truths of nature or of conduct out of that. (MW2: 282)

Many people seem to think that "child-centered" means letting the child do whatever they want. Steven M. Cahn makes it clear that the failures of an exaggerated "child-centered" method lie in allowing oneself to be guided uncritically by the child's impulses and diffuse interests alone; the curriculum is neglected and teachers are excluded from the learning process (cf. Steven M. Cahn in LW13: XII–XIII). Instead, good teaching is centered on connecting with the state of the child but never letting the child run wild. It means that teachers must understand the child's social, emotional, and cognitive state and the like.

However, this view of Dewey was not taken seriously for quite a long time. The so-called "child-centered" education was a target of further criticism. Zhao Xianglin and Wang Chengxu noted in 1981 that Dewey gave the child more weight than the curriculum (3f.). Recently, more and more researchers have become alert to this misunderstanding as it distracts educators from understanding Dewey's concept of experience-based learning and teaching methods. It has led to confusion in practice. Some researchers address this error openly (e.g., Zou & Mclaren, 2020). Tian (2017) points out that the root of the so-called "child-centered" method is dualism. Ding Daoyong (2016) concludes: "Defining Dewey's teaching ideas as 'child-centered' theory is not only a theoretical misunderstanding, but also misleading pedagogical practitioners."

4.1 Dewey's Experience-Based Approach

Dewey advocates an experience-based approach. The starting point of learning is experience. Dewey believes that we can only fully understand experience if we participate in an activity that involves an active phase of doing and a passive phase of undergoing. Only when both aspects are connected can we speak of a meaningful experience (Garrison, Neubert & Reich, 2012: 12). Learning from experience means:

> [T]o make a backward and forward connection between what we do to things and what we enjoy or suffer from things in consequence. Under such conditions, doing becomes a trying; an experiment with the world to find out what it is like; the undergoing becomes instruction – discovery of the connection of things. (MW9: 147)

By linking both aspects, "doing" and "undergoing," backwards and forwards, we learn. In this way, experience is constituted by the constant reconstruction of what already exists and what is new. The school environment should enable learners to experiment with their own world. The active process leads to one's own experience by showing relationships and connections from one's own actions ("doing") and observed effects ("undergoing"). Here the learner is not a passive recipient of abstract learning material but plays an active role, bringing their abilities, interests, and experiences into a learning context.

From this point of view, the primary task of school is not to impart cognitive knowledge but to promote intelligent action by providing "learning environments that offer sufficient freedom, opportunities and encouragement for a constructive extension ('reconstruction') of the learners' experience" (Neubert, 2012: 49). A successful teaching method "give[s] the pupils something to do, not something to learn; and the doing is of such a nature as to demand thinking, or the intentional noting of connections; learning naturally results" (MW9: 161). The art of teaching pragmatic education lies in shaping the environment that disturbs a student's experience so that students apply their existing emotional and cognitive dispositions to solving a problem situation and thus acquire new or refined dispositions (cf. Garrison, Neubert & Reich, 2016: 36). It is a challenge for teachers, as John J. McDermott summarizes in Introduction to the Later Work 11 (XVIII): Teachers must have a certain sense of the child's domestic experience in its social, family, and ecological environment, and they must be able to continue to feel the child's emotions and interests and then challenge it appropriately. In formal teaching, the wise teacher gives the students something to do that involves them in a critical-creative reflection that already takes place informally in out-of-school environments. The teachers must create opportunities to free children from their sole dependence on their familiar environment by proposing horizons that can create an imaginative reconstruction of their own experiences and encourage them to participate in different cultures, institutions, religions, ethical systems, politics, and social organizations.

Thus, the child's domestic experience gains new meaning. At the same time, their ability to better manage and control subsequent experimental situations increases (cf. Neubert, 2012: 50).

5 Consequences of the Three Misunderstandings

The three central misunderstandings and misinterpretations of Dewey's basic ideas had profound philosophical, educational, and political consequences in China, and they continue to have an impact today.

5.1 *Philosophical and Political Consequences*
Hu Shi's interpretation equates the method of inquiry to an "action plan" in which action is overemphasized while the decisive elements of reflection are not mentioned in the thought process. Without careful observation and reflection of the facts, this plan could be arbitrary. Although the action is freed from routine, it leads to another extreme: One acts blindly; the connections

between an action and its consequences and possibilities in the environment are not considered. The one-sided overemphasis on the active side of experience made Hu Shi neglect the connection between actions, context, and consequences, making them develop a dualism of action and intelligent thinking. The understanding of pragmatism is devalued in the sense of a maximum benefit principle. Obviously, this translation does not support Dewey but instead Sun Yat-sen.

After 1929, Hu Shi refuted Sun Yat-sen. He pointed out that the dualism embedded in Sun's theory was a fundamental flaw; it would result in the Chinese being divided into two classes: a small group of political elites to take the lead and the masses to follow them (cf. Hu, 1998d: 598). The driving force of "acting is easier" mobilized an attitude of following blindly; independent thinking was neglected. Hu Shi – with reference to Dewey's pragmatic theory of cognition – emphasized the inseparability of cognition and action. "The more you act, the greater your knowledge," Hu Shi wrote, and "knowledge is gained directly from practical action, and the function of knowledge is to support action, guide action and improve it" (Hu, 1998d: 597f.). With this argument, Hu Shi expressed one of the most important deviations from Dewey's idea. However, in terms of the history of ideas, reductionism was not without consequence. The lectures translated by Hu Shi were equated with Dewey's thinking. They were received by the wider audience as a confirmation and kind of recognition of Sun's theory. Sun Yat-sen's theory became a weapon of the National Revolution according to Ou Tsuin-chen (1978: 10) and Hu Shi (1998d: 597). Dewey's pragmatism should indirectly contribute to the rise of the nationalists to power, something Dewey would never have agreed with.

For the reformers Tao Xingzhi, Hu Shi, Jiang Menglin, action and activity were of multiple significances against the background of the drastically changing age in China at that time: practical and theoretical scientific experiments, overcoming forces of nature, adapting to the constantly changing living conditions, transforming society, fighting for national liberation in times of war against the Japanese (cf. Gu, 2000: 39). The experimental method became "methodology, life philosophical point of view, epistemology and political statement in one" (Frick, 2002: 224), which went beyond the framework of Dewey's concept of inquiry and experience and should be regarded as a factor distorting Dewey's ideas.

5.2   *Social and Pedagogical Consequence*
The influence of Dewey's democratic ideals remains limited over time and has been overshadowed by mistranslations of his lectures in China. There were considerable distortions in the interpretation of Dewey's basic ideas;

the philosophical and comprehensive democratic aspects were especially neglected so that the essence of his pragmatic approach based on democratic education was lost. In the widespread version of Dewey's lectures in China, Dewey's conception of the individual's relationship to society was completely misunderstood.

Dewey supporters Hu Shi, Jiang Menglin, and Liang Qichao interpreted the relationship between individual and society as "small-self "and "big-self." Their intellectual effort was far removed from the basic ideas of Dewey, and these intellectuals directly opposed Dewey's ideals. Social Darwinism was offered as an analytical model for China's situation and had a profound influence on the view of society and the individual. Transforming Spencer's social Darwinism in the view of the relationship between individual and society, the "big-self" and "small-self" model becomes more radical. Under the perspective of this dichotomy, society and the individual are not only in opposition but also in a hierarchical relationship, society being interpreted as the stronger and the individual as the weaker. In the contradictory framework of the two parties, society takes precedence. As the stronger, it "must" overcome the individual so that the society would survive in general. In a determinist meaning for the individual, there is no opportunity but to sacrifice themselves. In the end, this concept led to division between the individuals and the society, it promoted absolute submission of the individual to external authority, and it caused multiple burdens for individuals. Its practical use for building a new society was severely impaired.

With the outbreak of the Japanese-Chinese War in July 1937, the threat to national survival increased. The intellectuals emphasized the need for a collective identity instead of individual consciousness. Thus, intellectuals lost their critical attitude when it came to questioning the basis of national identity. The need to defend a collective identity at all costs overshadowed that of individual autonomy (cf. Schwarcz, 1986: 230–236). The emphasis on the primacy of the nation facilitated the rise of nationalist and socialist forces who overwhelmed the individualistic trend (Chow, 1960: 360). Thus, cultural and spiritual reorganization ultimately became an instrument for promoting patriotism or national consciousness as well as an instrument for strengthening a dictatorial government.

Educators demanded "nationalist education," considering education a function of the state, in order to strengthen the state against foreign intervention. It is the prerogative of the state to use education as a tool to train citizens, promote national characteristics, and serve the state. Ou Tsuin-chen was a representative of this trend among the Dewey scholars of the time. Ou assumed that the method of democratic education according to Dewey was not suitable for China's national conditions. He recommended the nationalist ideology of Sun

Yat-sen as the correct orientation for Chinese education. Ou was convinced that Chinese education should be reshaped, focusing on discipline, organization, duty, and self-sacrifice (Ou, 1972: 254–257). This school policy found support from Jiang Menglin, who also demanded patriotic moral education in the school policy concept (cf. Jiang, 2001: 113f.).

Tao Xingzhi's educational concept *Life as Education*[3] developed into *National Crisis Education* or *War Education* in the 1930s. For him, it was such a catastrophe that the importance of society outweighed that of the individual so that individuals are obliged to act productively for country and society (cf. Tao, 1985: 15–17). In Chen Heqin's concept of childhood, the child is given an important role in social reforms and in strengthening the country against foreign aggression. Since Japan's aggression from the 1930s onwards, his educational ideas were partly overlaid by patriotic emotions and promoted anti-Japanese resistance (cf. Chen, 1999a, 1999b).

It should be pointed out that with the concept of school as society Dewey proposes in his work *The School and Society* (MW1: 1–109), he provides a necessary conceptual tool for education. This approach encourages participation of schools in social life and reconstruction in response to changing social needs and constellations. Notably, Dewey's concept is consistently aligned with the idea of democracy, resisting any attempt of appropriation by authoritarian or totalitarian ideologies (Neubert, 2008: 229). However, if society determines the framework and contents in schools but does not provide them with sufficient options for participation and mutual exchange, it represents a reversal of Dewey's concept. There is a constant danger that social elites with powerful interests will define what they consider to be the best forms of common living for everyone. Then they could impose their goals and curriculum content on learners and make them fit their purposes while channeling their experiences and energies into utilitarian opportunities. In this case, schools cannot contribute to the useful reconstruction of society. Individual and societal progress could be restricted and the actual goal of the reform and democratization counteracted.

5.3 Consequences for Today

Over the past three decades, China has undergone profound social and economic transformation. Social researchers observe that modernity has an even more complex face in China than in the West. Currently, Chinese society is undergoing what Beck and Edgar (2010) characterize as "compressed modernization," a juxtaposition of pre-modern, modern, and post-modern states (Yan, 2010: 35). If we compare these conditions with Dewey's observations 100 years ago, we have to conclude that social divisions have grown significantly in Chinese society, and other associated forms of social division are constantly taking on new shapes: e.g., a growing gap between the country and city, the rich and poor, urban laborers and peasant workers, the lower classes and billionaires, etc. While diversity and plurality increase, ambivalence has emerged, and now they go hand in hand as modern life becomes more complex.

Bauman (2000) observes insightfully that there is a turn from a "heavy," "solid," hardware-focused modernity to a "light," "liquid," software-based modernity. He warns that in the social life of liquid modernity, there is a growing gap between "individuality de jure"—i.e., "the tasks of individualization that men and women are socially required to take upon themselves"— and "individuality de facto"—i.e., "their abilities, dispositions, chances, and resources to make, articulate, and realize the choices they really want to make" (Garrison, Neubert & Reich, 2012: 131). This gap has a more complex and profound dimension in current Chinese society. Today, China is lacking in the relationship between individual and state, "a domain of inviolable individual basic rights" (cf. Beck & Beck-Gernsheim, 2010: XVII). Individualization in Chinese society is mainly limited to the areas of economic activities. The possibilities of democratic participation are strictly limited. At the same time, an increasing capitalization in all areas of life is accompanied by division and exclusion, which jeopardize participation and equal opportunities and thus stand in the way of intellectual progress. Such divisions favor the development of a ruthless atomistic individual. A lack of participation in public life does not as fully allow for the development of individuality as it should.

From a democratic perspective, we see the necessity to help individuals to cope with these crises as an essential challenge for education to bridge this gap. This is effectively what we learn from Dewey. Dewey's approach was aimed at overcoming social transformation, counteracting the dark side of an expanding industrial society, and overcoming current and future challenges and risks through intellectual and cultural growth. As Garrison, Neubert and Reich (2016) point out:

> The aim of education in a pluralistic, participatory, and communicative democratic society is individual and social growth. This implies that each unique individual should have sufficient opportunity to make their unique social contribution. This can only be realized if steps are taken towards more equal chances and equitable support for all not only in education but in all areas of social life. That remains as much of a challenge for democracy and education today as in Dewey's time. (123)

However, the misinterpretations of Dewey's philosophies still have an impact on the thought of Chinese scholars today. The ideas associated with these three misunderstandings could be used to justify the current framework conditions that prevent individual and social progress. In contemporary political structure, we find similar characteristics that relate to dualism in Sun Yat-sen's thoughts which—as Hu Shi pointed out in 1929—would divide Chinese people (Hu, 1998d: 598). The dichotomy of "big-self" and "small-self" still has an impact on social life in modern China (cf. Yan, 2010: 15–31). This dualism stands as an obstacle to the cultivation of a healthy individuality (Zhang, 2013: 543). This hierarchical model of "big-self" and "small-self" has a root in social Darwinism. Its approach led to a division between individuals and society, promoting absolute submission of the individual to external authority. It could be used to justify the current framework conditions that deny or even eliminate diversity and variety, leading to exclusion.

The most recently published translations of Dewey's China lectures are still equated with Dewey's actual thinking. These three central misinterpretations remain unidentified and unexamined, which has seriously negative implications for the contemporary research literature. In my opinion, a critical revision of the edition of Dewey's China lectures is very necessary.

6 Conclusion

This paper explores and clarifies three crucial and powerful misunderstandings in the Chinese reception of Dewey's basic ideas of democratic education. It highlights their philosophical, educational, and political consequences and emphasizes their impact for today.

Sun Yat-sen took Dewey's concepts of inquiry and experience as justification for his hierarchical ideology, which called for blindly following political leadership and thus favoring nationalism. With his misinterpretation, Hu equates the method of inquiry as an "action plan." His reductionism leads to a dualism of action and intelligent thinking. The understanding of pragmatism is devalued in the sense of a principle of maximum benefit. Obviously, this misinterpretation supported Sun Yat-sen.

The influence of Dewey's democratic ideals remains limited over time and has been overshadowed by mistranslations of his lectures in China. In his lectures in China, Dewey's view of the relationship between individual and society was completely misinterpreted. This was transferred to the educational goals so that the essence of his pragmatic approach, based on democratic education, was lost. Hu Shi and other Dewey supporters interpreted the relationship between individual and society as "small-self" and "big-self." The intellectual effort supported by Hu Shi as an example was far removed from the basic ideas of Dewey, and these intellectuals directly opposed his ideals. This hierarchical model of "big-self" and "small-self" has a root in social Darwinism.

THE CHINESE RECEPTION OF DEWEY 71

Its approach led to division between the individuals and the society, promoting absolute submission of the individual to external authority. The over-emphasis on a one-sided child-centered approach was also a misunderstanding. Indeed, the overemphasis on the status of the child ended up being a tool for the benefit of the social state.

Undoubtedly, these misunderstandings were not unrelated to the historical context of the time. However, their consequences did not lose their significance with the end of this historical chapter. They are still evident in today's political, philosophical, and educational spheres. Today, China has undergone profound social and economic transformation. The challenges are increasing as the transformation from traditional to modern configurations continues and accelerates. Compellingly, in contemporary political structure, we find similar characteristics that relate to dualism in Sun Yat-sen's thoughts, which would divide Chinese people. The dichotomy of "big-self" and "small-self" still has an impact on social life and education. The publishing of Dewey's China lectures and interpretation of Deweyan ideas continues to lead to the widespread misunderstanding. The broader consequences are that these ideas will be used to defend claims that Dewey originally opposed. Further, it could also be used to justify the current framework conditions that prevent individual and social progress, or it could even be used to justify, deny, or eliminate diversity and variety, leading to exclusion.

In conclusion, I think the main lesson from the current pandemic crises is that we should recognize how valuable the individual mind (i.e., each person's ability to think, feel, and create) is. In addition, it is critical that we understand how important it is to enable and encourage this participation to advance sustainable development in the interest of the common good and how fatal it is to exclude participation—even eliminate it with power, censorship, or through sanctions—both for society and for the individual. These lessons remind us of what we learn from Dewey. His proposal for China—cultivating cooperative intelligence towards democracy and education to cope with current and further challenges—is still as relevant as it was 100 years ago and is gaining more and more credence and validity today. Obviously, to clarify and correct these crucial and powerful misunderstandings becomes even more important.

Acknowledgments

This manuscript has benefited from valuable comments and suggestions. I would like to express my sincere gratitude to Dr. Jim Garrison, Dr. Yuning Liu at Virginia Tech, and Dr. Huajun Zhang at Beijing Normal University.

Notes

1. All of Dewey's speeches and lectures were translated into Chinese by interpreters and later published in Chinese newspapers and periodicals.

   Anthologies in the Chinese language include:

   - His lecture series at Peking University (1919–1920) were translated by Hu Shi and published by the Peking Morning Paper under the title *Dewey's five famous lectures* (杜威五大演讲). This was the most common version at that time, which was published in 13 editions with over 100,000 copies within one year. Today, the anthology of *Dewey's five famous lectures* is still actively published.
   - The lecture series at Nanjing Normal University (1920) were translated by Liu Boming and published under the title *Dewey's three great lectures* (杜威三大演讲).
   - In 2004, Yuan Gang, Sun Jiaxiang and Ren Bingqiang collected about 170 manuscripts and compiled them into *John Dewey, Democracy and Modern Society. The Full Transcript of Dewey's Lectures in China* (民治主义与现代社会. 杜威在华演讲集).

   In the English language published lectures, there is a concern about (re)translations on the basis of the Chinese minutes, which had been orally translated by Hu Shi and other interpreters.

   - On the basis of the Chinese manuscripts, Robert W. Clopton and Tsuin-chen Ou (re)translated two lecture series into English in 1973, which was published under the title "John Dewey. Lectures in China 1919–1920." The series consists of 16 lectures on the topics "Social and Political Philosophy" and "A Philosophy of Education," given at the University of Peking from 1919–1920.
   - Tsuin-chen Ou translated and published a second volume in 1985, under the title "John Dewey. Lectures in China 1919–1920. On Logic, Ethics, Education and Democracy." The series consists of lectures on logic, ethics, education and democracy given in Peking, Shanghai, and Nanking.
   - Robert W. Clopton and Tsuin-chen Ou (re)translated a series of six lectures on the subject of *Three Contemporary Philosophers about William James, Henri Bergson and Bertrand Russell*, given in Peking in 1919–1920. This was included in the Critical Complete Edition of John Dewey's collected works (ed. by Jo Ann Boydston) in Middle Work 12.

   A part of Dewey's original manuscript of the "Social and Political Philosophy" lecture series delivered at Beijing University (1919–1920) (The Lectures I, II, III, IV, VI, X, XI, XII, and XVI) has been discovered by Chiang Y.C. in Hu Shi Archive, Institute of Modern History, Chinese Academy of the Social Sciences, in Beijing. The old existing lectures were published for the first time in 2015 by *European Journal of Pragmatism and American Philosophy* (Vol. 7, Issue 2, 2015, pp. 7–44). Roberto Frega (2017) and Michael A. Peters (2019) give critical reviews.

2. In the late Qing Dynasty, adherents of the basic ideas of Chinese nationalism formed. They wanted to try to transform China into a strong modern state by establishing and building a republic. This movement was led by Sun Yat-sen （孙中山, 1866–1925). In 1911, they succeeded in overthrowing the emperor – in history this event is called the Xinhai Revolution (辛亥革命). This ended the reign of the Chinese Empire, which was over 2000 years old. The first Chinese republic was established, but the road to democracy was rocky and difficult. The young republic was founded on extremely shaky foundations and had to struggle with huge problems from the very beginning: The first president, Yuan Shikai (袁世凯, 1859–1916), who had previously been a senior official in the imperial Qing government, was fundamentally hostile to democratic government. Further, he had little understanding of the revolutionaries' new ideas. After taking office, Yuan had the opposition persecuted and even murdered, and the National Assembly and provincial parliaments were dissolved. He established a

THE CHINESE RECEPTION OF DEWEY

dictatorial regime in which he possessed unlimited power. Ultimately, he proclaimed himself emperor (December 1915). China's hope for democracy was completely destroyed.

The result was mass protests and a military rebellion against Yuan's regime. Yuan was forced to abdicate and died shortly thereafter (June 1916). With his death, the last central power in China ended and a long period of destabilization, disorientation, and fragmentation of the country followed. The Beiyang army fragmented into factions from which regional military rulers asserted themselves, fighting against each other for their own interests and power. The country sank into a civil war that lasted for decades.

3 *Life as Education* according to Tao Xingzhi, is characterized by three central statements: "Life as education," "Society as a school," and "Teaching, learning and acting form a unity." It became the basis for various projects initiated by Tao Xingzhi to support "popular education," "rural education," "work and study education," "national crisis education," "war education," and "democratic education." A comprehensive handling of Tao's concepts and their connection to Dewey's ideas in Wang L. (2019, chapter 8).

References

Complete Edition of the Works of John Dewey

Quotations from the Critical Complete Edition of John Dewey's works are taken from the edition published by Southern Illinois University Press. The volume and page numbers follow the initial letters of the series. Abbreviations for the edition are:

– Dewey, John: Collected Works (edited by Jo Ann Boydston)
– MW *The Middle Works* (1899–1924)
– LW *The Later Works* (1925–1953)

John Dewey's Lectures in China

Clopton, R. W., & Ou Tsuin-chen (Eds. and Trans.). (1973). *John Dewey, Lectures in China, 1919–1920*. The University Press of Hawaii.

Yuan, Gang et al. (Eds.). (2004). [元刚等编] *Democracy and modern society. The full transcript of Dewey's Lectures in China* [民治主义与现代社会. 杜威在华演讲集]. Peking University Press [北京大学出版社].

Dewey, J. (2015). Lectures in social and political philosophy, 1919–21. Symposia. John Dewey's Lectures in Social and Political Philosophy (China). *European Journal of Pragmatism and American Philosophy, 7*(2), 7–45.

Other Literature

Bauman, Z. (2000). *Liquid modernity*. Polity Press.

Beck, U., & Beck-Gernsheim, E. (2010). Foreword: Varieties of individualization. In H. H. Mette & S. Rune (Eds.), *iChina. The rise of the individual in modern Chinese society* (pp. xiii–xx). Nordic Institute of Asian Studies (NIAS).

Beck, U., & Grande, E. (2010). Varieties of second modernity: Extra-European and European experiences and perspectives. *British Journal of Sociology, 61*(3), 409–443.

Campbell, J. (1995). *Understanding John Dewey: Nature and cooperative intelligence.* Illinois Open Court Publishing Company.

Chen, H. [陈鹤琴]. (1999a). My position (A. Stehen, Trans.). In H. Frick, M. Leutner, & N. Spakowski (Eds.), *"Die Befreiung der Kinder". Konzepte von Kindheit im China der Republikzeit* (pp. 307–321). LIT Verlag.

Chen, H. [陈鹤琴]. (1999b). How the "living education" should be carried out (A. Stehen, Trans.). In H. Frick, M. Leutner, & N. Spakowski (Eds.), *"Die Befreiung der Kinder". Konzepte von Kindheit im China der Republikzeit* (pp. 371–376). LIT Verlag.

Chen, Y. [陈妍], & Ren, Q. [任强]. (2017). From "children-centered" to "students-focused" – The influence of Dewey's "children centeredness on China's education" [从"儿童中心"到"学生为本". 略论杜威 "儿童中心论"对中国教育的影响] *Journal of Shaanxi Xueqian Normal University* [陕西学前师范学院学报], *33*(11), 25–28.

Chiang, Y.-C. (2015). Appropriating Dewey: Hu Shi and his translation of Dewey's "social and philosophical philosophy" lectures series in China. *European Journal of Pragmatism and American Philosophy, VII*(2), 71–97.

Chow, T.-t. (1960). *The May Fourth Movement. Intellectual revolution in modern China.* Harvard Universität Press.

Ding, D. [丁道勇]. (2016). The child is not the center. A review of John Dewey's Theory of education [儿童不是中心 对杜威教学思想的再认识]. *Global Education Magazine* [全球教育展望], *11*, 110–128.

Ebertshäuser, G. (2001). *Perspektiven nationaler und staatlicher Neugestaltung Chinas: Gu Yanwu und Sun Yat-sen.* LIT Verlag.

Frega, R. (2017). John Dewey's social philosophy: A restatement, symposia. John Dewey's Lectures in social and political philosophy (China). *European Journal of Pragmatism and American Philosophy, VII*(2), 98–128.

Frick, H. (2002). Kindheit als gestalteter Akt: Tao Xingzhi und die Priorität des Handelns. In H. Frick (Ed.), *"Rettet die Kinder!": Kinderliteratur und kulturelle Erneuerung in China, 1902–1946* (pp. 199–244). LIT Verlag.

Garrison, J., Neubert, S., & Reich, K. (2012). *John Dewey's philosophy of education. An introduction and recontextualization for our times.* Palgrave Macmillan.

Garrison, J., Neubert, S., & Reich, K. (2016). *Democracy and education reconsidered. 100 years after Dewey.* Routledge.

Grieder, J. (1970). *Hu Shi and the Chinese Renaissance: Liberalism in the Chinese Revolution, 1917–1937.* Harvard University Press.

Gu, H. [顾红亮]. (2000). *The misunderstood pragmatism* [实用主义的误读]. East China Normal University Press [华东师范大学出版社].

Hu, S. [胡适]. (1998a). Ibsenism [易普生主义]. In *HSWJ* [胡适文集] (2) (pp. 475–489). Peking University Press [北京大学出版社].

THE CHINESE RECEPTION OF DEWEY 75

Hu, S. [胡适]. (1998b). Experimentalism [实验主义]. In *HSWJ* 胡适文集 (2) (pp. 208–248). Peking University Press [北京大学出版社].

Hu, S. [胡适]. (1998c). Non-individualistic new life [非个人主义的新生活]. In *HSWJ* [胡适文集] (2) (pp. 564–572). Peking University Press [北京大学出版社].

Hu, S. [胡适]. (1998d). Knowledge is difficult, action is not easier [知难, 行亦不易]. In *HSWJ* [胡适文集] (5) (pp. 589–600). Peking University Press [北京大学出版社].

Huang, K. [黄克武]. (2012). *Wei Shi Zhi An: Yan Fu and the cultural transformation of Modern China* [惟适之安: 严复与近代中国的文化转型]. Social Sciences Academic Press [社会科学文献出版社].

Jiang, M. [蒋梦麟]. (2001). The educational concept for the development of a new country [建设新国家之教育观念]. In Jiang Menglin [蒋梦麟] (Ed.), *Essays on teaching and culture* [蒋梦麟学术文化随笔] (pp. 131–132). China Youth Publishing Group [中国青年出版社].

Klein, T. (2007). *Geschichte Chinas. Von 1800 bis zur Gegenwart.* UTB.

Leutner, M. (1999). Entwürfe zur Vorschulerziehung in der Republikzeit und der besondere Beitrag Chen Heqins. In H. Frick, M. Leutner, & N. Spakowski (Eds.), *"Die Befreiung der Kinder". Konzepte von Kindheit im China der Republikzeit* (pp. 75–116). LIT Verlag.

Neubert, S. (1998). *Erkenntnis, Verhalten und Kommunikation: John Deweys Philosophie des "experience" in interactionistisch-konstruktivistischer Interpretation.* Waxmann.

Neubert, S. (2012). *Studien zu Kultur und Erziehung im Pragmatismus und Konstruktivismus.* Waxmann.

Ou, T.-c. [吴俊升]. (1972). Preface to educational philosophy [教育哲学大纲渝版自序]. In T.-c. Ou [吴俊升] (Ed.), *Selection of Ou Tsuin-chen about education and culture* [教育与文化文选] (pp. 254–257). Taiwan Commercial Press [台湾商务印书馆].

Ou, T.-c. (1978). *Dewey's influence on China's efforts for modernization.* St. John's papers in Asian studies, No. 24. Center of Asian Studies at St. John's University.

Peters, M. A. (2019). 100 years of Dewey in China, 1919–1921 – A Reassessment. *Beijing International Review of Education, 1*(1), 9–26.

Ross, R. (1990). Introduction. In *The Middle Works of John Dewey 12* (pp. iii–xxx). Southern Illinois University Press.

Schulte, B. (2011). The Chinese Dewey: Friend, fiend, and flagship. In R. Bruno-Jofre & J. Schriewer (Eds.), *The global reception of John Dewey's thought: Multiple refractions through time and space* (pp. 83–115). Routledge.

Schwarcz, V. (1986). *The Chinese enlightenment. Intellectuals and the legacy of the May Fourth Movement of 1919.* University of California Press.

Schwartz, B. (1964). *In search of wealth and power. Yen Fu and the West.* Harvard University Press.

Spence, J. D. (2013). *The search for modern China* (3rd ed.). Norton & Company.

Steven, M. C. (1990). Introduction. In *The later works of John Dewey 13* (pp. ix–xviii). Southern Illinois University Press.

Su, Z. (2019). John Dewey and Chinese education: Comparative perspectives and contemporary interpretations. *Beijing International Review of Education, 1*(4), 714–745.

Sun, Y.-c. [孙中山]. (1994). On psychological reconstruction [心理建设]. In *The reconstruction of the state* [建国方略]. Liaoning People's Publishing House [辽宁人民出版社].

Tao, X. [陶行知]. (1985). A great school for national liberation [民族解放大学校]. In *TXZQJ* [陶行知全集] (Vol. 3, pp. 15–17). Hunan Education Press [湖南教育出版].

Teng, D. [藤大春]. (1990). Dewey and his democracy and education [杜威和他的民主主义与教育]. In C. Wang [王承绪] (Ed.), *Dewey. Democracy and education* [杜威民主主义与教育] (pp. 4–42). People's Education Press [人民教育出版社].

Tian, L. [田良臣], & Hu, B. [胡冰洁]. (2017). Misinterpretation and clarification of Dewey's educational thought in the Chinese context [中国语境下杜威教育思想的误读与澄清]. *Educational Science Research* [教育科学研究], *11*, 89–92.

Wang, C. [王成兵]. (2015). The understanding on the classical texts of the idea of experience in Dewey's "The need for a recovery of philosophie" [对杜威《哲学复兴的需要》中经验观念的理解]. *Academic Monthly* [学术月刊], *47*(7), 19–24, 41.

Wang, C. [汪楚雄]. (2010). *Qixin yu Tuoyu. Study on the movement for new education in China (1912–1930)* [启新与拓域 中国新教育运动研究 (1912–1930)]. Shangdong Education Press [山东教育出版社].

Wang, J. C.-S. (2007). *John Dewey in China: To teach and to learn.* SUNY Press.

Wang, L. (2019). *John Dewey's democratic education and its influence on pedagogy in China 1917–1937.* Springer VS.

Yan, Y. (2010). Introduction: Conflicting images of the individual and contested process of individualization. In H. H. Mette & S. Rune (Eds.), *iChina. The rise of the individual in modern Chinese society* (pp. 1–38). Nordic Institute of Asian Studies (NIAS).

Yang, J. Z. (2016). *When Confucius "encounters" John Dewey: A historical and philosophical analysis of Dewey's visit to China* [Dissertation]. University of Oklahoma Graduate College.

Yuan, Q. [元青]. (2001). *Dewey and China* [杜威与中国]. People's Publishing House [人民出版社].

Zhang, H. (2013). Individuality beyond the dichotomy of "small self and big self" in contemporary Chinese education: Lessons from Hu Shi and Liang Shuming. *Frontier of Education in China, 8*(4), 540–558.

Zhao, K. (2019). Why did Hu Shi introduce Deweyan pragmatism to China as only a method. *Beijing International Review of Education, 1*(4), 658–672.

Zhao, X. [赵祥霖], & Wang, C. [王承绪] (Eds.). (1981). *Dewey's writings in pedagogy* [杜威教育论著选]. East China Normal University Press [华东师范大学出版社].

Zhou, H. (2005). *The spread and impact of Deweyan educational philosophy in China* [Presentation]. Centre on Chinese Education, Teacher's College, Columbia University. Retrieved January 31, 2020, from https://citeseerx.ist.psu.edu/viewdoc/download?doi=10.1.1.564.1723&rep=rep1&type=pdf

Zou, H., & McLaren, P. (2020). Four issues in the centennial study of Dewey's "Child-centered" in China: A critical review [中国杜威"儿童中心"百年研究的四个问题 一个批判性考察]. *Education Science* [教育科学], *36*(5), 49–55.

CHAPTER 4

Why Did Hu Shi Introduce Deweyan Pragmatism to China as Only a Method?

ZHAO Kang

Abstract

Before and during John Dewey's visit to China, Hu Shi, who was one of the most famous and influential Chinese intellectuals of the time, intensively introduced pragmatism to China. Hu stressed that pragmatism was only "the scientific method applied to philosophy." This interpretation of Deweyan pragmatism not only caused insufficient understanding and even misunderstandings of Dewey's philosophy (including his philosophy of education), but has also been considered by many Chinese scholars today as a kind of transformation of Dewey's pragmatism. This essay explores why Hu introduced Deweyan pragmatism as only a method in China. Hu's reception and interpretation of Deweyan pragmatism was a complicated process; thus, it must be investigated from Hu's worldview, the particular sociopolitical context in China at the time as well as his life history. The paper concludes that labeling Hu Shi as an advocator of the total Westernization of China is not accurate.

Keywords

Dewey – Hu Shi (Hu Shih) – pragmatism – philosophy of education – social reform – educational reform

1   Introduction[1]

Before and during John Dewey's visit to China, Hu Shi (or Hu Shih), once a Dewey's PhD student and later one of the most famous and influential Chinese intellectuals of his time, introduced pragmatism to China systematically and intensively. However, instead of using the term "pragmatism," Hu used "experimentalism" to express this philosophy to his Chinese audience. Hu (1998 [1919]) claimed that "experimentalism is simply the application of scientific method to philosophy" (213). This interpretation of Deweyan pragmatism not

© KONINKLIJKE BRILL NV, LEIDEN, 2019 | DOI:10.1163/9789004511477_005

HU SHI'S INTRODUCTION OF DEWEYAN PRAGMATISM TO CHINA 79

only caused insufficient understanding, and even misunderstandings of Dewey's philosophy (including his philosophy of education) by his Chinese readers. It also has been identified by scholars today with Hu's transformation and even distortion of Dewey's pragmatism.

In this essay, I first explore how Hu Shi interpreted Deweyan pragmatism as a method and what impact this had on the educational and intellectual fields in China over the years. Second, I argue that Deweyan pragmatism is not simply a method, that is, Deweyan pragmatism, as a school of philosophical thought, had its own system with many branches of philosophy, including theories of knowledge, metaphysics, aesthetics, and ethics. Third, based on the observation mentioned above, I explore why Hu Shi introduced Deweyan pragmatism by merely focusing on its method from philosophical, social historical, and biographical perspectives. Finally, I conclude that Hu's reception and interpretation of Deweyan pragmatism was a highly complicated process that was limited by his world view, motivated by the social historical situation, and influenced by his own academic inclinations. Although some misunderstandings were caused by Hu's interpretation of pragmatism, his contribution to introducing pragmatism to China for its social, educational, and academic reform cannot be neglected or underestimated.

2 Hu Shi's Interpretation and Advocacy of Pragmatism as a Method

In the spring of 1919, Hu Shi introduced pragmatism in general and Deweyan pragmatism in particular, to the Chinese public by delivering a series of lectures at the Ministry of Education in Beijing. In his lecture titled "Experimentalism," instead of translating pragmatism as "实用主义" (pragmatism) as used today in Chinese, Hu used the term "实验主义" (Experimentalism) to translate its name. As Hu (1998 [1919]) argued, "pragmatism" only stresses "real effects" in its meaning; however, "experimentalism" not only pays attentions to "real effects," but also highlights that "what this philosophy cares about most is the *experimental method*" (208–209, emphasis added). Hu claimed that "the laboratory attitude of mind" is the overarching attitude of the different pragmatists within this school of philosophical thought. Hu further stressed that experimentalism is the result of the progress of both natural science and the influence of Darwin's theory of evolution, both of which developed in the Western world in the 19th century. Thus, Hu (1998 [1919]) described experimentalism demanding both scientific and genetic attitudes, and concluded that "experimentalism is simply the application of scientific method to philosophy" (212–213). In 1921, Hu (1998 [1919]) also delivered an address at the farewell party held for Dewey and his family in Beijing, claiming that "he (Dewey) leave us a philosophical method, which we use to solve our special problems. This method is experimentalism, and it can be further categorized as historical method and experimental method" (279).

Not only did Hu (1998 [1919]) apply the pragmatist method to his academic project and to his conception of social reform, but he also considered that Dewey's philosophy of education could mainly be seen as a method for reforming the traditional education system. For Hu (1919; cf., Zhang, 2013), a key role of the pragmatist philosophy of education is to cultivate "intellectual individuality" through the experimental method. In his lecture titled "Dewey's Philosophy of Education," Hu (1998 [1919]: 247) suggests that Dewey's philosophy of education could be a method for reforming China's educational system. A key principle of this philosophy of education is what Hu called "experimentalism." Hu then commented that the experimental method was beginning to work very well in the Chinese education system. As Hu (2003 [1919]) wrote, "His [Dewey's] advocacy of the experimental method in education has shattered our belief in a rigid and uniform educational system, and challenges us to carry on innovations and experiments without which an educational system is lifeless" (253).

Many scholars today have mentioned the issue of Hu's mere focus on the method in his interpretation of Deweyan pragmatism. Zhao (1996) observed that Hu fragmented Deweyan pragmatism and transformed it into part of his own thought. Deng (2001), a distinguished philosopher who is specialized in Western philosophy in today's China, noted that Hu accepted Deweyan pragmatism as only a method, that is, experimentalism, instead of receiving it as a philosophy as it is. Deng considered this a kind of "cultural malposition," that is, to interpret a Western philosophy mainly from a Chinese cultural perspective. Liu (2015) also expressed a similar point. Wang (2003) showed that in introducing and interpreting Deweyan pragmatism, Hu turned Dewey's empirical ontology into simply cognitive experimentalism. These scholars all believe that Hu transformed Dewey's philosophy to support his own academic ambitions and his conceptions of sociocultural reform during a particular historical period in the Chinese context. Tan (2004) also argued that ever since Hu began to study Dewey's philosophy in America in the summer of 1915, "[w]hat would occupy a central position in his thinking and practice in the years to come was actual application of Dewey's method of thinking" (46). She also demonstrated that "[t]hough his interpretation of pragmatism as method has considerable support from Dewey's writing, Hu sometimes exaggerated Dewey's own emphasis on method" (Tan, 2004: 51). In a similar vein, Wang (2007) noted that Hu "understood and promoted Dewey's pragmatism as a method of social inquiry" (34).

For a long time, Hu's interpretation of Dewey's philosophy as merely an experimental method caused other aspects of Deweyan pragmatism to become invisible, which led to numerous misunderstandings of Dewey's philosophy in China. In philosophical circles, Liang Shuming (梁漱溟), who was a contemporary of Hu, criticized Dewey's philosophy for merely focusing on changes without paying due attentions to certainties and moral principles (Liang, 1934). Qu Shiying (瞿世英) blamed Dewey's philosophy for its sole concern on the "process" without caring about "ideals" and "purposes" (Qu, 1940). In the field of education, Huang Yanpei (黄炎培), based on his understanding of Dewey's lectures in China, tended to read Dewey's philosophy of education as a somewhat utilitarian view of education and stressed its linkages to vocational education (Huang, 1921). Then, from the mid-1950s to the end of the 1970s, with ideological attacks launched on Hu Shi, Deweyan pragmatism also suffered from severe political criticisms. Although these misunderstandings of Dewey should not be solely ascribed to Hu, what cannot be neglected is that Hu's mere focus on introducing pragmatism as a method is one of the sources that led to those misunderstandings, not least because Hu was a very important figure in China's intellectual field and a very early interpreter of Deweyan pragmatism. It was not until the early 1980s that Deweyan pragmatism came to be understood and discussed more openly and respectfully in both the fields of philosophy and education.

3   Deweyan Pragmatism: Only a Method?

Without doubt, Deweyan pragmatism is not simply a method; otherwise it can hardly be called as a philosophy. Apart from stressing the pragmatist method, Dewey actually developed pragmatist theories of knowledge, pragmatist metaphysics, aesthetics, and ethics. Although some of them were fully developed after Hu's interpretation of Dewey's philosophical ideas in China, we can still find traces of them in their formative period before and during Hu's interpretation of Dewey's pragmatism. While Dewey indeed regarded "pragmatism as primarily a method" in his early article "What pragmatism means by practical" in 1908, this does not mean that he considered pragmatism as *only* a method. In fact, Dewey's claim concerning pragmatism as a method, that is, what he often called *the scientific method*, should be understood in the context of Dewey's theory of knowledge and his framework of pragmatic metaphysics.

In the modern history of Western philosophy, the question of knowledge is understood in the Cartesian dualism of mind and matter, viz., a dualistic scheme of an inner mind and matter "out there," but both are separate from each other and exist independently. In this scheme, the question of how mind gets in touch with the "outside" world to gain knowledge of that world has become a branch of philosophical studies, that is, epistemology, ever since Descartes. Dewey attempted to challenge this philosophical tradition. In rejecting this dualistic scheme, he developed a transactional approach to the question of knowledge, which he considered could not be formulated as "epistemology," but rather as "theories of knowledge," "theories of inquiry," or "experimental logic." In his book *Studies in Logic Theory*, Dewey (1903) offered a detailed analysis of the process of inquiry using an interactive naturalistic approach and he categorized his theory of knowledge as a *kind* of pragmatism, though he sometimes also called it "instrumentalism." This is when pragmatism as a *method* began to take shape. In the years that followed, Dewey continued to develop his theory of inquiry by exploring the process of the *intelligent* inquiry, and finally produced another book, *Logic: The Theory of Inquiry* (Dewey, 1916). Dewey contended that we should reject the "spectator" theory of knowledge, but consider a transactional theory of knowledge, or in today's language, transactional constructivism (see Biesta & Burbules, 2003: 11–12). In this theory of knowledge, the object of knowledge is created by the process of inquiry and is known in and through experience; that is, through the transactions between human beings as agents and the world. Therefore, knowing is a mode of experience, which Dewey called cognitive experience.

Parallel to the same period or perhaps a little bit later, Dewey developed his philosophy of metaphysics for his theory of knowledge to fit into. Metaphysics is the philosophy of characterizing existence or reality as a whole, or studies on ultimate origins or traits of the world. Shook's (2004) interpretation of reasons why Dewey worked on metaphysics is that after Dewey built up his theory of experience, he started to "seek a naturalism in which existence possesses traits similar to those of experience" (740). This is echoed by Gale's (2010) interpretation that Dewey's later work on metaphysics in *Experience and Nature* (1925) is a "transcendent argument for what nature must be like if it is to be possible for inquiry to take place in it" (Gale, 2010: 57).

Congruent with his theory of inquiry, Dewey rejected traditional metaphysics that assumed that only an immutable, unchangeable, stable, and reliable object can be real and hence be a foundation for knowledge. Traditional metaphysical philosophers consider these qualities as "ultimate traits" of the world. Dewey took a naturalistic approach to shape his philosophy of metaphysics. For Dewey (1905), the reality is a world of interaction between organism and environment, and what is real is the result of our experience gained by and through such interaction, as he argued, "things are what they are experienced as" (158). In the years that followed, Dewey developed his metaphysical ideas in a series of article, including "The Postulate of Immediate Empiricism" (1905) and "Does Reality Possess Practical Character?" (1908). In his essay, "What Does Pragmatism Mean by Practical" (1908), Dewey argued for an empirical basis for his metaphysics. In "The Realism of Pragmatism" (1905) and "Brief Studies in Realism" (1911), Dewey expressed his metaphysics as a kind of "naïve realism" to be distinguished from what he called "presentational realism."[2] In his 1915 essay, "The Subject-Matter of Metaphysical Inquiry," Dewey (1998 [1915]) asserted that "irreducible traits" of the world are "specifically diverse existences, interaction, change" (177). And he added, "the evolution of living and thinking beings out of a state of things in which life and thought were not found is a fact which must be recognized in any metaphysical inquiry into the irreducible traits of the world" (Dewey, 1998 [1915]: 179). This article anticipates his claim in his later book *Experience and Nature* that "metaphysics is cognizance of the generic traits of existence" (Dewey, 1925: 50). In this masterpiece, Dewey fully elaborated and clarified his own metaphysics by offering discussions on the problems of traditional metaphysics. He proposed to understand the human mind as a result of communication among human beings and as a result of interaction between human beings and the natural and social world.[3] In describing this worldview, Dewey preferred naturalism to materialism because the latter still hints at the world view of the dualistic scheme.

Despite the rich discussion on metaphysics in Dewey's work before Hu introduced Deweyan pragmatism to China, little about Dewey's philosophy of metaphysics can be found in Hu's introduction of his mentor's philosophy in Chinese. Hu should have read most of Dewey's works published before and while he introduced pragmatism to China (see Zhou, 2010). However, Hu surprisingly did not choose to introduce these philosophical ideas to the Chinese public. Dewey's metaphysical principles are employed in his theories of inquiry, aesthetics, ethics, and religion, but these principles were all absent from Hu's introduction of Deweyan pragmatism. Clearly, Hu's introduction of Deweyan pragmatism was *selective* and *partial*. Thus, the question arises: Why did Hu Shi introduce Deweyan pragmatism to China as only a method?

4 Why Did Hu Shi Introduce Deweyan Pragmatism as Only a Method?

As above, the immediate question that emerges is why Hu introduced Deweyan pragmatism to China as only a method. This question is certainly important given Hu's relationship with Dewey, but it is surely also complicated because of Hu's highly complicated role in Chinese and international modern history.

However, this question can be answered from at least three interconnected aspects: Hu's philosophical position, his sociocultural concerns, and his academic inclinations.

4.1 A Philosophical Divergence: Metaphysical Differences

Although being an ardent student of Dewey and calling himself as a pragmatist throughout his life, Hu had his own worldview which differed to his mentor's worldview. This difference largely led Hu to only choose pragmatism in terms of method in his introduction of Dewey's philosophy. Basically, Hu can be metaphysically seen as being materialistic because he holds a view of naturalism with a strong emphasis on scientism and natural laws, which differs from Dewey's empirical naturalism or metaphysics of experience.

In 1923, Chinese intellectuals engaged in a science–metaphysics debate (科玄之争). In this debate, Hu strongly opposed the metaphysics of idealism and took a scientific position. At the end of the debate, important essays on the topic were collected and published in a book prefaced by an essay written by Hu. The preface is titled as "Science and the Philosophy of Life,"in which Hu claimed that his view of the world and life "is a hypothesis founded on the generally accepted *scientific knowledge* of the last or three hundred years. To avoid unnecessary controversy, I propose to call it, not 'a scientific credo,' but merely 'the Naturalistic Conception of Life and Universe'" (Hu, 1998 [1923]: 164). In this article, Hu (1998 [1923]) claimed that "In this naturalistic universe, where every motion in the heavens has its regular course and every change follows *laws of nature*, where *causality* governs man's life and the struggle for existence spurs his activities – in such a universe man has very little freedom indeed" (164–165, emphasis added). In Hu's later English essay, "My Credo and Its Evolution," which was published in 1931, Hu (2001 [1932]) insisted on the same materialist-oriented naturalistic view.

Clearly, both Hu and Dewey hold naturalism as their worldviews, but they have very different rationales. While Hu's (2001 [1932]) naturalism stressed the natural laws, or what he called "absolute universality of the law of causality" (254) in the world, what Dewey (1929) tried to elaborate is the "metaphysics of event," a world of "interaction" between organism and environment taking place in nature, and nature itself is understood as "a moving whole of interacting parts" (232). For Dewey (1915 [1998]), the world is not characterized as purely physical and when things "are brought into more and complex interactions, they exhibit capacities not to be found in an exclusively mechanical world. To say, accordingly, that existence of vital, intellectual, and social organization makes impossible a purely mechanistic metaphysics is to say something which the situation calls for" (179–180).

There are also different understandings of the role of human beings in relation to the world. In Hu's materialist-oriented naturalistic worldview, the human being has "little freedom" and is forced to find and use the universe's natural laws to adapt to the natural world and exert technical control over it. In contrast, the importance of communication, of the human experience resulting from the interaction between human beings in nature, as well as between human beings and their environment, is emphasized in Dewey's transactional realism. Dewey also stressed the role of human mental activities, which can transform experience to create new knowledge, rather than representing the "reality" out there. For Dewey, the knowledge about the relationships between human actions and their consequences does not stand for certainty, but only possibility. Knowing is just one mode of human experience among the diversity of modes of human experience, including practical, ethical, aesthetic, and religious modes of experience. In his later works, Dewey called his naturalism "cultural naturalism" (1938), while Gale (2010) characterizes Dewey's naturalism as "anthropomorphic or humanistic naturalism" (55).

Although Hu's naturalism may partly come from Dewey, the different rationales of their naturalism suggest that Hu's naturalism has different sources. In 1925, in a speech titled "Difficulties Encountered by Christian Education in China," Hu pointed out that "ever since the introduction of modern Western scientific thought to China, the naturalist philosophy inherent in Chinese ancient philosophy gradually came back into view. The combination of these two thoughts brings about the current naturalist movement" (freely translated, Hu, 1998[1925]: 636). As a matter of fact, since his childhood days, Hu was deeply influenced by the Chinese ancient naturalist ideas advocated by such great philosophers as Lao Zi (老子) and Fan Zhen (范缜). Lao Zi, the founder of Taoism, is a naturalist who believes that everything follows the law of nature independent of human subjectivity. Fan Zhen is an atheist and materialist in the Southern and Northern Dynasties in Chinese history and his thought made Hu become an atheist from his very early years. Hu found that ancient Chinese naturalism was in great congruence with the spirit of Western modern science; therefore, he tried to integrate them. In his biographical essay "My Credo and Its Evolution," Hu (2001 [1931]) wrote: "My slight knowledge of the evolutionary hypothesis of Darwin and Spencer was easily linked up with the naturalism of some of the ancient Chinese thinkers" (239). Noticeably, despite the fact that Hu was famous for being critical of some ethical principles of Confucianism, Neo-Confucianism emerged in the 12th century as a school of philosophical thought drawing upon ancient Chinese naturalism had a deep influence on Hu's belief in atheism, as Hu (1998 [1933]: 59–60) recalled in his autobiography.

The Eastern and Western sources of Hu's naturalism can explain why his naturalism is mixed with scientism and positivism, and metaphysically speaking, why Hu is even materialist-oriented. Dewey clearly rejected the term "materialism" because it still assumes a dualistic perspective of mind–matter. Although Dewey stresses the *scientific method* in his works, he maintained a critical attitude toward *scientific rationality*; therefore, he cannot be considered as being a positivist (see Biesta & Burbules, 2003: 14–16). Although Dewey took a critical attitude towards traditional metaphysics, he did not give it a total "overthrow" and simply suspended it. However, Hu (1998 [1919]: 228) claimed that Dewey considered questions of traditional metaphysics as totally worthless and can be completely eliminated from philosophical discussions. Here, Hu misunderstands Dewey. Thus, the differences in worldviews between Hu and his mentor led Hu to focus only on the method of Deweyan pragmatism.

Others may argue that the practical reason for Hu's neglect of Dewey's philosophy of metaphysics might be that Dewey did not give a systematic clarification of his pragmatic metaphysics until he published his book *Nature and Experience* in 1925, whereas Hu's introduction of Deweyan pragmatism to China was intensively concentrated between 1919 and 1921. Nevertheless, Dewey's thought on metaphysics developed over years and was published in a range of articles since early 1900s until the early 1920s. Therefore, Hu's ignorance or negligence of Dewey's pragmatic metaphysics can still be seen as an optional activity.

4.2 *A Sociopolitical Concern: The Need for Social Inquiry*

Hu's introduction of Dewey's philosophy as a method is clearly motivated by his practical concern with Chinese social needs. After the 1911 Revolution, China became a republic, but it only had a *de jure* democracy rather than a *de facto* democracy, and the Chinese people suffered hugely from severe social injustice, political turmoil, and military harassment. Hu was deeply aware of this social malaise ever since he studied at America. After he returned back to China in 1917, one of his ambitions became to save his country from the terrible social conditions.

Thus, in his social inquiry, Hu conceived a new way to reform Chinese society into a real democratic society. Alongside his colleagues, he advocated the *New Cultural Movement*, a nonpolitical movement, to lay the cultural foundation for a future democratic China. Meanwhile, before Dewey started his great tour of China in 1919, Hu and his colleagues had invited Dewey to deliver lectures to the Chinese people. Apart from his philosophy of education, Hu hoped that Dewey would also bring his sociopolitical philosophy to China, and thus inspire new ways to save China and ameliorate its society. As early as 1914, Hu

(2001 [1914]) had already expressed his great concerns about methods in his diary: "What our country urgently needed today is not novel theories, not profound philosophical ideas, but methods that can be applied to pursue knowledge, to observe things, and to govern the country" (222, freely translated).

One of Dewey's key pragmatist ideas from the "Lectures of Social and Political Philosophy" presented in Beijing is the piecemeal reform of society to improve the community by gradually resolving all kinds of social problems. For Hu, this means that people need to reform the society incrementally; that is, specifically, people need to study concrete social problems and find methods to solve them "drop by drop." This is why Hu insisted on reforming society by studying social problems and issues; thus, Hu focused on methods to be formed and used for solving these problems instead of talking about many different kinds of "isms" or doctrines as different theories in efforts towards wholesale way of social and political revolution. Hu was clearly inspired by Dewey's pragmatist method of thinking, which he linked to his conception of reformation of China's sociocultural fabric, for example, Chinese language renovation, in order to lay a new cultural foundation for a future democratic China. Hence, the method Hu stressed is exactly the method of five steps of thinking in the process of inquiry elaborated by Dewey in his works, particularly in his book, *How We Think*. This partly explains why Hu chose to import Deweyan pragmatism as a method to China, that is, to meet China's urgent need for social reform at that time. What Hu could not do is to announce pragmatism as a doctrine because this is exactly what pragmatism is trying to overcome; therefore, this is also why Hu took up it as a method.

Hu started his social reform by applying the pragmatist method to the Chinese language renovation through experiments with writing poems in vernacular Chinese. Taking a cultural approach to social reform also led Hu to acknowledge the importance of education. Thus, following Dewey, Hu also considered education as a means, or we may say a *method*, of social reconstruction. This further led Hu to believe that educational reform should proceed before political reform, and hence it is necessary to separate education from politics. But what Hu seemed to neglect is that for Dewey, the claim of education as a means of social reconstruction should not be taken as a dogma, but rather as a hypothesis to verify through action.

4.3   *A Biographical Element: An Enduring Academic Inclination*
The third aspect that explains why Hu only focused on the method dimension of Deweyan pragmatism can be found in his life history or his biography, in particular, his academic life over his lifetime. Hu grew up in an area of China that kept a long academic tradition of working on *kaojuxue* (考据学), that is,

roughly in English, textual research or textology. This field of learning is considered as a Chinese academic discipline with a tradition of nearly one thousand years; it is the academic study using texts or documents to check, verify, and explain the documentary and historical problems. Hu grew up in a family in Jixi (绩溪), a town in southern Anhui Province, which is where he received his complete training in Chinese classical texts. Hu spent 9 years reading and memorizing Chinese Classics in one of the nine village schools in Jixi. It was not until Hu was 13 years old that he left his hometown for his secondary education in several modern schools in Shanghai.

Hu's father, Hu Chuan (胡传 1841–1895), "was a classical scholar and a stern follower of the Neo-Confucianist Rational Philosophy of Zhu Xi (朱熹 1130–1200)" (Hu, 2001[1931]: 232). The school of Neo-Confucianism in the 12th Century adopted much Chinese ancient naturalism, and advocated *ge wu qiong li* (格物穷理), that is, investigating the truth by approaching materials thoroughly, which is an idea that is very similar to the scientific attitudes and skeptical spirits in the modern Western world in Hu's understanding. Through his contact with Neo-Confucianist thought and memorizing his father's Neo-Confucianist work, Hu became an atheist when he was 11 or 12 years old (Hu, 1998 [1933]: 59–60). Meanwhile, the classic Confucian texts that Hu studied were interpreted by Zhu Xi (朱熹), who was an outstanding textual researcher on the Four Books of Confucian Classics and developed his own method on textual analysis during the Song Dynasty. Following this tradition, during the Late Qing Dynasty, Jixi, where Hu grew up, became famous for its Qianjia School of Textology (乾嘉学派). Thus, many outstanding scholars in this area were big names in textology. Hu was socialized and educated in his early years in a milieu pervaded by textological tradition. This exerted a significant influence on his academic inclinations. As can be seen, although Hu received a systematic education and training in Western philosophy, his major academic work was largely drawn upon his expertise in textology. Throughout his life, Hu' s main academic achievements were predominantly reflected by his linguistic and historical investigations into the evidences for particular understandings of classical Chinese works.

When Hu came into contact with Deweyan pragmatism, he was attracted and convinced by the modern scientific method elaborated in Dewey's work. Hu considered that what was severely lacked in China's academic research was exactly scientific method. In his PhD thesis, *The Development of the Logical Method in Ancient China*, Hu (1998 [1917]: 8) claimed that the reason why China was in a serious shortage of scientific research is simply because of the problem of method. Therefore, Hu advocated using pragmatist methods of thinking in China's academic fields. Inspired by Deweyan pragmatism, Hu asserted that the methods used in Chinese traditional textology bear a great resemblance to modern scientific methods, which had not yet been noticed by modern Chinese scholars. Later in his life, Hu recalled:

> He [Dewey]helped me [understand]the research methods of classical science and of the historians from the last one thousand years – in particular, the last three hundred years – such as 'kaojuxue,''kaozhengxue,' etc. I translate these into English as 'evidential investigation,' since it is an investigation on the basis of evidence. There were at this time only very few people (virtually none) who notice these commonalities between the principles of modern science and our classical kaoju, kaozheng method. I was the first to have expressed these statements. And the reason why I could do so was really thanks to Dewey's theories. (Hu, 1959, cited in Schulte, 2011: 86–87)

By combining textology methods from Chinese academic traditions and the modern scientific method clarified in Deweyan pragmatism, Hu created a method for academic research. In his short autobiography, *My Credo and Its Evolution*, Hu claimed that:

> Dewey has given us a philosophy of thinking which treats thinking as an art, as a technique. And in *How We Think* and *Essays in Experimental Logic* he has worked out this technique, which I have found to be true not only of the discoveries in the experimental sciences, but also of the best researches in the historical sciences, such as textual criticism, philological reconstruction, and higher criticism. In all these fields, the best results have been achieved by the same technique, which in its essence consist of a boldness in suggesting hypotheses coupled with a most solicitous regard for control and verification (大胆的假设，小心的求证). (Hu, 2001[1931]: 246–247)

5 Conclusion

In this essay, I have shown that Hu Shi received Deweyan pragmatism as only a method, which causes insufficient understanding and even misunderstanding of Dewey's philosophical and educational ideas. Many Chinese scholars today have taken note of this; however, the reason why Hu's reception, interpretation, and even advocacy of pragmatism only focused on Deweyan pragmatism as a method has not yet been analyzed systematically or adequately.

As has been shown, Hu's reception and interpretation of Deweyan pragmatism was complicated because Hu was influenced by his materialistic naturalism, motivated by the need for sociocultural reform in China, and determined by his academic inclinations cultivated during his early years. Hu's introduction of Dewey's philosophical and educational ideas again shows that any foreign ideas or thought are very likely to be interpreted in a way that is different from their original meaning. This transformation of ideas may be caused by the interaction between receivers and the context they are in, by the cultural differences encountered in this process, and even by the urgent and practical needs in a particular sociopolitical situation. In particular, the important people interpreting those ideas into their local contexts are surely key "filters" or "floodgates" in this transmitting process. Nevertheless, through this process, the refraction or deviation of those ideas occurs (Schriewer, 2012).

Although there might be some misunderstandings caused by Hu's interpretation of pragmatism, that is, his partial reception of pragmatism as only a method, his contribution to introducing pragmatism to China at that time for cultural, social, academic and educational reform cannot be ignored or underestimated. Although Hu's endeavor to conduct social reform through pure cultural and educational reform failed because of unsuitable circumstances of China at the time, Dewey's philosophical ideas had greatly influenced China since then and are still working even today in China, particularly in the field of education. As Wang (2019) says, it is "an unfinished task" (34). Finally, Hu's motivations to bring pragmatism as a method into the early republic of China indicate that it is inaccurate to label Hu as a pure advocate of the total Westernization of China in contemporary Chinese history.

Acknowledgment

This chapter is a reprint from: ZHAO, Kang. (2019). Why did Hu Shi introduce Deweyan pragmatism to China as only a method? *Beijing International Review of Education, 1*(4), 658–672.

Notes

1   This paper was funded by the Teaching and Research Development Program for Teachers of Liberal Arts in Zhejiang University. The research project title is "Contemporary Studies in Deweyan Educational Thought" (project number: 104000-541903/026).
2   Dewey's view of realism is also described as transactional realism (see Biesta & Burbules, 2003: 13), although the word "transaction" was used by Dewey relatively later in his life.
3   Dewey's metaphysics is also regarded as metaphysics of *presence* (see Biesta, 2012: 35).

References

Biesta, G. (2012). *The beautiful risk of education.* Routledge.

Biesta, G., & Burbules, N. (2003). *Pragmatism and educational research.* Rowman & Littlefield Publishers, Inc.

Bruno-Jofré, R., & Schriewer, J. (Eds.). (2011). *The global reception of John Dewey's thought: Multiple refractions through time and space.* Routledge.

Deng, X. (2001). Eight cultural mal-positions of one hundred years of studies in western philosophy in China. *Fujian Forum, 5,* 10–16. [in Chinese]

Dewey, J. (1903) Studies in logic theory. In J. A. Boydston (Ed.), *John Dewey. The middle works (1899–1924)* (Vol. 2). Southern Illinois University Press.

Dewey, J. (1905). The realism of pragmatism. In J. A. Boydston (Ed.), *John Dewey. The middle works (1899–1924)* (Vol. 3). Southern Illinois University Press.

Dewey, J. (1908). What pragmatism means by practical. In J. A. Boydston (Ed.), *John Dewey. Middle works (1899–1924)* (Vol. 5). Southern Illinois University Press.

Dewey, J. (1925). Experience and nature. In J. A. Boydston (Ed.), *John Dewey. Later works (1899–1924)* (Vol. 1). Southern Illinois University Press.

Dewey, J. (1929). The quest for certainty. In J. A. Boydston (Ed.), *John Dewey. The later works (1925–1953)* (Vol. 4). Southern Illinois University Press.

Dewey, J. (1905). The postulate of immediate empiricism. In J. A. Boydston (Ed.), *John Dewey. Middle works (1899–1924)* (Vol. 3). Southern Illinois University Press.

Dewy, J. (1911). Brief studies in realism. In J. A. Boydston (Ed.), *John Dewey. Middle works (1899–1924)* (Vol. 6). Southern Illinois University Press.

Dewy, J. (1915). The subject-matter of metaphysical inquiry. In J. A. Boydston (Ed.), *John Dewey. Middle works (1899–1924)* (Vol. 8). Southern Illinois University Press.

Gale, R. (2010). The naturalism of John Dewey. In M. Cochran (Ed.), *The Cambridge companion to Dewey.* Cambridge University Press.

Hu, S. (1959). *Dr. Hu Shi's personal reminiscences: An oral history.* Columbia University, East Asia Institute.

Hu, S. (2001[1931]). My credo and its evolution. In *The Chinese renaissance.* Foreign Language Teaching and Research Press.

Hu, S. (1998[1919]). Experimentalism. In *Collected works of Hu Shi* (Vol. 2). Beijing University Press.

Hu, S. (1998[1919]). Dewey's philosophy of education. In *Collected works of Hu Shi* (Vol. 2, pp. 239–248). Beijing University Press.

Hu, S. (1998[1923]). *Science and the philosophy of life.* In *Collected works of Hu Shi* (Vol. 3). Beijing University Press.

Hu, S. (1998[1933]). Autobiography of my forty years. In *Collected works of Hu Shi* (Vol. 1, pp. 59–60). Beijing University Press.

Hu, S. (2001[1914]). *Complete collection of Hu Shi's diaries* (Vol. 1). Anhui Educational Press.

Hu, S. (1998[1917]). The development of the logical method in ancient China. In *Collected works of Hu Shi* (Vol. 6). Beijing University Press.

Hu, S. (1998[1925]). The present crisis in Christian education. In *Collected works of Hu Shi* (Vol. 4). Beijing University Press.

Hu, S. (2003[1919]). Intellectual China 1919. *The Chinese Social and Political Science Review*, 6(4) 345–355. In *Complete works of Hu Shi* (Vol. 35). Anhui Education Press.

Huang, Y. (1921). Vocational education. *Educational Journal (JiaoyuZazhi)*, 13(11), 61–63.

Keenan, B. (1977). *The Dewey experiment in China: Educational reform and political power in the early republic*. Harvard University Press.

Liang, S. (1934). Fundamental ideas of Dewey's philosophy of education. *Rural Construction*, 6, 1–10.

Liu, H. (2015). A look into the differences between Chinese and Western cultures through Hu Shi's interpretation of John Dewey's pragmatism. *Academic Research Journal*, 10, 14–18.

Qu, S. (1940). *The ABC of philosophy of education*. World Book Company.

Schulte, B. (2011). The Chinese Dewey. In R. Bruno-Jofré & J. Schriewer (Eds.), *The global reception of John Dewey's thought: Multiple refractions through time and space*. Routledge.

Shook, J. (2004). Dewey's empirical naturalism and pragmatic metaphysics. Transaction of the Charles S Perice society. *A Quarterly Journal in American Philosophy*, XL(4), 731–742.

Tan, S. (2004). China's pragmatist experiment in democracy: Hu Shih's pragmatism and Dewey's influence in China. *Metaphilosophy, XXXV*(1/2), 44–64.

Wang, J. (2007). *Dewey in China. To teach and to learn*. State University of New York Press.

Wang, J. (2019). What should we learn about Dewey in China? An unfinished task. *Beijing International Review of Education, I*(1), 32–34.

Wang, Y. (2003). From John Dewey to Hu Shi – variations of pragmatism. *Journal of Hebei Normal University (Philosophy and social sciences Edition)*, 26(3), 18–22. [in Chinese]

Zhang, H. (2013). Individuality beyond the dichotomy of "small self and big self" in contemporary Chinese education: Lessons from Hu Shi and Liang Shuming. *Frontier of Education in China*, 8(4), 540–558.

Zhao, X. (1996). Hu Shi and pragmatism. *Twenty-First Century Bi-Monthly, 6*, 88–93. (Chinese)

Zhou, X. (2010). The influences of Dewey on Hu Shi: A perspective based on Hu Shi's collection of Dewey's work. *Newsletter of Hu Shi Studies, 3*, 1–8.

CHAPTER 5

New Confucian Liang Shuming's Transformation of John Dewey's Philosophy in Chinese Rural Education

James Zhixiang YANG

Abstract

During the May Fourth period, the clash of ideas of democracy and science with Confucian tradition had a great impact on the Chinese intellectual community, consisting of modern intellectuals and traditional scholars. In response to the prevailing anti-traditionalism during the May Fourth period, Liang made great efforts to retain and reform Confucianism. This paper highlights the effects of Confucian tradition and John Dewey's pragmatism on Chinese rural education during the Republican period by studying Liang Shuming's educational thought and practice. By exploring a philosophical 'dialogue' between Liang Shuming and John Dewey, this paper demonstrates how the intersection of traditional and modern aspects shaped Chinese rural educational reform during the 1930s.

Keywords

New Confucian – Liang Shuming – transformation – John Dewey's philosophy

1   Introduction

John Dewey's sojourn in China from 1919 to 1921 overlapped with the May Fourth/New Culture Movement in Chinese history. Such a historical coincidence brought about a fascinating conversation between Deweyan pragmatism and the May Fourth era. During this period, the clash of the ideas of democracy and science with Confucian tradition divided the Chinese intellectual community into two opposite camps: liberal intellectuals and traditional scholars. However, in different ways, both camps reached out to the philosophy of John Dewey in the context of the May Fourth movement.

© KONINKLIJKE BRILL NV, LEIDEN, 2019 | DOI:10.1163/9789004511477_006

Most of Dewey's Chinese followers were pro-liberalism intellectuals who advocated for the substitution of Confucianism with a Western value system. Throughout the 1920s and 1930s, a group of Chinese educators, most of whom had studied with John Dewey at Columbia University, strived to adopt, transport and apply Deweyan pragmatism to Chinese education on a wide range of issues, including literary revolution, higher education reform, civic education cultivation, and rural reconstruction. Hu Shi (Hu Shih, 胡适), Jiang Menglin (蒋梦麟), Guo Bingwen (郭秉文), Tao Xingzhi (陶行知), and Chen Heqin (陈鹤琴) were notable representatives of this group.

Unlike the majority of John Dewey's Chinese students, Liang Shuming (梁漱溟 1893–1988) never studied abroad during his lifetime. Compared to Dewey's Chinese followers, Liang took a firm stance in favor of cultural traditionalism. His unrelenting effort in practicing and disseminating Confucianism in modern China led to some scholars calling him 'The Last Confucian' (Alitto, 1979). Dewey had been dubbed the 'Modern Confucius' by some Chinese intellectuals, on his arrival in China (Keenan, 1977). Liang had pursued the Chinese rural reconstruction movement in the late 1920s, and intensively studied Dewey's pragmatism, writing about his reflections on the American educator's idea of education.

In this paper, I examine the ways in which Confucian teachings and Deweyan learnings interacted in Liang Shuming's educational thought and practice. The purpose of the paper is to answer a crucial question: How did Liang find a way to combine his educational experience in Confucianism with his journey into Dewey's pragmatism? The answer to this question relies on examination of Liang's interpretation and application of Dewey's educational philosophy to the dimension of his New-Confucian views. By exploring a philosophical 'dialogue' between Liang Shuming and John Dewey, this paper demonstrates how the intersection of traditional and modern aspects shaped Chinese rural educational reform in the 1930s.

2 Neo-Confucian Father Figure and the Formula of *nei sheng* and *wai wang*

During Liang Shuming's formative period, his father, Liang Ji (梁济 1958–1918), played a critical role in shaping and strengthening his belief in Confucianism. As a former Neo-Confucian official-scholar of the late imperial period, Liang Ji advocated the pathway "from being the sage on the inside" (*nei sheng* 内圣) to "being kingly on the outside" (*wai wang* 外王) in the face of China's unprecedented challenges. *Wai wang*, a concept from Confucianism strongly emphasizes Confucian scholars' commitment to achieving outstanding accomplishments in political affairs, which could bring order and prosperity to the entire empire. Following this conviction, Liang Ji believed that all learnings or teachings were futile unless they were beneficial to empowering the country (Liang, 1989). Therefore, the Neo-Confucian father rejected the classical civil service-oriented examination and instead supported a new style of education (Liang, 1989). In 1906, one year after the ending of the imperial civil service examination, Liang Ji sent 13-year old Liang Shuming to a new middle school in Beijing, the capital, where the teenage boy could learn practical knowledge (*shi xue*, 实学). Inspired by his father, Liang Shuming then embarked on a life-long dedication to the cause of national salvation (Ma, 1992).

Of the twin neo-Confucian concepts, *nei sheng* had a greater impact on Liang Ji compared with *wai wang*. In fact, the discourse of Neo-Confucian philosophy since the Song-Ming period (960–1644) revolved around this very idea. In contrast to *wai wang*, *nei sheng* mainly focuses on the perfection of individual inner morality, which was regarded by Neo-Confucian scholars as the root of all things good. Consequently, when emphasizing the significance of the spread of practical knowledge in Chinese society, Liang Ji asserted that "the purification of people's hearts" (*zheng ren xin*) should be the determining factor for achieving the goal of national salvation (Alitto, 1979). From the Neo-Confucian father's perspective, the development of a Confucian scholar into being 'sage inside' should become a requirement for the realization of being 'kingly outside.' Under Liang Ji's influence, the *nei sheng–wai wang* formula became a framework, within which Liang Shuming could develop his own thinking.

The advent of the Republican period in 1912 did not bring about the economic prosperity and social stability in China that most Chinese intellectuals had hoped for. Frustrated by national difficulties and his mother's death, Liang became immersed in studying and practiced Buddhism for a time. In November 1918, Liang Ji, in the depths of despair, committed suicide by drowning himself in a lake in Beijing. The last words of the Neo-Confucian scholar revealed his anxiety about the future of China, as well as his faith in Confucian ethics (Alitto, 1979). Liang Ji's suicide further strengthened Liang Shuming's attachment to Confucianism. Liang Shuming understood his father's life journey was a reflection of a moral principle in Confucianism: "scholar-apprentices (*shi* 士) should never be ashamed of their unrefined clothing and coarse food. Instead, they should be ashamed of their incompetence in bringing a happy life to common people" (Liang, 1989, vol. 2: 664). Inspired by the spirit of Liang Ji's sacrifice for his Confucian belief, Liang Shuming dedicated himself to exploring a pathway through which he could achieve national salvation through the rejuvenation of the Confucian tradition (Liang, 1989).

2.1 *Liang Shuming's Defense of Confucianism during the May Fourth Period*

One of the most significant themes embraced by the May Fourth/New Culture Movement was to re-evaluate the role of Confucianism in Chinese society. From the perspective of Chinese iconoclasts of the May Fourth era, Confucianism became an obstruction that prevented China from transforming itself into a modern state. In their critiques, traditional bonds of the family system, predicated on Confucian/Neo-Confucian morality and virtue, had psychologically poisoned Chinese people.

Perhaps the most famous iconoclast was Lu Xun (鲁迅 1881–1936), who in 1918 published his short fiction, 'The Diary of a Madman.' In the story, Lu Xun presented the diary entries written by a fictitious madman (in a first person narrative), who wanted to cure his paranoia through reading classical Confucian canons (Grieder, 1983). Satirically, while reviewing the books, the madman found nothing except the Chinese characters "Eat People" displayed between the lines of the texts in the classical writings (Grieder, 1983). Here, the word "Eat People" hinted at the fact that Confucian ethics was devouring the spirit of Chinese people.

In the meantime, some influential scholars treated Confucian legacy as a foe to the spreading of modern democratic ideas. For instance, Chen Duxiu (陈独秀 1879–1942), a professor from National Peking University, declared that Confucianism had been in complete contradiction to modern civilization. Chen (1984) asserted: "The essence of Confucian 'Three Cardinal Bonds' is a class system" (108). He further stated: "If we want to embrace democracy, we definitely need to oppose Confucianism and its other sociopolitical derivatives, including Confucian ritualism, the cult of women's purity, traditional ethics and politics" (317). Clearly, the Confucian tradition, from Chen's perspective ran directly counter to modern democracy.

Influenced by the idea of democracy and science, National Peking University, under the leadership of Cai Yuanpei (蔡元培 1868–1940), abolished most of the Confucian classical learnings in its curricula. For the majority of modern Chinese intellectuals, Confucianism was treated as a degenerate element in Chinese history that should be abandoned in the modern period. They believed that the yoking of the cultural stock of Confucianism to millions of Chinese people placed obstacles in the way of actualizing the modernization of China. Overall, the May Fourth/New Culture Movement undermined the dominance of Confucianism in Chinese culture and thought.

However, even though Confucianism had indeed lost its gloss among the Chinese intellectual community during the early Republican period, its influence in Chinese history never completely vanished. The May Fourth period provided scholars of New Confucianism[1] with an unparalleled opportunity to reform Confucianism (He, 1988). Unlike those scholars attempting to upgrade Confucianism into a national religion, New Confucian scholars opposed any endeavors to politicize Confucianism in modern times. As one of the founders of the school of New Confucianism, Liang Shuming thought that liberal intellectuals' critiques of Confucianism were unnecessarily harsh. Under the influence of Confucianism, the Chinese nation had avoided developing a religious tyranny over scholarly thought unlike European countries of the medieval period (Liang, 1989). Unfortunately, since the Song dynasty, with the transformation of the philosophical school into an official ideological dogma (*li xue* 理学), the sense of joy in life and dynamic thought had completely vanished from Confucianism (Liang, 1989). Thus, the dogmatized Confucian value system merely became 'a spiritual opium' used by emperors of dynasties past to poison the minds of Chinese people (Liang, 1989). In response to Confucius' critics of the May Fourth time, Liang (1989) concluded:

> ...What Confucius's critics want to attack is "Three Cardinal Bonds and Five Ethical Webs (*san gang wu chang* 三纲五常)." They regarded these things as the essence of Confucianism. In fact, all of them (Three Cardinal Bonds and Five Ethics) have nothing to do with the truth of Confucianism.... (vol. 4: 770)

Accordingly, Liang (1989) pointed out that it is unfair that Chinese people ascribed all of China's failures since the late nineteenth century to Confucianism. To search for the truth in Confucianism should be the most urgent task for modern Chinese intellectuals (Liang, 2004). As a result, Liang Shuming did not think of Confucianism as a cultural liability in Chinese history. Quite the contrary, he set himself the task of exploring the cultural assets of Confucianism, which could be applied to modern society.

Views of cultural conservatives also diverged significantly from liberal intellectuals in terms of scientism. As one of the most powerful ideas from the West, the thought of scientific empiricism shook the Chinese intellectual community to its core at the turn of the century. In particular, since the early Republican period, the erosion in the legitimacy of Confucianism opened a pathway for increasing popularity of science in Chinese society (He, 1990). From the perspectives of modern Chinese intellectuals of the May Fourth period, science went far beyond the realm of a system of foreign knowledge based mostly on verifiable hypotheses. In their view, science could be a miracle cure to all the ills afflicting China (Grieder, 1983).

This pro-scientism view was forcefully advocated by Ding Wenjiang (丁文江 1887–1936), a well-known geologist of the May Fourth era. Ding (1997) argued:

> Scientific method has been adopted by scientists to achieve remarkable accomplishments in the natural world. Therefore, we can expand the method to other fields in the human world. We need to treat science as a religious beacon, which can award us an honest mind and an instrument for exploring the truth of the world, as well as a strong will and the skills to illuminate human virtue. (205)

Ding's conviction about scientism was echoed by most of the liberal Chinese intellectuals of the May Fourth time, with some of them even taking a scientific approach to reorganizing Chinese tradition, including classical Confucian canons. To pro-scientism Chinese scholars, all Chinese classical learning was dead knowledge, the value of which could be scientifically categorized or dismissed as a 'historical fossil' (Mao, 1919).

Not surprisingly, the modern Chinese intellectuals' zeal for scientism provoked counterattacks from the cultural conservatives. For example, while visiting Europe in 1919 after WWI, the Master Liang Qichao (梁启超 1873–1929) was shocked by a distressing scene of material impoverishment and spiritual decadence there. In Liang's argument, Europeans' worship of scientism led to a disregard of human spiritual life, inspiring the relentless pursuit of wealth and power that ended in the catastrophe of the Great War (Grieder, 1983).

Liang Qichao's argument was strongly bolstered by his followers, including Zhang Junmai (张君劢 1887–1969), an influential philosopher and political figure who proclaimed that no matter how developed science is, it could never solve the problems of the philosophy of life, which depend completely on humans themselves. Another well-known philosopher, Zhang Dongsun (张东荪 1886–1973), elaborated that although the scientific method is analytical and controlled by the laws of reason, its usefulness is limited to improving our understanding of relationships that can be viewed objectively (Grieder, 1983). In general, most of the Chinese cultural conservatives argued against Ding Wenjiang, as they simultaneously endeavored to defend Confucian tradition against attacks by Chinese iconoclasts. This standpoint of cultural traditionalism was most eloquently explicated in Liang Shuming's works during the May Fourth/New Culture Movement period.

3 Liang Shuming's *The Cultures of East and West and Their Philosophies*

To defend Confucianism against the May Fourth Chinese iconoclasts' attacks, Liang Shuming published his famous book entitled *The Cultures of East and*

West and Their Philosophies in 1922. In this book, Liang attempted to examine the unique value of traditional Chinese culture in the context of world civilization. Liang (2015) defined culture as a 'way of life,' and life as the relationship between the individual and his/her environment. In Liang's terms, culture has been shaped by will. Following this statement, Liang (2015) categorized world civilization into three types: Western culture, Chinese culture, and Indian culture. Western culture, in Liang Shuming's mind, was the prototype of the first stage of the evolution of world civilization (Liang, 2015). The cultural system was derived from basic needs and the material requirements of human survival. The 'will' of this culture is to look forward to seeking the pleasure of satisfaction, emphasizing reason, utility, scientific knowledge and the conquest of nature, and a life of ceaseless struggle (Liang, 2015).

In contrast with Western culture, Liang argued that Chinese culture represents the second stage, which takes the middle path. It accommodates the relationship between humans and the environment in its view (Liang, 2015). This cultural type was based on the will's self-adjustment, self-sufficiency, and the cultivation of inner peace. By maintaining a balance between their desires and the environment, the Chinese people could achieve great spiritual happiness while enduring material poverty (Liang, 2015). The third stage of cultural development is represented by Indian culture. Within this culture, the will of the people was to turn backward for ultimate enlightenment. Liang (2015) pointed out that Indian people believe that the world is an illusion. Therefore, both self-denial and austerity play an important part in their religious practice.

After a comparative analysis, Liang characterized Chinese culture as a premature culture. Before developing the first stage of allowing the pursuit of material well-being and rationality, China had already fallen back on the second stage of having the will to be in equilibrium with nature. For the cause of national salvation, China should avoid taking the path of India, but instead borrow the idea of democracy and science from the west.

More to the point, when comparing Western culture with Chinese culture, the Neo-Confucian formula *nei sheng – wai wang* penetrated Liang's thinking. Alongside the idea of Neo-Confucianism, Liang's work displayed an intention of dividing a person's life into outer and inner spheres. Liang considered that in Western culture, intellectual calculation in taming the outer world led to the development of science; and, individual self-interest and desire for one's rights resulted in democracy (Allito, 1979). Liang's writings implied that all accomplishments in the West belonged to the category of 'being kingly outside' (*wai wang*).

In contrast, Liang argued that Chinese culture, which was mostly based on Confucianism, attached importance to the inner workings of the mind (Grieder, 1970). Moral and spiritual cultivation became the main theme running through a person's life so that the life goal was to pursue a spirit of happiness and tranquility instead of outer material achievement (Liang, 2015). Through practicing music and ritual, a Confucian individual could develop the character of benevolence (*ren*), and this was the foundation of all happiness (Liang, 2015). In this sense, Liang (2015) believed that although Chinese culture did not create democracy and science as the West did, Confucian life was morally superior to the deplorable Western obsession with material progress. In light of the perceived spiritual destruction of Western civilization since WWI, Liang thought only Confucianism could lay claim to becoming the teacher of the West. He made confident predictions in *The Cultures of East and West and Their Philosophies*:

> Confucius wholeheartedly focused upon the emotional aspect of humanity… The difference between Confucius and Westerners and their basic point of conflict lies precisely in this! Westerners never paid attention to this in the past. Now, they should start sidling up to the school of Confucianism. Therefore, I will not doubt that Westerners will take the path prescribed by Confucius. (2015: 184)

Liang's writing demonstrates his cultural pride in Confucianism. *The Cultures of East and West and Their Philosophies* laid a solid foundation for the development of his New Confucian philosophy. In this work, Liang emphasized the revival of Confucianism and its crucial role in empowering China for the future. At the same time, Liang (1989) wisely realized that the reconstruction of Confucianism in a modern period demanded some fresh thoughts and ideas from the Western world. Thus, the New Confucian scholar was devoted to opening a pathway for Confucianism to connect with Western cultures (Liang, 1989).

4 Intellectual Connections among Liang, Bergson, and Dewey

During the May Fourth period, as foreign ideas competed and interacted with each other in China, both new and conservative intellectuals were in search of new cultural stocks to enrich their own thoughts. Through intensively studying the schools of Western philosophy, Liang Shuming eventually found useful cultural assets from the philosophy of Henri Bergson (1859–1941). Bergson's philosophy emphasized the importance of intuition in human life, and criticized the belief of the supremacy of scientism (Dewey, 2004). The essential concept of Bergson's work is a vital impetus, which aimed to explain evolution in a dynamic way. In connection with vitalism, Bergson created the term 'duration' as an entirely qualitative multiplicity, an absolute heterogeneity of element, which comes to melt into one another (Dewey, 2004). As one of the most influential Western thinkers, Bergson emphasized the permanent flowing of free will and vital force in the world, as opposed to the worship of scientism. This philosophical approach was widely accepted by the conservative Chinese intellectuals of the May Fourth period. In particular, the idea of Bergson's vitalism struck a deep chord with Liang Shuming who stated that:

> Henri Bergson strongly criticized any fixed and measurable idea from the supremacy of scientism. He believed that metaphysical philosophy requires a soft and flowing idea, which was opposed to the thought of scientism. His philosophy opened a pathway for the development of the Chinese style of thought.... (2015: 127)

Liang argued that Bergson, through his vitalism, had tried to reach the same end point as Confucius. As Liang (2015) affirmed: "Only the spiritual life embraced by Confucius, which played a somewhat religious role in Chinese people's lives, can match the Western School of Vitalism" (164). In *The Cultures of East and West and Their Philosophies*, Liang (2015) also held that Confucius's ideas, to a large extent, embodied vitalism.

Consequently, Liang connected Bergson's thinking with Confucian philosophy. For Liang, Confucius – like Bergson – understood life as a continuous flow during which only intuition can appear (Alitto, 1979). That was why Confucian scholars always followed an intuition to live a life that rejected calculation and rationality (Liang, 2015). For instance, while gaining insight into Mencius's ideas, Liang introduced the idea of intuition from Bergson into the realm of Confucian moral education. He wrote:

> Everyone has an intuition and instinct to pursue goodness. Therefore, Mencius said: 'All people have a heart which cannot stand to see the suffering of others... Why do I say all human beings have a heart which cannot stand to see the suffering of others? If an infant were about to fall into a well, anyone would be upset and concerned. This concern would not be due to the fact that the person wanted to get on good terms with the baby's parents, or because he wanted to improve his reputation among the community or among his friends. Nor would it be because he was afraid of the criticism that might result from a show of non-concern. (134)

Based on his analysis, Liang Shuming (2015) affirmed that the core ethical idea of Confucianism, the character of *ren* (仁), is in fact derived from human intuition. In his explanation, *ren* is an inner state of being, peaceful yet full of vitality. Following this conviction, Liang (2015) concluded that: "the thought of Confucianism completely follows intuition. The most important mission that Confucian scholars want to achieve is to sharpen their intuition... Consequently, Confucius encouraged people to pursue '*ren*'" (137).

In sum, Liang Shuming was able to infuse Confucianism with the spirit of modernity during the May Fourth period by invoking Henri Bergson's vitalism. By "vitalizing" Confucianism, Liang transformed this classical philosophical system from a "dead" ideology into a spirited philosophy of life. In the meantime, Liang was looking forward to finding common ground among the ideas of Bergson, Dewey, and Confucius. To achieve this, the first important step for Liang Shuming was to explore an intellectual bond between Bergson and Dewey. As Liang (1989) stated:

> Although Bergson does not share the same school with William James and John Dewey, his vitalism has contributed to the development of the two thinkers' philosophies. Both thinkers have been affected by the theory of biology, which underpins their theories. If one reads over Dewey's works, one will find out where the philosophical root of the American educator's thought is located, and what logic he has adopted to create such a theory. (vol. 2: 126)

From Liang's perspective, Bergson's vitalism formed a foundation on which he could approach John Dewey's pragmatism. Furthermore, Liang stressed that there was a strong philosophical bond between his own ideas and the thoughts of Dewey and Bergson. He pointed out:

> There is a continuity between my thought and Dewey's idea. Dewey's theory is based on the field of biology. Likewise, Bergson's thought has a tremendous impact on my thinking. Bergson is a biologist. When elaborating on his own thought, Dewey repeatedly talks about "life" (*sheng ming* 生命). Although Dewey's theory is rooted in biology, his idea is not a result of studying biology. What he studies is indeed education... he has really done a great job on studying education! (1989, vol. 7: 685)

It is fair to say that Bergson's vitalism formed a platform for a philosophical dialogue between the "last Confucian" and the "American Confucian." Influenced by Bergson's ideas, Liang's understanding of Dewey's educational philosophy is compatible with his interpretation of Confucianism. When discussing Confucian philosophy, Liang (1989) recapitulated:

> ...[In Confucianism] the universe is the sum of all living beings. The main thread from biological development to evolutional history of human society is a relentless creation of 'big' life (*sheng ming*). All living things are supposed to be the embodiment of this 'big' life (*sheng ming*). (vol. 2: 94)

It is not surprising that Liang's writing used a similar tone to explicate the essence of Dewey's educational thought. According to Liang (1989):

> From the standpoint of Dewey's educational philosophy, the universe is a "big" life (*sheng ming*). An understanding of the universe demands an understanding of life (*sheng ming*). Although life (*sheng ming*) is every-where, the core of the big life (*sheng ming*) of the universe is a human being. This life (*sheng ming*) is full of vitality, and the most vital thing in the universe is people's heart. For Dewey, if we can soundly perceive people's heart, we can understand the meaning of life (*sheng ming*) in the universe. (vol. 7: 686)

Here, Liang views "perceiving people's heart" as a prerequisite to "understanding the meaning of life in the universe." That is to say, education shall start with the "purification of people's heart" (*zheng ren xin* 正人心). This way of interpreting Dewey's educational philosophy was in agreement with a Neo-Confucian formula of 'being the sage on the inside' (*nei sheng*) and 'being kingly on the outside' (*wai wang*). Following this mode of thinking, the New Confucian scholar (1989) believed that Dewey's educational philosophy offered insight into the cultivation of "inner growth first," and then made a strong connection between the individual and society.

In view of these convictions, Liang Shuming encouraged readers to use a unique way to study Dewey's *Democracy and Education*. Compared with other chapters in the book, Liang preferred to read chapter four ("Education as Growth") first. He explained:

> Chapter four paid more attention to individual life. It would be better for us to read this chapter in advance while studying the book so that we can have an understanding of the essence of individual life. This is the foundation of human education. (1989, vol. 7: 686)

Obviously, Bergson's vitalism had a strong influence on Liang's interpretation of Dewey's work. After discussing the significance of chapter four, Liang believed that it would be beneficial for readers to then review chapters one, two and three. In these chapters, Liang stated that Dewey aimed to explore the connection between individual life and social life. The focus of chapter seven considers how education can develop social life. Liang pointed out that this chapter should become the final section that readers need to study.

Liang interpreted vitalism as the main theme pervading all chapters of Dewey's *Democracy and Education*. Just as he had done to Confucianism, Liang also "vitalized" Dewey's educational philosophy. More meaningfully, based on the notion of vitalism, Liang eventually yoked his Confucian thought to Dewey's pragmatism. He argued:

> ...what his [Dewey's] book explored is a word *huo* (change 活). He completely understood that life is about change... what he discussed is not an innovative thing. Instead, it is supposed to stay where it should stay. In his opinion, life should follow its own way; the only thing we can do is to exactly grasp the essence of life. This notion is the same as Confucianism. (1989, vol. 7: 700)

It is clear that a basic assumption of Liang's understanding of Dewey's educational philosophy is aligned with his New Confucian way of thinking. In the following sections, I seek to uncover how Liang synthesized Confucian education with Deweyan learning in pursuit of his rural educational reform.

5   Liang Shuming's Reflection on Chinese Education

After completing the final chapters of *The Cultures of East and West and Their Philosophies*, Liang Shuming focused on how to implement his cultural theory in the Chinese reality. He considered:

> The philosophy of life of Confucius and Yan Hui (one of Confucius' favorite students) can resolve those problems of life anguishing Chinese young people, and eventually open a right pathway for them... Only the restoration of Chinese [Confucian] philosophy of life can revive Chinese people's force of vitality, which is disappearing and fading. A real vital force should come from the Chinese inner spirit... Since the May Fourth Movement, some scholars regard the New Culture Movement as the renaissance of Chinese civilization. In fact, this movement is only a result of the rise of Western

culture in China... The renaissance of Chinese civilization should be based on the restoration of their own philosophy of life.... (2015: 228–229)

Evidently, for Liang, the revival of Confucianism became a key factor in reconstructing Chinese people's spirit and morality. Inspired by such an ideal, Liang resigned his faculty job at National Beijing University in 1924. From 1924 to 1936, he experimented with his educational and cultural philosophy in rural counties in Henan and Shandong provinces. The most extraordinary accomplishment in his rural reconstruction was represented by his efforts in Zhouping county of Shandong province where Liang paid considerable attention to rural educational reform. Unfortunately, in 1937 when he began promoting his work in Zhouping, the second Sino-Japanese war erupted. As the Japanese army took over Shandong province in the following year, Liang's rural reconstruction movement came to a reluctant end.

A combination of specific factors shaped Liang Shuming's educational ideas about rural reconstruction. First, Liang felt very disappointed in the modern educational system in China, which was blindly modeled on the Western style. Development of the modern school system in China was a result of the imitation of a foreign style of education from the late Qing. During the period of the May Fourth movement, Chinese educators increasingly believed that the development of a new education system based on the Western model would be a good way to spread the ideal of democracy and science among Chinese youth. John Dewey's arrival triggered Chinese educators' enthusiasm to introduce an American-style school system. Even though Western-oriented Chinese educators made great progress in the modernization of Chinese education, some wise scholars still spoke out harshly about the new school system. Liang Shuming was one of them. He remarked:

...Current school education only taught students some knowledge and skills at the expense of all things of their lives... how can the formal school system help students understand their lives if our education only focuses on regular hour curriculum and subject materials? It is not correct for educators to only emphasize the importance of the acquisition of "knowledge," ignoring students' mental and physical growth... In my view, education should aim to lead students to view all aspects of their lives, then help them take a correct pathway... the building up of both spiritual mind and lively body are essential to education. (1989, vol. 4: 778)

Liang conceptualized education very broadly, embracing all items of a cultural inventory in human society. Following such a notion, he proceeded to elaborate on his educational philosophy based on the cultural perspective stemming from his work, *The Cultures of East and West and Their Philosophies.* Liang (1989) argued that the West and China formed their own respective educational ideals. Western education emphasizes the significance of the development of human intelligence, whereas Chinese or Confucian education pays considerable attention to the cultivation of human emotion and character. While the former aims for the acquisition of knowledge, the latter directs students to focus on the lives of human beings (Liang, 1989).

Liang Shuming's understanding of the uniqueness of Chinese society also contributed to the formation of his educational ideas. In Liang's view, an agricultural country like China could not cope adequately with the new education. He argued:

> ...In fact, the current school system is not in sync with our social reality... within the new school system or modern society, our students easily develop an urban way of life. In cities, they are totally alienated from the lifestyle and interest of the masses. [Through new education] they only study some subjects (such as superficial knowledge of English, Mathematics and Chemistry) that are unrelated to their real lives. They don't have the opportunity to acquire any basic knowledge of rural life... they don't know how to deal with farm labor... all the things that they learn through the new education are remote from their actual lives... the purpose of the new education only serves to produce brilliant persons for another society rather than for Chinese society. (1989, vol. 4: 837)

In Liang's revelation, the Westernized educational system had failed to modernize the state by discarding all that was of value in traditional Chinese education. As new education spread, Chinese society deteriorated further.

Liang's prescription for Chinese education was compatible with his thoughts of New Confucianism. In his eyes, Chinese culture was deeply rooted in rural domains (rather than urban enclaves) and the fundamental difficulties were caused by the problem of cultural disorder within these regions (Liang, 1989). Consequently, the rise of China would rely heavily on the revival of Confucianism in rural areas. In addition, Liang's educational ideas corresponded with the logical Confucian pathway from 'being sage inside' (*nei sheng*) to 'being kingly outside' (*wai wang*). As he wrote:

> Education aims to improve human creativity. It once paid considerable attention to the spiritual maturation of innumerable living individuals. For them, the mission of education is to pursue inner growth. External

achievements were merely the embodiment of their moral development. (1989, vol. 2: 96)

Apparently, Liang treated the 'purification of people's heart' as a foundation for achieving educational goals. In pursuit of such a New Confucian ideal, Liang made great efforts to engage in spiritual and moral reconstruction during the period of rural reconstruction.

6   Liang Shuming's Synthesis of Confucianism and Deweyan Pragmatism in Rural Educational Practice

One of Liang's famous reform endeavors was to revitalize the custom of academic lectures (*jiang xue* 讲学), which were used by Confucian scholars during the Song and Ming dynasty. The ultimate model for classical academic lectures was based on the relationship between Confucius and Mencius and their disciples. Generally speaking, this educational model combined moral and intellectual cultivation with mutual interaction, encouragement, and criticism in an intimate student-teacher setting. More importantly, in Liang's view, *jiang xue* became an excellent way to realize Confucius's philosophy of life in his rural reconstruction. Through the acquisition of the spirit behind Confucian ritual and music, each villager was supposed to develop the character of *ren*, which was derived from Liang's term 'human intuition,' and educated to become an exemplary person.

In reference to the classical educational model, Liang wanted to restore a Confucian human relationship among the masses in rural areas. Liang's New Confucian thought became an inner logic throughout his educational ideals toward rural reconstruction. The focal point of his rural educational reformation was to retain the superiority of Confucian civilization in the face of serious cultural and ideological challenges from the West. Focusing on the historical and cultural context is important for understanding Liang's absorption of John Dewey's educational philosophy.

Liang Shuming's application of Dewey's educational philosophy together with his application of Confucianism to rural reality, served his purpose of Chinese rural reconstruction. In his critiques of the modern educational system of the Republican period, Liang Shuming regarded Dewey's educational thought as a cultural asset to enrich his own discourse on the rural reconstruction movement. For instance, to justify his reflection on Western culture, Liang (1989) referenced some ideas from Dewey's *Democracy and Education*:

As Dewey thought, although today's [Western] society is in (a) great progress (ion), it is still encumbered by a large number of drawbacks. For many people, their relationships have been becoming more and more mechanical. For example, there is no communication between workers and capitalists... Although they reside in the same society, there are insufficient social interactions among them. If there was a society, where all people share a common value and organize themselves with the ability of reasoning, this society would be the most advanced and ideal.... (vol. 7: 694)

From the New Confucians' stance of anti-scientism, Dewey's attack on Western urban society greatly resonated with Liang Shuming. Dewey's educational idea also left a deep mark on Liang's ideas about rural educational reformation. While engaging in reforming rural society, Liang frequently highlighted the concept of growth in his explanation of the implication of his rural reconstruction movement. He stated:

...the goal of our rural reconstruction is to establish a social institution. I frequently treat this social institution as a growth... It gradually develops from the bud; it starts from a tiny thing... It will grow up from a rural area, then develop and spread to big society. (1989, vol. 2: 337)

In this short paragraph, the logical pathway from individual growth to social development somewhat mirrored the influence of Dewey's idea of 'Education as Growth' in Liang's view. Moreover, Dewey's view of balancing school education with social education in *Democracy and Education* also contributed to Liang Shuming's rural educational philosophy. In *Foundational Ideas of John Dewey's Educational Philosophy*, Liang disclosed that in Dewey's educational thinking, school education and social education are complementary. Liang (1989) argued:

[According to Dewey] social education can correct the disadvantages of school education. The most important thing is to find an equilibrium between the two styles of education... it is necessary to transform today's school into a mini-community, establish a continuity between the life of school and society, and get rid of certain artificial parts of current school life irrelevant to social reality.... (vol. 7: 696)

More meaningfully, as a follower of Confucius, Liang (1989) acutely realized that for both Dewey and Confucius, societal life and human education are in interplay. Consequently, when stating the idea of social education in Dewey's philosophy, Liang's writing (1989) simultaneously presented an example of Confucius's attempts to create ancient private schools, by breaking up the royal court's monopoly over mass education.

In keeping with Dewey's ideas, Liang attempted to foster intimacy between the school education and villagers' social life by establishing the Peasant School (*xiang nong xue xiao* 乡农学校) during the 1930s. The school was expected to play both roles of educational and social institution in the Chinese rural domain (Liang, 1989). To achieve this goal, the curriculum in the school encompassed the diversity of educational programs, including literacy education, mathematics, music, medical care, professional training, and character and civic education. Students were simultaneously taught to learn the basic three R skills (reading, writing, and arithmetic), as well as some knowledge of modern agricultural science and technology (Ma, 1992). After school they were strongly encouraged to develop a sense of cooperation and autonomy through participating in a variety of farming activities (Ma, 1992).

The Peasant School was the embodiment of Liang's Confucian idealism. For Liang Shuming, the development of the character of *nei sheng* was the most important thing in Chinese rural education. Liang emphasized the leadership of the school should be comprised of a group of exemplary Confucian people who are held in high prestige in the village for their morality. Following the custom of academic lectures (*jiang xue*), the teachers serving the school were also supposed to become role models for the students (Liang, 2012).

Correspondingly, moral cultivation played a crucial role in the students' educational life. For instance, the idea of 'the rural compact' (*xiang yue* 乡约) was adopted by the Peasant School to educate the students. Briefly speaking, *xiang yue*, which originated from the Song dynasty (960–1279), embraces social and educational functions in Chinese history. It was revived at the beginning of the Qing in the mid-seventeenth century for the edification of a wider audience than could be reached by ill-attended and irregular lectures at the school temples (Bothwick, 1983). Local officials appointed scholars to expound the maxims of the emperor at public lectures. The core of the *Xiang Yue* was to inculcate Confucian value among Chinese people (Bothwick, 1983).

After removal of an officially dogmatic aspect of the rural compact, Liang endeavored to retain the component of moral teaching and cultural transmission in the model. In the school community, Confucian ritual became an important guide to regulate student behavior instead of law. At the same time, students were required to practice a mutual exhortation of moral cultivation, together with developing an interdependent relationship to get through any hardship (Ma, 1992).

Liang planned to have the model of the peasant school spread from the village to provincial level, eventually forming one great nationwide social-educational-cultural system. Within a Confucian atmosphere, millions of exemplary persons were expected to develop out of the system. He believed that once rural reconstruction had built up its strength, a utopian Confucian

110   YANG

society would eventually replace government (Alitto, 1979). Liang Shuming's experiment with the Peasant School was a reflection of his synthesis of the educational thoughts of John Dewey and Confucianism in the rural reconstruction movement.

7   Conclusion

This paper has highlighted the effects of Confucian tradition and John Dewey's pragmatism on Chinese rural educational reform by studying Liang Shuming's intellectual development and his educational practice. Before approaching Dewey's philosophy, Liang had already developed his system of thought using the framework of *nei sheng–wai wang*. This Confucian formula drove Liang to undertake surveys of Western, Chinese, and Indian cultures. After investigating the uniqueness of Chinese civilization, Liang's book, *The Cultures of East and West and Their Philosophies,* highlighted his stance of cultural nationalism. During the May Fourth/New Culture period, Liang's nurturing of a sense of cultural superiority stemming from Confucianism shaped his vision of Deweyan education.

Overall, Liang (1989) portrayed Dewey's educational thought as a cultural asset, which could be instrumental in bringing about rural educational reform. Liang took a very positive view of Dewey's educational idea. He even announced: "I will stand by Dewey to resist the trend toward anti-humanity in contemporary Western philosophy..." (1989, vol. 7: 688). However, after reviewing Dewey's *Democracy and Education,* Liang found that there were still obvious limitations to Dewey's educational philosophy. He pointed out that:

> ...he [Dewey] only understands the changing side of life. He does not perceive the unchanging part of life. The unchanging part is the substance (*ti* 体) of changing part, and changing part is the function (*yong* 用) of unchanging part. He only understands the "*yong*" of life. Instead, he does not understand the "*ti*" of life... what he studies is about everything outside life itself. He cannot understand the essence of life... All things he said are quite moral but he has not discovered the truth of morality. His idea is close to Confucianism, however, he missed the most important part of it. (1989, vol. 7: 701)

This final statement was a reflection of the influence of the Confucian *ti-yong* formula on Liang's mind. Alongside such a formula, Liang implied that Dewey's educational thought should belong to the realm of *yong* (function), which can only serve as a complement for Confucianism. On the contrary, Confucianism was believed to be a *ti* (substance), which became a cultural and moral foundation for

Chinese people's living. Thus, Liang (1989) maintains Dewey guided people only towards applying intelligence in dealing with the practicalities of life, instead of reflecting inwardly upon the value of life. Liang (1989) thought that even though Dewey took a very critical view of Western society, the American educator failed to find a real solution to cure Western social ills because his philosophy was mostly rooted in Western civilization. Liang exhibited great self-confidence in helping Dewey through his theoretical dilemma. He declared: "…Dewey needs our assistance from the East. If I have surplus energy, I will help him out" (1989, vol. 7: 688). Liang's statement strongly emphasized his motivation to correct the deficiencies of Dewey's educational philosophy by means of Confucian philosophy. Liang's application of Dewey's educational thought had been fashioned by his stance as a cultural nationalist. In other words, the sources that Liang relied on in his reception of Dewey's idea derived from his New Confucian thought in *The Cultures of East and West and Their Philosophies.*

Liang Shuming's educational thought and practice during 1920–1930 denote a fascinating philosophical dialogue between Confucianism and John Dewey's pragmatism. This fruitful dialogue mirrors the cultural vision in Jane Roland Martin's *Educational Theory as Encounter.* As Martin (2011) points out in *Education Reconfigured: Culture, Encounter, and Change,* cultural stock can attach to individual capacities in a variety of ways that fall along a continuum from dead relic to living legacy. She further notes: "Depending on the individuals, the coupling and uncoupling of stock and capacities can lead to that stock or other items of stock being reinterpreted, refigured, reconstructed, or even rejected" (23). When Liang yoked himself to the cultural stock of China and the West, both Confucianism and Dewey's philosophy experienced a reinterpretation and reconstruction in his educational practice.

Acknowledgment

This chapter is a reprint from: YANG, James Zhixiang. (2019). New Confucian Liang Shuming's transformation of John Dewey's philosophy in Chinese rural education. *Beijing International Review of Education, 1*(4), 673–694.

Note

1   New Confucianism (新儒家) is an intellectual movement of Confucianism initiated in the early 20th century in Republican China, and further developed in post-Mao era contemporary China. It has been greatly influenced by the neo-Confucianism of the Song and Ming dynasties. New Confucianism aims to synthesize Confucianism, Buddhism, and Taoism. It also emphasizes the significance of the introduction of Western philosophy to Confucian

scholarship. The first generation of New Confucians (1912–1949) consisted of Xiong Shili (熊十力 1885–1968), Liang Shuming (梁漱溟 1893–1988), Ma Yifu (马一浮 1883–1967), Feng Youlan (冯友兰 1895–990), and Qian Mu (钱穆 1895–1990).

References

Alitto, G. S. (1979). *The last Confucian: Liang Shu-ming and the Chinese Dilemma of modernity.* University of California Press.

Bothwick, S. (1983). *Education and social change in China.* Hoover Institution Press.

Chen, D. (1984). *The selective works of Cheng Duxiu* (Vol. 1). Sanlian Press [陈独秀《陈独秀选集》.北京：三联出版社].

Dewey, J. (2004). The contemporary three philosophers. In G. Yuan, S. Jiaxing, & R. Bingang (Eds.), *Democracy and modern society: John Dewey's lecture in China.* Beijing University Press.

Ding, W. (1997). Metaphysics and science. In *Science and philosophy of life.* Shandong People Press [丁文江：玄学与科学.《科学与人生观》. 济南：山东人民出版社].

Grieder, J. B. (1970). *Hu Shih and the Chinese renaissance: Liberalism in the Chinese Revolution, 1917–1937.* Harvard University.

Grieder, J. B. (1983). *Intellectuals and the state in Modern China: A narrative history.* Simon and Schuster.

He, L. (1988). *Culture and life.* Commercial Press [贺麟《文化与人生》.北京：商务印书馆].

He, X. (1990). *One hundred years of misery: The destiny of Chinese intellectuals and modernization.* Orient Publishing Center [何晓明《百年忧患：知识分子命运与中国现代化进程》.上海：东方出版中心].

Keenan, B. (1977). *The Dewey experiment: Educational reform and political power in the Early Republic.* Harvard University Asia Center.

Liang, S. (1989). Morning lectures: Differences between Chinese and Western scholarship. In *Collected works of Liang Shuming* (Vol. 2, p. 126). Shangdong People Press [梁漱溟《朝话：中西学术之不同》，《梁漱溟全集》济南：山东人民出版社].

Liang, S. (1989). Self-introduction. In *Collected works of Liang Shuming* (Vol. 2, p. 10). Shandong People Press [梁漱溟《自述》，《梁漱溟全集》济南：山东人民出版社].

Liang, S. (1989). History of my self-taught. In *Collected works of Liang Shuming* (Vol. 2). Shandong People Press [梁漱溟《我的自学小史》，《梁漱溟全集》济南：山东人民出版社].

Liang, S. 溟 (1989). Theory of rural reconstruction. In *Collected works of Liang Shuming* (Vol. 2). Shandong People Press [梁漱溟《乡村建设理论》，《梁漱溟全集》济南：山东人民出版社].

Liang, S. (1989). Life is a creation. In *Collected works of Liang Shuming* (Vol. 2). Shandong People Press [梁漱溟《人生在创造》，《梁漱溟全集》济南：山东人民出版社].

Liang, S. (1989). My proposal of running school. In *Collected works of Liang Shuming* (Vol. 4). Shandong People Press [梁漱溟《办学意见述略》，《梁漱溟全集》济南：山东人民出版社].

Liang, S. (1989). A philosophical foundation of John Dewey's educational idea. In *Collected works of Liang Shuming* (Vol. 7). Shandong People Press [梁漱溟《杜威教育哲学之根本观念》，《梁漱溟全集》济南：山东人民出版社].

Liang, S. (1989). My worries. In *Collected works of Liang Shuming* (Vol. 4, p. 837). Shandong People Press [梁漱溟《我心中的苦闷》，《梁漱溟全集》济南：山东人民出版社].

Liang, S. (1989). Intellectual transformations during my early years. In *Collected works of Liang Shuming* (Vol. 7). Shandong People Press [梁漱溟《自述早年思想之再转再变》，《梁漱溟全集》济南：山东人民出版社].

Liang, S. (1989). How to find out the truth of Confucius. In *Collected Works of Liang Shuming* (Vol. 4). Shangdong People Press [梁漱溟《如何求孔子的真面目》，《梁漱溟全集》济南：山东人民出版社].

Liang, S. (2004). The rejuvenate of Confucian thought. In *Liang Shuming's lectures about Confucianism, Buddhism, and Taoism.* Press of Guang Xi University [梁漱溟《孔子学说之重光》，《梁漱溟先生论儒佛道》.桂林：广西大学出版社].

Liang, S. (2015). *The cultures of east and west and their philosophies.* Zhong Hua Shu Ju [梁漱溟《东西方文化及其哲学》北京：中华书局].

Liang, P. (2012). *The last Confucian master in China: My father Liang Shuming.* Jiang Su Wen Yi Press [梁培恕《中国最后一个大儒：记父亲梁漱溟》南京：江苏文艺出版社].

Ma, D. (1992). *Biography of Liang Shuming.* Dongfang Press [马东玉《梁漱溟传》北京：东方出版社].

Mao, Z. (1919). National antique and the spirit of scientism. *New Tide, 1*(5), 745. [毛子水《国故和科学精神》，《新潮》].

Martin, J. R. (2011). *Education reconfigured: Culture, encounter, and change.* Routledge Publisher.

CHAPTER 6

A Seed Found Its Ground

John Dewey and the Construction of the Department of Education at Beijing Normal University

LIU Xing

Abstract

Education did not exist as an independent field of studies in Chinese universities before Dewey's visit to China in 1919. Dewey's support accelerated the establishment of the Department of Education at Beijing Normal University (BNU), which was the first one in China. Dewey's book *Democracy and Education* was used as a textbook, encyclopedia, and introduction to this modern discipline during his one-year BNU course, "Philosophy of Education." BNU survived the 1922 Act and its Department of Education became a stable and growing institution where Dewey's ideas were studied and taught, which helped to keep Dewey's influence in China strong and long lasting.

Keywords

John Dewey – Beijing Normal University – *Democracy and Education* – Chang Daozhi

1 Introduction[1]

It is undeniable that John Dewey has greatly influenced Chinese education ever since 1919, when he and his wife Alice began their 2-year visit to Japan and China (Tian, 2013: 185). Dewey's visit of China is constantly being discussed in historical and educational studies (Peters, 2019; Wang, 2007; Zhang, 2013).

In the mainstream education discourse, it is said that Dewey and his pragmatic educational theory, to a great extent, have "an anti-traditional and progressive character" (Tian, 2013: 184). If there is a so-called "new–old" spectrum of education, Dewey will undoubtedly be placed at the "new" end of the spectrum. Most studies of Dewey's Chinese stay also view his educational influence in China from this angle; i.e., the narrative of Dewey's influence in China is always presented from "anti-" or "pro-" perspectives. In a widely read

© KONINKLIJKE BRILL NV, LEIDEN, 2019 | DOI:10.1163/9789004511477_007

A SEED FOUND ITS GROUND

textbook, e.g., "Dewey advocated an American democracy of capitalism, criticizing the feudalist system" in China and "he went against any dogmatic education, emphasizing the importance of combination of education and society" (Tian, 2013: 308–310).

This prevailing idea is partly correct because education was not a formal discipline in China before Dewey's arrival and his educational theory had no rivals at that time. More importantly, Dewey contributed to the founding of the first education department in a Chinese university and of education as a discipline in China. Based on this starting point, this article will offer a different narrative of Dewey's influence in China.

2   The Emerging Idea of Education as a Discipline in China

In 1901, Japanese scholar Tachibana Sensaburo's (立花铣三郎) book, *Education*, which was translated by Wang Guowei (王国维), was published in Shanghai.[2] This event was generally recognized as the starting point for the introduction of foreign educational ideas into China. In the next year, the Imperial University of Peking was re-established after the Boxer Rebellion (1899–1901)[3] and comprised a Normal School (师范馆) and an Officials School (仕学馆).[4] The former school, which is the predecessor of today's Beijing Normal University (BNU), was the earliest teacher training institute in China. Some Japanese professors were hired to teach courses on education and psychology. It is worth noting that these education courses were only supplemental courses at the Imperial University. Students in history or physics only attended these courses to learn some basic educational ideas or methods to assist their future teaching work (Hao, 2013: 226–227). Even in 1908, when the Normal School separated from the Imperial University of Peking and became an independent institution of higher education,[5] this curriculum structure did not change at all.

There may be several reasons for this lack of change in the curriculum structure, but the most important reason might be that education had not yet been recognized as a field of professional studies worthy of an independent major or university department. At that time, "few intellectuals recognized the value of educational studies" (Hou, 2009: 110). Chinese classical scholars who received strict academic training for several decades and enjoyed a great reputation among intellectuals always disparaged education as a kind of less-prestigious "practical" knowledge. In her excellent monograph, *An Elusive Science: The Troubling History of Education Research*, Lagemann (2002: 7–17) described a similar story in the United States during the 1890s. Education scholars in this time had to struggle very hard to obtain respect for their identities and positions among their university colleagues. Teachers College at Columbia University played a pathfinding role in this process and its most iconic figure, John Dewey, gradually became famous in educational studies since about 1902, when *The Child and the Curriculum* was officially published. In the early 1900s, Dewey emerged in the fields of logic and the philosophy of education "as a leading progressive intellectual and a national figure" (Rockefeller, 1991: 223).

In this sense, it is quite difficult to say whether there were any "old" ideas or schools of education in China when Dewey arrived. Nevertheless, education was always a hot topic for public discussion. In particular, "in 1905, the Chinese government abolished the Imperial Examination (科举), which brought a burst of articles on education" (Zuo, 2017: 22). Nevertheless, there was no institution for educational studies and education was not treated as a problem that needed professional or systematic analyses, i.e., educational discussions were conducted solely at the practical level. The emerging idea of education as a discipline had not yet fully developed at this stage.

3 Dewey and BNU

The five institutions that officially invited Dewey to China did not include BNU. A leading higher education institution in South China, Nanjing Normal University (NNU), played a more active role in this process in cooperation with National Peking University (NPU) from the very beginning. These institutions invited Dewey to China mainly because the president of NNU, Guo Bingwen (郭秉文) and a leading figure at NPU, Hu Shi (胡适) were both Teachers College graduates from Columbia University who had studied with Dewey. However, most BNU professors of the time had graduated from Japanese universities. As Dewey discovered himself, the returned students from Japan were "all at loggers with the returned students from America" (Hickman, 2002, no. 11757). These two former students of Dewey invited him to come to China when they learned that he would be visiting Japan. Dewey "entertained the idea of visiting China in the summer before returning to the United States, but he did not know how long he could stay" and "needed to evaluate the prospects in China to make an informed decision" (Wang, 2007: 3). In a letter to his adopted son, Sabino, Dewey expressed his mixed feelings: "the only trouble is that I shall have to lecture all the time to help even up. I don't know the program exactly, but I know it calls for lectures in Shanghai, Nanking and Peking and I assume other places. You look up your geography and you will see how far apart the places are" (Hickman, 2002, no. 03892).

A SEED FOUND ITS GROUND

However, history intervened with its own dramas. Dewey encountered the May Fourth Movement[6] in China, which was the climax of the student movement in China. He was greatly impressed and moved by this movement and felt that there was a possibility of democracy as "a mode of associated living, of conjoint communicated experience" in China. He then decided to extend his stay (Liu, 2016: 26–29).

In some BNU professors' eyes, Dewey's coming was probably a ray of hope because the field of education was facing a serious identity crisis. In the 1915 National Educational Meeting, some delegates questioned whether a normal university deserved to be an independent institution and should not just become a school of education in a comprehensive university. Not only was education as a subject disdained, normal university, as its matrix, also faced a similar situation. A fierce debate had raged since 1915 and finally after the 1922 Act (壬戌学制),[7] all six national normal universities were abolished or combined into comprehensive universities, with the exception of BNU.[8] The president of BNU, Chen Baoquan (陈宝泉), fought a lonely battle in his painstaking efforts to help his university survive from the reform. One of these efforts was to found a new Department of Education, because Chen (1996) realized that "our graduates were trained to teach subjects; but without a department of education, our educational academic would have no progress" (91). This department was set up to prove the value of modern educational studies and the value of the normal university, which should be considered equal to any other universities. Chen probably had this idea in 1915 when he tried but failed to establish a preparatory department of education (Zhang, 2011: 113). Therefore, when Dewey became a nationally recognized icon of education in China, Chen did not hesitate to take this opportunity to strengthen BNU's status.

Dewey arrived in Shanghai on April 30, 1919. After a one-month stay in South China, he came to Beijing on May 31st. It is hard to date when the BNU faculty first contacted Dewey. Since the focus of Dewey's first lecture in China (Shanghai, May 3, 1919) was on education and a nationwide Dewey fad had formed in a short time through the media, it is reasonable to presume that the BNU faculty were aware of Dewey's presence in China. The earliest record related to Dewey and BNU is that he visited BNU on July 4th with the invitation of "the head of the industrial department"[9] to celebrate the students who had built "three new school buildings" by themselves (Hickman, 2002, no. 10769). On November 12th, Dewey wrote a letter to his American friend William A. Wirt, who was the superintendent of public schools in Gary City, Indiana, to introduce the BNU president, Chen Baoquan, who was going to visit the States to investigate American education (Hickman, 2002, no. 05021).

Three years later, on April 3rd, 1922, when 16 graduates obtained the first bachelor degrees of education in China, Prof. Deng Cuiying (邓萃英) from BNU said at the graduation ceremony that "dystocia happened quite a lot of times before our department was born," and he added, "before that, President Chen discussed with me about the establishment of the department of education quite a lot, and Mr. Dewey lent us a hand" (Huang, 1922a: 32).

As stated above, Dewey did not have a clear program for his lectures even when he first arrived in China. His great fame brought him numerous invitations to speak. Dewey was exhausted by delivering numerous speeches to unknown audiences out of politeness. While his affection of China deepened during the May Fourth Movement, the unsettled situation of this great student movement also caused difficulties for his series of lectures on "Philosophy of Society and Politics" at NPU. In an August 1, 1919 letter to his Colombia colleague, Wendell Bush, Dewey complained that "it still isn't certain under just what auspices my lectures will be given" (Hickman, 2002, no. 05019).

Against this background, Dewey had sufficient reason to accept BNU's invitation to give a one-year course on the philosophy of education from 1920. This would have relieved the economic pressure, with no need to accept invitations to deliver exhausting public speeches.[10]

On November 8, 1919, the new Department of Education at BNU was approved by the Ministry of Education as the first education department in China.[11] In December 1919, BNU published a new journal called *The BNU Educational Record* (《北京高师教育丛刊》). The opening article of the first issue was BNU President Chen's "A Plan to reform Normal Education" (《改革师范教育之意见》), in which he emphasized that the newborn Department of Education would promote educational studies instead of pedagogical training for particular subjects. Following Chen's article, half of the remaining articles in the first issue of the journal were about Dewey's thought. Some articles introduced Dewey's ideas on vocational education ("Dr. Dewey's opinion of vocational education," 《杜威博士对于实业教育之意见》), while one article translated a note from Dewey's lectures in Japan[12] ("Dewey's Lecture: The Objectives of Science Education," 《杜威演讲理科教育之目的》), which was originally published in Japanese. Although most of the BNU teachers were trained in Japanese higher education institutes, this journal showed that they were eager to innovate educational studies in China with the foundation of the new Department of Education and the active introduction of Dewey's educational theory.

In the spring of 1920, 18 students[13] were enrolled in the BNU Department of Education. Their program of studies was recorded on their official transcripts,

A SEED FOUND ITS GROUND

which were collected in Box No. 1-0123-0001 in the BNU Archives. A leading student is Chang Daozhi (常道直) who later became a famous expert on Dewey in China. His courses included Philosophy, Philosophy of Education, Aesthetics, Educational Theory, History of Education, Modern Education, Sociology, Educational Hygiene, Elementary Pedagogy, English, and Biology. These subjects were marked with an asterisk, which referred to an interesting marginal note in his transcript: "* means before June 1921, those courses had no examinations. Therefore, these credits were given directly" (ABNU, no. 1-0123-0001).[14] Box No. 1-0124-0001 belongs to the 1923 Alumni and clearly shows that all courses adopted the centesimal system. Considering the crisis of legitimacy that BNU was facing in that period, it can be reasonably presumed that the BNU Department of Education was established in such haste that its curriculum was not prepared completely, particularly on the method of evaluation. The BNU faculty did not establish a fixed evaluation system until the following year. Chang took the Philosophy of Education course taught by Dewey in addition to Elementary Pedagogy taught by Alice Dewey (ABNU, no. 1-0087-0001), with only two asterisks in his transcript. We can imagine that Dewey's audience at his formal lectures from September 1920 at BNU (ABNU, no. 1-0087-0001) comprised a group of young students[15] from the newborn education department.

4   Democracy and Education

Dewey was fortunate in having Chang as his student at BNU because Chang took notes from Dewey's lectures and serialized them over almost a whole year in a BNU journal, *Democracy and Education* (《平民教育》) from December 20, 1920 to November 10, 1921.[16] Those notes were assembled into a book and published in 1922 as *Democracy and Education* (《平民主义与教育》)[17] similarly to Dewey's most famous monograph *Democracy and Education*, originally published in 1916. Dewey (2016) wrote an introduction and thanked Chang "for the pains he has taken in reporting his lectures and in translating them into Chinese in order to make them available to a larger audience" (11).

In his preface, Chang clearly explained that Dewey used his 1916 *Democracy and Education* as the textbook for his course. Most records of Dewey's teaching style suggest that his teaching method was somewhat dull because he just read the prepared materials to his audience in most instances (Rockefeller, 1991: 353). Therefore, we may reasonably assume that Dewey also read his book during his BNU course, but with additions or deletions corresponding to the Chinese context. Therefore, Chang's notes were closely derived from Dewey's original 1916 English work and Dewey's teaching at BNU did not stray far from that text.[18]

Why did Dewey choose *Democracy and Education* as his textbook for BNU? Was it chosen randomly or with some specific considerations?

While we will not summarize Dewey's *Democracy and Education* here, the contents of the book were shown in Table 6.1. These contents indicate that this book was very close to being an encyclopedia of education for the time. Statements can be found for nearly all of the current theoretical or practical educational topics and problems. Both traditional and hot topics, such as Plato's educational ideas and vocational education, respectively, were also discussed. As used in university lectures, this encyclopedia becomes an education textbook because it introduces the whole field of education. In addition, *Democracy and Education* was originally published as a textbook. The first edition of this book was published in a textbook series[19] edited by Dr. Paul Monroe with the assistance of the publisher, Macmillan.

Writing a textbook differs from writing a scholarly monograph. The style of writing in most instances is strictly regulated and the author is expected to write in a more structured way to offer readers clear ideas and a complete structure for a particular field. From this perspective, Dewey's writing style in *Democracy and Education* is understandably a little different from his other works. For example, every chapter ends with a summary, which makes it a more reader-friendly textbook. Finally, it was a large book at over 400 pages. Thus, Dewey obviously wanted to cover nearly all educational topics in this volume.

Several years before writing *Democracy and Education*, Dewey was invited by Dr. Paul Monroe to contribute to *A Cyclopedia of Education*, which was published by the same publisher, Macmillan, from 1911. Dewey contributed lexical items, such as accommodation, activity, adaptation, and adjustment.[20] One example is presented here. "Adaptation" was defined by Dewey as:

> the maintenance of life requires an adaptation of the organism to its surroundings, of the human individual to the natural and social medium in which he is placed. Disturbance of adaptation means disease – physical, mental, moral; and though the capacity of human beings to adapt themselves to abnormal condition is very great, maladjustment, if extreme and long continued, results in death or arrest of growth. The entire process of EDUCATION man properly be regarded as a process of securing the conditions that make for the most complete and effective adaptation of individuals to their physical and moral environment." (Boydston, 1978, MW, Vol. 6: 364)

A SEED FOUND ITS GROUND

TABLE 6.1   The respective chapters of Chang Daozhi's note on Democracy and Education and Dewey's original book

Chapter	The notes (1922)	Corresponding chapter	The book (1916)
I	Education and Life	I	Education as a Necessity of Life
II	Education and Environment	II	Education as a Social Function
III	Education as Growth	IV	Education as Growth
IV, V	Criticisms on Different Educational Ideas	V	Preparation, Unfolding, and Formal Discipline
		VI	Education as Conservative and Progressive
VI, VII	Democracy in Education	VII	The Democratic Conception in Education
VIII	Aims of Education	VIII	Aims of Education
IX	Natural Development as Aim	IX	Natural Development and Social Efficiency as Aims
X	Social Efficiency as Aim		
XI	Culture as Aim		
XII	Interest and Discipline	X	Interest and Discipline
XIII	Experience and Thinking	XI	Experience and Thinking
XIV, XV	Thinking in Education	XII	Thinking in Education
XVI	The Nature of Method	XIII	The Nature of Method
XVII	The Nature of Subject	XIV	The Nature of Subject Matter
XVIII	Play and Work	XV	Play and Work in the Curriculum
XIX	Geography and History	XVI	The Significance of Geography and History
XX	Science	XVII	Science in the Course of Study

(cont.)

TABLE 6.1   The respective chapters of Chang Daozhi's note on Democracy and Education and Dewey's original book (*cont.*)

Chapter	The notes (1922)	Corresponding chapter	The book (1916)
XXI	Educational Value	XVIII	Educational Value
XXII	Labor and Leisure	XIX	Labor and Leisure
XXIII	Intellectual and Practical Subjects	XX	Intellectual and Practical Studies
XXIV	Physical and Social Subjects	XXI	Physical and Social Subjects
XXV	The Individual and the World	XXII	The Individual and the World
XXVI	Vocational Education	XXIII	Vocational Aspects of Education
XXVII	Philosophy of Education	XXIV	Philosophy of Education
XXVIII	Epistemology and Ethics	XXV	Theories of Knowledge
		XXVI	Theories of Morals

SOURCE: DEWEY (1916, 2016)

These sentences evoke the first chapter of *Democracy and Education*, "Education as a Necessity of Life":

> As long as it endures, it struggles to use surrounding energies in its own behalf. It uses light, air, moisture, and the material of soil. To say that it uses them is to say that it turns them into means of its own conservation. As long as it is growing, the energy it expends in thus turning the environment to account is more than compensated for by the return it gets: it grows. Understanding the word "control" in this sense, it may be said that a living being is one that subjugates and controls for its own continued activity the energies that would otherwise use it up. Life is a self-renewing process through action upon the environment. (Dewey, 1916: 1–2)

Dewey's fundamental concepts, like "adaptation," had already been shaped at least since 1911 and he had been training himself in the writing style we can find in *Democracy and Education* by contributing to *A Cyclopedia of Education*

A SEED FOUND ITS GROUND

before 1911. Thus, *Democracy and Education* combined both a textbook and an encyclopedia. In this sense, a contemporary philosopher of education, Biesta (2006) is correct when he says:

> I have to confess that when I first read the book [*Democracy and Education*] as an undergraduate, I found it quite boring. In its attempt to cover almost everything there was to say about education past and present, the book didn't stand out – or at least not to me and not at the time – as making a particular point in the educational discussion or taking a particular position in the educational field. (23)

However, Dewey was drawing on a blank canvas at BNU. He was teaching at a newborn education department, which was the first and only one in China. Therefore, when Dewey began his lectures for the first freshmen in educational studies, he was not eager to peddle his own or pragmatic ideas. He used *Democracy and Education* as a textbook to give his students a bird's eye-view of the field of education instead of "taking a particular position in the educational field."

The structure of Chang Daozhi's notes published in 1922 left some clues. For example, chapters V and VI of his 1916 book were rearranged into one chapter in the notes with a clearer title: "Criticisms on Different Educational Ideas." Dewey introduced six kinds of understanding about education and their relationship: "Preparation," "Unfolding," "Training of Faculties," "Formation," "Recapitulation and Retrospection," and "Reconstruction." Froebel, Hegel, Locke, Herbart, and Hall[21] were also introduced as representative theorists.

Another of Dewey's obvious revisions in the notes was that Chapter IX of his book was split up into three chapters. Thus, Dewey could have one independent presentation at BNU to deal with Rousseau under the title of Natural Development. In addition, Dewey had more time to introduce two prevailing American ideas to his students, i.e., social efficiency and culture.

In brief, Dewey attempted to ensure that every important theory and topic was introduced to his Chinese students during his one-year course. Therefore, Dewey did not teach his books with more Deweyan or pragmatic characteristics, like *Child and Curriculum* or *The School and Society*, nor his latest lecture at Tokyo Imperial University, *Reconstruction in Philosophy*.

This was the first time that Western educational theories were systematically introduced and educational problems were expressed and analyzed in such a systematic way in Chinese universities. The lexical items of Accommodation, Activity, Democracy, Experience, Education as Preparation, and Education as Reconstruction became critical concepts for those Chinese students when dealing with educational problems in China. When one of the students at the BNU Department of Education, Huang Gongjue (黃公觉), began to use what he had learned to write some educational reviews, he admitted that "for anyone who wants to study modern educational thoughts, it is better to start from Dewey" (Huang, 1922b: 8).

Thus, Dewey did not intend to advocate his own theories or oppose any traditional education models as the flagbearer of a new education model, as assumed by many. Dewey was introducing education as a modern university discipline to China, which is why he chose *Democracy and Education* for the BNU course textbook.

5   The Significance of the Department of Education

On June 30, 1921, before Dewey returned to America, a big farewell party in Beijing was attended by about 80 people. Hu Shi and Liang Qichao (梁启超) gave speeches appreciating Dewey's contribution to the communication between Western and Eastern philosophies and cultures. However, the BNU representative, Prof. Deng Cuiying talked from a different perspective. He said that "Mr. Dewey is an educator, while BNU is a university for pure educational studies. Therefore, we cooperated very well." Another adjunct professor at BNU, Wu Zhuosheng (吴卓生) observed that:

> Chinese people used to respect education, but they only respect teachers, instead of the profession of education. They thought teaching is a job with low professional status and everyone can do it. When I studied education in America, some people in China even suspected: does education need any study? (Hu, 2003: 329–333)[22]

Dewey's work at BNU changed some people's bias about educational studies. Different people comprehended Dewey's influences from different aspects. However, Dewey's most important contribution at BNU was the construction of an education department and building the idea of education as a modern discipline.

Dewey himself also had similarly warm feelings about his time at BNU. Eight days earlier, on June 22nd, when Dewey delivered his last speech to his BNU audience, he said:

> I will keep those students from the Department of Education at BNU in my mind forever. I feel very lucky, for I had a chance to teach them for more than one year and had close connections with all of them. They

had rich teaching experience, while now they are promoting educational scholarship. They come from different provinces, or we should call them representatives of their provinces. Their experience at BNU will make them the core force of the future reform. (Wang, 1921: 51)[23]

Thus, Dewey also expected his BNU students to realize their ideals as educational researchers in the future.

On April 3, 1922, a solemn ceremony was held at BNU to celebrate the graduation of the first 16 students to get a bachelor's degree from the Department of Education. After their graduation, most of these students did not disappoint Dewey and became pioneering Chinese educational scholars and practitioners, like Chang Daozhi who became a professor of education at East China Normal University, another leading Shanghai teacher training institution. Hu Guoyu (胡国钰) became a professor of educational psychology at Northwest Normal University, which still plays an important role in educational studies and teacher training in western China. Fang Yongzheng (方永蒸) was appointed as the principal of the High School affiliated with BNU and greatly influenced the way this high school was run. These graduates were the first generation of Chinese educational researchers to receive academic training in education in China.

The year of 1922 also witnessed a new Act, which led to five of the six national normal universities to close or be combined into comprehensive universities. This period was a great shock to Chinese education, particularly teacher training programs. Only BNU survived.[24] The BNU Department of Education, as President Chen foresaw, contributed much to the academic reputation of not only educational studies as a discipline, but also the perception of BNU as a normal university. The BNU Department of Education also became the only stable and lasting institution where educational studies were taught and conducted in this period. Therefore, Dewey's efforts to introduce education as a discipline at BNU were not in vain. Not only did the first graduate generation from this department, but also their successors, continue to read Dewey's *Democracy and Education* as their first textbook, and used Dewey's core concepts, like "experience" and "learning by doing,"[25] to analyze Chinese educational problems. More generations of educational researchers were trained here and consciously or unconsciously spread Dewey's ideas.

6   Conclusion

Education did not exist as an independent field of studies in Chinese universities until Dewey's visit to China in 1919. Dewey's fame accelerated the founding of the BNU Department of Education, which was the first education department in China. Dewey's book *Democracy and Education* was used at his one-year BNU course "Philosophy of Education" as a textbook, encyclopedia, and introduction to this modern discipline, which greatly shaped Chinese people's knowledge of education from the very beginning. BNU survived the 1922 Act and its education department became a stable and growing institution where Dewey's ideas were studied and taught. Thus, Dewey's influence in China was kept strong and long-lasting.

Acknowledgment

This chapter is a reprint from: LIU, Xing. (2019). A seed found its ground: John Dewey and the construction of the Department of Education at Beijing Normal University. *Beijing International Review of Education, 1*(4), 695–713.

Notes

1   This project was supported by China Postdoctoral Science Foundation (No. 2018M641232).

2   Recent studies have observed that *Education* was also a translation into Japanese of Swiss educationist Hans Rudolf Rüegg's (1824–1898) German language book. This will be an interesting tangent for further studies in educational history from a global perspective.

3   In 1900, Beijing was successively seized by the Boxers and foreign armies during the Boxer Rebellion. "The dormitories of the Imperial University of Peking were occupied and used as barracks by the Russian armies, while teachers and students of the Imperial University were scattered, books and experimental instruments either destroyed or lost. This caused the two-year suspension of teaching at the Imperial University" (Hao, 2013: 242).

4   The Officials School was "in fact an accelerated training class for government officials" (Hao, 2013: 269).

5   The Chinese name of Beijing Normal University changed slightly several times in correspondence to the dramatically changing nature of Chinese society in the last century. For convenience's sake, we refer to the institution in this English-language paper as Beijing Normal University (BNU) for consistency; however, readers should note that it was called Beijing Higher Normal School (北京高等师范学校 in Chinese) from 1912 to 1923.

6   "On May Fourth, 1919, the date by which the May Fourth Movement took its name, more than three thousand students in Beijing held a mass demonstration against the decision of the Versailles Peace Conference to transfer German concessions in Shantung to Japan. With their dream of world peace shattered by this unjust treaty, the students were mortified and outraged. To protest against Japanese imperialism and government corruption, they took to the streets and even burned the house of one corrupt pro-Japanese official. The students' expression of patriotism and zeal for reform triggered similar demonstrations throughout China over the next few weeks" (Liu, 2016: 21).

7   The 1922 Act was a national school reform act issued by the President of the Republic of China in 1922. Using learnings from the American experience, a 6–3–3 system based on 6

A SEED FOUND ITS GROUND

127

years of elementary school, 3 years of junior high school, and 3 years of high school was introduced into China with the 1992 Act. This 6–3–3 system was a great achievement of this Act and is still in use today. The 1922 Act allowed two ways for the development of normal universities: (1) to continue as an independent institution; or (2) to become a school of education in a comprehensive university, similarly to Teachers College at Columbia University. However, most normal universities could not obtain enough financial support and were at a serious disadvantage, which meant that the 1992 Act helped comprehensive universities to absorb most normal universities.

8 NNU (南京高师) was closed in 1922, Shenyang Normal University (沈阳高师) was closed in 1923, Guangdong Normal University (广东高师) and Wu Chang Normal University (武昌高师) was closed in 1924, and Chengdu Normal University (成都高师) was closed in 1931. Chengdu Normal University was the last because it was far from the central government's control (Wang, 2005: 91–97).

9 This department head was probably Samuel M. Dean, an American professor of industrial training program (ABNU, No. 1-0086-0001). His Chinese name is "丁蔭" (Ding Yin). He also worked for Yenching University (燕京大学) in China.

10 Dewey's family budget was insufficient even before going to Japan. "In fact, he could not have afforded the trip to Japan if his close friend, Albert C. Barnes, had not offered financial support" (Wang, 2007: 4). While in China, Dewey actually was not paid by NPU after he gave lectures there. In a September 12, 1920 letter to Barnes, Dewey said that, "last year I was paid by private societies, but this year by the Government University" (Hickman, 2002, no. 04102). Dewey continually asked about the status of his stocks in his letters to his family (Hickman, 2002, no. 03910), which was probably because of his financial concerns.

11 NNU provided a junior college degree of education (教育专修科) from 1918. In 1921, however, NNU was folded into National Southeastern University, which was a comprehensive university with five departments, including an education department. This was the second Department of Education in China. The third was established at Chengdu Normal University in 1929. The three other national normal universities did not have independent education departments.

12 This note was originally produced by Professor Yoshida Kumaji (吉田熊次) at Tokyo Imperial University. The Chinese translator was Chen Jianshan (陈兼善), a student at the Department of Zoology, BNU.

13 Two students discontinued their studies; therefore, only 16 students graduated in 1922.

14 It might be useful to note that Chang's other courses of History of Philosophy, Moral Philosophy, Psychology, Educational Psychology, Psychology of Children, Psychological Measurement, Applied Psychology, Educational Sociology, Educational Administration, Educational Statistics and Principles of Teaching had relevant scores, ranging from A to C. Those courses were taken in his second year. It helps us to understand those graduates' knowledge structure.

15 Chang Daozhi was born in 1897; therefore, he was 23 years old when attending Dewey's BNU course. He possibly could not even imagine in 1920 that his career would be very closely tied to Dewey for the rest of his life.

16 Before going back to America, Dewey once joked with his daughters: "Can you wonder I hate to leave a country where educational lectures are treated as news?" (Hickman, 2002, no. 03964).

17 The Chinese name of this book is *Pinminzhuyi yu Jiaoyu* (《平民主义与教育》). *Jiaoyu* means education, while in modern Chinese, *pinminzhuyi* is a little distant from "democracy," but closer to "education for the poor."

18 Unfortunately, the available space here does not permit a detailed comparative study between Chang's notes and Dewey's original monograph. However, it is worth noting that both of them actually share a similar structure. See Table 6.1.

19 The front page of the 1916 edition of *Democracy and Education* shows that the other contributors to this textbook series were Ellwood Cubberley, Edward Elliott, Ernest Henderson, and Willystine Goodsell.

20 Dewey's writings in *A Cyclopedia of Education* can be found in volumes 6 and 7 of the middle works of John Dewey, *Collected Works of John Dewey*, edited by Jo Ann Boydston.

21 Stanley Hall (1844–1924) was mentioned in the notes, but not in the book. Dewey probably wanted his Chinese students to learn about this famous contemporary psychologist.

22 The Dean of the NPU Department of Education during the 1930s, Wu Junsheng (1976) claimed that "Hu Shi himself did not view educational studies as important as it seems" (55).

23 Dewey's words were retranslated from Wang Zhuoran's Chinese note.

24 An independent normal university is not necessarily better than a school of education in a comprehensive university, but considering the situation of twentieth century China, the 1922 Act shocked Chinese education with the closing of normal universities. With government support, normal universities used to be free of charge, which attracted a lot of excellent students from poor families to become teachers. However, fewer people were attracted to them after the reform and teacher professionalism was delayed greatly (Liu & Xie, 2002: 99–100).

25 For example, Chang Daozhi was still studying Dewey's theory even in 1960. He guided a graduate student to write her dissertation under the title of *A study of Dewey's Learning by Doing* (《杜威"做中学"理论研究》). However, political changes disturbed the writing of her dissertation (Chang, 2018: VI).

References

Archives of Beijing Normal University (ABNU). (n.d.). Beijing Normal University.

Biesta, Gert (2006). "Of all affairs, communication is the most wonderful": The Communicative Turn in Dewey's Democracy and Education. In D. T. Hansen (Ed.), *John Dewey and our educational prospect: A critical engagement with Dewey's democracy and education.* State University of New York Press.

Boydston, Jo Ann. (Ed.). (1978). *The collected works of John Dewey.* Southern Illinois University Press.

Chang, Daozhi. (2018). *Educational writings of Daozhi Chang.* East China Normal University [常道直：《大夏教育文存·常道直卷》，上海：华东师范大学出版社，2018 年版。].

Chen, Baoquan. (1996). *Educational writings of Baoquan Chen.* People's Education Press [陈宝泉：《陈宝泉教育论著选》，北京：人民教育出版社，1996 年版。].

Dewey, John. (1916). *Democracy and education: An introduction to the philosophy of education.* The Macmillan Company.

Dewey, John. (2016). *Democracy and education* (Daozhi Chang, Trans.). Fujian Educational Publishing House [杜威：《平民主义与教育》，常道直译，福州：福建教育出版社，2016 年版。].

A SEED FOUND ITS GROUND

Hao, Ping. (2013). *Peking University and the origins of higher education in China* (Yuping Shen, Trans.). Peking University Press.

Hickman, Larry. (Ed.). (2002). *The correspondence of John Dewey* [CD-ROM]. InteLex.

Hou, Huaiyin. (2009). *The path of Chinese education.* Anhui Educational Publishing House [侯怀银：《中国教育学之路》，合肥：安徽教育出版社，２００９年版。].

Hu, Shi. (2003). *The collected works of Hu Shi.* Anhui Educational Publishing Press [胡适：《胡适全集》，合肥：安徽教育出版社，2003 年版。].

Huang, Gongjue. (1922a). The first educational bachelor degree conferral ceremony in China. *Democracy and Education, 51,* 25–32 [黄公觉：《中国第一次授教育学士学位典礼纪盛》，《平民教育》，1922 年第51号，第25–32页].

Huang, Gongjue. (1922b). The recent trends of educational thoughts. *The Chinese Educational Review, 14*(9), 1–8 [黄公觉：《最近教育思潮的趋势》，《教育杂志》，1922 年第14卷第9号，第1–8页。].

Lagemann, Ellen Condliffe. (2002). *An elusive science: The troubling history of education research.* University of Chicago Press.

Liu, Jie, & Xie, Weihe. (2002). *Inside and outside of the Fence: A reflection upon the 100 years Chinese normal education.* Beijing Normal University Publishing Group [刘捷，谢维和：《栅栏内外：中国高等师范教育百年省思》，北京：北京师范大学出版社，2002 年版。].

Liu, Xing. (2016). How history created its own dramas: A study of John Dewey's experiences in his 1919 visits in Japan and China. *The Journal of Northeast Asian History, 13*(2), 9–31.

Peters, Michael A. (2019). 100 years of Dewey in China, 1919–1921: A reassessment. *Beijing International Review of Education, 1* (1), 9–26.

Rockefeller, Steven C. (1991). *John Dewey: Religious faith and democratic humanism.* Columbia University Press.

Tian, Zhengping. (Ed.). (2013). *General history of Chinese education, Volume 12: Republic of China.* Beijing Normal University Publishing Group [田正平：《中国教育通史・第十二卷：中华民国卷》，北京：北京师范大学出版社，2003 年版。].

Wang, Dongjie. (2005). *Interaction between state and intellectual on the basic level: Nationalization of Sichuan University (1925–1939).* SDX Joint Publishing Company [王东杰：《国家与学术的地方互动：四川大学国立化进程（1925–1939）》，北京：生活・读书・新知三联书店，2005 年版。].

Wang, Jessica Ching-Sze. (2007). *John Dewey in China.* State University of New York Press.

Wang, Zhuoran. (1921): Dr. Dewey's farewell speech. *Gazette of Education, 8*(7), 47–51 [王卓然：《杜威博士之临别演讲》，《教育公报》，1921 年，第8卷第7期，第47–51页。].

Wu, Junsheng. (1976). *My sixty years in education*. Biographical Literature Press [吴俊升：《教育生涯一周甲》，台北：传记文学出版社，1976 年版。].

Zhang, Huajun. (2013). *John Dewey, Liang Shuming, and China's education reform: Cultivating individuality*. Lexington Books.

Zhang, Xiaoli. (2011). The historical situation of education research section in Beijing higher normal school. *Journal of Educational Studies, 7*(4), 111–120 [张小丽：《北高师教育研究科的历史境遇》，《教育学报》，2001 年第4期，第111–120页。].

Zuo, Songtao. (2017). *Rivalry between private schools (sishu) and academies (xuetang) in early modern China*. SDX Joint Publishing Company [左松涛：《近代中国的私塾与学堂之争》，北京：生活·读书·新知三联书店，2017 年版。].

CHAPTER 7

100 Years of Dewey in China, 1919–1921

A Reassessment

Michael A. PETERS

Abstract

This paper uses the centenary of Dewey' two years in China as an opportunity to reassess John Dewey's views on China, based mainly on his *Letters* and his *Lectures in Social and Political Philosophy*, 1919–21 given on invitation at the University of Peking. In particular, the paper makes some criticisms of Dewey's pragmatism (his lack of contextualism in not mentioning the significance of the May 4th Movement) and raises the question of the relationship of his thought with Chinese Marxism. The essay is given a critical reading by three scholars Jessica Ching-Sze Wang, Kang Zhao, and Zhang Huajun, all Dewey scholars.

Keywords

Dewey – China – May 4th Movement – political philosophy

1 Prologue: Dewey's Letters on China, 1919–1921 – The May 4th Student Movement

2019 marks one hundred years of John Dewey in China. It is ironic that Dewey spent several months in Japan in 1919, before traveling to China at the invitation of Cai Yuanpei and other scholars on behalf of Peking University and other universities to give some lectures during which time he witnesses first-hand both the Japanese imperialist expansion in China and the student protests against it. Writing home on May 12, 1919 he pens a letter with the following sentence: 'The Peking tempest seems to have subsided for the present, the Chancellor still holding the fort, and the students being released.' (He goes on to make unfavourable comparisons with Japan, commenting on corruption and the status of women.[1]) Dewey, his wife, Alice Chipman, and his daughter, Lucy Dewey travel to China arriving in Shanghai on April 30. Zou Zhenhuan

© KONINKLIJKE BRILL NV, LEIDEN, 2022 | DOI:10.1163/9789004511477_008

(2010: 43) who authors a paper on 'The "Dewey Fever" in Jiangsu and Zhejiang during the May Fourth Movement and Its Relation to the Cultural Tradition in Jiangnan' indicates that he 'gave over 120 lectures upon invitation in eleven provinces including Liaoning, Hebei, Shanxi, Shandong, Jiangsu, Zhejiang, Hunan, Fujian, and Guangdong and the three cities of Beijing, Shanghai, and Tianjin' with nearly half in nearly half of them in Jiangsu and Zhejiang, leading to 'Dewey fever' and 'Dewey schools.' He writes:

> They arrived in Shanghai from Japan on April 30. Welcoming them at the wharf were, among others, Hu Shi, Jiang Menglin, and Tao Xingzhi. The family was accommodated at Cangzhou Villa. Dewey stayed in China for twenty-six months to present more than two hundred lectures, traveling to eleven provinces and three cities, including the city of Beijing, and Liaoning, Hebei, Shandong, Jiangsu, Zhejiang, Fujian, Hunan, and Guangdong provinces. Dewey's emphases on science and education coincided with the pursuit of those of many Chinese thinkers around the May Fourth movement. These Chinese thinkers wanted to break away from the old and construct a new way of conceptualizing China. It is thus not surprising to see his philosophy highly respected and valued in China as new ideas from the West. (Zou, 2010: 44)

Dewey's *Letters* are a great source of background to Dewey's first impressions and understanding of China. They tell us as much about the man and his attitudes as they do a first-hand account of the historic May 4th student movement – one of the early models of new Chinese nationalism based on populist sentiments that galvanised the population and acted as an early precursor of revolutionary socialism. Sometimes in the *Letters* Dewey appears somewhat naïve and also he makes comments that from the perspective of today we might question on the basis of racial stereotypes. At other times the distorted view of events in China led Dewey to see revolutionary activity as 'the fascination of the struggle going on in China for a unified and independent democracy,' as his daughter expressed it in her Preface. This clearly expressed Dewey's American preference for a model of social reform over revolutionary Marxism while at the same time providing positive input on pragmatism (that has much to do with Marxism and praxis), and a new progressive philosophy of education based on democratic participation.

The first set of letters from February 10 when the Dewey family lands in Tokyo until April 2 on the *Kumano Maru* en route to China, some 27 letters, Dewey is both very impressed and polite about Japanese culture – the formality, the tea ceremony, the cult of the scholar, 'old' theatre, Noh, gardens, Buddhism, geisha, 'daily festivals that add so much to the joy of living' – and hopeful about social democracy and the prospect of representative government. May 1st they land in Shanghai. In the letters following China initially suffers in comparison to Japan – especially on the treatment of children.

> The Chinese are noisy, not to say boisterous, easy-going and dirty – and quite human in general effect. They are much bigger than the Japanese, and frequently very handsome from any point of view. The most surprising thing is the number of those who look not merely intelligent but intellectual among the laborers, such as some of the hotel waiters and attendants. (Letter, May 3)

Dewey records that he has dinner with the Chancellor of the University, who is forced from office, commenting 'American sentiment here hopes that the Senate will reject the treaty [of Versailles] because it virtually completes the turning over of China to Japan.' Actually, this is not the case as it concerns the district of Shandong which is turned over to Japan rather than China, representing a betrayal by the Allies. Dewey forms the opinion that the Treaty turning over a large area of Chinese territory to the Japanese ought to be rejected and indicates that if the war drifts on 'the world will have a China under Japanese military domination.' This is a fair enough speculation and signals aspects of the Second Sino-Japanese War to come during WWII, the largest Asian war of the twentieth century with some four million deaths. Dewey's letters following in the days after this communication in his letters home to his children he begins to detail the hopelessness and despair of the Chinese situation as the Japanese begin their imperialist take over.

In a letter dated Shanghai May 13, Dewey also comments on the students' protests and the boycotts of open air meetings and begins to form a political opinion maintaining that 'the United States ought to wash its hands entirely of the Eastern question' or hold Japan to account. He travels to Nanking on May 18, expressing concern at the level of poverty and lack of education for children. One emerging theme is the students' protests: 'The returned students from Japan hate Japan, but they are all at loggers with the returned students from America, and their separate organizations cannot get together' (May 22). He begins to document the student movement more seriously: 'The trouble among the students is daily getting worse, and even the most sympathetic among the faculties are getting more and more anxious' (May 23). He writes a comment that seems to sanction revolution: 'Certainly China needs education all along the line, but they never will get it as long as they try in little bits. So maybe they will have to be pushed to the very bottom before they will be ready to go the whole hog or none' (May 24). His letters start with political news and then trail off into tourist talk.

On June 1st he travels to Peking visiting a temple and museum and then intercedes: 'We have just seen a few hundred girls march away from the American Board Mission school to go to see the President to ask him to release the boy students who are in prison for making speeches on the street. To say that life in China is exciting is to put it fairly. We are witnessing the birth of a nation, and birth always comes hard' (June 1st). He details students' speech-making and their public flogging. On June 5th, he writes: 'This is Thursday morning, and last night we heard that about one thousand students were arrested the day before' ... 'No one can tell to-day what the students' strike will bring next; it may bring a revolution.' Again, on June 5th, he writes: 'The students were stirred up by orders dissolving their associations, and by the "mandates" criticising the Japanese boycott ... So they got busy – the students. They were also angered because the industrial departments of two schools were ordered closed by the police ....' 'Then the students inside held a meeting and passed a resolution asking the government whether they were guaranteed freedom of speech, because if they were not, they would not leave the building merely to be arrested again, as they planned to go on speaking ....' 'The students have now asked that the chief of police come personally to escort them out and make an apology.'

On June 7th, Dewey reports: 'The whole story of the students is funny and not the least funny part is that last Friday the students were speaking and parading with banners and cheers and the police standing near them like guardian angels, no one being arrested or molested.' On June 10th, it is clear that Dewey has started his lectures: 'The students have taken the trick and won the game at the present moment – I decline to predict the morrow when it comes to China. Sunday morning, I lectured at the auditorium of the Board of Education and at that time, the officials there didn't know what had happened.' Then he assertively writes: 'In talking about democratic developments in America, whenever I make a remark such as the Americans do not depend upon the government to do things for them, but go ahead and do things for themselves, the response is immediate and emphatic. The Chinese are socially a very democratic people and their centralized government bores them' (June 10). From June to August 4 Dewey continues to relate his experiences. Does this mean that Dewey's power of observation is tainted by his hopes for American style democracy?

Dewey witnessed the May 4th Movement, a student-led anti-Japanese, anti-warlord, multi-class movement that was sparked in protest to China's treatment at Versailles not long after the founding of the Chinese Communist Party (CCP) took place in 1921 in Shanghai. The May Fourth Movement (*Wǔsì*

100 YEARS OF DEWEY IN CHINA, 1919–1921

Yùndòng) was an anti-imperialist and political movement growing out of student protests in Beijing on 4 May 1919, against the government's response to the Treaty of Versailles that allowed Japan to receive territories in Shandong. China had entered the WWI on the side of the Allies on condition that all German territories in China including Shandong be returned, but the Treaty of Versailles in 1919 awarded the German rights to Japan. While the US promoted the ideal of self-determination and Wilson's Fourteen Points – a statement of principles of peace – the US did not follow through and Chinese intellectuals saw it as a US betrayal. It sparked a series of protests led by students who met in Beijing to oppose the concession of Shandong to the Japanese and to found a student union of the thirteen local universities. On May 4, over 3000 students met in Tiananmen Square to protest against the Allies betrayal and three Chinese collaborators. Student protests sparked general protests across the country with merchants, workers and peasant joining in. These demonstrations sometimes referred to as the New Culture Movement ignited an upsurge in Chinese nationalism, and symbolized the broad movement towards a new kind of political mobilization based on a populist base rather than the older cultural movement dominated by intellectual elites. While the success of the movement was largely symbolic as Japan retained Shandong, it demonstrated the power of national protest with appropriate political leadership. The May 4th Movement laid the basis for successful national protest and some saw it as an early forerunner of the Maoist revolution to come. In 1939, twenty years later, Mao Zedong (1939) wrote:

> The May 4th Movement twenty years ago marked a new stage in China's bourgeois-democratic revolution against imperialism and feudalism. The cultural reform movement which grew out of the May 4th Movement was only one of the manifestations of this revolution. With the growth and development of new social forces in that period, a powerful camp made its appearance in the bourgeois-democratic revolution, a camp consisting of the working class, the student masses and the new national bourgeoisie. Around the time of the May 4th Movement, hundreds of thousands of students courageously took their place in the van. In these respects the May 4th Movement went a step beyond the Revolution of 1911.[2]

Mao is surely right to mention the May 4th Movement in terms of the establishment and development of communism. After all, Britain and France abetted by USA decided to hand Shandong province to the Japanese dishonouring a former promise to return the province to China as previously agreed. It was not until 1922 that Shandong was returned to Chinese control.

Many of the extant works of scholarship on Dewey do not emphasise the differences between Dewey's position of liberal democracy and Chinese Marxism but tend to occlude discussion of this point to draw conclusions about the advocacy of his ideas by his Chinese students (mostly ex-Columbia University) and also the relationship of Dewey to Confucius. For instance, James Zhixiang Yang (2016) in his dissertation 'When Confucius "Encounters" John Dewey: A Historical and Philosophical Analysis of Dewey's Visit to China' focuses on the question 'What motivated Dewey's Chinese students to introduce Dewey's educational thought to China?' He argues that Dewey is the 'American Confucius' and begins his dissertation by making reference to, Cai Yuanpei's (Chancellor of Beijing University) banquet speech:

> Dr. Dewey's philosophy ... should be treated as the symbol of modern western civilization. Correspondingly, Confucius's philosophy ... can be thought of as the counterpart of traditional Chinese civilization. Confucius said respect the emperor, Dr. Dewey advocated democracy; Confucius said females are a problem to raise, Dr. Dewey advocates equal rights for men and women; Confucius said transmit not create, Dr. Dewey advocates creativity. These are fundamentally different. (as cited in Yang, 2016: 1)

And Cai goes on to note similarities and to see them as evidence of East-West confluence of thought. Some students went on to call Dewey a 'modern Confucius.' Hu Shih indicated that no Western scholar ever had or is likely to have the influence that Dewey has, especially with the emulation of his 'experimental' schools. This may or may not be true, especially if the claim is restricted to intellectual history, but it needs to be put into context of cultural exchange that includes Marco Polo, Thomas Huxley, Charles Darwin, and of course Karl Marx, even though he never set foot in China. Marxist theory was imported into China between 1900 and 1930, leading to the establishment of Chinese Marxist thought. Arguably, the true encounter with Dewey and Marx has not taken place in China, although it is well known that Mao drew on Dewey before his conversion to Marxism, and continued to echo a number of Deweyan themes: 'the political importance of education, the instrumentalist and pluralist conception of the relation between theory and practice, the invocation of a concept of inquiry' (Renault, 2013). Bertram Russell visited China at roughly the same time as Dewey. Both left indelible impressions but were eclipsed by the development of Marxism (Ding, 2007). Translation is a tricky business and open to the whims and the bias of translators as prisoners of their own age. Barbara Schulte (2011: 83) reveals how Dewey was transformed into the Chinese 'Duwei' – as she demonstrates, into 'a friend of the Chinese people, a friend of China and Marxism, and a flagship of modernization.' In '100 Years of John Dewey and Education in China,' Zhang Grace Xinfu and Ron Sheese (2017: 400) document the changing fortunes of the reception of Dewey in China from fame in the 1920s and 1930s, to infamy in the 1950 and 1960s, undergoing a restoration of sort in recent years:

> The changing attitudes of the Chinese to Dewey and his ideas are associated with the changing, and often tumultuous, cultural and political context for education in China from the time of his visit through the following century. Hu Shi and Tao Xingzhi, PhD students of Dewey at Columbia University, were prominent Chinese educators who adapted Dewey's educational concepts to the Chinese environment, and their work continues to influence educational debate in China today.

The relationship between Dewey and Marx is critical in understanding Dewey's perception of the May 4th movement. It seems clear that while Dewey was critical of Marx, he had no first-hand knowledge. However, they share a common history in Hegel, favouring naturalistic philosophy and an emphasis on practice. Philosophy is located in the world and both Dewey and Marx belong to the materialist tradition avoiding both reductive and mechanical versions. And they accept the existence of the external world and Darwin's evolution of living things and mind from organic matter while opposing, Plato's a priori essences and any form of dualism, especially of mind/body. The scope of human knowledge is limited but can attain truth which is provisional and fallible. They both reject the spectator view of epistemology to emphasise practical activity and agency as a source of understanding. This conception leads them both to accept a belief in the unity of theory and practice (Cork, 1949, 1950). Dewey had been to Soviet Russia after the 1917 Revolution and later seemed to confuse Marxism with Stalinism criticising it for its absolutism and dogmatism. He visited Soviet Russia in 1928 and admired the 'collectivistic mentality' and the collusion of school and state,[3] but on the rise of Stalinism, his optimism faded. It is clear that in his early philosophical development he came to the view that individualism offered a distorted view of freedom which could only be found in social cooperation. It was a view that came to occupy a central place in his mature view of democracy and eventually to put him in collision with capitalism. In his book *Democracy and Education* (1916), he embraced a democratic, egalitarian Darwinism against the social Darwinism of the market: Dewey's vision of free and equal human development became the basis for his democratic socialism, although the full statement was only given in his 1927 classic *The Public and its Problems.*

Jessica Ching-Sze Wang (2007) in her book *Dewey in China* begins the process of rethinking his visit to China reviewing two books on the extent to which Dewey influenced education in China (Clopton & Ou's, 1973, *Lectures in China 1919–20* and Keenan's, 1977, *The Dewey Experiment in China*) concluding that both books are simplistic, problematic, unrealistic and overestimate Dewey's influence. She notes to his credit that Dewey is aware that democracy in China cannot be imposed from outside. She refers to Robert Westbrook's (1991) view that the Chinese Deweyans unrealistic strategic weakness making the school the heart of democracy. She also debunks Alan Ryan's (1995) hypothesis that Dewey's popularity was due to his Confucian-type beliefs pointing out that Dewey saw himself as an alternative. She maintains that what Dewey was 'experiencing, thinking and learning' in China at this time has not been addressed. Wang (2007) maintains Dewey was received critically by radicals and traditionalists. The encounter with China was characterized by change, and uncertainty. It was confusing and he was not clear how he or his own country should respond to China. After the Revolution in the 1950s and 1960s allegedly China tried to purge the pragmatic influences of Dewey and his Chinese students. After the Open Door Policy in the 1980s, the dialogue was revived and Chinese scholars were ready to reevaluate Dewey's pragmatism. The history of Dewey criticism is a history of appropriation by traditionalists, liberals, and socialist who interpret Dewey as a means of legitimating their own belief systems. Wang's (2007) own researches search for the warrant to link Deweyan democracy and classical Confucianism to a notion of 'Confucian democracy.'

It was against the tumultuous political background of events of May 4th that Dewey postponed his return home to the USA to take a year's leave of absence from Columbia University, in order to stay in China where he gave a set of 16 lectures at Peking University, referred to as Dewey's Lectures of Social and Political Philosophy, which had been lost and only recently recovered.

2   Dewey's Rediscovered *Lectures in Social and Political Philosophy,* 1919–21

The full text of Dewey's *Lectures in Social and Political Philosophy* (the lectures he delivered in China) were published for the first time in 2015, in the *European Journal of Pragmatism and American Philosophy*. Dewey's original manuscript had been lost and a version has been reconstructed from a Chinese transcription. As the Editors Roberto Frega and Roberto Gronda (2015: 5) explain:

> The typescript of Dewey's "Social and Political Philosophy" lecture series has been discovered by Prof. Yung-chen Chiang ... and it is now deposited at the Hu Shi Archives ... Institute of Modern History, Chinese Academy of the Social Sciences, in Beijing. Dewey's "Social and Political Philosophy" lecture series consisted of sixteen lectures that he delivered at Peking University once a week on Saturday afternoons from 4 P.M. to 6 P.M., beginning on September 20, 1919. The lecture notes survived and now collected in the Hu Shi Archives consist of Lectures I, II, III, IV, VI, X, XI, XII, and XVI.

The extant lectures have the following structure moving from the function of theory and science, through topics on social conflict and reform, to a discussion of communication, the state, the government and political liberalism, and ending on intellectual freedom.

- *Lecture I* [Chapter The Function of Theory, pp. 45–53]
- *Lecture II* [Chapter Science and Social Philosophy, pp. 54–63]
- *Lecture III* [Chapter Social Conflict, pp. 64–71]
- *Lecture IV* [Chapter Social Reform, pp. 72–81]
- *Lecture VI* [Chapter Communication and Associated Living, pp. 90–98]
- *Lecture X* [Chapter The State, pp. 125–132]
- *Lecture XI* [Chapter The Government, pp. 133–140]
- *Lecture XII* [Chapter Political Liberalism, pp. 141–146]
- *Lecture XIV* [Chapter Intellectual Freedom, pp. 173–180]

Yung-chen Chiang (2015) investigates Hu Shi's translation of Dewey's Social and Political Philosophy (Lecture series in China) comparing it to the recently discovered lectures (given above) to demonstrate that given the problems of translation into the vernacular Hu Shi 'tweaked, rearranged, and even expunged at will the source text. He was translating Dewey, to be sure. But it would be more accurate to say that he was using Dewey to advance his own cultural and political agenda' (Chiang, 2015: 95).

In *John Dewey's Social Philosophy: A Restatement*, Roberto Frega (2015) makes a fresh examination of Dewey's social philosophy after the rediscovery of the missing manuscript. He indicates that for Dewey 'the aim of social philosophy consists in the conscious orientation of the social process, a process which Dewey sees as being always in flux, always in the making, hence always in need of being steered, controlled, directed through what he usually terms "intelligence," or social inquiry' (101). It is, in other words, *an instrument of social reform*. And Dewey delineates what he calls a 'third philosophy' by which he means his pragmatist method of inquiry. Dewey, following a kind of naturalistic explanation, in Lecture I determines 'The Function of Theory', arguing that thinking only occurs in situations when instinct, habit and customs do not provide answers, that is, philosophy only begins when established institutions break down. Once it has arisen, life cannot go on as before. As Dewey expresses the point: *'Ideas, theories are originally products, causes of non-intellectual forces*. Thinking arises so to speak only in the *thin cracks* of solid habits ...' (7, original emphasis). He distinguishes three different theories in which philosophy has practical effects: idealistic philosophy, both romantic and utopian in tone (Plato, Lao-Tze); and, conservative philosophy that aims at justifying the spirit of existing institutions (Aristotle, Hegel, Confucius). The third type of social and political philosophy is, of course, Dewey's pragmatism, a topic he picks up in the second lecture distinguishing it from the other two by two features: (i) *'The union of the scientific spirit with the moral and practical aim of philosophy'* (12), and (ii) 'It is pragmatic, instrumental. That is, it aims to be an art, an applied science, a form of social engineering. Politics is an art, but should not be a blind or routine or magical art, not directed by intrigue or vested interest etc. *It rests on the possibility of introducing more conscious regulation into the course of events in behalf of the general or public interests'* (13, original emphasis). Dewey maintains that social philosophy 'must be *specific,* not universal' (13) always aimed at improvement through an instrumental means-end rationality.

Reflecting on these first two lectures today, if we were to accept Dewey's elementary account we would have to supplement his account of pragmatic instrumental rationality with a stronger concept of practice, a story of the evolution of the brain over the last million years, and also perhaps a cognitive model of rational problem-solving as a learned system of logical inferences. That thinking begins in a crisis of some sort that cannot be resolved by existing social convention is pure speculation for which Dewey offers no argument or evidence.

When we compare Dewey's account to current historicist theories of scientific rationality we can get some indication of the historicist turn in philosophy of science that began with Thomas Kuhn, followed by Lakatos' methodology of research programs, Feyerabend's methodological anarchism, Laudan's pragmatic, problem solving, Toulmin's evolutionary model of scientific development to new-wave sociology of science (Nickles, 2017). This is not the space to attempt to critique Dewey but if we situate agents in real-life situation, what is it to be rational is a question that is by no means straightforward and is perhaps more contested today than at any previous time. Frankly, while I'm in tune with Dewey, I want to leave open that theory or thinking may originate in aesthetics and in story-telling. While I hold with Dewey that it is likely that thinking begins in practical situations, I doubt there is a single source.

Dewey begins the third lecture on social conflict with the observation: 'Theory began in disturbance, confusion, friction. It attempts to discover causes and project plans of reorganization that bring about unity, harmony, freer movement.' Social conflict and the need to regulate conduct gave rise to political society. Social philosophy is the means for resolving social conflicts. Lecture IV is devoted to Social Reform and Lecture VI to Communication and Associated Living (little over a paragraph only). By Lecture X, the next in the series recovered, Dewey comes to a discussion of the State, the nature and constitution of government, and the nature and scope of law and the systems of legal rights. He notes that the history of the state as the supreme political authority has not taken the same course everywhere. Here for the first time he mentions China in an example that mentions China's development and the way that it has been interfered by other more developed States. He is talking about the reneging in the Versailles settlement on return of territories that are given to the Japanese.

This is the first time that Dewey shows any awareness of the fact that the Chinese State was in turmoil and that he had witnessed the student movement but the reference is only a glancing one. For a pragmatist who is sensitive to context, this is perhaps surprising and a little disappointing. I would have thought that having witnessed the May 4th Movement and the on-going protests by students that Dewey would have more to say or that he would have drawn on his experience more systematically. It was an opportunity when Dewey might have drawn on his Chinese experience but he wanders off the topic to talk of moral and physical force in the administration of law. In Lecture XI Dewey tackles The Government: 'The Government should be an organ of the general interest, an expression of the public will.' In this lecture, he does contrast European and Confucian political philosophy:

> While the old Chinese theory was based upon faith in the intrinsic goodness of human nature, the orderliness and loyalty of the subjects, the wisdom and benevolence of rulers. Hence the Confucian political philosophy really assumed the supremacy of moral forces, while the European philosophies – at least of the liberal school – have assumed the need of physical backing in order to prevent the immoral forces from becoming supreme. (32)

He puts the argument tersely: 'No powerful government no state, no state no society, no society no stable human morals at all' (32). The necessity of political organization, i.e, the state, to the order of society became an axiom of

Continental thought as the foundation of morals. 'The state [through] government must foster art and science as well as promote education.' He picks up and develops the theme of the problem of the exercise of power by the state in the Lecture XII on Political Liberalism: how does it become a *right*? Through an excursus in liberal political theory, Dewey arrives at the following elements of political democracy (abridged below):

> (1) The people are the source of political power, that is, authority to govern, to legislate and administrate proceeds from them, not from any superhuman force, not from a ruling dynasty or family, nor from a selected class ...
>
> (2) The state exists for society, for promoting human intercourse, not society for the state. Rule, order, law and submission, are not valuable for their own sakes, but only for [the] sake of furthering of deepening and extending the processes of living together.
>
> (3) The government is *responsible* to the people. It must be so organized as to render an account, to be liable to the people for the way in which it administers its affairs in the interest of the people ... (38)

He offers a correction to political liberalism which sees government as a necessary evil to protect property 'In fact, the government is an organ or tool for the realization of public interests, the things that men have in common, that affect all in the way they work out, in their consequences' (39), and how the state handles this is a scientific rather than a moral question. The realization of public interest is achieved in term of a means-end instrumentality. The liberalism of Locke mistakenly holds that individuals are logically priori and separate from society, and that the individual is the best judge of his own interests. As he puts it: 'A public interest and public opinion rather than self-interest and judgment of what is to [be] the interests of the self must be the chief reliances of democratic government' ... 'Hence also education as a public charge' (40). His famous argument for education as a public good is summed up in the words:

> Political democracy thus runs into the broader moral and social democracy. The *ulterior* justification of political democracy, that is of popular government, is its educative effect. That is, its effect in broadening the interests and imagination, in extending sentiments from personal and local and family, clique interests, to take in the welfare of the country, producing a public conscience and civic loyalty; and its effect in stimulating thought, ideas and their expression about social matters. (40)

This chapter is by far the most substantive, the clearest and best written, especially where he engages the Continental traditions to argue for his own pragmatist version of democracy. In Lecture XIV Dewey in the last recovered chapter discusses Intellectual Freedom: 'the actual worth of any social arrangement lies in its educative effect: its release of thought, its nurture of the imagination, its refinement of emotions, in the persons who are influenced by it (41). Free speech is the cornerstone of education and democracy. He equates 'the whole society of humanity' with the 'communism of intelligence,' a lovely phrase and perhaps a recognition of the socialism of ideas and the intellect in a concept of the public mind (42–43). With great pertinence and relevance in the age of the internet and Trump, Dewey writes: 'Public and universal education is a social necessity in order to give a basis for this common sharing in knowledge and thought' (43).

Dewey's argument has run its course. It is unfortunate that we have only nine of the sixteen lectures. To my mind the early lectures are insubstantial, loosely argued and speculative. The last three are fully rounded philosophical expressions that eloquently state Dewey's case. His task was to formulate a pragmatist social philosophy that argues for the closest connection between democracy and education. I agree with Roberto Gronda (2015: 46) that Dewey's approach was 'far from being clear and consistent.' What is clear is that Dewey became aware of the historical significance of the students' movement and its role in "the transformation of the mind of China." Yet Dewey does not provide grounds for understanding the meaning of protest or its role in conditioning the establishment of the Chinese Communist Party in 1921. Accounting for the Chinese 'difference' is a problem for Dewey, because he does not have enough acquaintance with Chinese history and culture to understand its internal development.

The application of Western political concepts also seems a problem. Gronda quotes Dewey "If things are fairly well off, then let well enough alone. If they are evil, endure them rather than run the risk of making them worse by interference" (MW 12: 54), presumably without knowing anything of the doctrine of the Daoist notion of 'non-action' (*Wu wei*, 無爲) that some contemporary scholars argue exercised direct impact on the ideas of Spinoza, Leibniz, Voltaire, Quesnay and on Enlightenment ideas of *Laissez-faire* (McCormick, 1999; Dorn, 1998; Gerlatch, 2005). This example is worth dwelling on because on the one hand it speaks of cultural hybridity and exchange – a fact Dewey doesn't contemplate, and on the other, it speaks to misinterpretation and the difficulty of getting outside the Western frame of reference to make comparisons. Eric Goodfield (2011: 56) reviews this literature to argue that these frequent conceptual comparisons have often been inappropriate where touchstone humanist notions devoid of the *Dao de Jing's* fundamental spiritual and metaphysical commitments are brought forward as evidence of interconnection.

He begins with J.J. Clarke's (1997) *Oriental Enlightenment: The Encounter between Asian and Western Thought* as one source that juxtaposes 'the intimacy of Daoist and Enlightenment political thought' by quoting the following: 'The wise ruler knows that, at a certain level of operating, the best policy is in a sense to do nothing, a policy summed up in the central philosophical concept of wu-wei which is translated into French as laissez-faire' (1997: 50) (cited in Goodfield, 2011: 56). While these texts try to make Chinese and Western thought commensurable despite radically different cultural and economic contexts, the attempts are rife with misunderstandings that ignore sensitivities of tradition.

Dewey in 1919 is very much still a part of the ethnocentric bias of mainstream accounts of the 'Rise of the West' that assumes that Europeans engineered their own economic and political development into capitalist modernity with no help or influence from other civilizations, even if he holds that China must be understood in terms of its own cultural history. In *The Eastern Origins of Western Civilization*, John Hobson (2004) offers an Afro–Asia centric view of world history that decenters the myth of the European miracle or virgin birth (Peters, 2012) . This historical counterargument runs against the Eurocentric bias of world history common to both Marxist and non-Marxist accounts that deny the influence and significance of the non-West in the rise of capitalist modernity. It may not be surprising that Dewey strongly influenced by Hegel's *Lectures on the Philosophy of History* delivered in 1825, even though he shook himself free of transcendent realities, might see China as Hegel (2001: 123) did:

> a paternal Government, which holds together the constitution by its provident care, its admonitions, retributive or rather disciplinary inflictions – a prosaic Empire, because the antithesis of Form, viz., Infinity, Ideality, has not yet asserted itself.

Actually, what Dewey takes to be passiveness is really based on the fact that Chinese civilization had developed a rationality at odds with Dewey's pragmatic instrumentalism and, more broadly, Europe's emphasis on material progress. While he was correct to argue that the Chinese civilization was the outcome of particular choices taken in the past, it was not clear that Dewey had the intellectual resources to appreciate these deep cultural differences despite his turn to the ancient Chinese texts. Dewey detects the 'Chinese difference' but did not have enough detailed understanding of Chinese history and philosophy to give it a definite form.

He focuses on the environmental difference of population, specifically Chinese 'overpopulation,' as instrumental in in the cultural development of Chinese conservatism and the reason why Chinese authorities distrust reason to control events. Gronda (2015: 51) puts the following spin on this:

> Against the Western emphasis on creativity and initiative, regardless of any possible future consequences on the environment, the Chinese civilization advanced a different conception of life and nature, much more respectful of the soil and its fertility. The ultimate reason of the 'Chinese difference' relied precisely here, on the fact that, traditionally, China was "agrarian, agricultural"; and the success of the teachings of Laotze should be traced back to their capacity to express "something congenial to Chinese temperament and habits of life."

The relationship between environment and culture is an important part of Dewey's pragmatism and naturalism, but this description just will not stand up to scrutiny for it seems to forget a common evolutionary story, expects too much of 'philosophies of life' (whatever that term may mean) and advances differences in the understanding of social reality on flimsy grounds. Yet as Gronda points out, the Chinese experience helps Dewey to modify his views on thinking and the 'cultural contingency of thought' rather than treating it as a 'logical universal constant' (56). But if the Chinese experience led Dewey to modify his views on thinking to advance a more radically contingent view strongly influenced by culture and one that, accordingly, became more pluralist and anti-foundationalist, as Gronda (2017: 58) claims:

> His confrontation with the Chinese civilization reminded him of something which he had to know very well, that is, that much of what we are ready to assume to be natural is, in reality, second nature.

Dewey's lectures should remind us to become more suspicious as to what counts as 'natural' in the first instance. And this applies not only to cultures that do not possess a single trajectory or 'spirit' but are disrupted by multiple fractures, influences, and exchanges as something fundamentally partial and hybrid, but also that education is in part a reflection of cultural and intellectual histories that bears the traces of this complexity.[4]

Acknowledgment

This chapter is a reprint from: PETERS, Michael A. (2019), 100 years of Dewey in China, 1919–1921: A reassessment. *Beijing International Review of Education, 1*(1), 9–26. Zhao (2019), Wang (2019) and Zhang (2019) responded to Peters' article (see the same issue of the journal *Beijing International Review of Education, 1*(1)).

Notes

1 Taken from *Letters from China and Japan*, by John Dewey and Alice Chipman Dewey, The Project Gutenberg EBook, http://www.gutenberg.org/files/31043/31043-h/31043-h.htm
2 https://www.marxists.org/reference/archive/mao/selected-works/volume-2/mswv2_13.htm
3 See http://ariwatch.com/VS/JD/ImpressionsOfSovietRussia.htm
4 One engages in the critique of Dewey, even a benign updating, at one's peril, as I discovered after giving an invited keynote at International Conference on Democracy and Education, Taipei, November 4–5, in 2016. I revisited Dewey's *Democracy and Education. An Introduction to the Philosophy of Education* (1916/2001) in order to evaluate the growth and development of democracy against the decline of social democracy in the West. I identified three turns which separate democracy of Dewey's times and democracy of today – the global, the ecological, and the digital turn – and relate them to changing notions of citizenship. To some of liberal Deweyans in the audience updating Dewey especially in relation to the digital turn was not to be tolerated. They found it difficult to even contemplate the notion of digital democracy (Peters & Jandric, 2017).

References

Chiang, Y. C. (2015). *Appropriating Dewey: Hu Shi and his translation of Dewey's "social and philosophical philosophy" lectures series in China, Symposia* [John Dewey's Lectures in Social and Political Philosophy (China)]. *European Journal of Pragmatism and American Philosophy, VII*(2), 71–97.

Clarke, J. J. (1997). *Oriental enlightenment: The encounter between Asian and Western thought.* Routledge.

Clopton, R., & Ou, T.-C. (1973). Lectures in China 1919–20. *Philosophy East and West, 25*(3), 365–369.

Cork, J. (1949). John Dewey, Karl Marx, and democratic socialism. *The Antioch Review, 9*, 435–452.

Cork, J. (1950). John Dewey and Karl Marx. In S. Hook (Ed.), *John Dewey: Philosopher of science and freedom* (pp. 331–350). The Dial Press.

Dewey, J. (1916). *Democracy and education.* Macmillan. https://archive.org/stream/democracyandeduooodewegoog#page/n6/mode/2up

Dewey, J. (2015). *Lectures in social and political philosophy, 1919–21* [Symposia. John Dewey's Lectures in Social and Political Philosophy (China)]. *European Journal of Pragmatism and American Philosophy, VII*(2), 7–45.

Ding, Z. (2007). A comparison of Dewey's and Russell's influences on China. *Dao, 6*, 149. https://link.springer.com/article/10.1007%2Fs11712-007-9009-x

Dorn, J. A. (1998). China's future: Market socialism or market Taoism? *Cato Journal, 18*(1), 131–146.

Frega, R. (2017). *John Dewey's social philosophy: A restatement* [Symposia. John Dewey's Lectures in Social and Political Philosophy (China)]. *European Journal of Pragmatism and American Philosophy, VII*(2), 98–128.

Frega, R., & Gronda, R. (2015). *Introduction* [Symposia. John Dewey's Lectures in Social and Political Philosophy (China)]. *European Journal of Pragmatism and American Philosophy, VII*(2), 5–6.

Gerlach, C. (2005). *Wu-wei in Europe. A study of Eurasian economic thought.* Working Paper No. 032/2005. Department of Economic History, London School of Economics.

Goodfield, E. (2011, March). Wu wei East and West: Humanism and anti-humanism in Daoist and enlightenment political thought. *Theoria.* doi:10.3167/th.2011.5812603

Gronda, R. (2015). *What does China mean for pragmatism? A philosophical interpretation of Dewey's sojourn in China (1919–1921)* [Symposia. John Dewey's Lectures in Social and Political Philosophy (China)]. *European Journal of Pragmatism and American Philosophy, VII*(2), 45–70.

Hegel, G. (1825/2001). *The philosophy of history.* Batouche Books.

Keenan, B. (1977). *The Dewey experiment in China: Educational reform and political power in the Early Republic.* Council on East Asian Studies, Harvard University.

Mao, Z. (1939). *The May 4th Movement.* https://www.marxists.org/reference/archive/mao/selected-works/volume-2/mswv2_13.htm

McCormick, K. (1999). The Tao of laissez-faire. *Eastern Economic Journal, 25*, 331–341.

Nickles, T. (2017). Historicist theories of scientific rationality. In E. N. Zalta (Ed.), *The Stanford encyclopedia of philosophy* (Summer 2017 ed.). https://plato.stanford.edu/archives/sum2017/entries/rationality-historicist/

Peters, M. A. (2012). Eurocentrism and the critique of "universal world history": The eastern origins of western civilization [Keynote address at the 42nd annual conference of the Philosophy of Education Society of Australasia Inc.]. *Geopolitics, History, and International Relations, 6*(1), 63–77. http://pesa2012.blogspot.co.nz/

Peters, M. A., & Jandric, P. (2017). Dewey's democracy and education in the age of digital reason: The global, ecological and digital turns [Keynote at International conference on democracy and education]. *Open Review of Educational Research, 4*(1). https://www.tandfonline.com/doi/full/10.1080/23265507.2017.1395290

Renault, E. (2013). Dewey, Hook, and Mao: On some affinities between Marxism and pragmatism. *Actuel Marx, 54*(2). https://www.cairn-int.info/abstract-E_AMX_054_0137--dewey-hook-mao-on-some-affinities.htm

Ryan, A. (1995). *John Dewey and the high tide of American liberalism*. W. W. Norton & Company.

Schulte, B. (2011). The Chinese Dewey: Friend, fiend, and flagship. In R. Bruno-Jofre & J. Schriewer (Eds.), *The global reception of John Dewey's thought: Multiple refractions through time and space* (pp. 83–115). Routledge.

Yang, J. Z. (2016). *When Confucius "encounters" John Dewey: A historical and philosophical analysis of Dewey's visit to China* [Dissertation]. University of Oklahoma Graduate College.

Wang, C. (2019). What should we learn about Dewey in China? An unfinished task. *Beijing International Review of Education, 1*(1), 32–34.

Westbrook, R. (1991). *John Dewey and American democracy*. Cornell University Press.

Zhang, H. (2019). Some dialogue not yet happened – A response to Michael A. Peters, "100 years of Dewey in China, 1919–1921: A reassessment." *Beijing International Review of Education, 1*(1), 35–38.

Zhang, X., & Sheese, R. (2017). 100 years of John Dewey and education in China. *The Journal of the Gilded Age and Progressive Era, 16*(4), 400–408.

Zhao, K. (2019). Democracy, student movement and thinking: A response to Michael Peters' article. *Beijing International Review of Education, 1*(1), 27–31.

Zou, Z. (2010). The 'Dewey fever' in Jiangsu and Zhejiang during the May Fourth Movement and its relation to the cultural tradition in Jiangnan. *Chinese Studies in History, 43*(4), 43–62. doi:10.2753/CSH0009-4633430403

PART 2

Philosophical Reflections

∵

CHAPTER 8

Mahayana Buddhism and Deweyan Philosophy

Jim GARRISON

Abstract

My paper examines some of the many similarities between Mahayana Buddhism and Deweyan philosophy. It builds upon two previously published works. The first is my dialogue with Daisaku Ikeda President of Soka Gakkai International, a UN registered NGO currently active in one hundred ninety-two countries and territories, and the Director Emeritus of the Center for Dewey Studies, Larry Hickman (see Garrison, Hickman, & Ikdea, 2014). My paper will first briefly review some of the many similarities between Buddhism and Deweyan pragmatism. Second, I will also briefly review additional similarities in the published version of my Kneller Lecture to the American Educational Studies Association (see Garrison, 2019). In the present paper, I will introduce some new similarities of interest to educators. Among these are Dewey's surprisingly Buddhist notions of language and logic as merely useful conventions. Secondly, I examine Dewey's argument that "causation as ordered sequence is a *logical* category," not an *ontological* category (LW 12: 453). The similarity to the opening chapter of Nagarjuna's *Madhyamaka*, or Middle Way, is striking. I will suggest a logical reading has some interesting implications for student-teacher relations.

Keywords

Buddhism – causation – Dewey – Ikeda – Nagarjuna – metaphysics

• • •

I think it shows a deplorable deadness of imagination to suppose that philosophy will indefinitely revolve within the scope of the problems and systems that two thousand years of European history have bequeathed to us. Seen in the long perspective of the future, the whole of western European history is a provincial episode. (LW 5: 159)

My paper puts John Dewey's philosophy into dialogue with Mahayana Buddhist thought. It does so by pointing out a surprising array of shared beliefs and commitments. The first part of my paper is a review and extension of previously published work. The extension involves showing how Dewey agrees with the Buddhist insight that our linguistic and logical constructions are only useful conventions that are harmless if we do not reify them as antecedently existing things. The second section introduces another new comparison. Nagarjuna is the leading philosopher of the Mahayana tradition. The opening chapter of his *Madhyamaka*, or "Middle Way" is titled "Examination of Conditions." It is a devastating argument against causation as a metaphysical substance that has the power to bring about its effect. Nagarjuna's argument is remarkably like Dewey's argument that claims, "causation as ordered sequence is a *logical* category," not a metaphysical category (LW 12: 453).[1] For Nagarjuna and Dewey there are only dependent, co-originating conditions and their consequences. A logical understanding of causation has important implications for understanding the student-teacher relationship. Teachers are not the metaphysical cause of students' learning; instead, while important, they constitute just one among a multitude of dependent co-originating conditions required for learning to occur.

I first became aware of the similarities between Dewey and Buddhism while in a dialogue with Larry Hickman, director emeritus of the Center for Dewey Studies, and Daisaku Ikeda, the third president of Soka Gakkai and the current president of Soka Gakkai International (see Garrison, Hickman, and Ikeda, 2014). Ikeda is influential both as an educator and in the troubled context of Chinese-Japanese relations. He is the founder of the largest system of private schooling on the island of Japan, including Soka University Japan. As of the publication of this paper both the Chinese and the Russian ambassadors to Japan were educated there. Ikeda is known and respected in China for meetings with Zhou Enlai in which he acknowledged Japanese atrocities in China during ww ii. Among his published dialogues is one with Mikhail Gorbachev.

One in every eight native resident of Japan is a member of the Soka Gakkai (meaning "value creating society"), which is a form of Nichiren Buddhism, a Japanese variant of Mahayana Buddhism established through the teachings of Nichiren, a thirteenth-century Japanese priest Nichiren. It is based on the *Lotus Sutra*, perhaps the most popular of the Mahayana Sutras. Analysis of the Chinese and Sanskrit versions of the Sutra suggest its earliest parts date back over two-thousand years.

At the conclusion of my dialogue with Hickman and Ikeda, I acknowledge, "This surprising compatibility between Nichiren Buddhism and Deweyan pragmatism has made an enduring impression on me" (LL 272). Some of the compatibilities I mention are "dependent origination," "anti-dualism," "ameliorative action," "humanism," and Ikeda's own observation identifying "Dewey as a follower of the Middle Way" (LL 272, see also 205). I address all these compatibilities just mentioned and more in a paper titled, "Nichiren Buddhism and Deweyan Pragmatism: An Eastern-Western Integration of Thought," which is based on my 2018 Kneller lecture to the American Educational Studies Association (Garrison, 2019). The next section draws from and expands on that paper.

1 Buddhism and Deweyan Pragmatism: The Middle Way

All forms of Buddhism emphasize the following universal truths: (1) everything is impermanent, (2) there is no permanent and unchanging substantial self; and (3) the impermanence of the self and of the world causes suffering. They also share the Four Noble Truths, namely that life is suffering, suffering is caused by attachment, suffering arises from dependent, co-arising conditions and, it ceases when those conditions no longer exist.

In a chapter titled "Existence as Precarious and Stable," Dewey asserted: "A thing may endure *secula seculorum* and yet not be everlasting; it will crumble before the gnawing tooth of time, as it exceeds a certain measure" (LW 1: 63). Dewey cited the renowned Greek philosopher, Heraclitus, who proclaimed that "there is nothing permanent except change" over 2,000 years ago (LW 17: 131). He went on to state that "today it seems to me, looking back over my fourscore years of work and study, that too few men have recently paid attention to this great truth" (131). Every "thing" is impermanent. Hence, as Dewey observed, "even the solid earth mountains, the emblems of constancy, appear and disappear like the clouds" (LW 1: 63). Moreover, what is true for "everything" is true for the self.

Dewey famously rejected the spectator stance toward existence, instead favoring a participant stance in which the mind and the self are a part of an ever-changing universe:

> The essential difference is that between a mind which beholds or grasps objects from outside the world of things, physical and social, and one which is a *participant*, interacting with other things and knowing them provided the interaction is regulated in a definable way. (LW 4: 161)

Instead of passively contemplating an antecedent reality, participants recognize their transactional, dependent co-origination. From an epistemological perspective, knowledge is not about discovering something that already exists; rather, it is something produced by arranging interactions in diverse ways while always remembering:

> What is known is seen to be a product in which the act of observation plays a necessary role. Knowing is seen to be a participant in what is finally known. Moreover, the metaphysics of existence as something fixed and therefore capable of literally exact mathematical description and prediction is undermined. (LW 4: 163)

There is no creation *ex nihilo*; existence precedes essence, but without makers of meaning, knowing, and value, there is no meaning, knowledge, or value in the universe. As participants in an ever-changing universe, we ourselves are continually changing, and will eventually vanish as the relationships that sustain us begin to "crumble before the gnawing tooth of time" (op. cit.). We are as impermanent as the rest of existence.

The purpose of knowledge is to enable individuals and their progeny to live long and well amidst the flux of existence. Dewey declared that "the great vice of philosophy is an arbitrary 'intellectualism'," implying that knowledge is *not* our primary relation to reality (LW 1: 28). Mere intellectualism leads to "the denial to nature of the characters which make things lovable and contemptible, beautiful and ugly, adorable and awful" and much more" (LW 1: 28). Our noncognitive relations with existence provide the context for knowledge. The function of knowledge is to help put us into the right relationship with surroundings so that we may live long and prosper while providing a better world for future generations. Of course, the process of acquiring knowledge may itself be a creative and pleasurable pursuit. Dewey claimed that "science is one among the arts and among the works of art" (LW 1: 287). The artifact of the scientific art is knowledge. Knowledge is useful for other arts, so "science itself is but a central art auxiliary to the generation and utilization of other arts" (LW 10: 33). Dewey further argued that "science states meanings; art expresses them" (LW 10: 90). Statable meanings are useful for creating expressive meanings. Still, for all the artifacts of art, we and all we love shall perish; hence, we suffer.

Knowledge contributes to ameliorating suffering. Many misunderstand Dewey's progressivism. He does not think we are progressing to some ideal end rather, although we may always make progress toward ameliorating suffering. He writes:

> Meliorism is the belief that the specific conditions which exist at one moment, be they comparatively bad or comparatively good, in any event may be bettered. It encourages intelligence to study the positive means of good and the obstructions to their realization, and to put forth endeavor for the improvement of conditions. It arouses confidence and a reasonable hopefulness as optimism does not. (MW 12: 182)

MAHAYANA BUDDHISM AND DEWEYAN PHILOSOPHY

The only alternative to *tuche* (i.e., luck) is *techne* (i.e., the arts of production). Dewey asserts, "Art is the sole alternative to luck; and divorce from each other of the meaning and value of instrumentalities and ends is the essence of luck" (LW 1: 279). Nevertheless, wisdom is beyond knowledge. Wisdom comprehends the good of knowledge because it perceives ameliorative possibilities beyond the actual. We must work hard to actualize ideal values:

> An ideal is a sense of the possibilities of a situation and is of value only as inspiring action and directing of ameliorating its evils; meliorism as compared with optimism and pessimism. Happiness is found not in possession or fixed attainment, but in the active process of striving, overcoming and succeeding; failures are to be turned to account, and are not incompatible with moral happiness. (MW 11: 348)

According to Thomas A. Alexander (2013), Dewey's book, *A Common Faith*, expresses a "spirituality of possibility" (354). Ideals as imaginary ends-in-view serve as goals of artful ameliorative inquiry.

One consequence of Dewey's participant stance is strident anti-dualism. Hinayana Buddhism tends to emphasize the extinction of desire as the key to overcoming suffering and entry into Nirvana. As with most of Mahayana Buddhism, Nichiren Buddhism identifies sources of suffering other than desire including, among others, arrogance, negligence, hatred, and vilification, while finding the supernatural notion of Nirvana at best a sometimes useful expedient means.[2] Nichiren Buddhism emphasizes the proper appeasement of desires, not their extinction.[3] In Western terms, the proper appeasement of desires would involve the education of eros to desire the genuinely good (see Garrison, 1997). In his *Theory of Valuation*, Dewey distinguishes between value and the truly valuable, desire and the truly desirable. Distinguishing an immediate object of desire from a genuinely desirable object is the task of intelligent inquiry. Dewey rejected a rigid fact versus value dualism as Hilary Putnam (2002) observes in his book *The Collapse of the Fact/Value Dichotomy* (9). Any parent or educator understands that if their offspring or charges possess the wisdom to pursue only the genuinely good, everything else would be fine. Overcoming the fact/value dualism contributes considerably to intelligent amelioration.

Buddhism emphasizes the oneness of life and the environment; their separation is a distorting illusion. In Deweyan terms, it is a false dualism: "Life (or functions, activities) includes within itself the distinction of Environment and Organism" (MW 6: 467). In *Art as Experience*, Dewey says:

> As the developing growth of an individual from embryo to maturity is the result of interaction of organism with surroundings, so culture is the

product not of efforts of men put forth in a void or just upon themselves, but of prolonged and cumulative interaction with environment. (LW 10: 35)

Understood transactionally, organisms and their environments, individuals and their social environments, or nature and culture are merely useful methodological distinctions.

Dewey presents his entire philosophy as "empirical naturalism or naturalistic empiricism, or, taking 'experience' in its usual signification, naturalistic humanism" (10). Presumably, "naturalistic humanism" renders Dewey susceptible to post-modern critiques of humanism. However, these critiques totally ignore Eastern philosophies, which are not especially susceptible to the post-modern onslaught.

The first of Ikeda's works that I encountered was *A New Humanism* (2010), which is a compilation of lectures delivered at various universities worldwide, including Fudan University and Peking University. In one lecture, Ikeda asks: "Does religion make people stronger, or weaker?" (171). Referring to Marx's description of religion as the "opiate of the masses" (171), he expressed concern over the "dogmatism and insularity" of many religions that "run counter to the accelerating trend toward interdependence and cross-cultural interaction" (171). While appreciating the accomplishments of science, Ikeda worries about "the omnipotence of reason" and those "blindly convinced of the power of technology" that can lead to the "hubris of assuming that there is nothing we are unable to accomplish" (158). Ikeda urges "a third path, a new balance between faith in ourselves and recognition of a power that is greater than we are" (158). He cites Nichiren, "Neither solely through one's own efforts ... nor solely through the power of others" (158).

Steven C. Rockefeller (1991) subtitles his book on Dewey's philosophy of religion, "*Religious faith and democratic humanism.*" In *A Common Faith*, Dewey is especially concerned with "the exclusive preoccupation of both militant atheism and supernaturalism with man in isolation;" whereas supernaturalism is obsessed with the "lonely soul of man" while the atheist envisages affirms "man living in an indifferent and hostile world and issuing blasts of defiance" (36). He thinks, "The essentially unreligious attitude is that which attributes human achievement and purpose to man in isolation from the world of physical nature and his fellows. Our successes are dependent upon the cooperation of nature" (LW 9: 18). Dewey argued that beyond resignation to the natural world, conceived as being fully determined, and unquestioning belief in supernatural beings and ideals, imaginary ideals of the possible beyond the actual may assume prominence in our lives, providing ideal ends-in-view that guide moral action. He distinguishes dogmatic faith in the supernatural from "aggressive atheism" which he finds lacks "natural piety" (LW 9: 36). Ikeda (2010) identifies Dewey's *A Common Faith* as also advocating the middle way of religious humanism (171–172). Dewey's practice of the middle way was discussed in my dialogue with Hickman and Ikeda (2014: 205).

Critics ranging from Fredreich Nietzsche to Martin Heidegger, Michael Foucault, and Jacques Derrida have supposedly devastated humanism. They have demonstrated that concepts such as human nature and humanity are hopelessly metaphysical and historically relative. There is simply no metaphysical substance of humanity whether conceived in terms of rationality, the possession of 46 chromosomes or being featherless bipeds. In *A New Humanism*, Ikeda (1996) cites Dewey statement that "Everything which is distinctly human is learned" (54; see LW 2: 331). If everything distinctly human is learned, then it is evident that human subjects are entirely contingent on historical socio-cultural constructions born into a world of pre-existing institutional, social, and linguistic practices that condition the very habits of their bodies and the feelings those habits channel into emotions. Culture has us before we have it. The human sciences may help us understand how cultural practices condition our conduct, and subjects may use the knowledge to reconstruct their culture and thereby themselves, but these sciences cannot disclose some unalterable foundation of self, if only because they are themselves cultural practices requiring reflective inquiry to be understood. They cannot be used to complete what Dewey calls "the quest for certainty" (see LW 4). In the first paragraph of an essay titled, "Does Human Nature Change?" Dewey proclaims in the first paragraph that "the proper answer is that human nature *does* change" (LW 13: 286). This is true simply because everything changes. Education is the effort to change things for the better.

Both the Nagarjuna and Dewey are anti-foundationalists that reject metaphysical substance; there are no eternal immutable essences underlying the impermanent and ever-changing flux. Nagarjuna sought the middle way between two metaphysical extremes. Richard Hayes (2019) explains that Nagarjuna "avoids the two extremes of eternalism – the doctrine that all things exist because of an eternal essence – and annihilationism – the doctrine that things have essences while they exist but that these essences are annihilated just when the things themselves go out of existence" (1). The former defends the absolute, eternal, and immutable continuity of metaphysical essences, abstract concepts, or universals; the latter are those materialists, atomists, nominalists, and mechanists that nihilistically assert the transient, mutable discontinuity of metaphysical essences annihilated when things vanish on the other. Both are committed to the metaphysics of substance (i.e., *svabhava*).

All commentators agree that the central idea of the middle way fundamentally entails the rejection of a metaphysics of substance underlying an impermanent, ever-changing flux. However, Jan Westerhoff (2009) argues that we must distinguish two fundamental kinds of *svabhava,* the first of which is not metaphysical. They are essence-*svabhava* and substance-*svabhava.* The former refers to "the *specific quality* that that is unique to the object characterized and therefore allows us to distinguish it from other objects" (21). He concludes:

> The notion of essence-svabhava, which equates svabhava with the specific qualities of an object and contrasts them with those qualities it shares with other objects, serves mainly epistemological purposes. It provides a procedure for drawing a line between a variety of objects with shared qualities and thereby allows us to tell them apart. (23)

Dewey concurs.

Dewey claims that "objects are the *objectives* of inquiry" (LW 12: 122). He thinks objects are "produced" by the various social practices of inquiry, including science. Objects do not exist prior to the practices that produce them. He identifies what he calls "*the* philosophic fallacy;" that is, the "conversion of eventual functions into antecedent existence" (LW 1: 34). Objects are artifacts of inquiry. Dewey remarks that "*an enduring object is all one with the determination that it is one of a kind*" (LW 12: 248). Kinds are constituted by bundles of qualitative traits. Of themselves, "Immediate qualities in their immediacy are ... non-recurrent" (248). Hence, "qualities are not recurrent in themselves but in their evidential function. As evidential, they are characteristics which describe a kind" (351). Further, "the existential traits employed to determine descriptively a kind should be conceived in terms of modes of interaction" (LW 12: 425). These modes of interaction are dependent co-originating transactions:

> The traits or characteristics which describe a kind are taken to go together in existence. The ground of their selection is logical but the ground of their going together is existential. The ground is that, as a matter of existence, they do go together or are existentially so conjoined that when one varies the other varies. (268)

When one quality or set of qualities are present, another quality or set of qualities comes to be. When one quality or set of qualities are absent, another quality or set of qualities does not come to be.

Substance-*svabhava* is metaphysical primary existence: "Primary existents constitute the irreducible constituents of the empirical world. Secondary existents, on the other hand, depend on the linguistic and mental construction for their existence" (24). Essence-*svabhava* has only conventional (conceptual, linguistic, logical, etc.) existence; they are constructed to serve our finite, human (sometimes all too human) purposes (20 and 30). Secondary existence conceptually constructed for practical epistemological purposes (essence-*svabhava*) is not the point of Nagarjuna or Dewey's criticisms if we do not ontologically reify our contingent constructions by committing "*the* philosophic fallacy" (op. cit.).

Supposedly, there are three ways substance-*svabhava* subsists in complete *existential* independence. First, there is causal independence, implying that the substances' existence does not depend on causes and conditions. Second, there is mereological independence, meaning that such substances are not a part that depends on a larger whole. Finally, substance-*svabhava* is conceptually independent from a designating mind or linguistic designation (see Westerhoff, 2009: 27). Substance-*svabhava* is also *notionally* or descriptively independent. Westerhoff concludes:

> [T]he notion of substance-svabhava is much stronger than that of essence-svabhava. In particular we can assert the existence of the second without affirming the first. It could be the case that every object has some properties it could not lose without ceasing to be that very object ... and therefore be endowed with essence-svabhava. But at the same time everything could in some way (either existentially or notionally) be dependent on something else so that substance-svabhava did not exist at all. (29)

For Nagarjuna, all things are entirely empty of inherent, independent natures (substance-*svabhava*). There is only the dependent co-origination of all that arises and ceases. Everything is impermanent:

> How could there be becoming
> Without destruction?
> For impermanence
> *Is never absent from entities* (Madhyamaka, Chapter xx, Garfield, 1995)

Eventually, every object loses its characteristic qualities as the dependent co-originating conditions that gave rise to it alter. In Dewey's terms "it will crumble before the gnawing tooth of time, as it exceeds a certain measure" (op. cit.).

Like Nagarjuna, Dewey's emergent empirical naturalism rejects ultimate substances or what classical metaphysics calls *ousia*. Indeed, one of the leading commentators on Nagarjuna's middle way reads him as a Jamesian radical empiricist (Kalupahana, 1986). William James, including his radical empiricism wherein relations as well as the things being related appear and disappear in the stream of consciousness, greatly influenced Dewey. As Thomas M. Alexander (2013) remarks, Dewey's version of radical empiricism in such essays as "The Postulate of Immediate Empiricism" challenges one of the principle dogmas of twenty-five hundred years of western thought arising from Parmenides's identification of Being and knowing: "For it is the same thing, To-Be and To-Know" (Parmenides cited in Alexander, 2013: 34). Essence-*svabhava* is not substance-*svabhava*.

The impermanency posited in the theory of evolution presents a dramatic challenge to Western metaphysics. In "The Influence of Darwinism on Philosophy," Dewey declares:

> In laying hands upon the sacred ark of absolute permanency, in treating forms that had been regarded as types of fixity and perfection as originating and passing away, the Origin of Species introduced a mode of thinking that in the end was bound to transform the logic of knowledge, and hence the treatment of morals, politics and religion. (MW 4: 3)

He could have added education to this list.

Before Darwin, Dewey argued, "the conception of εἶδος, species, a fixed form and final cause, was the central principle of knowledge as well as of nature" (MW 3: 6). Dewey did for fixed and final nonlogical, essences (substance-*svabhava*) what Darwin did for species. Usually metaphysical essences (*eidos*) are teleologically determined by their ultimate end states. A *telos*, and especially a perfect *telos* or an *entelecheia* (ultimate purpose), is a critical aspect of classical metaphysics. From Aristotle to Piaget, rationality has constituted the essence of "man," the final cause, the *entelecheia*. Every individual mind and self is emptiness devoid of substance. Having rejected the notion of a human metaphysical essence (*eidos*) and (*entelecheia*), Dewey has no choice but to assert: "Since growth is the characteristic of life, education is all one with growing; it has no end beyond itself" (MW 9: 56).

Given his anti-foundationalism, Dewey rejects the idea of a metaphysical *arche,* wherein ultimate principles, beginnings, or endings; first or final causes; or any causes can be conceptualized as latent or active power. The opening chapter of Nagarjuna's *Madhyamaka*, titled "Examination of Conditions" is a refutation of metaphysical causation as substance, self-nature, or *svabhava*. It refutes the metaphysical concept of self-acting or inter-acting entities with an intrinsic, nondependent nature or essence, including human selves, or any other metaphysical forces.

MAHAYANA BUDDHISM AND DEWEYAN PHILOSOPHY 161

Nothing possesses an intrinsically self-moving power. This is an important insight because in the words of the Buddha, "He who perceives causation ... perceives the dharma [the Law]" (cited in Kalupahana, 1976: 30). The Buddha proclaims:

> When this is present, that comes to be;
> From the arising of this, that arises.
> When this is absent, that does not come to be;
> On the cessation of this, that ceases. (Cited in Kalupahana, 1976: 28)

Instead of change due to metaphysical causal powers, the Buddha only acknowledges dependent co-arising, or what Dewey identifies as the conditions and consequences of emergent trans-actions.

Sleeper (1986) argues that Dewey advocated "transactional realism" (3). Transactionalism is dependent co-arising: "But all changes occur through inter-actions of conditions. What exists co-exists, and no change can either occur or be determined in inquiry in isolation from the connection of an existence with co-existing conditions" (LW 12: 221). In a section of my dialogue with Hickman and Ikeda (2014) titled "Dependent Origination," Ikeda highlighted the following passage written by Dewey: "[N]othing in the universe, not even physical things, exists apart from some form of association; there is nothing from the atom to man which is not involved in conjoint action" (175, fn. 12; see LW 7: 323).

Dewey rejected self-action and, later in life, inter-action. By self-action he means some intrinsic power or force "where things are viewed as acting under their own powers (LW 16: 101). Aristotelian physics and metaphysics are examples. By "inter-action" he means the notion of two separate things operating on each other: that is, "where thing is balanced against thing in causal interaction" (101). Newtonian elastic collisions, wherein for every action there is an equal and opposite reaction, is a good example. So too is organism and environment inter-action. The emphasis here is on "transactional observation of the 'organism-in-environment-as-a-whole'" (103). Transactional observations do not require synthesis if the various aspects and phases can be envisioned together.

Dewey argued that common sense "is given to ascribing ... consequences to some 'power' inherent in the things themselves (an ingredient of the popular notion of substance), and to ignoring *inter*action with other things as the determining factor" (LW 12: 440). Here, we can discern Dewey's earlier use of "interaction," considered as transactional and entailing avoidance of "attribution to 'elements' or other presumptively detachable or independent 'entities,' 'essences,' or 'realities,' and without isolation of presumptively detachable 'relations' from such detachable 'elements'" (LW 16: 101–102). The transactional realist views all transactions as reciprocally transformative, evolving (or developing), and emergent.

Transaction involves "functional observation of full system" (71). When proceeding "in the *transactional,*" it is always possible to "see together, extensionally and durationally, much that is talked about conventionally, as if it were composed of irreconcilable separates" (67). Seeing together poses the greatest challenge to thinking transactionally; it is also perhaps the greatest challenge to understanding dependent co-origination. One might observe a bird in flight, but transactional observation allows the observer to "take in not just a bird while in flight but bird nest-building, egg-laying and hatching" (50). Recalling that "the subject matters of observation are durational and extensional," it may even be possible to "see" birds together with the dinosaurs (most likely theropods) from whence they evolved and which they visibly resemble (83). Similarly, we should strive to see teachers, students, and the teacher-student relationship together within a single transaction.

2 Buddhism, Causation, and the Teaching Transaction

For Dewey, "mind" is "an added property assumed by a feeling creature, when it reaches that organized interaction with other living creatures which is language, communication" (LW 1:198). Language and its consequences, accordingly, "are characters taken on by natural interaction and natural conjunction in specified conditions of organization" (145). In Dewey's realism, minds and selves emerge from physically and biologically dependent co-originating transactions without any breach of continuity:

> A requests B to bring him something, to which A points ... There is an original mechanism by which B may react to A's movement in pointing. But natively such a reaction is to the movement, not to the pointing, not to the object [O] pointed out. But B learns that the movement is a pointing; he responds to it not in itself, but as an index of something else. His response is transferred from A's direct movement to the object to which A points .... He perceives the thing as it may function in A's experience, instead of just ego-centrically ... Something is literally made common in at least two different centres of behavior. To understand is to anticipate together ... [It is] a transaction in which both participate. (141–142)[4]

As in any dependent co-arising transaction, A, B, and O *emerge* and are transformed together. When this [A and B] is present, that [O] comes to be. From the arising of this [O], that [A and B] arises. Think of A and B as teacher and student and O as some object, the subject matter, or curriculum and remember: "Everything which is distinctly human is learned" (op. cit.). Human beings not only learn from each other, they *co-create* each other's minds (and selves) and worlds in the process.

As in any dependent co-originating transaction, teacher and student, or in Buddhist terms mentor and disciple, is merely a useful distinction. In my dialogue with Ikeda and Hickman, the former observed that "Buddhism considers the disciple the cause and the mentor the result. Though we say, 'mentor and disciple,' the disciple is the key, and everything depends on the disciple. The two are inseparably united and nondual" (LL, 36). For "A" to be a teacher there must be a student "B." One could say that the student is the "cause" of the teacher. Mentor and disciple arise and cease together in a single, co-transformative transaction.

Learning is an instance of dependent co-arising involving a vast array of conditions. However, here, I will examine only two of them: the teacher and the student. The first verse of the "Examination of Conditions," which is the opening chapter of Nagarjuna's *Madhyamaka*, presents the following tetralemma:

> Neither from itself nor from another,
> Nor from both
> Nor without a cause,
> Does anything whatever, anywhere arise. (Garfield, 1995: 105)

There is no such thing as a power of self-causation ("from itself") or of a self-caused thing that causes something else ("from another"). The third alternative is either a combination the first two forms of causation; that is from both," or as Dewey says, "where thing is balanced against thing in causal interaction" (op. cit.) or a subtle concession that every "thing" that arises does so from co-dependent conditions, which is Nagarjuna's point. Ultimately, nothing arises spontaneously.

Teaching is not a substance. Therefore, teaching is not self-caused (i.e., self-action), which would not require a student. Nor does the teacher have some intrinsic power to force students to learn. Moreover, in the student–teacher transaction, there are not two separate substances, powers, or forces that are balanced against each other in causal interaction. Finally, student learning is not simply spontaneous, although learning can occur without teaching because there are dependent co-arising conditions of learning that do not involve teachers at all. For example, a sage in the social role of teacher could simply create a good learning environment. There is no such thing as metaphysical causation; there are only dependent, co-originating conditions (including students, teachers, and their natural and cultural environments) and consequences including, hopefully, learning. A cause never arises without an effect; it could be posited that the effect is the cause of the cause. Cause and effect, like organism and environment, mind and body, knower and known, or mentor and disciple is merely a useful distinction among co-arising events.

Recall that for Dewey, "causation as ordered sequence is a *logical* category," in the sense that it is an abstract conception of the indefinitely numerous existential sequences that are established in scientific inquiry (op. cit.). Consequently, Dewey's concludes:

> For when events are taken strictly existentially, there is no event which is antecedent or "cause" any more than it is consequent or "effect." Moreover, even when an event is taken to be an antecedent or a consequent [a condition or consequence] ... it has an indefinite number of antecedents and consequents with which it is connected, since every event is existentially connected with some other event without end. Consequently, the only possible conclusion upon the basis of an existential or ontological interpretation of causation is that everything in the universe is cause and effect of everything else – a conclusion which renders the category completely worthless for scientific purposes. (LW 12: 453)

Nevertheless, in a practical context, we need to "see together" some aspects of the infinite vastness to grasp what must be done.

While we are finite participants in what appears to be an infinite universe, we must simplify in practice, and in service to our contextualized human needs, desires, and purposes. However, "no event comes to us labelled 'cause' or 'effect.' An event must be deliberately *taken* to be cause or effect. Such taking would be purely arbitrary if there were not a particular and differential problem to be solved" (LW 12: 453). When we call something "the" cause or effect, what we are really saying is that to accomplish our finite human purposes, we have selected certain aspects of the vast universe that we know how to use as conditions from whence certain consequences follow. For practical purposes within this logic of inquiry, calling such *conventions* causes is not harmful unless we reify them as ontological substances existing antecedent to and apart from their taking and use in an inquiry.

For Dewey, logic is "the generalized idea of the means-consequence relation" (17). In an inquiry, the inquirer searches for conditions as a means of bringing about the desired consequences. Dewey defined inquiry as "*the controlled or directed transformation of an indeterminate situation into one that is so determinate in its constituent distinctions and relations as to convert the elements of the original situation into a unified whole*" (LW 12: 108; original emphasis). A situation becomes problematic for individuals because they participate in it. Consider, for example, the case of a teacher in a student–teacher transaction that is not proceeding smoothly. A good teacher will strive to transform the indeterminate situation into a harmonious, fully unified whole. If that is not possible, she or he will strive to ameliorate the situation.

It is a mistake to assume that an antecedently existing cause exists as a metaphysical substance. What can be identified are dependent co-originating conditions (the means) for bringing about desirable pedagogical consequences (the ends). Dewey declared that "every intelligent act involves selection of certain things as means to other things as their consequences" (LW 12: 454). What should the inquirer choose? The choice would be "purely arbitrary if there were not a particular and differential problem to be solved" (op. cit.).

If the inquirer chooses not to ameliorate troubled student–teacher relations, then the search for conditions and consequences may end up simply being the evasion of responsibility. Bad teachers often look for deficiencies in their students, blaming failure on them, perhaps by claiming that the student is simply too lazy or too dumb. Bad school administrators often do the same thing with teachers. Sometimes students, teachers, or administrators assign blame to the parents or to the wider community. In such cases, no inquiry toward seeking amelioration occurs.

When student-teacher transactions fail there is a temptation to look for the cause "inside" the student or teacher as a self-acting power. However, both the student and the teacher are among a vast array of the dependent co-arising conditions, which is not to say some change in one, the other, or both student and teacher may not be required if they are to coordinate their transaction. However, we must not forget that the student-teacher transaction is only one part of a much larger situation. There is also a temptation to simply blame the interaction. Practically, it might be best to assign a student to a new teacher. However, again, the wider transactional situation must be considered.

Often a failed student–teacher transaction arises from differences in personal and cultural histories and traditions, social classes, ethnicities, genders, and so on. Here it becomes especially important to "see together, extensionally and durationally, much that is talked about conventionally as if it were composed of irreconcilable separates" (op. cit.). The complexity is immense, but because we must act, we cannot let such complexity paralyze us. While identifying appropriate means for ameliorating consequences requires considerable intelligence, ultimately it requires wisdom. We must avoid the "vice of arbitrary 'intellectualism'" (op. cit.). Although wisdom requires knowledge, it extends beyond knowledge alone.

In artful ameliorative inquiry, it is sometimes more important to be than to know; being perceptive, sympathetic, intuitive, reflectively aware, imaginative, and much more may be essential. Rather than considering the daunting complexity of student–teacher relationships as a burden, good teachers view them as opportunities to exercise their creativity to connect better with their students.

Acknowledgment

This chapter is a reprint of: GARRISON, Jim. (2019). Mahayana Buddhism and Deweyan philosophy. *Beijing International Review of Education, 1*(4), 609–625.

Notes

1　Nowhere has emphasis been added to citations.
2　According to the final part of chapter 8 of the *Lotus Sutra*, "the Buddhas in their capacity as leaders preach nirvana to provide rest. But when they know you have become rested, they lead you onward to the Buddha wisdom" (Watson, 1993: 142).
3　Dewey himself seems to think all Buddhist sought to extinguish desire and enter a heaven-like state of Nirvana (see MW 14: 198).
4　We now know the "original mechanism" involves mirror neurons.

References

Alexander, Thomas M. (2013). *The human eros: Eco-ontology and the aesthetics of existence*. Fordham University Press.

Dewey, John. References are to the critical edition published by Southern Illinois University Press. Volume and page numbers follow the initials of the series. Abbreviations for the volumes cited are:

MW *The Middle Works* (1899–1924).

LW *The Later Works* (1925–1953).

Garfield, Jay L. (1995). *The fundamental wisdom of the middle way*. Oxford University Press.

Garrison, Jim. (1997). *Dewey and eros: Wisdom and desire in the art of teaching*. Teachers College Press. Reissued by Information Age Press, 2010.

Garrison, Jim, Hickman, Larry, & Ikeda, Daisaku. (2014). *Living as learning*. Dialogue Path Press. LL in the text.

Garrison, Jim. (2019). Nichiren Buddhism and Deweyan Pragmatism: An eastern-western integration of thought. *Educational Studies, 5*(1), 12–27.

Hayes, Richard. (2019). Madhyamaka. In E. N. Zalta (Ed.), *The Stanford encyclopedia of philosophy* (Spring 2019 edition). https://plato.stanford.edu/archives/spr2019/entries/madhyamaka/

Ikeda, Daisaku. (2010). *A new humanism*. I.B. Tauris.

Kalupahana, David J. (1986). *Nagarjuna: The philosophy of the middle way*. State University of New York Press.

Putnam, Hilary. (2002). *The collapse of the fact/value Dichotomy*. Harvard University Press.

Rockefeller, S. C. (1991). *John Dewey: Religious faith and democratic humanism*. Columbia University Press.

Sleeper, R. (1986). *The necessity of pragmatism*. Yale University Press.

Westerhoff, Jan. (2009). *Nagarjuna's Madhyamaka*. Oxford University Press.

Watson, Burton. (1993). *The Lotus Sutra*. Columbia University Press.

CHAPTER 9

Confucianism and Deweyan Pragmatism
A Dialogue

Roger T. AMES

Abstract

In rethinking the concept of persons, Dewey retrofits familiar terms in unfamiliar ways-individuality, democracy, experience, equality, personality, and so on. And in this process offers a unique understanding of the lives of irreducibly social persons that is such a radical departure from the received tradition it has taken philosophers some half a century to grasp. This relationally-constituted notion of "individuality" resonates importantly with one of the most prominent ideas in Confucian philosophy: the aesthetic project of learning to become consummately human captured in the term *ren*. Dewey and Confucianism can again be compared on their understanding of an "a-theistic" human-centered conception of religiousness that makes no appeal to the conventional understanding of a supernatural Supreme Being.

Keywords

Confucianism – Deweyan pragmatism – religiousness – authoritative person – individuality

• • •

There is a set of complementary and interpenetrating conditions that has set the stage for a conversation between a newly revised Deweyan pragmatism and a Confucianism that is returning to prominence with a growing Chinese self-esteem and pride in its traditions. To begin, since both of these terms – Deweyan "pragmatism" and "Confucianism" – are rather contested placeholders for the rich and varied resources that define in some degree the predominant and persistent cultural sensibilities of their native soils, we might want to stipulate how we understand them before proceeding with any attempt at a comparison between them (Thompson & Hilde, 2000; Fei, 1992).

© JOHN WILEY AND SONS, 2003 | DOI:10.1163/9789004511477_010

CONFUCIANISM AND DEWEYAN PRAGMATISM 169

1   Defining Our Terms: "Confucianism" and "Deweyan Pragmatism"

What is Confucianism? Elsewhere I have argued for a *narrative* rather than an *analytical* understanding of Confucianism (Ames, 2001). In short, framing our question as "What is Confucianism?" in analytical terms tends to essentialize Confucianism as a specific ideology – a technical philosophy – that can be stipulated with varying degrees of detail and accuracy. *What* is a question that is perhaps more successfully directed at attempts at systematic philosophy where through analysis one can seek to abstract the formal, cognitive structure in the language of principles, theories, and concepts. However, in evaluating the content and worth of a fundamentally aesthetic tradition that takes as its basic premise the uniqueness of each and every situation, and in which the goal of ritualized living is to redirect attention back to the level of concrete feeling, the *what* question is at best a first step. Beyond the "what" question, we need to ask more importantly after method: *how* has "Confucianism" functioned historically within the specific conditions of an evolving Chinese culture to try to make the most of its circumstances?

However we might choose to characterize "Confucianism," it is more than any particular set of precepts or potted ideology identified post hoc within different phases or epochs of China's cultural narrative. Confucianism is not as much an isolatable doctrine or a commitment to a certain belief structure as it is the continuing narrative of a community of people – the center of an ongoing "way" or *dao* of thinking and living. Approaching the story of Confucianism as a continuing cultural narrative presents us with a rolling, continuous, and always contingent tradition out of which emerges its own values and its own logic. A *narrative* understanding of Confucianism is made available to us by drawing relevant correlations among specific historical figures and events. Confucianism is importantly biographical and genealogical – the stories of formative models. And in reflecting on the lives of Chinese *philosophes* – a survey of often passionate, sometimes courageous intellectuals who as heirs to the tradition of the "scholar-official (*shi*)" advance their own programs of human values and social order – we become immediately aware that any account of the existential, practical, and resolutely historical nature of this tradition makes it more (and certainly less) than what would be defined as "philosophers" doing "philosophy" within the contemporary Western context.

If we take Dewey on his own terms, the same distinction between narrative and analysis – method and ideology – might be directed at the question, "What is Deweyan pragmatism?" Robert Westbrook recounts how the early critics of pragmatism attacked it condescendingly as a "would-be philosophical system" with distinctively American characteristics, and how Dewey responded by readily allowing the relationship between philosophical ideas and the cultural sensibilities within which they are embedded (Westbrook, 1991: 147–149). The American sensibility is not to be found in an assessment of notions such as "fundamental principles," "system of values," "ruling theories," or "core beliefs." The term "sensibility" is best understood dispositionally as a nuanced manner of anticipating, responding to, and shaping the world about us. Sensibilities are complexes of *habits* that both create and are created by *habitats* and that promote specific, personal manners of *in-habiting* a world. Cultural sensibilities are not easily expressed through the analysis of social, economic, or even political institutions. Such sensibilities reside in the prominent feelings, ideas, and beliefs defining the culture.[1] Richard Rorty certainly reminds us that while our American sensibility may be characterized partly through the description and analysis of ideas, it is perhaps most readily available through the indirection and evocation associated with poetry and literature.

At a personal level, the philosopher Dewey was a lifelong advocate of "democracy," where his understanding of democracy was nothing more or less than the advocacy of the consummate, even spiritual, way of living that he sought to embody. Democracy is the flourishing community as it emerges concretely and processively through the "equality" and "individuality" of its specific members. The proper occupation of philosophy thus understood, must "surrender all pretension to be peculiarly concerned with ultimate reality, or with reality as a complete (i.e. completed) whole: with *the* real object." In this respect, Dewey's long career as a social activist, taking him from the underbelly of Chicago to a simmering revolution in China to educational reform in Turkey to the Trotsky trials in Mexico City, was fair demonstration of his commitment to what in fact he called "the recovery of philosophy":

> Philosophy recovers itself when it ceases to be a device for dealing with the problems of philosophers and becomes a method, cultivated by philosophers, for dealing with the problems of men. (MW 10: 46)

In the Confucian tradition too, philosophical "knowing (*zhi*)," far from being some privileged access to a Reality lying behind the everyday world, is an attempt to "realize" a world in the sense of orchestrating the existing conditions to "make a desirable world real." Speaking in the broadest terms, Confucianism is a meliorative aestheticism concerned with appreciating the world – adding value to it – through the cultivation of a meaningful, communicating, human community. And the prominence of ritual as a primary level of communication in this process suggests that the site of realizing this world is ritualized, concrete feeling. In general terms, we can observe that the self-understanding of many Chinese philosophers approximates Dewey's vision of the philosopher as the purveyor of considered, intelligent practice to adjust situations and improve upon the human experience.

In exploring some of the more specific Deweyan vocabulary of consummatory experience below – concepts like "individuality," "equality," "habit," "human nature," "religiousness" – we will discover that Dewey, like the Confucians, remains painfully vague until we recover the insistent historical particularity that provides concrete exemplification of personal growth and articulation. In the case of Confucius, he is certainly "The Sage." However, he is best remembered by history not only through the episodes of his life depicted in the *Analects*, but also dispositionally by the specific personal habits as they are recounted in the middle books of this same text. For Dewey too, his own life-experience and the cultivated habits of his heart and mind are perhaps the best measure of his philosophical profundity (Lloyd, 1996: 3–6).[2] It is no accident that the most sophisticated representations of his ideas are to be found in the philosophical biographies of interpreters such as Rockefeller and Westbrook.

2 Deweyan Pragmatism and Confucianism: Points of Comparison

What are the resonances between a Deweyan pragmatism and Confucianism that might make a dialogue between them illuminating? In the earlier collaborative work David Hall and I have done, and in this brief essay too, an attempt has been made to reconnoiter and make suggestive forays into some promising terrain rather than to try to "cover the territory." This being said, we might begin from the relational and radically contextualized Confucian notion of person, an embeddedness that we have tried to express in the language of "focus and field." In *The Democracy of the Dead* chapters 8–10 – "Confucian Democracy: A Contradiction in Terms," "The Chinese Individual," and "The Role of Ritual in a Communicating Community" – we summarize what we would suggest are some of the defining sensibilities of the irreducibly social Confucian person. While good scholars certainly disagree, there is, on my reading, minimal dispute with respect to our understanding of notions such as the symbiotic relationship that obtains among the radial spheres of personal, communal, political, and cosmic cultivation, the process of self-cultivation through ritualized living, the centrality of communication and the attunement of language, the inseparability of the cognitive and affective dimensions of experience, an understanding of the heart-and-mind (*xin*) (or "thinking and feeling") as a disposition to act rather than a framework of ideas and beliefs, the construal of knowing as an epistemology of caring – of trust rather than truth, the prevalence of correlative (rather than dualistic) thinking, the pursuit of self-realizing as authentication in practice, the familial nature of all relationships, the centrality of family and filial deference, the high value of inclusive harmony, the priority of ritual propriety to rule or law, the role of exemplary modeling, the didactic function of sage as virtuoso communicator, the expression of sagacity as focusing and enchanting the familiar affairs of the day, a recognition of the continuity between humanity and the numinous, and so on.

There is much in this model of human "becoming" as a communal "doing and undergoing" that sounds like Dewey. One virtue of pursuing a comparison between Dewey and Confucianism is that until now much of the recent discussion of Chinese philosophy both within China and without tends to take place within the framework and categories of the Western philosophical tradition. Dewey's attempt to reconstruct philosophy largely abandons the technical vocabulary of professional philosophy in favor of ordinary language, although an ordinary language that is used at times in rather extraordinary ways.

3   The Deweyan Notion of Person

An example of the use of ordinary language in extraordinary ways is Dewey's notion of "individuality." Individuality is not a ready-made given, but rather arises qualitatively out of ordinary human experience. By this I mean that "individuality" like "character" is an accomplishment, and since it emerges relationally out of associated living, far from being discrete, has implicated within it a "field of selves." And "experience" as Dewey uses this term will not be resolved with any finality into familiar dualistic categories such as "subjective" and "objective" or "fact" and "value." Indeed, the inseparability of subject and object is a function of what Dewey understands to be the intrinsic and constitutive nature of personal relations, and the inseparability of fact and value is entailed by the affective content of these relations as what they really are. Situated experience for Dewey is prior to any abstracted notion of agency. Experience, like the terms "life" and "history" and "culture," is both the process and the product of the interaction between human organism and the social, natural, and cultural environments:

> "Experience" ... includes *what* men do and suffer, what they strive for, love, believe and endure, and also *how* men act and are acted upon, the ways in which they do and suffer, desire and enjoy, see, believe, imagine – in short, processes of *experiencing*. (LW 1: 18)

CONFUCIANISM AND DEWEYAN PRAGMATISM 173

For Dewey, "individuality" is not quantitative: it is neither a pre-social potential nor a kind of isolating discreteness. Rather, it is qualitative, arising through distinctive service to one's community. Individuality is "the realization of what we specifically are as distinct from others," a realization that can only take place within the context of a flourishing communal life (EW 3: 304). "Individuality cannot be opposed to association." said Dewey, "It is through association that man has acquired his individuality, and it is through association that he exercises it" (Dewey, 1892: 38). An individual so construed is not a "thing" but a "patterned event," describable in the language of uniqueness, integrity, social activity, relationality, and qualitative achievement.

How radical is Dewey in this social construction of the person? He certainly rejects the idea that the human being is in any way complete outside of the association one has with other people. But does he go too far in claiming that "Apart from the ties which bind him [the human being] to others, he is nothing" (LW 7: 323)? As James Campbell observes, this passage is easily and often misunderstood as a negation of the individual (Campbell, 1995: 53–55). But as we have seen with Dewey's notion of emergent "individuality," to say that persons are irreducibly social is not to deny the integrity, uniqueness, and diversity of human beings; on the contrary, it is precisely to affirm these conditions.

In commenting on Dewey and the social processes in which persons are created, Campbell avers Aristotle's vocabulary of "potential" and "actual":

> Dewey's point is not just that what was potential becomes actual when provided with the proper conditions, as, for example, the growth of a seed into a plant is sometimes understood (Cf. LW 9: 195–96). His point is rather that persons are incomplete without a social component and develop into what they are – individual members of groups, socially grounded selves – in the ongoing process of living in a social environment. (Campbell, 1995: 40)

In fact, from Dewey's processual and radically contextualized perspective, Aristotle has missed the point that most acorns, far from becoming oak trees, in fact become squirrels.

How does the community grow its persons? Dewey invests enormously in the centrality of language and other modes of communicative discourse (including signs, symbols, gestures, and social institutions):

> Through speech a person dramatically identifies himself with potential acts and deeds; he plays many roles, not in successive stages of life but in a contemporaneously enacted drama. Thus mind emerges. (LW 1: 135)

For Dewey, mind is "an added property assumed by a feeling creature, when it reaches that organized interaction with other living creatures which is language, communication" (Dewey, 1958: 133). In reflecting on Dewey's emergent mind, Westbrook observes that "it is not because they had minds that some creatures had language, but because they had language that they had minds" (Westbrook, 1991: 336).

For Dewey, then, heart-and-mind is created in the process of realizing a world. Heart-and-mind, like world, is *becoming* rather than *being*, and the question is how productive and enjoyable are we able to make this creative process. The way in which heart-and-mind and world are changed is not simply in terms of human attitude, but in real growth and productivity, and in the efficiency and pleasure that attends this process. The alternative – for a community to fail to communicate effectively – is for the community to wither, leaving it vulnerable to the "mindless" violence and "heartless" atrocities of creatures that have failed to become human.

Dewey's notion of "equality" is also evocative. As we would expect, given his qualitative notion of "individuality," equality is active participation in communal life forms that allows one the full contribution of all one's unique abilities. Commenting on this departure from the common meaning of the term, Westbrook allows that Dewey

> advocated neither an equality of result in which everyone would be like everyone else nor the absolutely equal distribution of social resources, ... (Westbrook, 1991: 165)

Dewey, instead, insists that:

> Since actual, that is, effective rights and demands are products of interactions, and are not found in the original and isolated constitution of human nature, whether moral or psychological, mere elimination of obstructions is not enough. (LW 3: 99)

Equality so construed is not an original possession. Again, attaching a most unfamiliar interpretation to a familiar term, Dewey insists that:

> Equality does not signify that kind of mathematical or physical equivalence in virtue of which any one element may be substituted for another. It denotes effective regard for whatever is distinctive and unique in each, irrespective of physical and psychological inequalities. It is not a natural possession but the fruit of the community when its action is directed by its character as a community. (MW 12: 329–330)

CONFUCIANISM AND DEWEYAN PRAGMATISM

In interpreting this passage, Raymond Boisvert underscores the fact that for Dewey, "equality is a result, a 'fruit,' not an antecedent possession" (LW 11: 168; Boisvert, 1998: 68–69). It is growth in contribution. Further, like freedom, equality has no meaning in reference to a discrete and independent person, and can only assume importance when "appropriate social interactions take place." Indeed, equality is qualitative equity rather than strict identity. In Dewey's own words, equality can only take place by

> establishing the basic conditions through which and because of which every human being might become all that he was capable of becoming. (Boisvert, 1998: 68–69)

Again, Dewey offers a novel alternative to classical forms of teleology that, by definition, entail a means/end driven dialectic. In place of some predetermined and preassigned design, Dewey's notion of ideals entail aspirational ideas projected as meliorative goals for social action that "take shape and gain content as they operate in remaking conditions" (Dewey, 1993: 87). As Campbell observes:

> For Dewey, ideals like *justice* or *beauty* or *equality* have all the power in human life that the proponents of 'abstract,' 'fixed,' or 'remote' senses of such ideals claim for them. The problem that he sees is with their interpretation, one that presents ideals as some sort of finished and unchanging Existents placed in a realm other than the natural world of hunger and death, secure from the problems and confusions of day-to-day existence ... Our ideals are connected to the ongoing processes of living: they are rooted in particular difficulties and draw upon presumptive solutions. (Campbell, 1995: 152–153)

Without fixed ideals, how does disposition lead to action within a Deweyan world? For Dewey, it is not ideals that guide conduct as ends in themselves. Rather the direction for action comes from the interface between a particular problem and its resolution, where the sometimes consummatory experiences that emerge in the process of problem-solving are the context in which such ideals are revealed. And such consummatory experiences when they do occur are a shared expression of social intelligence dealing with unique situations as they may arise within the communicating community.

In process philosophy, change will not be denied. And relentless temporality vitiates any notion of perfection or completion. The world of experience entails genuine contingency and the emergent possibilities that always changing circumstances produce. It is the pursuit of the "as yet only possible" that makes the end inhere in the means for achieving it.

Even human nature is not exempt from process. Dewey in presenting his understanding of human nature uses John Stuart Mill's individualism as his foil. He cites Mill at length, who claims that "all phenomena of society are phenomena of human nature"; that is, "human beings in society have no properties but those which are derived from and may be resolved into the laws of the nature of individual man." While expressing appreciation for Mill's motives in liberating the common man from a powerful landed aristocracy, Dewey is unwilling to embrace his notion of person that for Dewey's is another example of "*the* philosophical fallacy" (Tiles, 1988: 21).[3] In fact, Dewey wants to invert Mill's assumptions about the relationship between the person and the society. For Dewey, discussion of the fixed structure of human nature independent of particular social conditions is a non-starter because it "does not explain in the least the differences that mark off one tribe, family, people, from another – which is to say that in and of itself it explains no state of society whatever" (Dewey, 1993: 223). For Dewey, then:

> ... the alleged unchangeableness of human nature cannot be admitted. For while certain needs in human nature are constant, the consequences they produce (because of the existing state of culture – of science, morals, religion, art, industry, legal rules) react back into the original components of human nature to shape them into new forms. The total pattern is thereby modified. The futility of exclusive appeal to psychological factors both to explain what takes place and to form policies as to what *should* take place, would be evident to everybody – had it not proved to be a convenient device for "rationalizing" policies that are urged on other grounds by some group or faction. (Dewey, 1993: 223–224)

For Dewey, the human being is a social achievement, an adaptive success made possible through the applications of social intelligence. Given the reality of change, this success is always provisional, leaving us as incomplete creatures with the always new challenge of contingent circumstances. And yet this success is progressive and programmatic. "We *use* our past experiences to construct new and better ones in the future" (MW 12: 134).

In distinguishing the aristocratic model from democracy, Dewey is equally explicit about how the personal dimension expressed by notions such as "individuality" and "equality" are essential to the kind of harmony that defines a flourishing democracy, and about how the life forms of the society are the stimuli and the media through which such personality is achieved:

> In one word, democracy means that *personality* is the first and final reality. It admits that the full significance of personality can be learned by the

individual only as it is already presented to him in objective form in society; it admits that the chief stimuli and encouragements to the realization of personality come from society; but it holds, none the less, to the fact that personality cannot be procured for anyone else, however degraded and feeble, by any one else, however wise and strong. (EW 1: 244)

As Westbrook observes, "The critical point is that, for Dewey, the relationship between the individual capacities and environments was one of *mutual* adjustment, not the one-sided accommodation of individual needs and powers to a fixed environment" (Westbrook, 1991: 43).

4   The Confucian Notion of Person

To pursue a comparison of the Deweyan conception of person with Confucius, we need some Confucian vocabulary. And if we allow with Wittgenstein that the limits of our language are indeed the limits of our world, we need some more language (Ames and Rosemont, 1998; Ames and Hall, 2001). We can begin with the term *ren* that we have chosen (to the chagrin of many) to translate as "authoritative conduct," "to act authoritatively," and sometimes, as "authoritative person." *Ren* is the foremost project taken up by Confucius, and occurs over one hundred times in the *Analects*. It is a fairly simple graph, and according to the *Shuowen* lexicon, is made up of the elements *ren* "person," and *er*, the number "two." This etymological analysis underscores the Confucian assumption that one cannot become a person by oneself – we are, from our inchoate beginnings, irreducibly social. Herbert Fingarette has stated the matter concisely: "For Confucius, unless there are at least two human beings, there can be no human beings" (Fingarette, 2008: 217).

An alternative explanation of the character *ren* we might derive from oracle bone inscriptions is that what appears to be the number "two" is in fact an early form of "above, to ascend *shang*," that like the number "two" was also written as two horizontal strokes (Karlgren, 1950: 191). Such a reading would highlight the growing distinction one accrues in becoming *ren*, thereby setting a bearing for one's community and the world to come: "those authoritative in their humanity enjoy mountains ... are still ... [and] are long-enduring (*Analects* 6.23; see also 2.1 and 17.3).

Ren is most commonly translated as "benevolence," "goodness," and "humanity," occasionally as "human-heartedness," and less occasionally by the clumsy and sexist "manhood-at-its-best." While "benevolence" and "humanity" might be more comfortable choices for translating *ren* into English, our decision to use the less elegant "authoritative person" is a considered one. First, *ren* is one's entire person: one's cultivated cognitive, aesthetic, moral, and religious sensibilities as they are expressed in one's ritualized roles and relationships. It is one's "field of selves," the sum of significant relationships that constitute one as a resolutely social person. *Ren* is not only mental, but physical as well: one's posture and comportment, gestures and bodily communication. Hence, translating *ren* as "benevolence" is to "psychologize" it in a tradition that does not rely upon the notion of *psyche* as a way of defining the human experience; it is to impoverish *ren* by isolating one out of many moral dispositions at the expense of so much more that comes together in the complexity of becoming human.

Again, "humanity" suggests a shared, essential condition of being human owned by all members of the species. Yet *ren* does not come so easy. It is an aesthetic project, an accomplishment, something done (12.1). The human *being* is not something we are; it is something that we do, and become. Perhaps "human *becoming*" might thus be a more appropriate term to capture the processional and emergent nature of what it means to become human. It is not an essential endowed potential, but what one is able to make of oneself given the interface between one's initial conditions and one's natural, social, and cultural environments. Certainly the human being as a focus of constitutive relationships has an initial disposition (17.2). But *ren* is foremost the process of "growing (*sheng*)" these relationships into vital, robust, and healthy participation in the human community.

The fact that Confucius is asked so often what he means by the expression *ren* would suggest that he is reinventing this term for his own purposes, and that those in conversation with him are not comfortable in their understanding of it. Confucius' creative investment of new meaning in *ren* is borne out by a survey of its infrequent, and relatively unimportant usage in the earlier classical corpus. *Ren* is further ambiguous because it denotes the qualitative transformation of a *particular* person, and can only be understood relative to the specific, concrete conditions of that person's life. There is no formula, no ideal. Like a work of art, it is a process of disclosure rather than closure, resisting fixed definition and replication.

Our term "authoritative person" as a translation of *ren* then, is a somewhat novel expression, as was *ren* itself, and will probably prompt a similar desire for clarification. "Authoritative" entails the "authority" that a person comes to represent in community by becoming *ren*, embodying in oneself the values and customs of one's tradition through the performance of ritual propriety (*li*). The prominence and visibility of the authoritative person is captured in the metaphor of the mountain (6.23): still, stately, spiritual, enduring, a landmark of the local culture and community, a bearing for those who have lost their way.

At the same time, although the authoritative person serves the world as a beacon, the way of becoming human (*dao*) is by no means a "given"; indeed, the population inspired by the authoritative person must be "road-builders," participants in "authoring" the culture for their own place and time (15.29). Observing ritual propriety (*li*) is, by definition, a process of internalization – "making the tradition one's own" – requiring personalization of the roles and relationships that locate one within community. In so doing, one reauthorizes the traditions for oneself, and thereby becomes the true author of one's own life story. It is this creative aspect of *ren* that is implicit in the process of becoming authoritative for one's own community. The contrast between top-down and impositional "authoritarian" order, and the bottom-up, deferential sense of "authoritative" order is also salutary. The authoritative person is a model that others, recognizing the achievement, gladly and without coercion defer to and appropriate in the construction of their own personhood. Confucius is explicit in expressing the same reservations about authoritative relations becoming authoritarian as he has been about a deference-driven ritualized community surrendering this non-coercive structure for the rule of law (2.3).

A second Confucian term that has relevance in our comparison with Dewey is *xin*, translated as "heart-and-mind." The character *xin* is a stylized pictograph of the aorta, associating it quite immediately with the "heart" and the emotional connotations that attend it. The fact that the character *qing* that we translate as "emotions" or "feelings" is a combination of this *xin* and a phonetic element, *qing*, justifies this understanding. In fact, many if not most of the characters that entail "feeling" have *xin* as a component element.

However, given that *xin* has as often been rendered as "mind" should alert us to the inadequacy of simply translating it as "heart." Many, if not most, of the characters that refer to different modalities of "thinking" are also constructed with *xin* as a component. Indeed, there are many passages in the classical Chinese texts that would not make sense in English unless the *xin thinks* as well as *feels*. The point of course is that in this classical Chinese world view, the mind cannot be divorced from the heart. The cognitive is inseparable from the affective. To avoid such a dichotomy, we translate *xin* rather inelegantly as "heart-and-mind" with the intention of reminding ourselves that there are no altogether rational thoughts devoid of feeling, nor any raw feelings altogether lacking in cognitive content.

In the classical Chinese world view, process and change have priority over substance and permanence. Thus, it is frequently observed that, with respect to the human body, physiology has priority over anatomy, and function takes precedence over simple location. This being the case, it might well be argued that *xin* means "thinking and feeling," and then, derivatively and metaphorically, the organ with which these experiences are to be associated.

Since feelings define the quality of one's interactions, the proper expression of such feelings is a singularly important value in early Confucian conception of person. *Qing* is "what something really is" in the sense that the relatively unmediated experience itself resides in affective transactions that become selective and abstract when reduced to the cognitive structures of language. It is to the concreteness of affective experience that Whitehead nods when he observes that "... mothers can ponder many things in their hearts that words cannot express." *Qing* is the content of the life experience that is constantly reforming our natural tendencies as human beings. More broadly, *qing* takes on particular importance in the *Zhongyong* because of the dramatic role that properly focused human affect is assumed to have on cosmic order. As the *Zhongyong* 1 discussion of emotions concludes: "When [human] equilibrium and focus is sustained and harmony is fully realized, the heavens and earth maintain their proper places and all things flourish in the world."

Again, *qing* is important in understanding the radically contextualized and perspectival nature of human co-creativity itself. Because persons are constituted by their relationships, and because these relationships are valorized in the process of bringing their fields of experience into focus, the creative interactions among such persons disclose their feelings for one another, and for their environs. Affective tone and the subjective form of feeling are always entailed in the uniquely perspectival locus of the creative process.

The final Confucian term relevant for the notion of person that we might want to explore briefly is *he*, conventionally translated "harmony." The etymology of the term is culinary. Harmony is the art of combining and blending two or more foodstuffs so that they mutually enhance one another without losing their distinctive flavors. Throughout the early corpus, the preparation of food is referenced as a gloss on this sense of elegant harmony. Harmony so considered entails both the integrity of the particular ingredient and its ease of integration into some larger whole, where integrity is to be understood as "*becoming* whole in relationships" rather than "*being* whole." Signatory of this harmony is the endurance of the particular ingredients and the aesthetic nature of the harmony. Such harmony is an elegant order that emerges out of the collaboration of intrinsically related details to embellish the contribution of each one.

In the *Analects*, this sense of harmony is celebrated as the highest cultural achievement. Here, harmony is distinguished from mere agreement by defining it in terms of eliciting the optimum contribution of each particular to its context. The family metaphor pervades this text, encouraged by the intuition that this is the institution in which the members usually give themselves most

CONFUCIANISM AND DEWEYAN PRAGMATISM

fully and unreservedly to the group nexus, in interactions that are governed by those ritualized observances (*li*) most appropriate (*yi*) to the occasion. Such a commitment to family requires the full expression of personal integrity, and thus becomes the context in which one can most effectively pursue personal realization. The two passages in the *Analects* that best express the inseparability of ritual life forms and personal contribution in the achievement of communal harmony are as follows:

> Achieving harmony (*he*) is the most valuable function of observing ritual propriety (*li*). In the ways of the Former Kings, this achievement of harmony through observing propriety made them elegant, and was a guiding standard in all things large and small. But when things are not going well, to realize harmony just for its own sake without regulating the situation through observing ritual propriety will not work. (1.12)

> Yan Hui inquired about authoritative conduct (*ren*). The Master replied, "Through self-discipline and observing ritual propriety (*li*) one becomes authoritative in one's conduct. If for the space of a day one were able to accomplish this, the whole empire would defer to this authoritative model. Becoming authoritative in one's conduct is self-originating – how could it originate with others?"
> Yan Hui said, "Could I ask what becoming authoritative entails?" The Master replied, "Do not look at anything that violates the observance of ritual propriety; do not listen to anything that violates the observance of ritual propriety; do not speak about anything that violates the observance of ritual propriety; do not do anything that violates the observance of ritual propriety." (12.1)

In the *Zhongyong*, this Confucian sense of harmony (*he*) is further stipulated with the introduction of "focus" or "equilibrium" (*zhong*) as in "focusing (*zhong*) the familiar in the affairs of the day (*yong*)."

5   Dewey's Religious Humanism

The final topic that I want to explore briefly is Dewey's not uncontroversial sense of religiousness. Quite early in his career, Dewey rejects conventional "religion" as institutionalized dogmatism competing with equally misguided modern science in its claims about "Truth." Yet Dewey insists on retaining not only the term "religious," but also "God," to connote "the sense of the connection of man, in the way of both dependence and support, with the enveloping world that the imagination feels is a universe" (LW 9: 36).

In the recent Dewey scholarship, summarized and interpreted in Michael Eldridge's *Transforming Experience*, we have a range of divided and even conflicted readings of Dewey's religious sensibilities. On one end of the spectrum, we have scholars such as Jerome Soneson and Richard Bernstein, the former seeing Dewey as "a fundamentally religious thinker" and the latter regarding Dewey's "treatment of the religious attitude and quality" as "the culmination of his entire philosophy." Perhaps the most nuanced presentation of this position that tries to explain and appreciate Dewey's unique and often misunderstood "democratic form of spirituality" is Steven Rockefeller's philosophical and religious biography (Rockefeller, 1991).[4]

At the other end of the spectrum are a disappointed Michael Eldridge and Alan Ryan who want to argue that the cake that Dewey's would "have" is all but eaten. That is, in Ryan's words, "We may wonder whether, in fact, it is possible to have the *use* of religious vocabulary without the accretion of supernaturalist beliefs that Dewey wishes to slough off" (Ryan, 1995: 274).[5] Eldridge, in invoking the language of "secularity" and "humanism" to challenge the appropriateness of using "religious" to describe Dewey's project, insists that "the 'steady emotion' aroused by a 'clear and intense conception of a union of the ideal ends with actual conditions' did not have to cross a very high threshold to count as religious for Dewey" (Eldridge, 1998: 162).[6]

This debate is not surprising given that, in his use of the term "religious," as with "individuality" and "equality," Dewey again inverts popular wisdom. He does not begin from the familiar conception of Deity that infuses social forms with religious meaning – a Godhead that stands as the ultimate arbiter and guarantor of truth, beauty, and goodness. Rather, Dewey starts from ordinary social practices that, when they achieve a certain breadth and depth of meaning, reveal a religious sensibility that emerges out of full contribution to one's own cultured human community, that further emerges out of one's solidarity with a continuing humanity, and, importantly, that emerges out of one's reverence for the natural world. Later in his career, Dewey would make the same argument for art as experience where art, as an aspiration that properly suffuses and elevates every human activity, is much more than an exclusive, professionalized, institutionalized part of the human experience.

What seems to dissuade Dewey from secular humanism is both an unwillingness to take an unqualified and general notion of humanity itself as an object of worship and the radicalness of Dewey's contextualism. Religiousness is a *qualitative* possibility of consummate experience where, indeed, "both the means employed and the ends sought are within experience" (Eldridge, 1998: 170).

CONFUCIANISM AND DEWEYAN PRAGMATISM

Although Dewey specifically rejects "atheism" because it pretends to too much confidence in human understanding, Dewey's sense of the religious might be fairly described as "a-theistic" in that has no need for positing the existence of a supernatural supreme being:

> Nature, as the object of knowledge, is capable of being the source of constant good and a rule of life, and thus has all the properties and the functions which the Jewish-Christian tradition attributed to God. (LW 4: 45)

In fact, although Dewey occasionally refers to "God" as a sense of continuity, any notion of a temporarily prior, transcendent source and architect of the human experience, lawgiver and judge, is anathema to the substance of Deweyan pragmatism. What Dewey does want to preserve of traditional religiousness is natural piety: a sense of awe and wonder and modesty that precludes any temptation to seek control, and in its stead, encourages an attitude of cooperation and coordination with the natural complexity that surrounds us. His adjustment to the "religious" lies in replacing institutionalized worship with the creative role that deliberate human activity has in the appreciation and enchantment of experience for the flourishing community. In Rockefeller's description of Dewey's "religious humanism," he cites a passage from Dewey's *Individualism, Old and New* (1929) that testifies to the inseparability of the secular and the sacred, the individual and the communal, the social root and its religious flower:

> Religion is not so much a root of unity as it is its flower or fruit ... The sense of wholeness which is urged as the essence of religion can be built up and sustained only through membership in a society which has attained a degree of unity. (Rockefeller, 1991: 449)

6   Confucianism's Human-Centered Religiousness

Regardless of which side of the debate we come down on – that is, we might claim that Dewey is still profoundly religious in spite of his rejection of so much of what has been understood conventionally as religious, or we might insist that he has indeed thrown out the baby with the holy bath water – the question I would pose is this: Does a Confucian perspective have something to contribute here? It is interesting that a generation ago Herbert Fingarette chose *Confucius: The Secular as Sacred* as the title of his small book that has had such a big impact on Confucian studies. In this essay, Fingarette argues rather persuasively that it is the ritualization of the human experience that is the source of what is sacred in the Confucian world (Fingarette, 1972).

Again, we need to understand what is entailed by "ritual propriety (*li*)" as a term of art in Confucian philosophy. *Li* has been conventionally translated as "ritual," "rites," "customs," "etiquette, "propriety," "morals," "rules of proper behavior," and "worship." Properly contextualized, each of these English terms can render *li* on occasion. In classical Chinese, however, the character carries *all* of these meanings on every occasion of its use. The compound character is an ideograph connoting the presentation (*shi*) of sacrifices to the primarily ancestral spirits at an altar to them (*li*), suggesting the profound religious significance that this term entails. It is defined in the *Shuowen* lexicon paronomastically (by phonetic and semantic association) as *li*, meaning "to tread a path," and hence "conduct, behavior" – that is, parsed in its narrowest sense, it is "how to serve the spirits to bring about good fortune." This understanding of *li* as processional and eventful is a signature of the classical Confucian sensibility.

We choose to translate *li* broadly understood as "ritual propriety." Again, this rendering is a considered choice. On the formal side, *li* are those meaning-invested roles, relationships, and institutions that facilitate communication, and foster a sense of community. All formal conduct constitutes *li* – including table manners, patterns of greeting and leave-taking, graduations, weddings, funerals, gestures of deference, ancestral sacrifices, and so on. *Li* are a social grammar that provides each member with a defined place and status within the family, community, and polity. *Li* are life forms transmitted from generation to generation as repositories of meaning, enabling individuals to appropriate persisting values and to make them appropriate to their own situations. While we perform the *li* in the present, much of their efficacy stems from their being a link to the past and thereby, to the future as well. Without *li*, one might avoid a friend who has lost a loved one; with *li* one is prompted to be there.

On the informal and uniquely personal side, full participation in a ritually-constituted community requires the personalization of prevailing customs, institutions, and values. What makes ritual profoundly different from law or rule is this process of making the tradition one's own. The Latin *proprius*, "to have made something one's own" (as in "appropriate" and "property") gives us a series of cognate expressions that are useful in translating key philosophical terms to capture this sense of participation. *Yi* is not "righteousness" but "appropriateness," "a sense of what is fitting"; *zheng* is not "rectification" or "correct conduct," but "proper conduct"; *zheng* is not "government" but "governing properly"; *li* ("ritual propriety") is not just "what is appropriate," but "*doing* what is appropriate."

CONFUCIANISM AND DEWEYAN PRAGMATISM   185

Ritual propriety, like most things Confucian, begins at home. That is, *Zhongyong* 20 is explicit in identifying the familial source of *li*:

> The degree of devotion due different kin and the degree of esteem accorded those who are different in character is what gives rise to the observance of ritual propriety.

Li, thus understood, aggregates within the human community, defining the appropriate relationships between the present population and its forbearers (*Zhongyong* 19), and the proper relationships between social and political authority and those who govern and are governed by it (*Zhongyong* 20).

Perhaps the greatest obstacle to understanding what *li* means in the world of Confucius is thinking that "ritual" is a familiar dimension of our own world, and that we fully understand what it entails. "Ritual" in English is often pejorative, suggesting compliance with hollow and hence meaningless social conventions. A careful reading of the Confucian literature, however, uncovers a way of life carefully modulated down to appropriate facial expressions and physical gestures, a world in which a life is a performance requiring unrelenting attention to detail. Importantly, this *li*-constituted performance begins from the insight that personal refinement is only possible through the discipline provided by formalized roles and behaviors. Form without creative personalization is coercive and dehumanizing; creative personal expression without form is randomness at best, and license at worst. It is only with the appropriate combination of form and personalization that family and community can be self-regulating and refined.

In reading the *Analects*, we have a tendency to give short shrift to the middle books 9–11 that are primarily a series of intimate snapshots depicting the events in the life of the historical person, Confucius. Yet it is precisely these passages that are most revealing of the extent to which the appropriate behaviors of a scholar-official participating in the daily life of the court were choreographed in and through the slightest gesture, the cut of one's clothes, the cadence of one's stride, one's posture and facial expression, one's tone of voice, even the rhythm of one's breathing:

> On passing through the entrance way to the Duke's court, he would bow forward from the waist, as though the gateway were not high enough. While in attendance, he would not stand in the middle of the entranceway; on passing through, he would not step on the raised threshold. On passing by the empty throne, his countenance would change visibly, his legs would bend, and in his speech he would seem to be breathless. He

would lift the hem of his skirts in ascending the hall, bow forward from the waist, and hold in his breath as though ceasing to breathe. On leaving and descending the first steps, he would relax his expression and regain his composure. He would glide briskly from the bottom of the steps, and returning to his place, he would resume a reverent posture. (*Analects* 10: 4)

The *Analects* does not provide us with a catechism of prescribed formal conducts, but rather with the image of a particular historical person striving with imagination to exhibit the sensitivity to ritualized living that would ultimately make him the teacher of an entire civilization.

We might make one summary point that connects *li* rather immediately with Dewey's notions of "function" and "adjustment": the active relationship between the mutual accommodation of one's own capacities and the conditions of one's environment. First, *li* are by definition personalized and site specific. Further, as both performance and performative, *li* are both means and end in the sense that they are wholly meaningful within their own context and yet resist rationalization or explanation. They do what they mean.

Recently, I contributed an essay to a new volume on *Confucian Spirituality* entitled "*Li* and the A-theistic Religiousness of Classical Confucianism" in which I argue that classical Confucianism is at once a-theistic, and profoundly religious (Ames, 2003–2004).[7] It is a religious tradition without a God; a religious sensibility that affirms a spirituality that emerges out of inspired human experience itself. There is no church (except for the family), no altars (except perhaps for the dining room table), and no clergy (except for the exemplary models of one's community). Confucianism celebrates the way in which the process of human growth and extension both is shaped by, and contributes to, the meaning of the totality – a kind of "creativity" that in our translation of the *Zhongyong* we argue stands in stark contrast to *creatio ex nihilo* traditions (Tu, 1985).[8]

There are several profound differences between this kind of religiousness and that of the Abrahamic traditions that have largely defined the meaning of religion in the Western cultural narratives. And these differences it seems to me have at least a superficial resonance with Dewey's use of "religious." In my essay, I argue that, unlike the "worship" model that defers to the ultimate meaning of some temporally prior, independent, external agency – what Schleiermacher has called "absolute dependence" – Confucian religious experience is itself a *product* of the flourishing community, where the quality of the religious life is a direct consequence of the quality of communal living. It is a human-centered rather than a god-centered religiousness that emerges through conscientious attention to ritual propriety. And the religious in Confucianism is not the root of the flourishing community, not the foundation on which it is built, but rather is its intrinsic quality, its blossom.

A second way in which Confucian religiousness is distinct from the Abrahamic traditions is that Confucian religiousness is neither salvific nor eschatological. While it does entail a kind of transformation, it is specifically a transformation of the quality of human life in the ordinary business of the day that not only elevates and inspires our daily transactions, but further extends radially to enchant the world. The cosmos is wider and deeper when human feeding is elevated to *haute cuisine*; when stick markings are disciplined into fine calligraphy and breathtaking bronze designs; when coarse gestures are refined to become the sober cadence of ceremony and the exhilaration of the dance; when grunting interventions are amplified into sublime and haunting melody; when the heat of random copulation becomes the constant and reassuring warmth of hearth and family. It is this transformation – the ordinary and everyday made elegant – that seems at least in part to provide the mystery other religious expressions find in some transcendent, supernatural appeal.

7   Dewey and Confucius: Resonances and Differences

Now, for me at least, there is much in Dewey's vocabulary that resonates with the way in which I have come to understand the cluster of terms defining the classical Confucian sensibilities: "experience" and *dao*; "consummatory experience and democracy" and *he*; "personality, individuality, and equality" and *ren*, "religiousness" and *li*; "processual human nature" and *renxing*. And more broadly, there seem to be many points of convergence: the irreducibly social nature of human experience, the priority of situation to agency, the central importance of effective communication, and melioristic continuity as the alternative to teleology. At the same time, there are many more interesting differences, both substantial and in terms of emphasis.

Where should we look then for significant and productive differences?

One way in which Dewey was used to focus a lack in the Confucian tradition earlier in this century was with respect to "Mr. Science." Robert Westbrook is not alone when he claims that "at the heart of Dewey's effort to reconstruct the role of the philosopher was his view of the relationship between philosophy and science" (Westbrook, 1991: 138). One of the weaknesses that Chinese scholars themselves have directed at Confucianism as a tradition where Dewey might prove compensatory has been the Confucian tendency towards a kind of "voluntarism" that exaggerates the capacity of human purposes to transform the world. The Kantian scholar, Li Zehou, is one of China's more prominent social critics. Work being done by several contemporary interpretive scholars – particularly Woei Lien Chong and Gu Xin at Leiden, and Liu Kang at Penn State – makes much of Li's rejection of Maoist voluntarism: the idea that the power of the human will can accomplish all things.[9] Mao's voluntarism is not new, but emerges out of and is consistent with the traditional Confucian position that human realization lies with the transformative powers of the unmediated moral will. It is Li's claim that unbridled confidence in the moral will – a belief that translates readily into the image of ideologically driven mass mobilization campaigns – has been responsible for China's contemporary crises, from Western colonialization down to the Great Leap Forward and the Cultural Revolution (Chang, 1994).

The argument, simply put, is that Confucian philosophers from classical times have recognized a continuity between human beings, and their natural and numinous environments: *tianren heyi*. The nature of this continuity, however, has often been misunderstood, to the detriment of the natural sciences. Instead of being a continuity between subject and object, respecting both the ability of the collective human community to transform its environment productively, *and* the resistance of the natural world to this human transformation, it has been dominated by the belief that the moral subject holds almost absolute transformative powers over an infinitely malleable natural world. As such, this attitude has become a kind of raw subjectivism that discounts the need for collective human efforts in science and technology to "humanize" nature and establish a productive relationship between subject and object, a relationship that Li Zehou takes to be a precondition for human freedom.

The scientific and empirical demands of Deweyan inquiry might be a corrective on this perceived Confucian weakness. Can Confucianism repay the favor? Could the Confucian insistence upon ritualized living as instrumental to enchanting the human experience be borrowed as a sufficient conventional supplement to Dewey's notion of religiousness to assuage Ryan's and Eldridge's feeling that Dewey is using a much impoverished sense of religiousness? Would the centrality of the religious aspect of Confucian philosophy and its focus on ritualized living be a sufficient extension of Dewey's qualitative understanding of religiousness to persuade Ryan and Eldridge that there is a viable "a-theistic" religiousness that warrants a religious vocabulary, although one importantly different from that of theism? Does Confucianism offer a sufficiently robust example of such an alternative human-centered religious sensibility that could persuade us that what we have conventionally taken to be religious does not exhaust all of the possible examples of what is to be legitimately labeled "religious?"

Dewey suggests that a transcendental appeal offers little respite or real relief to the vicissitudes of the human experience:

> Were it a thousand times dialectically demonstrated that life as a whole is regulated by a transcendent principle to a final inclusive goal, nonetheless

CONFUCIANISM AND DEWEYAN PRAGMATISM

189

truth and error, health and disease, good and evil, hope and fear in the concrete, would remain just what and where they are now. (MW 4: 12)

But is there, in fact, a "cost" to transcendence? The power of the family to function as the radial locus for human growth might be much enhanced when natural family and communal relations are not perceived as being in competition with, a distraction from, or dependent upon some higher supernatural relations. Said another way, when human relations are subordinated to a personal relationship with a transcendent object of worship, whatever the benefits of such subordination might be, it is at a cost to the fabric of family and community. In ritualized living, it is from the family expanding outward that persons themselves emerge as objects of profound communal, cultural, and ultimately religious deference. Beyond the achievement of an intense religious quality felt in the everyday experience of their lives, these exemplary persons emerge as ancestors for their families and communities, and as contributors to the ancestral legacy – *tian* – that defines Chinese culture more broadly construed. It is the cumulative propensity of ancestors and cultural heroes over time that makes *tian* determinate and meaningful.

We can identify specific ways in which a dialogue between Confucianism and Deweyan pragmatism is enriching for both. At a more general level, I dare say most scholars who do comparative philosophy would agree that Western philosophical rigor is enabling when it comes to the study of Chinese philosophy. Students who have Western philosophical training bring new, often analytic, tools and fresh perspectives to the understanding and extension of the Chinese tradition. But the benefits are mutual. In *The Democracy of the Dead*, we argue that "Easternization," although until now a largely unannounced and certainly unacknowledged process, has been and will continue to be an implication of a relationship between China and America. In this same spirit, what only a few Western philosophers have realized is that while process thinking is relatively new within the context of Western philosophy, the *qi*-cosmology of the long Chinese tradition entails a process world view that begins historically as early as the *Book of Changes*. That is, our recent interest in process philosophy might be much enhanced by a closer look at a developed Chinese process sensibility. What are often construed as "alternative" traditions might better be seen as "complementary." Both worlds remain less by being exclusive.

If we are persuaded that there is a basis for dialogue and that such a dialogue would be mutually advantageous, how do we, inspired by the models of social activism provided by both Dewey and Confucius, move from an academic conversation among what some less kind than us might characterize as freeloading intellectuals, to thick social practices?

The real value that this discussion might have is in its immediate contemporary relevance as China moves ineluctably toward some Chinese version of democracy. There is an absence in both Confucianism and Dewey of many of the prerequisites for liberal democracy. Certainly notions such as autonomous individuality, and quantitative equality that provide a basis for individually conceived political rights, are anathema to both visions of the flourishing community. There are, on the other hand, resonances between Confucianism and the more communitarian model of democracy grounded in the process philosophy of Dewey, where the greatest guarantee of human liberty are not the entitlements guaranteed by rights-talk but a flourishing community, and where liberty is not the absence of constraint but full participation in self-governance. The question we have tried to ask in *The Democracy of the Dead* is: Can Chinese democracy best be served by encouraging an appeal to the specific kind of "communitarianism" ubiquitous in classical Confucianism, or need China abandon its cultural center and import a Western conception of liberal democracy?

Acknowledgment

This chapter is a reprint from: AMES, Roger (2003). Confucianism and Deweyan pragmatism: A dialogue. *Journal of Chinese Philosophy*, *30*(3–4), 403–417. Reprinted here with permission from the publisher.

Notes

1 In a manuscript on the history of American philosophy that David Hall was working on before his death he is intent on interpreting Jonathan Edwards as one of the principal architects of the American sensibility. In rehearsing aspects of Edwards' philosophical reflections, Hall begins by claiming that Edwards circumvents the modern problematic of subjectivity and self-consciousness in any of its familiar modes by proposing a model of individuality that is not predicated upon either knowing, acting or making as subject-centered. In fact, the dissolution of the subject is a function of the development in Edwards of a process vision of the world as an alternative to substance modes of thinking. Further, this process philosophy is informed by a dispositional ontology that understands natural and supernatural processes in terms of inclinations or habits of response that are to be normatively understood as inclinations toward or responses to beauty. For Edwards, the communication of beauty is the defining feature of both the Divine and Human realms. And for Hall, the de-subjectification of the individual by appeal to a processive, dispositional ontology, and the movement of beauty and the aesthetic sensibility from the margins to the center qualify Edwards to serve as an original American thinker.

CONFUCIANISM AND DEWEYAN PRAGMATISM 191

2 G.E.R. Lloyd (1996: 3–6) worries quite properly about "piecemeal" cross-cultural comparisons of "individual theories and concepts" based on the uncritical assumption that representative figures "were addressing the same questions." This concern is hugely important when moving between scientific traditions, and is still a cautionary consideration when dealing with the cultural narratives of philosophers so distant in time and place as Confucius and Dewey.

3 J.E. Tiles in his discussion of *the* philosophical fallacy cites Dewey: "Personality, selfhood, subjectivity are eventual functions that emerge with complexly organized interactions, organic and social. Personal individuality has its basis and conditions in simpler events" (LW 1:162). And from this Tiles infers that Dewey "will accuse those who assume individual human beings are constituted as conscious rational beings prior to, or independently of, their entering into social relations, of committing '*the* philosophic fallacy.'"

4 What makes Rockefeller's presentation so remarkable is his own reservation about a processual and creative religious sensibility that clearly raises but does not resolve the problem of ultimate meaning, a religious affirmation that is necessary for at least some people (Dostoevsky comes immediately to mind) in dealing with both personal existential challenges and the mindless horrors we witness as modern human beings.

5 In spite of Eldridge's (1998: 155–156) own strong convictions, he is very good about rehearsing all of the evidence. For example, he cites among Sidney Hook's reminiscences of Dewey's reasons for using the "term" God a Deweyan rejoinder that "there is no reason why the emotive associations of the sacred, profound, and ultimate should be surrendered to the supernaturalists."

6 The use of "secular" as a description of Dewey, if understood in its usual way, is an indictment that we might assume Dewey himself would resist. In its weakest form it would suggest an emphasis upon the self-sufficiency of the worldly and human and an indifference to the spiritual and religious. In a stronger sense as the opposite of sacred it might even imply a religious skepticism that seeks to exclude the religious from civil and public affairs. But Eldridge uses secular to mean "a thoroughgoing naturalism" as opposed to "supernaturalism" or "extranaturalism," interpreting Dewey as implying that the human experience and its entire history is located within nature, a characterization with which Dewey would certainly agree.

7 A more sustained argument for the profundity and legitimacy of this use of religiousness is found in Rosemont (2002).

8 Tu Weiming (1985, *passim*) develops this contrast between *creatio ex nihilo* and the continuous creativity of the Confucian world as it is directed by an "anthropocosmic vision."

9 I am indebted here to Woei Lien Chong's (1996) article and also to the responses to Chong's work by Li Zehou (1999) and Jane Cauvel (1999). For a bibliography of recent scholarship on Li Zehou, see Chong (1996: 142–143).

References

Ames, R. T. (2001). New Confucianism: A native response to western philosophy. In S. Hua (Ed.), *Chinese political culture*. M.E. Sharpe.

Ames, R. T. (2003–2004). Li and the a-theistic religiousness of classical Confucianism. In W.-m. Tu & M. E. Tucker (Eds.), *Confucian spirituality* (2 Vols.). The Crossroad Publishing Company.

Ames, R. T., & Rosemont, H. Jr. (1998). *The analects of Confucius: A philosophical translation*. Ballantine.

Ames, R. T., & Hall, D. L. (2001). *Focusing the familiar: A translation and philosophical interpretation of the* Zhongyong. University of Hawai'i Press.

Boisvert, R. D. (1998). *John Dewey: Rethinking our time.* State University of New York.

Campbell, J. (1995). *Understanding John Dewey.* Open Court.

Cauvel, J. (1999). The transformative power of art: Li Zehou's aesthetic theory. *Philosophy East and West, 49*(2), 150–173.

Chang, H. (1994). Roundtable discussion on W. T. de Bary's The trouble with Confucianism. *China Review International, 1*(1), 9–47.

Chong, W. L. (1996). Mankind and nature in Chinese thought: Li Zehou on the traditional roots of Maoist voluntarism. *China Information, 11*(2/3), 138–175.

Dewey, J. (1892). Lecture notes: Political philosophy. In *Dewey papers.* Morris Library, Southern Illinois University.

Dewey, J. (1958). *Experience and nature.* Dover.

Dewey, J. (1991). *John Dewey: The collected works* (J. A. Boydston, Ed.). Southern Illinois University Press. Volume and page numbers follow the initials of the series. Abbreviations for the volumes cited are: EW: The Early Works (1882–1899); MW: The Middle Works (1899–1924); LW: The Later Works (1925–1953).

Dewey, J. (1993). *The political writings.* Hackett.

Eldridge, M. (1998). *Transforming experience: John Dewey's cultural instrumentalism.* Vanderbilt University Press.

Fei, X. (Fei, Hsiao-t'ung). (1992). *From the soil: The foundations of Chinese xociety* (*Xiangtu Zhongguo*) (G. Hamilton & Z. Wang, Trans.). University of California Press.

Fingarette, H. (1972). *Confucius: The secular as sacred.* Harper and Row.

Fingarette, H. (2008). The music of humanity in the conversations of Confucius. *Journal of Chinese Philosophy, 10*(4), 331–356.

Karlgren, B. (1950). *Grammata Serica Recensa.* Museum of Far Eastern Antiquities.

Li, Z. (1999). Subjectivity and "subjectality": A response. *Philosophy East and West, 49*(2), 174–183.

Lloyd, G. E. R. (1996). *Adversaries and authorities.* Cambridge University Press.

Rockefeller, S. (1991). *John Dewey: Religious faith and democratic humanism.* Columbia University Press.

Rosemont, H. Jr. (2002). *Rationality and religious experience.* Open Court.

Ryan, A. (1995). *John Dewey and the high tide of American liberalism.* Norton.

Thompson, P., & Hilde, T. (Eds.). (2000). *The agrarian roots of pragmatism.* Vanderbilt University Press.

Tiles, J. E. (1988). *Dewey.* Routledge.

Tu, W. (1985). *Confucian thought: Self as creative transformation.* SUNY Press.

Westbrook, R. B. (1991). *John Dewey and American democracy.* Cornell University Press.

CHAPTER 10

Democratic Self-Cultivation

Leonard J. WAKS

Abstract

In this paper I draw on the concept of Confucian self-cultivation to strengthen John Dewey's democratic education project. For Dewey, democracy is primarily a form of associated living, marked by the broad sharing of interests and rich communication among social groups. In appealing to Confucian philosophy to bolster Dewey's educational project, I adopt the framework of global Intercultural philosophy, placing philosophical approaches from different cultural traditions together to augment intellectual resources and advance philosophical understanding. This approach initially dictates a comparative method: "setting into dialogue sources from across cultural, linguistic, and philosophical streams" (Littlejohn, n.d.). I draw particularly upon the *Analects* of Confucius, the collected works of John Dewey, and standard interpretive works. But I go beyond mere comparison, to argue for an enriched form of democratic education, bolstered by Confucian insights, and suitable for contemporary Western democracies.

Keywords

self-cultivation – intercultural philosophy – democratic education – Confucius – John Dewey – the literary canon in education – rituals in education

1   Introduction

Democratic values are under siege. In the West, far- right populist regimes with anti-democratic tendencies – nationalist hostility to immigrants and those with religious and ethnic differences, attacks on the free press – have recently led governments in Brazil, Colombia, Hungary, India, Poland, Turkey and the United States among other countries. According to the Economist Intelligence Unit (EIU)'s 2018 annual report on the state of democracy in 167 nations, "deep disillusionment with establishment politics means that the quality of democratic societies is eroding." The report "considers the U.S. under President

© KONINKLIJKE BRILL NV, LEIDEN, 2019 | DOI:10.1163/9789004511477_011

Donald Trump, a 'flawed democracy,' having been downgraded from a 'full democracy' when he was elected" (Rapoza, 2019).

Meanwhile, China's quest for democracy has, according to philosopher Sor-Hoon Tan (2007), "been a frustrating tale of broken promises and unfulfilled hope" (142). Since the May Fourth Movement (1919), many Chinese intellectuals and youth leaders have called for liberal, Western style democracy in China, but their Western-oriented democratic goals have been thwarted.

Despite many setbacks, democratic values remain attractive to many Chinese intellectuals, civil society leaders, and even members of the Chinese Communist Party. Scholars have recently been searching for forms of democracy suitable in light of Chinese cultural history. Fewer today think that democracy must assume the liberal Western form. Many look instead to Confucianism – as more in keeping with Chinese traditional values and a firmer ground for Asian democracy. As one influential scholar puts it, "In East Asian societies democracy would be most politically effective and culturally relevant if it were rooted in and operates on the 'Confucian habits and mores' with which East Asians are still deeply saturated ... if democracy were a *Confucian democracy*" (Kim, 2014: 4, original emphasis).

Some leading theorists of such a Confucian Democracy have drawn on the philosophy of John Dewey (Hall & Ames 1999; Tan, 2004), emphasizing both similarities between Deweyan and Confucian conceptions of the self as inherently social, and Dewey's notion of democracy itself as primarily social rather than political. This move opens a space for democratic reform efforts in civil society and education rather than in the state, and indeed, many of these democratic efforts have been encouraged by the current Chinese government.

2 Confucian Education for the West

This paper reverses the direction. Instead of turning to the West – and John Dewey in particular – to interpret Confucian democracy for China, I turn to the East – and specifically to Confucianism – to address the democratic crisis in the West, drawing on Confucian self -cultivation education to strengthen John Dewey's democratic education project.

For Dewey, democracy is primarily a form of associated living, marked by the broad sharing of interests and rich communication among social groups. These defining democratic values are particularly relevant in countering today's far right populism, which trades on antagonisms among ethnic and religious groups, and denies the authority of both scientific inquiry and investigative journalism.

DEMOCRATIC SELF-CULTIVATION   195

In appealing to Confucian philosophy to bolster Dewey's educational project I adopt the framework of global Intercultural philosophy (Brooks, 2013, Bai et al., 2014), placing philosophical approaches from different cultural traditions together to augment intellectual resources and advance philosophical understanding. This approach initially dictates a comparative method: "setting into dialogue sources from across cultural, linguistic, and philosophical streams" (Littlejohn, n.d.). I draw particularly upon the *Analects* of Confucius (Eno translation, 2015), the collected works of Dewey (see references for details), standard interpretive works, and secondary literature found through structured searches associating both philosophers with terms such as "classical study," "ritual" and "music." But I go beyond mere comparison, to argue for an enriched form of democratic education, bolstered by Confucian insights, and suitable for contemporary Western democracies.

My argument proceeds by first outlining the central aims and methods of Confucian self-cultivation education, emphasizing its two key elements – reverent study of literary classics as texts isolated for special study, and performance of customary ritual; and second, providing a similar outline of Dewey's democratic education for comparison, noting Dewey's rejection of both of these elements of Confucian self-cultivation education. I then argue that both classical study and ritual can nonetheless be incorporated in democratic education in the Deweyan spirit to strengthen democratic values.

3   Confucian Self-Cultivation Education

3.1   *Background*
Confucius (551–479 BCE) belonged to the *shi* (士) – originally the class of chariot-riding warriors and archers governed by a strict, ritualized ethical code. As rulers turned to a professional military after the Chinese iron age (officially dated as starting in approximately 600 BCE), the *shi* were transformed into an administrative and scholar class known for their proficiency at ritual ceremonies and stringent code of conduct.

Confucius came of age during the Spring and Autumn period (771 to 476 BCE), a time of great turbulence and disorder. Here some background is in order. The Zhou dynasty began when King Wu, son of King Wen of Zhou (the "cultivated King"), defeated the Shang dynasty rulers in 1046 BCE. When King Wu died, his young son Cheng became king and his brother Dan, the Duke of Zhou, became regent. Dan is widely regarded as both a capable ruler and culture hero -the legendary creator of the *i Ching*, the *Book of Poetry*, and the basic texts of Chinese classical music, as well as the founder of the *Rites of Zhou* (周礼).

In a long decline after 970 BCE, the Zhou kings eventually became figure-heads. In 771 BCE, after the death of You, the twelfth Zhou King, and the near destruction of his capital at Haojing, the Zhou court, devoid of power, relocated eastward to Luoyang. This date marks the beginning of the Eastern Zhou Dynasty, the first stage of which is known as the Spring and Autumn period (771–476 BCE). During this period, the nobles fought among themselves for power, and the traditional Zhou culture languished.

Confucius's father belonged[1] to the lower aristocracy of the state of Lu, which prided itself on counting among its founders Dan, the Duke of Zhou. After the decline of the Zhou court, Lu became the repository of Zhou aristocratic culture (Eno, 2015: 11). It was thus natural that Confucius would look back to the presumed golden age when Zhou culture thrived, when Zhou sage kings ruled, ritual codes were observed, and society was well-ordered and harmonious.

Like others in his family, Confucius was deeply impressed by the Zhou ritual practices as representations of proper relations among people with different social statuses. The neglect of ritual practice, he felt, had undermined the normative social order, and Confucius set out to preserve and re-establish Zhou knowledge and ritual behavior among leaders and their ministers (Ivanhoe, 2000). The *Analects* provides Confucius's vision of legitimate Zhou culture, and his account of why it's pattern contained the basis for a new utopia (Eno, 2015: 111). He said of the Zhou "How splendid was its pattern! And I follow the Zhou" (3.14); "The virtue of the Zhou may be said to be the utmost of virtue" (8.20).

3.2 *The Ideal of the Junzi*

Confucius's moral ideal was the *junzi* (君子) – literally "ruler's sons" or "princes," but in common usage, superior persons or noblemen – as opposed to *xiaoren* (小人)- petty, servile commoners. Confucius *ethicized* the term *junzi;* he reconceived *junzi* not as men of noble *pedigree*, but of noble *character* (Pines, 2017). He urged his students to aim at the highest virtue -to become *junzi* and rise above pettiness (6.13). *Junzi* possessed humaneness or benevolence (*ren*, 仁), an over-arching virtuous character incorporating such component virtues as ritual propriety (*li*, 礼), filial piety (*xiao*, 孝), wisdom (*zhi*, 智), sympathy (*shu*, 恕), cultural refinement (*wen*, 文), and charisma (*de*, 德) among other virtues suited for leadership (Olberding, 2013: 21). Confucius in the *Analects* tells us that *Junzi* are concerned with lifelong learning and self-improvement; not about obtaining full bellies or comfortable homes (1.14). They are always inclusive and never partisan (2.14). Their virtue is truly radical: "The *junzi* works on the root – once the root is planted, the *dao* (道) is born" (1.2). They are moral through and through: "they insist on nothing and refuse nothing, but simply align themselves with the right" (4.10). Once learners grasp Zhou patterns and constrain their behavior by ritual practice, they can never turn back – their moral transformation is permanent (6.27).

Confucius noted that despite his unstinting efforts even he did not fully exemplify *junzi* perfection (7.33). The *junzi* is thus a moral *ideal,* but one that served as a guide light in fostering *ren* in his students. By dedication to the ideal, they in turn could exert moral authority as teachers and ministers, spread Zhou learning and practice, and restore peace and harmony to "all under heaven" (*tianxia*, 天下).

3.3   *The Confucian Curriculum*

Confucius sought to transform young men into *junzi* through a curriculum of reverential learning of literary classics (*xue*, 学), and ritual observance (*li*, 礼). According to legend, Confucius was the editor of the six Zhou classics: *The Classic of Poetry, The Book of History, The Book of Changes* (*i Ching*), *The Book of Rites, The Classic of Music* (now lost) and *The Spring and Autumn Annals.* Students in self-cultivation education read these texts closely, and reflected on them with teachers and peers to disclose their deeper meanings. The educational ideal expressed in this tradition have recently been synthesized by Charlene Tan (2017) as follows:

> The aim of education is to inculcate *ren* (humanity) through li (normative behaviours) so that learners could realise and broaden *dao* (Way). To achieve this aim, the curriculum should be holistic, broad-based and integrated where students constantly practise what they have learnt through self-cultivation and social interaction.

3.3.1   Classical Study

In Confucian self-cultivation education, the Zhou classics were the initial focus of learning, and students were expected to master them. But the aim of study was not merely to memorize them or grasp their literal meaning, but rather to absorb, through discussions and reflection about them, the ancient wisdom they depict. As Barry Allen (2017) puts this point, in Confucian education, "classical learning is a school of experience … The Classics are the works of ancient sages and a record of their experience. The study of this material is a method for establishing an intuitive continuity between that experience and our own." Through reading and reflection the students were to attain a larger view of the world and greater flexibility and responsiveness of behavior (Ivanhoe, 2000: 2).

The knowledge gained through close study of the classical texts is thus inherently *moral*. Confucian thought makes no sharp distinction between thinking and doing. Elliot and Tsai (2008) note:

> For Confucius, 'pursuing knowledge' or 'knowing' refers to a dynamic process of becoming intelligent, of 'realizing' new possibilities for action within a specific set of circumstances of which he is a participant ... Knowledge is not determined independently of action in the circumstances of everyday life; the relationship between knowledge and action is a non-instrumental one. Knowledge is only fully achieved in action.

The aim of classical learning is effectiveness in action. As Confucius in the *Analects* explains,

> You can recite the 300 poems from the *Book of Odes*, but when you try to use them in administration, they are not effective, and in handling the outlying regions, you cannot apply them, then even though you know a lot, what good is it? (13.5)

Confucius expected students to do the heavy lifting: "Where there is no agitated attempt at thinking, I do not provide a clue; where there is no stammered attempt at expression, I do not provide a prompt. If I raise one corner and do not receive the other three in response, I teach no further" (7.8). Self-cultivation education was in this way learner-centered – the learners cultivated *themselves* – within a group of peers bound by filial bonds of mutual regard and support.

Classical study was also aimed at inculcating a deep love of learning – the development of lifelong study and practice as a source of edification and joy (*le*, 乐): Confucius says of textual learning, "Knowing it is not so good as loving it; loving it is not so good as taking joy in it" (6.20). The opening statement in the *Analects* sounds this keynote: "to study and at appropriate times, to practice what one has studied, is this not a pleasure?" (1.1). (For more on the role of joy in Confucian self-cultivation, see Shun, 2017.)

3.3.2   Ritual Practice

Classical study was united with ritual practice in self-cultivation education. Confucian rituals represented normative human relations – between ruler and ruled, father and son, elder brother to younger brothers, husband to wife, teacher to student and friend to friend – in symbolic form. In the hierarchical relations subordinates showed obedience to their superiors, who in turn showed benevolent regard for their subordinates; thus everyone had respected

DEMOCRATIC SELF-CULTIVATION   199

and satisfying roles, symbolizing a harmonious society. These rituals were supplemented with music and dance – augmenting the beauty and joy to be found in ritual performances (Ji, 2008; Liu, 2014; Yi, 2017).

Some Confucian rituals had profound educational significance. One example will suffice. In the crown prince's school entrance ceremony – consisting of a 'request for lessons' and 'offering simple presents' and 'bowing to teachers.' in Tang dynasty China, the crown prince bows twice to the teacher, who bows once to the crown prince. The crown prince represents all children, and the ritual symbolizes respect for teachers (Park, 2019). Even today, school children in China bow at the beginning of each class and say "good morning (afternoon), teacher," and bow at the end of class and say "thank you, teacher."

4   Dewey and Democratic Education

4.1   *Background*

Dewey first took up democratic education in the American socially stratified multi-ethnic industrial cities of the late 19th and early 20th centuries. As he states in *The School and Society* (MW 1: 1–92),[2] many peoples had been drawn from all corners of the earth to work as laborers in huge capitalist enterprises in the industrial cities, transforming the United States from a frontier society of roughly-equal, enterprising individuals (plus former slaves and other excluded minorities) to a vastly unequal society of elites and ethnically and socially distinct workers struggling for basic democratic rights. This was also a time of great turbulence and disorder. Dewey's concerns – poverty, class warfare, racial discrimination, child welfare, women's rights, free speech and press, and world peace – were shared by other intellectuals and activists of the American Progressive Era (1890–1920) such as Upton Sinclair, Jane Addams, Lester Ward, Florence Kelley, Grace Abbott and Richard T. Ely. Dewey was active in the fight for equal justice in all of these interconnected areas, for example, as a founding trustee in 1899 of Jane Addams' Hull House (a social settlement house for immigrants), a founding member in 1909 of the National Association for Colored People (NAACP), a prominent early member of the American Civil Liberties Union (founded in 1920), and a member in other movements for peace and social harmony for all.

4.2   *Dewey's Ideal Democracy and Democratic Personality*

Dewey conceived democracy ideally as a "form of associated living" with shared interests within and rich communication between social groups and classes (MW9: 94f). In such a society, while conflicts were inevitable, they could be resolved peacefully, through discussion and negotiation, rather than violence. Dewey's most detailed discussion of democracy as a form of associated living is found in Chapter 7 of *Democracy and Education* (MW9: 88f). In this chapter, he both analyses the concept of democracy and explains the moral value of the democratic way of life.

Dewey begins by explaining that any modern society, democratic or otherwise, is in concrete reality a collection of many interrelated groups, and thus a society is a kind of complex super group, with individuals belonging to various overlapping sub-groups – economic, political, religious, and cultural. He asks what the standard of value for any group is, and answers that in any group we will find some common interests – for otherwise what would hold the group together – and interactions with other groups (MW 9: 88–89). We then can thus evaluate any group along two dimensions: how numerous and varied are the interests shared by members; and how full and free are the interactions of the group with other groups.

He then provides two examples, and evaluates them to demonstrate his point. In a criminal band, the members share only a single interest – in plunder. This narrow interest in turn limits its free exchange with other groups – they cannot let their potential victims know about the one thing that holds them together. The criminal band is thus an impoverished form of group life. A healthy family, on the other hand, shares many mutual interests – in health, economic and cultural development and more. And the progress of any member in advancing these interests is felt as valuable by all of the others. Their lives bring them into contact with many other groups and organizations – economic, cultural, educational, and political; they actively support these groups which, in turn, support them in achieving their shared aims.

Dewey then moves from these examples of well-contained groups to modern societies. In a non-democratic society some groups have inordinate power and use it to dominate other groups for their own narrow aims. The ruling class sends directives to those in subordinate groups but has no interest in taking their thoughts and feelings into account, so there is no communication. The lack of equitable intercourse limits the growth of both classes, because diversity of stimulation creates novelty and provokes thinking. Both groups remain stagnant, ignorant, fearful, and antagonistic.

What, then, is a *democratic* society. Dewey says that the two criteria of social value, taken together, "point to democracy." They do not, however, sufficiently *define* it, a fact which has sometimes been neglected. I will shortly turn to the significance of this neglect.

Democratic society is precisely characterized by two features: First, in a democratic society, not only are there numerous and varied shared interests,

DEMOCRATIC SELF-CULTIVATION 201

but also greater reliance on the *recognition of these shared interests as a factor in social control.* That is, the shared *experiences* of mutual interest and cooperative activity by themselves are not sufficient; members also have consciously to *recognise* mutuality as a factor in sustaining and enhancing group life; they must *consciously* engage in both self-direction and social influence by explicit reference to the ends of others beyond their immediate circle of family and friends, and must have *self-consciousness* of doing so.

Second, not only do groups interact freely and fully, but there must also be a consequent *change in social habit* – the *continuous readjustment* of both individuals and groups as they meet new situations produced by their ever-increasing variety of social contacts. This requires a self-conscious, even loving, *embrace* of new challenges and the behavioral changes required to meet them (LW11, 549–561).

Democracy thus understood requires specific educational arrangements. The interests of members are mutually interpenetrating, and all share an interest in continual re-adjustment under changing conditions. As they seek to be self-governing, and reject external authority, they must find a substitute in voluntary disposition – self-government through communication and mutual concern. These dispositions are not "natural" even though they have roots in deep human instincts. They need to be developed through an education of a specific sort – one based on *shared activities* requiring *communication and cooperative action.* Even more important, as in a modern society citizens have to communicate over large distances and across many differences to refer their own actions to those of others, they must actively cooperate in breaking down all barriers and obstacles of race, class, ethnicity and gender that keep individuals or groups from perceiving the full impact of the aims and actions of others.

The goal of democratic education at the individual level is to foster the democratic personality (Dewey's *junzi*) – marked by such virtues as intelligent sympathy for those from all social groups and active concern to break down social barriers (MW9: 128); flexibility of re-adjustment to new situations (LW11: 550); and "attitudes of open- mindedness, intellectual integrity, observation and interest in testing opinions and beliefs that are characteristic of the scientific attitude" (LW9: 100).

5   Dewey's Curriculum

For Dewey, every course in every subject should have as its chief end the cultivation of democratic personality (LW9: 100). Knowledge in all fields – from history, literature, and science to mathematics – originated in human efforts to solve problems and enhance life. Each field makes a unique contribution to moral development (MW 4: 206–214). The arts, for example, provide vivid, intense models of consummatory value. History and geography provide records of human attempts to meet ends in concrete natural and social circumstances and hence are rich with lessons for effective action.

All intellectual learning, at all levels, should thus begin in cooperative endeavors with shared ends that call out for knowledge inputs. As Dewey puts this in his most concentrated summary:

(a) "Every educative process should begin with *doing something* ... something inherently significant, and of such a nature that the pupil appreciates for himself its importance enough to take a vital interest in it" (MW 4: 186). In a surprisingly dogmatic tone, he adds that "All intellectual instruction would grow – *all of it* – out of the needs and opportunities of activities engaged in by the students themselves. This principle would be *universal*" (MW 4: 188, emphasis added).

(b) These activities in turn inevitably call out for communicated knowledge inputs, which must:
cluster about the development of activities. Some information is immediately required in order to do anything successfully; a child cannot garden intelligently without learning about soils, seeds, measures, plants and their growth, the facts of rain, sunshine, etc. Interest in the continuous carrying on of such an activity would, however, generate curiosity and openness of mind about many things not directly related to the immediate needs. (MW 4: 189)

When teachers share information or direct students to written materials, it is only educative to the extent that it grows naturally out of questions the students are raising, and fits into their own frames of experience to increase their practical efficacy in, and deepen their grasp of, practical situations out of which it grows (MW 9: 195).

(c) The communicative exchanges should culminate in presentation of organized, systematic knowledge, of the sort drawn upon by adult professionals in their occupations. This knowledge should be scientific – that is, grounded in experience and held as tentative and subject to further test and modification. Because it has a firm rational basis grounded in prior experience, it can be used to enrich subsequent cooperative activities. It is taken on board for use. "What is known, in a given case, is what is sure, certain, settled, disposed of; that which we think with rather than that which we think about" (MW 9: 197). This organized subject matter knowledge then serves as the intellectual ground in further practical activities. It is settled, but not certain – it is thus always, at least indirectly, subject to test in subsequent experience.

For Dewey, subject matters should never be isolated in separate disciplines (science, mathematics, literature) but always coordinated around human problems and their cooperative resolution (MW 7: 114–128; MW 9: 259). This is especially true for literary study, which marks Dewey's approach in stark contrast with Confucian self-cultivation education. Indeed, a central plank of Dewey's "Pedagogic Creed" is that literary study must follow upon, not precede, human problems in curricular learning (EW 5: 90). This reverses the order in the Confucian curriculum.[3]

A striking example is Dewey's discussion of the uses of Defoe's *Robinson Crusoe* in primary education. Because, he says, American colonial history and Defoe's novel address the same problem – the man who, having first "achieved civilization" is "suddenly thrown back upon his own resources" – the work should not be studied in isolation as literature, but used "as an imaginative idealization" of a type of problem (MW 1: 107) in coordination with other subject matters. Works of imaginative literature should not be studied as such, and in isolation, but should always be brought into the curriculum alongside of, and in interaction with, the literatures of other scientific, artistic, commercial and industrial fields bearing upon human problems (MW 9: 259).

5.1 Democratic Self-Cultivation

At first glance, Deweyan democratic education excludes both special study of literary classics and repetitive rituals. Self-cultivation through classical study, for Dewey, has "usually been futile, with something rotten about it" (MW 9: 130), producing "only a feebly pretentious snobbishness of culture" (MW 10: 182). Customary rituals, by the same token, he says, are akin to irrational magic spells and charms. Rather than breathing meaning into natural human relations, such rituals obscure the values inherent in human relations and block inquiries to enhance these values (LW 9: 48–49).

Dewey would further reject Confucian rituals as anti-democratic, not only because they assign unequal roles to those in subordinate positions, but because these roles – which symbolize the roles obtaining in actual social life – are not self-chosen and self-shaped through personal initiative and effort of their occupants, but imposed upon them (EW 1: 244).

Nonetheless, as I will now argue, both reverential study of classics and repetitive rituals – akin to those in Confucian self-cultivation – can enhance the Deweyan democratic education project.

5.2 Study of Democratic Classics

The present crisis of democracy in the West demonstrates that our established educational practices have failed broadly to inculcate democratic values. Today we see citizens in the liberal democracies of the West fall prey to populist demagogues preaching division. Leaders attack the free press that exposes their corruption and anti-democratic conduct as "fake news," and their devotees enthusiastically embrace propaganda. Writing in *Freedom and Culture* (1939) during the rise of fascism in the West, Dewey warned that we see "supposedly free institutions in many countries not so much overthrown as abandoned willingly, apparently with enthusiasm" (LW 7:67). He forewarned that the conventional schooling practices in modern democracies could not protect us, because while political and educational leaders *preach* rational discussion and scientific method, they in fact rely upon arbitrary dictate:

> In homes and in schools, the places where the essentials of character are supposed to be formed, the usual l procedure is settlement of issues, intellectual and moral, by appeal to the "authority" of parent, teacher, or textbook. Dispositions formed under such conditions are so inconsistent with the democratic method that in a crisis they may be aroused to act in positively anti-democratic ways for anti-democratic ends. (LW 13: 155)

Dewey's democratic alternative – starting with habitual participation in cooperative activities at school – might be expected to engender a larger range of mutual interests, greater exchange among groups. In his approach, democratic values would develop gradually, incidental to experiences of shared interests and inter-group cooperation in activities increasingly enriched by discipline-based knowledge.

All of this is fine as far as it goes. But what about the conscious recognition of mutuality as a factor in social control? What about the conscious recognition of continual readjustment in the face of changing circumstances, and the conscious adoption of scientific reason to generate and test the value of proposed changes? These are necessary conditions for democratic living. Democratic values are *paramount for Dewey*. We must, he says, "use education to promote our national idea – which is the idea of democracy" (MW 10: 210–11); "The necessity for a frame of reference (for education) must be admitted.

DEMOCRATIC SELF-CULTIVATION

There exists in this country such a unified frame. It is called democracy" (LW11: 416). Or as he states "Upon one thing we take our stand. We frankly accept the democratic tradition in its moral and human import. That is our premise ..." (LW8: 77).

Dewey, nonetheless, does not make specific space in his normative curriculum sequence (see, for example, MW 4: 179–192; MW9: 189–202) for *conscious reflection on* the democratic tradition and democratic values, grounded in the canonical democratic texts. When the knowledge inputs called forth in practical activities are eventually presented in organized scientific form, it is the science content, not knowledge of democratic classics, that is organized for further use. For example, after a cooperative garden project, soil chemistry – not cooperation – is studied systematically.

So the question remains: why not illuminate the democratic frame of reference itself? Why not give democratic values pride of place in the curriculum? A special site for reading and reflection on democratic classics with peers – adjusted for different nations and regions – can bring democratic values to the fore and thus deepen democratic learning. Like Confucian self-cultivation, democratic self- cultivation can thus be a school of experience; it can establish continuity between the leaders who forged these values, in the crucible of democratic struggle, and today's youth. It can provide a larger view and promote greater flexibility and responsiveness in behavior – hallmarks of democratic personality. Even if we wished, we could never achieve such results through indoctrination. In democratic self-cultivation, as in Confucian self-cultivation, the students will have to do the heavy lifting, taking the lessons on board and making them their own. That is what makes it "*self*-cultivation." Democratic self-cultivation is simply, in Dewey's words, the opportunity for "deeper loyalty to intelligence, pure and undefiled, and to the intrinsic connection between it and free communication: the method of conference, consultation, discussion" pooling the net results of experience (LW14: 277).

In the United States, such classics might include – George Washington's farewell address, Madison's Federalist #10, the Emancipation Proclamation, the Seneca Falls Declaration, Frederick Douglass' "What to the Slave Is the Fourth of July?", selections from Whitman's poetry and *Democratic Vistas*, Emma Lazarus's "The New Colossus," Dewey's "Creative Democracy: The Task Before Us," Woody Guthrie's "This Land is Your Land" – all selected and edited for students at different levels.

In this light, we should note that Dewey himself urged, in his essay "Presenting Thomas Jefferson" (LW 14: 202–224) that we should be "amazed, as well as grateful, at the spectacle of the intellectual and moral calibre of the men who took a hand in shaping the American political tradition" (LW 14: 204). He calls out Washington, Jefferson, Hamilton, Madison, Franklin, John Adams and Monroe as "giants." Nothing, he says, should "create indifference to what they contributed to American institutions and to what we still may learn from them" (LW 14: 204). And given his other portraits, we know he would add Emerson, Horace Mann, Whitman, Jane Addams, and others to this list of giants.

This leaves open the question of just how school students should be introduced to them. Here it is necessary to recall and reconsider Dewey's concerns about studying literary documents in isolation from concrete human problems. He insists that communicated subject matters must be "organized into the existing experiences of the learners" (MW9: 196–197). Fair enough. But in considering the core democratic canonical texts I would argue that we have no need to *combine* the texts with *new* activities. School students are surrounded daily by experiences which resonate with such texts: Are students from early ages not familiar with factions (Federalist 10)? Or Immigrant experiences (Lazarus)? Or unequal treatment of minorities or females (Douglas, Seneca Falls)? Even from the earliest grade levels, students – especially those in multi-class, multi-ethnic schools – encounter barriers to the formation of shared interests and inter-group communication and cooperation. It is an important plank in the democratic education tradition that such experiences be taken up as school subject matters and augmented with further reading and reflection, and a well-selected democratic canon provides the key reference points.

Despite Dewey's frequent insistence that intellectual learning should *always* begin with cooperative activities, in a noteworthy passage in "The Way out of Educational Confusion" (LW 6: 76–90) he offers (somewhat begrudgingly) an alternative approach in line with the program of Democratic self-cultivation.

Dewey begins the passage with a sharp defense of project-based and problem based learning and the activity curriculum, making it clear that the educational values of cooperative problem-solving activities are found not only in primary education, but also in the high school and college (LW 6: 86–89).

But then, contradicting his earlier statement that all intellectual learning must *always* begin with cooperative activity (MW 4:188f), he says that he "does not urge" the project based on problem based activity "as the sole way out of educational confusion, not even in the elementary school." Rather, he says, it is possible (if second best) to include great works in a multi-disciplinary curriculum which merely "takes account of interdependencies of knowledge and connection of knowledge with use and application." Using as an example the works of H.G. Wells on the sciences of life, he says that these great works "cut across all conventional divisions in the field: yet not at the expense of scientific accuracy but in a way which increases both intellectual curiosity and understanding, while disclosing the world about us as a perennial source of esthetic delight"(LW 6: 88–89).

DEMOCRATIC SELF-CULTIVATION

To be clear, it is the works themselves that increase understanding, intellectual curiosity and delight. Cooperative problem and project-based activities, while for Dewey arguably the *best* pathways into subject matter knowledge, are, by 1931, no longer *necessary* even for Dewey himself.

5.3 *Democratic Rituals*

Schooling is filled with customary rituals. Lining up outside the building, filing in under tight control and taking an assigned seat – what is this but a ritual that establishes a specific place in a social order? Or consider school football, where alpha-males struggle for the glory of the school while females – selected for beauty and sexual allure – cheer them on, broadcasting toxic messages about gender roles and ideals (Jane, 2017; Macur, 2018; Fortin, 2019).

Not all rituals, however, are customary; new rituals can be invented. While customary rituals like football cheerleading look backward to values we now on reflection might reject, new rituals can look forward to a world of democratic social relationships we hope to build. Originating in the Ivy League around 1880, football cheerleading was an exclusively male activity until 1920, with female squads dominating only after 1950. The cheerleading ritual can be modified in a democratic direction – e.g., with male cheerleaders for female teams – or replaced by new rituals better symbolizing democratic values. Or consider the ritual established by fifth grade teacher Barry White Jr. of Ashley Park Elementary School in Charlotte, North Carolina; rather than lining his students up outside the building, he greets all students by name with a convivial handshake every day as they enter class while they are cheered on by all the students already present (Good Morning America, 2017).

Dewey was an unapologetic critic of customary rituals. Nonetheless, he strongly endorsed the establishment of religious and quasi-religious rituals representing and reinforcing the values actually to be found in natural human relations through social inquiry (LW9: 55). And his followers should welcome them in schools. This point is argued in detail by Nikkanen & Westerlund (2017). Drawing on the work of Christoph Wulf et al. (2010), they argue that "it is through rituals that a school reveals its core values ... (including) how the school sees the student." Ultimately:

> school rituals are expressions of emotions and relationships that tend to create a community by using playful elements ... through rituals children and young adults learn which values and modes of behavior are important for both the school and society. (117)

The authors consider a Finland middle school that changed the selection process for roles in the annual Christmas play. Instead of selecting on the basis of physical appearance and talent, they adopted ritual inclusion of all students, including those with disabilities, in valued roles (here, remember the cheerleading example above).

Acknowledging that such individual ritual performances can at first glance be downplayed as insignificant, the authors argue that, on the contrary, they require careful planning and practice over time, and thus can impact the entire structure and content of the music and arts curriculum. Thus targeted rituals can eventuate in intentional change in the values consciously and demonstratively embraced by the school (Nikkanen & Westerlund, 2017: 122).

Educators working in the spirit of Dewey should be following such examples and devising new democratic rituals exemplifying respected, satisfying, equal and self-determined roles for all students. Combined with music, dance, drama, and other creative and performing arts, these ritual performances can be joyful occasions fostering democratic values.

6 Concluding Comment

This paper challenges the supposition that democratic education along Deweyan lines leaves no place for either reverential study of literary classics or ritual performance. It also proposes two further projects for democratic education: (i) the preparation of *Classics of Democracy* in forms suitable for school learners at various grade levels, and (ii) the investigation, modification, or replacement of anti-democratic school rituals and the invention of new, consciously conceived democratic school rituals that can be tested and modified through inquiry and carried on with great joy by students.

Acknowledgment

This chapter is a reprint from: WAKS, Leonard J. (2019). Democratic self-cultivation. *Beijing International Review of Education, 1*(4), 626–644.

Notes

1 All references to the *Analects* are drawn from Eno (2015). I retain the standard chapter and paragraph number citations, so that e.g., (3.14) refers to chapter 3, paragraph 14.

2 All citations to the works of Dewey in the text and bibliography are from *The Collected Works of John Dewey*, 1882–1953, ed. by Jo Ann Boydston (Carbondale and Edwardsville: Southern Illinois University Press, 1967–1991), published in three series as *The Early Works* (EW), *The*

DEMOCRATIC SELF-CULTIVATION

Middle Works (MW) and *The Later Works* (LW). These designations are followed by volume and page number. In the bibliography I also include the original year of publication.

3   An exception is found in the educational theory of Wang Yangming (1472–1529). Wang, the leading Ming dynasty philosopher and leader of the 'school of heart' (also called the 'school of mind') opposed the view of both Confucius and the Song dynasty philosopher Zhu Xi (1130–1200), founder of the 'school of principle, or 'rationalist school.' For Zhu Xi, as for Confucius, investigating the classic works was the *preliminary stepping stone* to action as a wise person. Wang, like Dewey, conceived on the contrary that thought and knowledge grew directly out of action situations, and that thought and action were always discrete facets of one complex action-thought-action complex. As Wang put this, "If you want to know bitterness, you have to eat a bitter melon yourself" (Kim, Y., n.d.).

References

Allen, B. (2017, December). *Pragmatism and Confucian empiricism* [Proceedings]. Fudan University [会议 | "实用主义与儒学思想" 国际学术研讨会会议日程]. http://deweycenterchina.org/nd.jsp?id=57

Bai, H., Eppert, C., Scott, C, Tait, S., & Nguyen, T. (2014). Towards intercultural philosophy of education. *Studies in Philosophy of Education.* http://citeseerx.ist.psu.edu/viewdoc/download?doi=10.1.1.1029.7709&rep=rep1&type=pd

Brooks, T. (2013). Philosophy unbound: The idea of global philosophy. *Metaphilosophy,* *44*(13), 254–266.

Communist Party of China. (1981). Resolution on certain questions in the history of our party since the founding of the People's Republic of China, Adopted by the Sixth Plenary Session of the Eleventh Central Committee on June 27, 1981.

Dewey, J. (1888). The Ethics of Democracy, EW 1: 228–250.

Dewey, J. (1899). The School and Society, MW 1: 1–92.

Dewey, J. (1900). The Aim Of History In Elementary Education, MW 1: 106–110.

Dewey, J. (1908–1909). The Bearing of Pragmatism upon Education, MW 4: 179–192.

Dewey, J. (1909). The Moral Significance Of The Common School Studies, MW 4: 206–214.

Dewey, J. (1916). Democracy and Education, MW 9.

Dewey, J. (1916). Our Educational Ideal In Wartime, MW 10: 182.

Dewey, J. (1916). Nationalizing Education, MW 10: 210–11.

Dewey, J. (1931). The Way Out of Educational Confusion, LW 6: 76–90.

Dewey, J. (1934). A Common Faith, LW 9: 4–59.

Dewey, J. (1933). The Supreme Intellectual Obligation, LW 9: 97–102.

Dewey, J. (1937). Education and Social Change, LW 11: 409–418.

Dewey, J. (1940). Presenting Thomas Jefferson, LW 14: 202–224.

Dewey, J. (1941). The Basic Values and Loyalties of Democracy, LW14: 277.

Dewey, J. (1937). Boyd H. Bode, William Heard Kilpatrick, An Active Flexible Personality, LW11: 549–561.

Elliot, J., & Tsai, C. t. (2008). What might confucius have to say about action research? *Educational Action Research, 16*, 569–578.

Eno, R. (1989). *Confucian creation of Heaven, The: Philosophy and the defense of ritual mastery.* SUNY Press.

Eno, R. (2015). *The analects of Confucius: An online teaching translation.* Version 2,21. http://www.indiana.edu/~p374/Analects_of_Confucius_(Eno-2015).pdf

Fortin, J. (2019, March 28). Wisconsin school Bans Mock cheerleading awards after aarassment accusations. *New York Times.* https://www.nytimes.com/2019/03/28/sports/wisconsin-cheerleaders-body-shaming-banned.html

Goldin, P. R. (Ed.). (2017). *A concise companion to Confucius.* Wiley Blackwell.

Good Morning America. (2017). *Teacher has personalized handshakes with every single one of his students.* https://www.youtube.com/watch?v=IojgcyfC2r8&fbclid=IwAR2LmsYZNHC_w8882sf5K8idsz500QngxZLr4RKa_cYkdwpMXHmDdtW-W2Q

Hall, D., & Ames, R. (1998). *Thinking from the Han.* State University of New York Press.

Hall, D., & Ames, R. (1999). *The democracy of the dead: Dewey, Confucius, and the hope for democracy in China.* Open Court.

Ivanhoe, P. J. (2000). *Confucian moral self cultivation.* Hackett Publishing Company.

Jane, E. A. (2017). Is Debbie Does Dallas dangerous? Representations of cheerleading in pornography and some possible effects. *Feminist Media Studies, 17*(2), 264–280.

Ji, Z. (2008). Educating through music from an "initiation into classical music" for children to Confucian "self-cultivation" for university students. *China Perspectives, 3*, 107–117.

Kim, S. (2014). *Confucian democracy in East Asia: Theory and practice.* Cambridge University Press.

Kim, Y. (n.d.). *Wang Yangming, Internet encyclopedia of philosophy.* https://www.iep.utm.edu/wangyang/

Littlejohn, R. (n.d.). Comparative philosophy. *Internet Encyclopedia of Philosophy.* https://www.iep.utm.edu/comparat/

Liu, J. (2014). Art and aesthetics of music in classical Confucianism. In V. Shen (Ed.), *Dao Companion to classical Confucian philosophy.* Dao Companions to Chinese Philosophy, Book 3, Springer.

Macur, J. (2018, May 2). Washington redskins cheerleaders describe topless photo shoot and uneasy night out. *New York Times.* https://www.nytimes.com/2018/05/02/sports/redskins-cheerleaders-nfl.html?action=click&module=RelatedCoverage&pgtype=Article&region=Footer

Nikkanen, H. M., & Westerlund, H. (2017). More than just music: Reconsidering the educational value of music in school rituals. *Philosophy of Music Education Review, 25*(2), 112–127.

Olberding, A. (2013). *Moral exemplars in the analects: The good person is that!* Routledge.

Park, J.-B. (2019). School rituals and their educational significance in the Joseon period – Rituals as one of the pedagogical pillars of Confucian school education. *Educational Philosophy and Theory, 51*(9), 949–957.

Pines, Y. (2017). Confucius' elitism: The concepts of junzi and xiaoren revisited. In P. R. Goldin (Ed.), *A concise companion to Confucius* (p. 164). Wiley Blackwell.

Rapoza, K. (2019, January 9). Democracies in crisis: Has the west given up on democracy? *Forbes.* https://www.forbes.com/sites/kenrapoza/2019/01/09/democracies-in-crisis-has-the-west-given-up-on-democracy/#172b6f221242

Shun, K.-l. (2017). Le in the Analects Goldin, ed. *A Concise Companion to Confucius,* 133.

Tan, C. (2017). Confucianism and education. In G. Noblit (Ed.), *Oxford research encyclopedia of education* (pp. 1–18). Oxford University Press. https://www.researchgate.net/publication/326412668_Confucianism_and_Education

Tan, S.-H. (2004). *Confucian democracy – A Deweyan reconstruction of Confucianism.* State University of New York Press.

Tan, S.-H. (2007). Confucian democracy as pragmatic experiment: Uniting love of learning and love of antiquity. *Asian Philosophy, 17*(2), 141–166.

Wulf, et al. (2010). *Ritual and identity: The staging and performing of rituals in the lives of young people.* Tufnell Press.

Yi, X. (2017). Understanding curriculum based on the study of Chinese "Gu Qin". *International Journal of Music Education, 35*(3), 403–413.

CHAPTER 11

John Dewey and Early Confucianism on the Idea of Self-Cultivation

ZHANG Huajun

Abstract

As many scholars have already argued, although Dewey spent more than two years in China from 1919 to 1921 and executed tremendous influence on Chinese social movements in the early 20th century, Dewey's thought was mis-received, to a great extent, by focusing on his idea of "the scientific method." By carefully reviewing Dewey's philosophy of experience in his later works, mainly his books *Experience and Nature* (1925) and *Art as Experience* (1934), I argue that Dewey's philosophy of experience is about the development of individuality. By realizing the potential values and meanings in experience, the individual creates an inclusive and transactive relationship with the world. This understanding of experience can be connected to the tradition of early Confucianism on the idea of self-cultivation, which is a creative and dynamic process of interaction between the individual and the world. Thus, I suggest that emphasizing Dewey's philosophy of experience in his later works provides a new vision for Dewey's reception in contemporary Chinese scholarship. Also, the dialogue between Dewey and early Confucian thoughts on the idea of self-cultivation creates new space for the development of individuality through educational interventions in the context of global conflicts.

Keywords

Dewey's reception and mis-reception in China – John Dewey – Early Confucianism – self-cultivation

•••

The American philosopher John Dewey (1859–1952) is considered a very important and influential figure in China's modernization, not only in the field of education but also in more general areas of social sciences. Even though Dewey has been hotly studied in China in the first decades of the twentieth century and after the 1980s until now, there is still more space for the discussion on Dewey's reception in China. In the previous reception of Dewey's thought, his idea of the scientific method of thinking is his most well-known, which may bring some misunderstanding of Dewey's thought and lead people to narrowly categorize him as only a philosopher of logic. In recent years, more domestic and international scholars have noticed Dewey's connection to Confucian thoughts (Hall & Ames, 1999; Ames, 2003; Grange, 2004; Tan, 2012; Zhang, 2013; Yang, 2016; Waks, 2019). This is a very important direction of study. The study of self-cultivation in Confucianism, especially early Confucianism, may help us to realize Dewey's thought on the development of individuality as an essential concern. It then can draw the attention of Chinese scholars to seriously study Dewey's philosophy of experience, which was richly developed in his later works. This perspective will contribute to a better understanding of Dewey's idea of self-cultivation for individual development. Without this perspective, the study and application of Dewey's philosophy in social studies, and especially in the field of education, might be misleading in Chinese scholarship.

In this chapter, I will first briefly review Dewey's (mis-)reception in China in the past century. Then, I will closely study Dewey's philosophy of experience in his later works and how it relates to the idea of self-cultivation. Furthermore, I will discuss the idea of self-cultivation in early Confucianism by reviewing some of Confucius's dialogues and quotations in *Analects* and *Zhongyong*. I conclude that both Dewey and Confucius emphasize immediate sensibility to others by focusing on the familiar affairs in daily life for an inclusive, creative, and dynamic process of self-cultivation. In the practice of education, it is important to promote sensibility and awareness to others in the development of individuality.

1 Dewey's Reception and Mis-Reception in China

1.1 Dewey's Initial Reception in the 1920s and 1930s
It is a historical event that Dewey visited China in 1919 just a few days before the May Fourth Movement. He and his wife Alice Dewey spent more than two years in China and delivered thousands of lectures and speeches in different cities. With the efforts of his eminent and influential Chinese disciples, the most famous of which being Hu Shi (1891–1962) and Tao Xingzhi (1891–1946), Dewey executed tremendous influence on China's educational modernization.[1] In this book, Su Zhixin (2019) specifically discussed Dewey's reception in China in different periods in the past hundred years. Also, Liu Xing (2019)

took a historical study on Dewey's role in establishing the Department of Education at Beijing Normal University, the first educational department in Chinese universities. However, more contemporary scholars argue that Dewey was mis-interpreted or mis-received in the 1920s and 1930s for various reasons. In this book, Zhao Kang (2019) explains why Hu Shi only introduced Dewey's philosophy as a method, focusing mainly on the 1920s. Lei Wang (2019) points out three misunderstandings on Dewey's philosophy in the Chinese reception of his thought in the early half of the twentieth century.

1.2 *Deweyan Studies in Contemporary China after the 1980s*

The enthusiastic reception of Dewey's philosophy did not last long and was replaced by an enthusiasm for Marxism in the 1930s with the rising of the Communist Party. During the period of 1949–1976, Dewey's philosophy was completely rejected in mainland China for ideological and political reasons. However, after China initiated the open-and-reform policy after 1978, Dewey was once again acclaimed and recognized as an important western thinker. Dewey's philosophy acquired renewed value among scholars from different disciplines and was re-introduced to Chinese audiences. It is conceivable that scholars and students in the field of education may be the most appreciative members of Dewey's readership.[2]

Dewey's philosophy was well received and applied not only in the field of education but also in other fields of humanities and social sciences. For example, in the field of philosophy, Dewey's complete collection of work was translated and published in Chinese in the first years of the 2010s with the leadership of the Chinese contemporary philosopher Liu Fangtong. Dewey's philosophy was the subject of comparative studies regarding Marxism and Confucianism, the two mainstream thoughts in contemporary China (Liu, 2014; Chen, 2015). But in the disciplines of social sciences, Dewey's pragmatism was still considered a way of scientific thinking that focused more on the logic of hypothesis-testing-conclusion (Qu, 2021). The misunderstanding of Dewey in the social sciences was echoed in Hu Shi's deliberate efforts to introduce Dewey's philosophy only as a method in the 1920s.

1.3 *New Understandings on Dewey in Contemporary Chinese Scholarship*

Though the misunderstanding of Dewey still endures in contemporary Chinese academia, new understandings are emerging. For example, the Confucian scholar Liang Shuming's review of Dewey's *Democracy and Education* in 1934 is recognized and highlighted by some contemporary scholars (Gu, 2010; Zhang, 2013). Gu (2010) suggested that Liang shared some important commonalities with Dewey on the philosophy of life. Both Dewey and Liang agree that the meaning of life is endless growth, which requires the individual's efforts to realize the potentiality for building more connections with the world that the individual is in. Also, Dewey's later works are discussed more, especially those regarding his theory of aesthetic experience (Chen, 2019). Because Dewey's later works were largely ignored in Chinese scholarship, it is important to highlight Dewey's thoughts in his later works; for example, in *Experience and Nature* (EN) and *Art as Experience* (AE), his concept of experience was significantly developed.

In the following section, I will review Dewey's concept of experience mainly from EN and AE. I will highlight the process of the development of *an experience* and how the development of an experience relates to the development of individuality. By doing so, I suggest that Dewey's concept of experience could connect to the thoughts of early Confucianism on the idea of self-cultivation.

2 Dewey's Thoughts of Experience and Individuality in His Later Works[3]

Dewey's philosophy of experience in his later works, especially in AE, kept consistency with his earlier works (Miedema, 1994–1995). However, in AE, Dewey made significant efforts to provide his richest and most complete concept of experience (Alexander, 1987: 183). Alexander (1987: 184) urged readers to take AE not as a book on aesthetics *per se* but as the one through which to understand the core idea of Dewey's philosophy. The understanding of Dewey's concept of experience in his later works helps readers to avoid the common misunderstanding of Dewey, which is the categorization of his thought as mechanical intelligence or the rigid scientific method. Also, the idea of experience Dewey developed in his later works, first in EN and then in AE and *A Common Faith* (1934), was a strong response to the critique that Dewey was ignorant on the religious aspect of human being (Wieman, 1925).

In a short essay titled "I believe" written in 1939, Dewey said, "I should now wish to emphasize more than I formerly did that individuals are the finally decisive factors of the nature and movement of associated life" (LW 14: 91). Dewey realized that it was individual minds (LW 1: 169), not institutionalized organizations, that best guarantee a democratic society. We may consider that it is Dewey's motivation to develop the concept of experience in a more sophisticated way in his later works.

In the following section, I will review the idea of experience Dewey developed in his later works. I try to highlight the dynamic process of the development of an experience, which was not sufficiently discussed in Chinese contemporary scholarship on Deweyan studies. So, the intention is to close the gap between Dewey's philosophy and the understanding of his thought in Chinese contemporary context. This effort may provide some potential possibilities for a fruitful conversation between Dewey and Confucianism.

I will first briefly point out that the disruption of experience is the preparation for the evolving of an experience. Dewey did not ignore this reality that life is full of disruption and that we live in a disrupted world. Instead, Dewey's major concern is how to overcome the disruption by revealing the potential reality in the experience. Therefore, he emphasizes that an experience is a flow, that it overcomes the disruption and reaches continuity. We not only need the methods of intelligence to reach the continuity, but we also need imagination, the immediate experience in the present moment, to build the connection between old and new experience. I show that Dewey's concept of experience emphasizes self-cultivation for an inclusive idea of individuality.

2.1 *The Disruption of Experience and the Efforts of the Individual for Connection*

Dewey was often criticized for his optimism by focusing on the continuity and interaction of experience in the environment. He was often blamed for ignoring the discontinuity and non-interaction of experience as the real situation of existence of many people. However, if we read AE or some other later works by Dewey, it is obviously a misunderstanding of his philosophy. He had a full sense of the tragedy of human life. His care of the qualitative living situation of individual beings is the motive of his thought. In the first chapter of AE titled "The Live Creature," he points out that an energetic life is "the moment of passage from disturbance into harmony" (LW 10: 22), and the process of living is "one that brings with its potency of new adjustments to be made through struggle" (LW 10: 23). The recognition of the split "between their present living and their past and future" (LW 10: 23) became the initial motivation for Dewey's philosophy of experience. In his intellectual biographical essay "From Absolutism to Experimentalism," Dewey reflected that his conflicted mind when he was young was something that everyone might experience. The deep concern of realizing the vital sense of life permeated through his long life of intellectual adventure (LW 5: 147–160).

Here, we have to recognize two different aspects of experience: one is we generally take, and the other is Dewey deliberately develops. We often take any events we experience as "experience" even though that "experience" may not bring new understandings and new connections from the past experience. That "experience" might be chaotic and disrupted, which could not lead to the heightened vitality of life (LW 10: 25). On the one hand, Dewey considers this kind of experience as conditions of human existence; on the other hand, he considers that this experience is the one that needs to be transformed into "an experience." "Having an experience" was what Dewey emphasized in AE.

Different from the general understanding of experience, *an experience* overcomes the interruption or disruption that one experiences and achieves continuity in the active interaction with the environment. Dewey said, "Because of continuous merging, there are no holes, mechanical junctions, and dead centers when we have *an* experience. There are pauses, places of rest, but they punctuate and define the quality of movement" (LW 10: 43). In other words, the energy of the individual is re-organized so it is moved with some pace and rhythm, and it will conclude when it reaches the consummation of the movement. An experience "is a whole and carries with it its own individualizing quality and self-sufficiency" (LW 10: 42). When the energy is not re-organized and works for the harmonious movement, it is not forming an experience. Dewey thus said that "the enemies of the esthetic are neither the practical nor the intellectual. They are the humdrum; slackness of loose ends; submission to convention in practice and intellectual procedure. Rigid abstinence, coerced submission, tightness on one side and dissipation, incoherence and aimless indulgence on the other, are deviations in opposite directions from the unity of an experience" (LW 10: 47).

In Dewey's idea of an experience, he is fully aware of the tragic condition of human existence, but he suggests the direction for human efforts to work on the disruption and to reach the continuity when the individual interacts with the environment. Therefore, the emphasis in Dewey's philosophy of experience is how to reach the continuity in the environment. This is also the realization of potentiality in reality.

2.2 *The Realization of Potentiality in Reality*

In EN, Dewey distinguishes two aspects of reality. One aspect of reality is the reality recognized and explicitly explained with the empirical methods. In this knowledge of reality, "the vague and unrevealed is a limitation" and "the obscure and vague are explained away" (LW 1: 27). However, Dewey argues that the reality of nature extends much further than the knowledge of reality. He reminds that "in any object of primary experience there are always potentialities which are not explicit; any object that is overt is charged with possible consequences that are hidden; the most overt act has factors which are not explicit" (LW 1: 28). Dewey further claims that the trait of experience is always "the visible is set in the invisible; and in the end what is unseen decides what happens in the seen; the tangible rests precariously upon the untouched and un-grasped. The contrast and the potential maladjustment of the immediate, the conspicuous and focal phase of things, with those indirect and hidden factors which determine the origin and career of what is present, are indestructible features of any and every experience" (LW 1: 44).

The highlight on potentiality as the reality waiting for further realization provides new space for the individual to build connections in the interaction with the environment. This new space is the space to connect the ideal with the reality. In other words, the ideal is not something outside of the reality but is the potentiality hidden *in* the reality. In AE, Dewey suggests that an experience is building the active relationship between the doing and the undergoing (LW 10: 50). What is undergoing is often hidden, vague, but with passion, emotion, and impulsion in the making. The philosophy of experience indicates that the world we live in is not the world with certain and final values and meanings. Instead, "there are many meanings and many purposes in the situations with which we are confronted ... Each offers its own challenge to thought and endeavor, and presents its own potential value" (LW 5: 272). Therefore, the evolution of experience means varied possibilities for new meanings and new growth. The joy of constant discovery and of constant growing is possible even in the midst of trouble and defeat (LW 5: 272).

In Dewey's philosophy of experience, the realization of potentiality creates new realities, which is different from the reality of disruption, disconnection, or humdrumness of the human existence. It is possible only when the individual is fully aware of the situation of unsatisfied human existence and is willing to make efforts to create alternative reality with new values and meanings. In other words, Dewey did not simply hold an optimistic position on human being, but he more heavily emphasized the deliberate efforts of the individual to be fully aware of the situation, go through the situation, and creatively find the new meanings in the reality. As Dewey said, "progress is not inevitable, it is up to men as individuals to bring it about" (LW 14: 113). The individual needs to be open to the uncertain and changing situation, and the faith in the hidden potentiality for an alternative reality indicates courage more so than blind optimism. The development of an experience is thus a process of creativity when the individual is fully engaged with the present time in the situation.

2.3   *Creativity in the Present*
As discussed above, to build new connections and create new meanings in reality, the individual must be willing to open the self to the present, which is still unknown and uncertain. In other words, the individual is entering a completely new time and space that is different from the old experience he/she might have had before. In this situation, the self is not only the one he/she

knows and owns based on the past experience, but the self is also unfinished, unrealized, and includes new possibilities waiting to be realized in the present situation. The self-renewal is realized when the deeper meanings of reality are perceived. Through the self-renewal in the present, life grows.

To understand the idea of creativity in the present, we need to clarify the meaning of time in Dewey's philosophy of experience. In the essay "Time and Individuality" (LW 14: 98–114), Dewey clarifies that the time he means is different from the way of measurement of motion in physical space. In physical time, change always happens but will not automatically lead to progress. The idea of time is meaningful only when it relates to the development of individuality, which is a creative process of the individual's interaction with the changing environment. He said,

> Genuine time, if it exists as anything else except the measure of motions in space, is all one with the existence of individuals as individuals, with the creative, with the occurrence of unpredictable novelties. Everything that can be said contrary to this conclusion is but a reminder that an individual may lose his individuality, for individuals become imprisoned in routine and fall to the level of mechanisms. Genuine time then ceases to be an integral element in their being. Our behavior becomes predictable because it is about an external rearrangement of what went before. (LW 14: 112)

In other words, the time of the present is not the repetition of the past but something new when the individual, with his/her own historical biography, enters into the present moment, which is unknown and completely new for the individual. Only when the individual is fully engaged with this present moment can he/she activate and renew the experience. In this present situation, time reaches continuity with the past, the present, and the future. In AE, Dewey said, "Only when the past ceases to trouble and anticipations of the future are not perturbing is a being wholly united with his environment and therefore fully alive. Art celebrates with peculiar intensity the moments in which the past reenforces the present and in which the future is a quickening of what now is" (LW 10: 24).

In Dewey's concept of time, the present situation is filled with creative potential. The understanding of creative individuality in the present is closely related to the understanding of Dewey's primary idea on human existence, which he called "immediacy of existence" (LW 1: 74). He claimed that "in every event there is something obdurate, self-sufficient, wholly immediate, neither a relation nor an element in a relational whole, but terminal and exclusive" (LW 1: 74). He further stated that "things in their immediacy are unknown and unknowable, not because they are remote or behind some impenetrable veil of sensation of ideas, but because knowledge has no concern with them" (LW 1: 74). Of course, Dewey had no intention to imply the mythical idea of experience, but he suggests that knowledge could not equal experience nor replace it: "Immediate things may be *pointed to* by words, but not described or defined" (LW 1: 75). In later chapters of EN, Dewey considers the immediacy of experience as an incommunicable stage preparing us to begin the cognitive mediation:

> There is a peculiar intrinsic privacy and incommunicability attending the preparatory intermediate stage. When an old essence or meaning is in process of dissolution and a new one has not taken shape even as a hypothetical scheme, the intervening existence is too fluid and formless for publication, even to one's self ... This process of flux and ineffability is intrinsic to any thought which is subjective and private. (LW 1: 171)

The immediate experience prepares us for the intermediate stage during which the individual's consciousness is sharpened by being fully engaged with the environment. This stage is also the critical stage for creativity. The religious philosopher Henry Wieman comments on EN and points out the immediate experience as the condition of the radical originality of human life to foster the mystic consciousness that we can also call religion. He said,

> It is the great regenerator, re-newer, and re-constructor of human life because it fosters that experience which provide for the extreme reconstruction of meanings. It revitalizes old meanings with new insight, brings on 'conversion,' and once in a while it lifts human history bodily into new channels. (Wieman, 1925: 536–537)

At this intermediate stage, consciousness is keen and focused on the subject that the individual is engaged with. It might be a very trivial thing – for example, a bee flying in an afternoon classroom – but it would "swell and swell" (LW 1: 236) and become the focus of the students' attention in that classroom. The engaged attention on the bee then becomes the immediate need for some of the students in the classroom.[4] In Dewey's words, "The *immediately* precarious, the point of greatest immediate need, defines the apex of consciousness, its intense or focal mode. And this is the point of *re*-direction, of *re*-adaptation, *re*-organization" (LW 1: 236; original emphasis).

But the immediate experience could not be described in words or other forms even though it has held the embryo of the new experience. Dewey suggests that we thus need imagination to bridge the old experience and the new experience, to provide an image of the immediate experience. Dewey says, "there is always a gap between the here and now of direct interaction and the past interactions whose funded result constitutes the meanings with which we grasp and understand what is now occurring" (LW 10: 276), and "imagination is the only gateway through which these meanings can find their way into a present interaction" (LW 10: 276). Without imagination as a creative digestion of the condensed consciousness in immediate experience, the inertia of habit will override the consciousness of new meanings, and the resulting experience will again become routine and mechanical (LW 10: 276).

However, the focus on immediate experience and imagination as the moment of creativity in the present does not mean that the development of an experience could not be reached with deliberate efforts, nor does it mean that it could only be enlightened by some transcendent power. Instead, Dewey's lifelong effort is to cultivate individuality that could create broadened meanings for the progress of the society. As he says in "Time and Individuality": "While progress is not inevitable, it is up to men as individuals to bring it about. Change is going to occur anyway, and the problem is the control of change in a given direction. The direction, the quality of change, is a matter of individuality" (LW 14: 113).

2.4 Individuality and the Idea of Self-Cultivation

To summarize the process of having an experience, Dewey suggests that the development of individuality is realizing the potentiality of reality as the individual interacts with the environment (LW 10: 286). However, it is important to avoid mechanical interaction where the present moment is only the repetition of the past. The exercise of imagination in immediate experience brings new consciousness and new meanings so that the self is renewed and the energy of life is activated. Therefore, in Dewey's philosophy of experience, the development of individuality or the practice of self-cultivation does not happen secretly inside of one's mind nor in the mechanical interaction with the environment. Instead, it is a creative adaptation to the environment involving the creation of new meanings and knowings in trans-actions such that the world that the individual is engaged in is enlarged and enriched (Garrison, 2001). Dewey says in AE, "The self is created in the creation of objects, a creation that demands active adaption to external materials, including a modification of the self so as to utilize and thereby overcome external necessities by incorporating them in an individual vision and expression" (LW 10: 286–287). This is a process of active interaction of doing and undergoing so that a sophisticated and harmonious relationship between the two is gradually built up by relieving the various tensions of the two.

When Dewey claims that his concern is not the problem of philosophy but "the problem of men" (MW 10: 46), and his faith is in "the potentialities of individuals" (LW 14: 113), he is actually interested in an ethic of self-cultivation, an ethic of caring for the growth of the self (Uffelman, 2011: 320). Also, the idea of self-cultivation highlights that the development of individuality is not ready-made or pre-made but is always in the process of making. It is a continuous effort to overcome the barriers of inertia habits and mechanical repetition of old experience.

The practice of self-cultivation toward the development of individuality means that the sense of individuality is broadened while the individual opens to the larger world and builds various meaningful connections with others who are alien to him/her in the previous experience of the self. Dewey indicates that the sense of wholeness of the individual with the world is "the religious feeling that accompanies intense esthetic perception" (LW 10: 199). In the same chapter, he continued: "We are, as it were, introduced into a world beyond this world which is nevertheless the deeper reality of the world in which we live in our ordinary experience ... This whole is then felt as an expansion of ourselves" (LW 10: 199). In this dynamic relationship process of self-cultivation, the individual breaks through the barriers of an exclusive, closed, and pre-made sense of the reality and creates an inclusive, open, and new space for the mutual interaction of the individual with the world. That is the realization of potentiality in the reality and the creation of new realities. As Dewey claims, individuals are the final decisive factors of the nature and movement of associated life (LW 14: 91). Then, social amelioration is possible.

In the following section, I will review the idea of self-cultivation in Early Confucianism and suggest some connections of Dewey's philosophy of experience with the idea of self-cultivation in early Confucianism. I will mainly use the quotation of Confucius (BC 551–479) in *Analects* and *Zhongyong*, two main Confucian texts before Qin Dynasty (BC 221–AD 207). I refer the idea of self-cultivation only to early Confucianism because the thought of Confucianism develops in two thousand years of Chinese ancient history. The later development of Confucianism is considered to be the various re-interpretations of classic Confucianism set up by Confucius and his disciples before the Qin Dynasty.

3 The Idea of Self-Cultivation in Early Confucianism

It is the Confucian assumption that individuals learn to be human rather than are born human. The meaning of being a human is a moral, aesthetic, and spiritual endeavor. It involves a lifelong commitment and a continuous process of self-education (Tu, 1984). In *Analects,* which is considered the classical text of early Confucianism and reflects the original thoughts of Confucius, starts as below:

> The Master[5] said: "Having studied, to then repeatedly apply what you have learned – is this not a source of pleasure?" (Ames & Rosemont, 1998, 1.1:71)

This paragraph on learning appears as the first paragraph of *Analects.* The word "study/learn" (*xue* 学)[6] is so critical in *Analects* that it appears more than 60 times throughout the text, which only contains 20 thousand words total. It only appears less than the other word "humanness" (*ren* 仁), which appears more than 100 times. The two concepts of *xue* and *ren* in *Analects* compose the simple but powerful idea of Confucius: The individual needs to learn (*xue*) so that he/she becomes human (with humanity, *ren*). Confucius claimed that his lifelong enterprise was simply to learn (*xue*), and he confirmed his mind on learning when he was fifteen years old. In *Analects*, it is said,

> The Master said: "From fifteen, my heart-and-mind was set upon learning." (Ames & Rosemont, 1998, 2.4:76)

But what is the aim and the content of learning? In other words, learning what and learning for what? Also in *Analects*, there is a paragraph wherein Confucius clearly answers these questions, but this paragraph was not highlighted by Confucian scholars in the following dynasties until the rising of Neo-Confucianism in the Song Dynasty (960–1127). The paragraph is as below:

> The Master said, "Men of antiquity studied to improve themselves; men today study to impress others." (Lau, 1979, 14.24: 128)[7]

In early Confucianism, especially in the thought of Confucius, learning means learning about the self, and the aim of learning is to become a human. In other words, learning is about self-cultivation to become a profound man (*junzi,* 君子).[8] It is a deliberate and lifelong effort that happens in daily life so that the individual can gain inner strength for character building and the realizing of the various responsibilities of the family, the community, the state, and the universe (*tianxia* 天下). The individual's perspective on the world outside of him/her is an enlarging process, a process of self-cultivation. Tu (1984: 385) said, "self-cultivation, in this connection, involves a conscientious attempt to open oneself up to the universe as a whole by extending one's horizon of feeling as well as knowing. The more one knows, in the sense of being enlightened about external things, the more one is sensitized to relate meaningfully to the world outside."

In the following section, I will discuss a few points highlighted in early Confucianism, mainly in *Analects* and *Zhongyong*, a classic Confucian text written in the period of the Warring States (BC 475–BC 221).[9] Responding to the concept of experience in Dewey's later works, I find some points related to immediate sensibility and the role of imagination in the practice of self-cultivation for a broader and more inclusive self that could build connections to others in the world.

3.1   *Focusing on the Familiar Affairs in Daily Life*

In early Confucianism, it is emphasized that the practice of self-cultivation happens when the individual deals with familiar affairs in daily life. In other words, it is not separated from daily life, but it happens when the individual participates in various events (*wu* 物) in daily life. The word *wu* literally means objects or things. However, Ames (2002: 153) argues that the idea of *wu* in Confucianism is not related to discrete "things" but to radically contextualized events, which are always marked by continuous yet changing patterns. It is not separated from walking, talking, eating, or other routines in daily life. It is the routine itself. However, the routine is different from mindless habitual doing; it is rather serious, attentive, and deliberate care. In *Analects*, there are many detailed descriptions on how Confucius leads his routine life with care and mindfulness and thus builds a role model of a profound person (*junzi*) with propriety (*li* 礼).

Because the practice of self-cultivation happens in daily life, or is the way of living a daily life, it also means that it has no interval in the practice of self-cultivation. It should be the flow of the life itself. Therefore, Confucius often reminds his disciples that self-cultivation for humanness might be an easy thing because it is doing the familiar things in daily life. Meanwhile, it is also the most difficult thing in the world. Even the sage could not fulfill it since it has no interval. But it is still the worthiest thing that a profound person needs to do. In *Analects*, it is said:

> The gentleman never deserts benevolence, not even for as long as it takes to eat a meal. If he hurries and stumbles one may be sure that it is in benevolence that he does so. (Lau, 1979, 4.5: 72)

In the first chapter of *Zhongyong*, it is said:

> As for this proper way, we cannot quit it even for an instant. Were it even possible to quit it, it would not be the proper way. (Ames & Hall, 2001: 89)

Besides the two points regarding the easiness and difficulty highlighted above on the practice of self-cultivation in daily life, another element that needs to be highlighted is "focusing." The practice of self-cultivation requires a high level of attention and awareness to the potentially active interaction between the individual and the environment. In the context of Confucianism, the environment is taken in a mostly general way. Not only does it mean a physical space the individual is in, but it also means the psychological or even spiritual space that the individual holds. By focusing on the familiar things in daily life, the individual intensifies his/her awareness of the environment and gives close attention to it. This deliberate effort will help the individual to perceive the un-noticed or trivial things in the environment so that he/she could be engaged with a more enriched environment and attain richer meanings connected with the environment. In Confucianism, it is important to remember that this deliberate effort for self-cultivation in daily life often takes place when the person is alone with no presence of others. This is called *shendu* (慎独): literally, a radical subjectivity with the intensity of the attentiveness and responsiveness required in the appropriate observance of ritual propriety when one is alone and beyond the evaluating gaze of others (Ames, 2002: 154). In the first chapter of *Zhongyong*, it is said:

> Exemplary persons (*junzi*) are so concerned about what is not seen, and so anxious about what is not heard. There is nothing more present than what is imminent, and nothing more manifest than what is inchoate. Thus, exemplary persons are ever concerned about their uniqueness. (Ames & Hall, 2011: 89)[10]

By focusing on the familiar things in daily life, the individual cultivates the uniqueness of the self and then realizes the humanness of a profound person (*junzi*). The paragraph above highlights the intensity of the attentiveness and responsiveness as an internal status of the person when he/she is engaged with the environment. On the other hand, the individual will take the daily practice of propriety (*li* 礼), a kind of performance to some extent, for making the appropriate relations with his/her community and the environment in general.

3.2   *The Daily Practice of Propriety (li礼) through Imagination*
The word *li* (礼) used to be translated as "rites" or "rituals" and denotes a series of impersonal regulations for individual performance. It was often considered as the form of hierarchical order in Chinese society, which is hostile to unique qualities of individuals. The paragraph below by a prominent western scholar of Chinese culture Donald Munro is an example: "Confucianism, unlike

Western romantic thought, never viewed the unique qualities of individuals as a realm of philosophical interest" (Munro 1985: 6). This point of view on *li* as impersonal rituals that are hostile to unique individuality could trace its origins to the early contact of the Chinese and western cultures in the 19th century, but it is still a very powerful and influential idea today. It greatly impacted Chinese liberal intellectuals in the early twentieth century and developed into a common view through the May Fourth Movement. During that time period, *li* was even condemned as the beast that "swallow[s] human life" (*chi ren* 吃人). As a result, in the following century until today, *li*, the essential practice of self-cultivation in Confucianism, is rejected and almost disappears in people's daily lives.

In contrast, some contemporary scholars, both western and Chinese, realize the necessity of reviving the original meaning of *li* in daily life. Here, *li* does not mean a series of formal regulations but means a propriate and creative way of interaction of the individual with the environment. For example, Ames (2002: 147) suggests:

> The performance of *li* must be understood in light of the uniqueness of each participant and the profoundly aesthetic project of becoming a person. *Li* is an ongoing process of personal investment that, with persistence and effort, refines the quality of one's communal transactions ... We might want to think of it as producing an achieved, aggregating disposition, a sustained attitude, a defining posture, an identity in action.

Simply stated, *li* is an ethics of responding properly (Puett, 2004), and it is more precise to be translated as "propriety" rather than "rites" or "rituals" (Ames, 2002: 147). The new translation emphasizes that *li* is more about the creative and personal response to the concrete situations the individual is in. However, the sages, with the high level of self-cultivation, could respond to concrete situations in a highly ethical and aesthetic way and thus create artificial patterns as models for humans to follow so that it is possible to fully realize their natural potentiality in the interaction with the environment (Puett, 2004: 56). *Li* is thus the deliberately designed patterns for the appropriate response to the various situations in daily life. It has some form but is not ossified and always needs the person's full engagement and creative participation.

Actually, in the texts of early Confucianism, in the answers Confucius gives to his disciples on how to practice self-cultivation for the realization of humanness (*ren* 仁), Confucius does not emphasize the regulations or rites but reminds his disciples to pay more attention on the preparation of the mind-heart (*xin* 心) for the practice of *li*. In more detail, it is crucial to keep a pious and highly attentive attitude to the events that the individual is engaged in.

Through the imagination of connecting to the sage or the deity, the individual could develop a similar seriousness and intensity of feeling to the familiar affairs in daily life. Therefore, the imagination of the alternative realities could help the individual to focus his/her most serious attention and promote his/her awareness of the potentiality, or the minute and unseen things, in his/her engagement with the environment. Here is an example in *Analects*:

> "Sacrifice *as if* present" is taken to mean "sacrifice to the gods *as if* the gods were present." The Master, however, said, "Unless I take part in a sacrifice, it is *as if* I did not sacrifice." (Lau, 1979, 3.12: 69, emphasis added)

In the following paragraph in *Analects*, Confucius again emphasizes the possibility of building connection between the familiar affairs in daily life and an alternative reality with imagination. The practice of *li* is the realization of the imagination so that a new space for realizing the potentiality in the reality can be created. In the new space, the humanness of the individual can be realized through the seemed routine and mundane life.

Confucius' disciple Zhong Gong once asked about perfect virtue (or humanness, *ren* 仁). The Master said, "It is, when you go outside, to behave to every one *as if* you were receiving a great guest; to employ the people *as if* you were assisting at a great sacrifice; not to do to others as you would not wish done to yourself; to have no murmuring against you in the country, and none in the family." Zhong Gong said, "Though I am deficient in intelligence and vigor, I will make it my business to practice this lesson" (Legge, n.d., 12.2, emphasis added).

The phrase "as if" is the imagination for the alternative reality. Puett and Gross-Loh (2017: 32) argue that this "as if" of *li* in Confucianism helps us to create a small but new space in daily life. By practicing *li*, the individual thus breaks the routines of daily life and enters into this new space of life; thus, it may be more possible for us to find the new potentialities of ourselves and find new meanings in daily life. The imagination through the "as if" of *li* helps us to cultivate a pious attitude for deliberate efforts and seriousness to the events we are engaged in. In other words, in this newly imagined space through the practice of the "as if" of *li*, the individual learns to promote his/her awareness and intensive attention to interact with the environment. In this way, humanness could possibly be realized even though it might be realized in a more subtle way that no one else even would notice.

3.3   Self-Cultivation as a Way of Connecting to Others

As discussed above, Confucius' practice of self-cultivation focuses on the familiar affairs in daily life. Through the imaginative activity of *li*, the individual creates a new space of alternative realities through intensive attention and wide awakening to the interaction with the environment. Therefore, the practice of *li* is not only a formalized action by following the role models but also a highly creative and personalized activity to realize the potentiality of the minute and un-noticed events in daily life. Then, new meanings and a harmonious relationship are possibly built up between the individual and his/her environment. In early Confucianism, this is the dynamic process for enlarging the potentiality of humanness, which is the way (*dao* 道) or ultimate goal of living.

When the individual builds new meanings with the environment, he/she is creating new possibilities of making connections with others so that others become part of the self. As the contemporary Confucian Liang Shuming (2005: 135) said, "connection with no barriers when interacting with others in the universe is the ultimate humanness." Tu (1984: 385) commented that the profound person (*junzi*)'s ability "creatively to transform the world through personal realization is predicated not only his moral rectitude but also on his spiritual resonance with the cosmic transformation of Heaven and Earth. The moral community that the *junzi* creates in the world is therefore a microcosm of the dynamic universe." Therefore, the practice of self-cultivation by *junzi* is also a deliberate effort to build connections with others so that others become part of the self. In this perspective, the sense of responsibility is not a moral obligation from the community but the urgent need of the self for enlarging the sense of humanness and develop the unique individuality (Zhang, 2021). In *Analects*, the classical expression of the self-other relationship reflects the principle of humanness: "A benevolent man helps others to take their stand in so far as he himself wishes to take his stand, and gets others there in so far as he himself wishes to get there. The ability to take as analogy what is near at hand can be called the method of benevolence" (Lau, 1979, 6.30: 85).

The self-other relationship in Confucianism mirrors John Dewey's basic idea of individuality. He says: "In the realization of individuality there is found also the needed realization of some community of persons of which the individual is a member; and, conversely, the agent who duly satisfies the community in which he shares, by that some conduct satisfies himself" (EW 3: 323).

4 Conclusion: The Idea of Self-Cultivation and Its Educational Implication

In discussing John Dewey's philosophy of experience in his later works and the idea of self-cultivation in early Confucianism, a commonality emerges between the two schools of thought. For both, it is critical to cultivate the sensibility of the individual while interacting with the environment as a way of cultivating individuality. The development of individuality is a dynamic process of building meaningful connections with others in creative ways, so the potentiality of individuality is realized through the flourishing of humanness. In both schools of thought, it is emphasized that the preparation for the realization of potentiality relies on keen sensibility to the environment to focus on the intensive attention to the interaction with the environment. The sensibility is the care of the feelings of the self and the feelings of others in the environment. Here, others include not only human beings but everything in the universe. Moreover, it is a creative way to understand emotions, to transform the disrupted feelings into a more harmonious way of reaction. The cultivation of sensibility is not motivated by moral or social regulations but by impulsion for a more enriched and enlarged connection to a broader world.

This perspective of Dewey's thought above was not sufficiently discussed, or more precisely was generally ignored, by Chinese intellectuals since the early twentieth century when Dewey's works were initially introduced in China. However, there might be one exception even in the early twentieth century. The contemporary Confucian scholar Liang Shuming (1993) noticed the immediate sensibility of experience in Dewey's thought when he reviewed Dewey's *Democracy and Education* in 1934. The emphasis on the realization of potentiality through creative and imaginative practice of self-cultivation for an inclusive individuality from both schools of thought can provide insightful resources for the contemporary world that is full of dualism and conflicts.

Educators should learn to practice self-cultivation so that they can care better for others – mainly students in the schooling context. The focused attention on the present, which is an open and unknown space but connects to the past and the future, would help both teachers and students renew the self through the engagement with trivial things in the daily life of schooling. Through the engagement, trivial things might become mighty subjects for inviting the individual into an energetic and creative process of building meaningful relationships with others in the environment who are unknown and alien to him/her in the previous experience. It could be considered a way of practicing self-cultivation in daily life. With this perspective of understanding the interaction of the individuals with the environment, it is clear that both Dewey's thoughts, especially in his later works, and the thought in early Confucianism share a strong commonality on the practice of self-cultivation.

In today's world, which is full of conflicts and biases, it is even more important and more urgent to educate global citizens with sensibilities to build meaningful connections with others. Through the active engagement with trivial things in the present, it helps to develop the creative and open-minded way of thinking that has the potential to overcome bias, stereotypes, or abstract ideologies. By facing concrete situations that are full of rich potentialities of new meanings, it might be possible to create new realities of the world that are more inclusive and share more common interests.

Notes

1 In this chapter, I use the conventional order of Chinese names to show all the Chinese names. So, the family name appears first and the first name appears second.

2 John Dewey's book *Democracy and Education* is the most-read book for students of education in Chinese universities. For example, Chu Zhaohui, Guo Faqi, Shan Zhonghui, and Zhang Binxian are all the contemporary educational scholars who studied intensively on Dewey. They submitted short essays to review the study appeared in, the special issue on "John Dewey and Chinese Education: A Centennial Reflection," *Beijing International Review of Education*, Vol. 1, No. 4, 2019: 598–607.

3 I develop this part on Dewey's philosophy of experience based on the Chinese article I published on *Journal of Educational Studies* (Chinese); see Zhang (2016).

4 This is an example I explicitly discussed in the paper "Teaching by Making Spiritual Connection with Students towards Self-transformation." The paper was presented at American Educational Research Association Conference, Toronto, Canada, April 5–9, 2019.

5 In *Analects*, the master refers to Confucius.

6 The words "study" and "learn" can refer to the same Chinese character *xue* (学). However, the translators in this version distinguish the word "study" from "learning" with slightly different meanings. They refer to "study" as "task" or "process" but to "learn" as "achievement" and "success." In the original text of Confucius, the meaning of process or task of action is highlighted in the character of *xue*, so the word "study" was used in this sentence, but I prefer to make these two words interchangeable. Also, "learn to be human," rather than "study to be human," is more used in the discussion of Confucianism.

7 In this chapter, I will mainly use two resources of translation of *Analects*. One is by Lau (1979) and the other is by Ames and Rosemont (1998). I will use both and pick the translation that is more appropriate for the context of the interpretation.

8 There are various versions of translation on *junzi*: for example, good person, virtuous person, or exemplary person. I use "profound person" by Tu Wei-ming (1984) to highlight the quality of the person. This quality does not only refer to the moral quality, but also emotional, aesthetic and spiritual quality. Also, it indicates that the quality of the person is gained in a dynamic and accumulated process of human becoming with the degree of intensity.

9 It is still debatable about the period of the text *Zhongyong* (中庸), but it is generally agreed that the grandson of Confucius Zisi is the main author of this text. It appears as a chapter of *the Book of Rites* (*Liji*礼记). Some scholars consider that it appears before the book *Mencius*, a book on the thought of Mencius (BC 372–BC 289).

10 Because the concept of *shendu* (慎独) is very abstruse, other versions of translation could be a helpful reference. For example, James Legge's translation is more literal, and his version of translation can be helpful for the understanding: "The superior man does not wait till he sees things, to be cautious, nor till he hears things, to be apprehensive. There is nothing more visible than what is secret, and nothing more manifest than what is minute. Therefore, the superior man is watchful over himself, when he is alone."

References

Alexander, T. (1987). *John Dewey's theory of art, experience, and nature: The horizon of feeling*. State University of New York Press.

Ames, R. T. (2002). Observing ritual "propriety (*li* 禮)" as focusing the "familiar" in the affairs of the day. *Dao: A Journal of Comparative Philosophy*, *1*(2), 143–156.

Ames, R. (2003). Confucianism and Deweyan pragmatism: A dialogue. *Journal of Chinese Philosophy*, *30*(3/4), 403–417.

Ames, R., & Hall, D. (2001). *Focusing the familiar: A translation and philosophical interpretation of the Zhongyong*. University of Hawaii Press.

Ames, R. T., & Rosemont, Jr. H. (1998). *The Analects of Confucius: A philosophical translation*. Ballantine Books.

Chen, J. (2019). "Does the deed that breeds the emotion": An interpretation on John Dewey's aesthetic theory of expression [由"行动而生出情感"：杜威美学表现观解读]. *Academic Monthly* [学术月刊], *51*(6), 143–151.

Chen, Y. (2015). Pragmatism as an intermediary between Chinese and Marxist philosophy [作为"居间者"的实用主义——与中国哲学、马克思主义哲学的对话]. *Academic Monthly* [学术月刊], *47*(7), 5–12.

Dewey, J. (1981). *The later works, 1925–1953, Vol. 1: 1925*. Southern Illinois University Press.

Dewey, J. (1984). *The later works, 1925–1953, Vol. 5: 1929–1930*. Southern Illinois University Press.

Dewey, J. (1987). *The later works, 1925–1953, Vol. 10: 1934*. Southern Illinois University Press.

Dewey, J. (1988). *The later works, 1925–1953, Vol. 14: 1939–1941*. Southern Illinois University Press.

Garrison, J. (2001). An introduction to Dewey's theory of functional "trans-action": An alternative paradigm for activity theory. *Mind, Culture, and Activity*, *8*(4), 275–296.

Grange, J. (2004). *John Dewey, Confucius, and global philosophy*. State University of New York Press.

Gu, H. (2010). Liang Shuming and John Dewey's philosophy of life [梁漱溟与杜威的生命哲学]. *Xuehai* [学海], *5*, 74–80.

Hall, D. L., & Ames, R. T. (1999). *The democracy of the dead: Dewey, Confucianism, and the hope for democracy in China*. Open Court.

Lau, D. C. (1979). *Confucius: The Analects (Lun Yu)*. Penguin Classics.

Legge, J. (n.d.). *The Analects of Confucius*. Chinese Text Project. https://ctext.org/analects/yan-yuan

Liang, S. (1993). The fundamental thoughts of John Dewey's philosophy of education [杜威教育哲学之根本观念]. In *The complete collection of Liang Shuming's work* [梁漱溟全集] (Vol. VII). Shangdong People Press [济南：山东人民出版社].

Liang, S. (2005). *Mind and life* [人心与人生]. Shanghai People's Press [上海：上海人民出版社].

Liu, F. (2014). On evaluation of pragmatism: The commonality and difference between Dewey's and Marx's philosophies [再论重新评价实用主义—兼论杜威哲学与马克思哲学的同一与差异]. *Tianjin Social Sciences* [天津社会科学], 2, 11–12.

Liu, X. (2019). A seed found its ground: John Dewey and the construction of the Department of Education at Beijing Normal University. *Beijing International Review of Education, 1*(4), 695–713.

Miedema, S. (1994–1995). The beyond in the mist: The relevance of Dewey's philosophy of religion for education. *Studies in Philosophy and Education, 3*, 229–241.

Munro, D. (1985). *Individualism and holism: Studies in Confucian and Taoist values.* University of Michigan Press.

Puett, M. (2004). The ethics of responding properly: The notion of *Qing* 情 in early Chinese thought. In H. Eifring (Ed.), *Love and emotions in traditional Chinese literature.* Brill.

Puett, M., & Gross-Loh, C. (2017). *The path: A new way to think about everything* [哈佛中国哲学课]. Zhongxin Press [北京：中信出版社].

Qu, J. (2021). The humanness of Chinese social sciences [中国社会科学的人文性]. *Open Times* [开放时代], 1, 80–84.

Su, Z. (2019). John Dewey and Chinese education: Comparative perspectives and contemporary interpretations. *Beijing International Review of Education, 1*(4), 714–745.

Tan, S.-h. (2012). The pragmatic Confucian approach to tradition in modernizing China. *History and Theory (Tradition and History), 51*(4), 23–44.

Tu, W.-m. (1984). Pain and suffering in Confucian self-cultivation. *Philosophy East and West, 34*(4), 379–388.

Uffelman, M. (2011). Forging the self in the stream of experience: Classical currents of self-cultivation in James and Dewey. *Transactions of the Charles S. Peirce Society, 47*(3), 319–339.

Waks, L. (2019). Democratic self-cultivation. *Beijing International Review of Education, 1*(4), 626–644.

Wang, L. (2019). *John Dewey's democratic education and its influence on pedagogy in China 1917–1937.* Springer VS.

Wieman, H. N. (1925). Religion in Dewey's "experience and nature." *The Journal of Religion, 5*(5), 519–542.

Yang, J. Z. (2016). *When Confucius "encounters" John Dewey: A historical and philosophical analysis of Dewey's visit to China* [Dissertation]. University of Oklahoma Graduate College.

Zhang, H. (2013). *John Dewey, Liang Shuming and China's education reform: Cultivate individuality.* Lexington Books.

Zhang, H. (2016). A whole self: An education review of John Dewey's idea of religion in his later works [整全的自我：教育视角下杜威晚期思想中的宗教观解读]. *Journal of Educational Studies* [教育学报], *12*(3), 68–78.

Zhang, H. (2021). *Individuality as responsibility: Insights from early Confucianism and John Dewey* [Virtual paper presentation]. American Educational Research Association Conference.

Zhao, K. (2019). Why did Hu Shi introduce Deweyan pragmatism to China as only a method. *Beijing International Review of Education, 1*(4), 658–672.

CHAPTER 12

Humanities Education in the Age of AI

Reflections from Deweyan and Confucian Perspectives

Sor-hoon TAN

Abstract

Artificial Intelligence (AI) is transforming our world: today machines not only can mimic human actions but out-perform human agents in many activities, including learning and thinking. AI offers revolutionary solutions and new possibilities in transportation, business, communication, medicine, law, and other domains. While some welcome this brave new world, others fear the threats AI pose to people's livelihoods, social relations, individuality, freedom, and perhaps even the very survival of the human species. No doubt some of this existential angst is exaggerated, but AI does raise questions for our understanding of the world and ourselves that require serious reflection, including questions about adequacy of education in various aspects.

This chapter offers, from the perspectives of John Dewey's Pragmatism as well as Confucianism, some reflections on the role of the humanities in education in response to the opportunities and challenges of the development and widespread use of AI. It shows that Dewey and Confucius share similar views regarding the humanistic purpose of education and their philosophies of education offer arguments for why humanities education will be relevant, if not more important, when many jobs we are familiar with become obsolete. Their attitudes toward the economic motive in education will help us rethink the meaning of work in a "world without work." At the same time, they offer a critical evaluation of contemporary humanities education, which have failed to realize their visions of personal cultivation and growth. Among its failings is the continued dichotomy between the humanities and the sciences. In the age of AI, it has become even more vital to integrate them to so that science and technology would not become materialistic and anti-human and the humanities not become merely literary and without any means to transform the world.

Keywords

Dewey – technology – artificial intelligence – digital humanities – science – purpose of education – personal cultivation

© KONINKLIJKE BRILL NV, LEIDEN, 2022 | DOI:10.1163/9789004511477_013

HUMANITIES EDUCATION IN THE AGE OF AI   235

...

During his visit to China from 1919 to 1921, John Dewey often gave lectures on education, as the main aim of his former students who invited him was to enlist his help in education reforms, which they believed were the key to save China from its predicament at that time. In those lectures, he discussed the necessity of both education and a philosophy of education. For Dewey, "a philosophy of education produces conscious criticism and evaluation of educational endeavor, creates a desire for improvement, and affords criteria by which improvement may be assessed" (Clopton & Ou, 1973: 184). While education is necessary at any time, a philosophy of education is very important during times of rapid change, if we are to chart our way forward amid complex and conflicting trends that affect education and its relation to society. While the specific challenges his Chinese audience faced then were different, his words remain relevant today as we confront the fourth industrial revolution (Schwab, 2016), with technologies that have transformed many aspects of our lives, from self-driving cars to smart homes and robots that care for the elderly. More than ever before, "we must reconstruct the traditional aims, methods, and subject matter of education so that it may adequately serve the needs of our age" (Clopton & Ou, 1973: 188).

1   AI's Impact on the Future of Work and Humanities Education

What kind of education will ensure that its beneficiaries will function well, even thrive, in the age of AI? Most of us spend a large part of life working, as few are rich enough not to have to worry about earning a living, and furthermore, career accomplishments provide meaning, a sense of purpose, and social esteem. It is therefore not surprising that people are troubled, if not panicked, to find studies by academics and business consultants alike predicting that nearly half the income-earning activities today can be computerized.[1] Driving in traffic was once thought unsusceptible to automation (Levy & Murnane, 2004), but AI has made autonomous vehicles a reality that will render human drivers redundant. The risk of redundancy is not limited to low-skill low-wage occupations, as AI goes beyond automation of routine tasks and opens up new frontiers for machines to replace humans. Studies indicate a hollowing out of middle-income jobs, which have been filled hitherto by university graduates. Computers have already proven their superiority at diagnosing cancer and neurological disorders, and algorithmic systems are performing within minutes and with greater precision tasks that take financial analysts many hours to complete (Popper, 2016; Dixon, 2018; Huang et al., 2020). Experts canvassed by the Pew Research Centre in 2014 are deeply divided as to whether new jobs created will keep pace with those destroyed, but there is consensus that most education systems are currently doing a poor job of preparing students for work of the future.[2]

Does this mean that policy makers should shift limited resources into disciplines directly related to new technologies and cut the already inadequate budgets of humanities departments and schools? Should parents advise their children to study computer science or engineering rather than pursue their interests in the humanities? Such reactions are unwarranted by the trends of both technological development and transformation of economic activities. In the United States, the most recent survey by the National Association of Colleges and Employers shows that technical skills are ranked 10th out of 20, among key attributes they seek in students' resumes, lower than written (5th) and verbal (7th) communication skills. Problem-solving skills, ability to work in a team, and strong work ethic are the top three attributes employers looked for (NACE, 2020). While technology and data literacies are necessary for a digitized world, knowledge and skills acquired in the humanities are far from obsolete. Microsoft and other tech companies have been hiring graduates from the liberal arts and the humanities and will hire even more in the future, as their skills are critical in making AI and robots as "human" as possible, to ensure seamless interactions between machines and humans ("Liberal arts, humanities shine in the age of AI," 2019). As technologies transform various domains of our lives and challenge existing institutions and social arrangements, an education in the humanities – philosophy, history, literature, law, among others – will equip us with the knowledge and skills to ensure that technological advancements will benefit rather than harm human beings and civilizations.

Kathryn Hume, who has worked in tech start-ups since completing her PhD in comparative literature at Stanford University, and gives lectures around the world on AI, including guest lectures at Harvard Business School, Stanford, University of Toronto and MIT, argues that "the right educational training and curriculum for the AI-enabled job market of the 21st century should create generalists, not specialists" (Hume, 2017a). The skills she identifies as AI-resistant include flexibility and adaptability, interdisciplinarity, model thinking, synthetic and analogical reasoning, and framing qualitative ideas as quantitative problems; these are skills of a rigorous humanistic education.[3] She goes so far as to claim that,

> As machines creep ever further into work that requires thinking and judgment, critical thinking, creativity, interpretation, emotions, and

reasoning will become increasingly important. STEM may just lead to its own obsoleteness (AI software is now making its own AI software), and in doing so is increasing the value of professionals trained in the humanities. (Hume, 2017b)[4]

Joseph E. Auon, President of Northeastern University in Boston, Massachusetts, USA, in his book, *Robot-Proof: Higher Education in the Age of Artificial Intelligence* (2017), suggests that the new literacies students need to thrive in a digitized world include data literacy, technological literacy, and human literacy, the last of which requires education in "the humanities, communication and design." The humanities have a key role to play in nurturing our unique capacities as human beings that machines could not replicate. The Dean of the College of Humanities and Social Sciences at the Southern University of Science and Technology, Chen Yuehong, delivered a guest lecture on "Technology and Humanities in the Age of Artificial Intelligence," on 7th April 2019, in which he maintained that AI needs the contribution of the humanities in content, ethics, and innovation (Edwards, 2019). And MIT's Schwarzman College of Computing – which according to its mission statement aims to reorient MIT to ensure, *inter alia*, that "the future of computing is shaped by insights from other disciplines"[5] – challenges the false dichotomy between technology and the humanities (Hao, 2019). Beyond preparation for new and transformed occupations, if AI does usher in massive technology-induced unemployment, it could be argued that, besides the need to deal with the economic and political fall-out, the existential questions that would arise also demand reflections for which an education in the humanities will prepare us (Tonar, 2018). In Daniel Suskind's words, "In a world with less work, though, we will need to revisit the fundamental ends once again. The problem is not simply how to live, but how to live well. We will be forced to consider what it really means to live a meaningful life" (Susskind, 2020: 224).

Humanities education will remain relevant in the age of AI not only because it offers knowledge and skills for making better AI or performing new jobs, but because the question of what it means for human beings to live a flourishing life remains an important question. The role of humanities education in the universities depends on what we understand to be the purpose of education. For those who see education – in particular attendance at an institution of tertiary education which has to be paid for, either with parents' or students' and taxpayers money – to be an investment in human resources, the primary purpose of education is to prepare students to become economically productive. This contrasts with how the humanities have understood education as development of human capacities – intellectual, emotional, aesthetic, and spiritual

– which would enable an educated person to live a flourishing life, and at the same time to contribute to society not only in economic terms but also in various other ways important to flourishing human communities. Both Dewey and Confucius share this humanistic approach to education without dismissing the importance of economic productivity in the purpose of education.

2 Confucius and Dewey on the Purpose of Education

Confucius remarked that "it is not easy to find students who will study for three years without their thoughts turning to an official salary" (*Analects* 8.12).[6] Among his students, Zi Zhang was specifically described in the text as studying for the purpose of career advancement (*Analects* 2.18); in contrast, Zixia declared that, "The various craftsmen stay in their shops so that they may master their trades; exemplary persons study so that they might promote their way" (*Analects* 19.7). At his most idealistic, Confucius believed that those who could be said to have a love of learning "do not look for a full stomach in eating, nor comfort and contentment in their lodgings" (*Analects* 1.14). Although the true rewards of learning for Confucius are joy and virtue (*Analects* 1.1, 6.11), Confucius was realistic enough not to disdain the acquisition of economically useful skills. His dismissal of Fan Chi as a "petty person" for the latter's interest in learning farming notwithstanding (*Analects* 13.4), he himself had acquired many skills not required of an exemplary person out of economic necessity (*Analects*, 9.6, 9.7).

The "exemplary person," as a contemporary translation for *junzi* (君子) in Confucius's teachings, is a person who has cultivated herself to become humane and wise, to interact with others sincerely and graciously, and to do what is most appropriate to any situation; she is therefore an exemplar for other human beings.[7] The Confucian *junzi* is an ethical ideal that remains relevant today, as most people still recognize that economic wealth alone is not enough if we wish to live a good life as a human being. The Confucian view of the good life is to cultivate oneself to become an exemplary person who would contribute to one's community, without which a truly human life is impossible. Confucian education is, first and foremost, personal cultivation, which is a life-long process and commitment; training to acquire skills to earn a livelihood is secondary and undertaken only out of necessity. A contemporary Confucian philosophy of education, as part of a larger ethical philosophy of living a good life by cultivating the ideal character of the exemplary person, would not dismiss student's career goals, but nevertheless would emphasize that education must aim to achieve more than marketable skills and knowledge. For

Confucians, regardless of what jobs a person may take up, unless she cultivates herself to become an exemplary person, her education is lacking.

Confucius did not merely prepare his students for jobs, he prepared them for a career in government, which should be undertaken not solely for its material rewards but because it was an excellent way for an exemplary person to practice his virtue of humaneness. This does not mean that Confucius would consider any student not in government a failure. An exemplary person is one who contributes to the well-being of others in whatever domains she finds herself, just as good governments should ensure the well-being of the governed in Confucius's philosophy. In today's context, AI's capacity to process huge volumes of data with accuracy and speed no human could match is very useful in many areas of government policy making as well as decision making and problem solving in various other domains with consequences for people's well-being. A modern Confucian education must therefore include learning the new technology, not necessarily to become a technical expert but to acquire a sufficient understanding of it and the capacity to work with technical experts to employ the technology for people's well-being.

Contrary to the recurrent fear of technology, which he attributes to the dualistic Western worldview, Roger Ames argues that Confucianism's "one-world" cosmology does not define the man-machine relationship as one of antagonistic interaction, and its ability to embrace new technologies has been manifested since the times of the ancient sages, whose accomplishments included what were among the earliest technological innovations – tools for fishing, hunting and farming (Ames, 2020). Confucians would welcome the age of the AI as far as the new technologies will benefit humans, and Confucianism could contribute its perspectives in ensuring that human-machine relationships turn out to be mutually beneficial. In contrast, Eliza Gkritsi, Technode's blockchain and fintech reporter, believes that Confucius would be more worried than impressed by the way AI is taking over so much decision making for humans.

> Regardless of how big the data AI could process, they could never grasp human emotion, and it is emotive intelligence that can bring about judgements, as opposed to decisions. Seeing the virtuous judge situations over time empowers and teaches ordinary people to become benevolent.
> (Gkritsi, 2019)

A contemporary Confucian education must include knowledge and skills suited to an increasingly digitized world, but such knowledge and skills are still secondary to cultivating the excellences of exemplary persons, who would be capable of making the virtuous judgments that Gkritsi insists machines are incapable of. While we cannot give a full account of Confucian personal cultivation here, suffice to say that the cultivating the excellences of the Confucian *junzi* is not a process comprising only of learning algorithmic cognitive tasks; it involves cultivating emotions, which have a role in deliberation. Confucians also recognize deliberation as an *embodied* experience – and hence the importance of ritual performance (*li* 礼) in Confucian ethical life – which is not replicable in machines or anything else that does not share the human organic life form.

Education understood as Confucian personal cultivation resonates strongly with Dewey's conception of education as growth (MW 9: 46–58).[8] Dewey rejected the common view of education as moving towards some fixed goal external to the learning activities and separate from the instinctive and native powers of the learner, which have to be suppressed or brought into conformity with external standards. Education as growth means "(i) that the education process has no end beyond itself; it is its own end; and (ii) that the educational process is one of continual reorganizing, reconstructing, transforming" (MW 9: 54). This has sometimes led his Chinese critics to accuse Dewey of promoting "education without a purpose."[9] Such accusations completely overlook the meaning and importance of the concept of "growth" in Dewey's philosophy. For him, "growth itself is the only moral 'end'" (MW 12: 181); and "life is growth" (MW 9: 56). Instead of being "without a purpose," all of life, how to improve it at every stage according to its intrinsic qualities is the purpose of education. Growth as the end of education differs from other ends in its organic continuity with the learner's abilities and dispositions; it is internal to the learning activity itself, a completion and fulfillment of what precedes it in that activity.

From Dewey's perspective, attempting to "robot-proof" education would be misguided if its *only* concern is to ensure that students could find jobs in the digitized world, as that would be an example of imposing an external end on education, insofar as that preoccupation is symptomatic of an economic individualism which measures the worth of a person in terms of material success (LW 8: 55), so that "chronic insecurity" and acquisitiveness, perceived as human nature, are the chief motives driving people to work (LW 8: 61).[10] Nevertheless, "the dominant purpose of school education was to prepare individuals for successful achievement, for getting on, in the struggle of life" (LW 8: 54), so Dewey acknowledged that education must prepare students for earning a living (MW 15: 164). However, he would agree with Confucius that education must go beyond this. While acknowledging the importance of earning a living, he maintained that "the problem of general public-school education is not to train workers for a trade, but to make use of the whole environment of the child in order to supply motive and meaning to the work" (MW 8: 265). Dewey

HUMANITIES EDUCATION IN THE AGE OF AI

spent an entire lecture on vocational education in his series of lectures on philosophy of education in China (Clopton & Ou, 1973: 279–285); and his publications of the early decades of the twentieth century include several discussions of vocational and industrial education as the American education system was struggling with new challenges due to socioeconomic changes.[11] He rejected narrowly defined vocational training for a specific trade or industry that was based on the needs and welfare of that trade or industry instead of being guided by the welfare of the learners and their communities. Then, as now, if students learn no more than what is necessary to get jobs, then not only does this increase the chances of obsolescence given the rapid changes in the jobs available and the precarious future of work, they would also be ill-prepared to take advantage of the time and energy released by use of technology (MW 9: 269; Clopton & Ou, 1973: 283).

Speaking to his Chinese audience, Dewey noted that humanities subjects, such as literature, history, geography, and the arts, had been associated with the education for an elite expected to rule but not engage in manual labour, and such formal education was denied to those engaged in economic production, who acquired the necessary skills on the job instead of formal institutions of learning (Clopton & Ou, 1973: 280). Rejecting the dichotomy between the education for the ruling elite and that for workers as a relic of a feudal society and unsuited to modern conditions, he stressed that vocational education must also develop intellectual capacities of individuals while it prepares them for work. Thus, "vocational education must be as much concerned with the worthy use of leisure as with the ability to perform a job" (Clopton & Ou, 1973: 280). Both education that prepares people for economic production and other useful service to society and education previously reserved for a class with leisure to enjoy cultural refinements and seek knowledge out of curiosity are equally relevant for everyone. Education is the reorganization and reconstruction of our experience in order to direct our activities more intelligently to achieve growth in all its dimensions – physical, emotional, intellectual, moral, and spiritual. Achieving growth in this sense includes contributing creatively to one's culture even as one benefits from it; and in the economic sense, it means being productive rather than merely producing under others' direction for external goals (Clopton & Ou, 1973: 210–211). It involves developing the intelligence to control the new technologies and one's own future economic endeavors rather than merely fitting in with the existing economic and technological regimes (MW 10: 150).

Besides being realistic, Dewey's and Confucius' similar attitudes toward the economic motive in education will help us rethink the meaning of work in the age of AI.[12] Both would consider a world where humans need not work out of economic necessity an improvement, if the prosperity resulting from new technologies could be equitably distributed to ensure economic sufficiency for everyone. Implicit in this approval is a belief that humans freed from economic want would not live in idle dissipation. From a Deweyan perspective, preparing students for adult working life should not be narrowly practical, and certainly not driven by merely pecuniary interest, if we recall Dewey's definition of a vocation as "such a direction of life activities as renders them perceptibly significant to a person, because of the consequences they accomplish, and also useful to his associates" (MW 9: 316). In a "world without work" (Susskind, 2020) – a scenario of AI putting human beings out of work that both inspires and worries many today – provided everyone could be assured of economic sufficiency through equitable distribution of wealth, human beings would be able to spend their time in creative and productive activities that give their lives meaning and worth, and contribute to their growth. When rejecting the blame cast on machines for unemployment during the depression era, Dewey saw in technology "the possibility of not merely doing away with the evils which result from our present economic regime but of ushering in an order of unprecedented security and abundant comfort as the material basis for a high culture in which all and not merely the few shall share" (LW 8: 68–69) – this possibility is also present in AI and related technologies today. He attributed the opposition between work and leisure – "which is thought of as a period of amusement and idle relaxation if not dissipation" (LW 8: 62) – to productive activities being carried out primarily for the external goal of financial rewards, pushing out all other motives for productive activities, including expanding one's labour and time because of a direct interest in the activity itself. It is productive activity as such, not work for pay, that constitutes growth and a truly human life.

For Dewey, social and educational reconstructions are closely connected, and both will be required to meet the challenges that AI poses to our current institutions and practices. Among the factors that Dewey believed such reconstructions must take into account is increased interdependence in society on a worldwide scale during his time. Unfortunately, his counsel that this requires rejecting the doctrine of competitive individualism has fallen on deaf ears among his own compatriots. While interdependence has increased further with the advent of the digital age, the world is arguably in a worse predicament than before, with the rise of unilateralism, xenophobic nationalism, global terrorism, and unsatisfactory responses to the current pandemic (Morris, 2020), *inter alia*, revealing how poorly we are handling this crucial aspect of the human condition. Not only has it not been curbed in Dewey's native land, the malaise of competitive individualism has spread with global capitalism, a

HUMANITIES EDUCATION IN THE AGE OF AI

trend that Confucian scholars such as Roger Ames (2021) and Henry Rosemont Jr. (2015), among others, have been fighting.

Confucians would agree with Dewey that we must "educate individuals to live in a world where social conditions beyond the reach of any one individual's will affect his security, his work, his achievements" (LW 8: 73). More than economic survival is at stake. For Confucians and Deweyans alike, human interdependence is constitutive of our humanity. Our relationships with other human beings, from family members, close friends, colleagues, neighbors, to strangers we pass on the street, and now even those we have never met face to face but could be connected to via the new media, shape our experience, which makes us the persons we are. Confucian personal cultivation – acquisition and exercise of the excellences of humaneness (*ren* 仁), appropriateness (*yi* 义), ritual propriety (*li* 礼), even wisdom (*zhi* 知) – is possible only in human relationships. For Dewey, human beings are not born with ready-made selves. One first distinguishes oneself from others through interaction with others. The self, which is synonymous with individuality in Dewey's philosophy, emerges from experience, from an individual's doings and undergoings. It is "essentially social, being constituted not by isolated capacity, but by capacity acting in response the needs of an environment – an environment which, when taken in its fullness, is a community of persons" (EW 3: 335).[13]

As we interact more with AI-driven machines, including robots that may appear more and more human-like, relations between humans become more vital to distinguish humanity. The most important replacement for economic production would be working on improving our relationship with those closest to us and extending that to other human beings – improvement in the quality of one's relationships would constitute personal cultivation for Confucians and growth in Dewey's philosophy. The humanities – philosophy, literature, and history – contain insights into human relationships, and an education in the humanities teaches us to reflect on those relationships, which is an important prelude to improving them. The moral growth of developing excellences of character – humaneness, appropriateness, ritual propriety, and wisdom – at the core of a Confucian education will become more rather than less relevant as AI transforms our lives. Dewey understands wisdom as a "moral term" which "refers to a choice about something to be done, a preference for living this sort of life rather than that. It refers not to accomplished reality but to a desired future which our desires, when translated into articulate conviction, may help bring into existence" (MW 11: 44). Such wisdom and excellences of character will be needed to respond to the impact of AI on the future of work, as Susskind (2020: 214) recognizes the need for education to go "beyond basic workplace competence" to cultivate a set of "virtues" for human flourishing in a "world without work."[14] The humanities – literature, history and philosophy among other subjects – help us access the civilizational wisdom of what it means to be human and how to become a human being. As we are shaped by our interaction with other human beings, so would we be shaped by our interactions with AI technologies. An education in the humanities, which explore human values and their relations, would also help us to understand such impact and to deliberate on which kinds of human-AI interactions would enhance our humanity and which should be avoided for their detrimental effects.

Confucius's and Dewey's philosophies of education, centered in personal cultivation and growth respectively, are humanistic in approach. While they do not dismiss the need of students to prepare to earn a livelihood and they understand the value of economic productivity both to the individual and to society, they stress the importance of developing human capacities – intellectual, emotional, aesthetic, and spiritual – which requires the knowledge and skills of philosophy, literature, and history, among other humanities subjects. However, this does not mean that humanities education could simply carry on "business as usual." Much of what passes for humanities education today does not realize the vision of either Confucius's or Dewey's philosophy of education as it is ineffective in contributing to Confucian personal cultivation and Deweyan growth.

3   Reuniting the Two Cultures

Education in the humanities suitable for the AI age would not be the liberal education that was opposed to vocational education, which was associated with science, in the debates in American education that Dewey addressed in the early decades of the twentieth century. Dewey had no patience with the reactionary opposition to science in favor of humanities reduced to literary and linguistics studies. "In a world which is largely what it is today because of science and technology ... Their proposal is so remote from the facts of the present world, it involves such a bland ignoring of actualities, that there is a temptation to dismiss it as idle vaporing" (LW 15: 257). Unfortunately, far from being harmless, the medievalism that perpetuates the opposition between the liberal and the vocational in education, between the humanities and the sciences, is responsible for keeping science "materialistic and anti-human" and strengthening "all the habits and institutions which render that which is morally 'ideal' impotent in action and which leave the 'material' to operate without humane direction" (LW 15: 257).

The very dichotomy between the humanities and the sciences in education fails to appreciate the role of science in education, which is not merely "a set

HUMANITIES EDUCATION IN THE AGE OF AI

of formal and technical exercises" (MW 9: 237), or the teaching of "readymade information and technical skills" (LW 15: 258). Dewey criticized the way science "is taught upon the whole not with respect to the way in which it actually enters into human life, and hence as a supremely humanistic subject, but as if it had to do with a world which is 'external' to human concerns" (LW 15: 258; see also MW 9: 227–239; Clopton & Ou, 1973: 252–260). He was even more critical of the purely scholastic way of teaching humanities focusing on the literary and linguistic, consisting in narrow training in techniques of reading texts and abstract discussions divorced from the human activities and concerns which give their subject matter meaning and significance – a pedagogy that produces "a feebly pretentious snobbishness of culture" (MW 10: 181) instead of "a social and socialized sense" that liberates and humanizes. The conflict between the sciences and humanities cannot be resolved by eliminating one of them from education (MW 1: 304; see also MW 9: 236–238). It is rooted in the common source of their pedagogical errors – the disassociation from real life problems – which blinds them to the oneness of knowledge as the outcome of social inquiry into those problems.

The humanities and the sciences are clearly not mutually exclusive choices in Dewey's understanding of education. Introducing volume 17 of Dewey's *Collected Works* with an essay on "The Relevance of John Dewey's Thought," Sidney Hook remarked, "A half century before C. P. Snow's superficial book on *The Two Cultures* (1959) appeared, Dewey had defined the problem facing reflective citizens concerned with education as 'how we are to effect in this country a combination of a scientific and a humanistic education'" (LW 17: XVIII; MW 10: 181). When he referred to the three-centuries long debate in European education over the relative importance of the humanities and the natural sciences while lecturing in China, Dewey concluded that, "Both sides in this quarrel fell into identical error; both separated man from nature; both made the one independent of the other" (Clopton & Ou, 1973: 254). For Dewey, an education is incomplete if it does not include both the sciences and the humanities, which must be taught through confronting real world problems, and such problems always have human as well as natural aspects (Clopton & Ou, 1973: 255–256). He was critical of humanistic studies which define themselves in opposition to the sciences – the humanities understood as an exclusively literary education, which he saw as primarily "the prerogative of the aristocracy" (Clopton & Ou, 1973: 255), quite unsuited to any actual or aspiring democratic society. In the Chinese context, he associated the traditional humanities with "dogmatic methods of instruction, such as indoctrination in old beliefs and traditions and memorization of the Chinese classics" – an impression that he probably obtained from his students who were leaders of the May Fourth movement, and standard bearers for its condemnation of Confucianism. Dewey certainly would not endorse a revival of Confucian studies on that model, although he would be sympathetic to the Chinese people's desire to build their future on the basis of their cultural traditions.[15]

Dewey's assessment of America's "educational situation" (MW 1: 305) at the beginning of the twentieth century proves to be prescient in that, instead of science being eliminated from education, empirical methods have contributed to the rise of new disciplines of social sciences studying the varied phenomena and fundamental values of human life. Technology has also transformed, to some extent but not as much as some would like, the disciplines that continue to be categorized as humanities. Since Jesuit Father Roberto Busa approached IBM to use computers to produce a concordance of the works of Thomas Aquinas in the late nineteen forties, the use of digital technology in humanities research and education has enabled many hitherto laborious tasks of working with literary and historical texts to be carried out with greater speed and accuracy. From this emerged a new field known as humanities computing; and it became digital humanities in the new millennium – a change of name to signify that the field has progressed beyond mere digitization of texts and automation of traditional research tasks, as technical support for humanities research, and should be considered "a discipline in its own right" (Schreibman, Siemens, & Unsworth, 2004: XXIII). Digital collections of texts has grown exponentially and expanded to include images, audio recordings, videos and now "born digital" materials as records of human activities, which humanities scholars could engage in ways previously unimaginable with a variety of digital tools from word search, word frequency count, sorting and comparing of texts, to automatic annotation, text-mining, GIS (geographic information system) mapping, and other forms of data visualization. According to the editors of the Blackwell *Companion* who renamed the field, digital humanities "is now much broader than it once was, and includes not only the computational modeling and analysis of humanities information, but also the cultural study of digital technologies, their creative possibilities, and their social impact" (Schreibman, Siemens, & Unsworth, 2016: XVII).

Academic discussions of digital humanities began in the People's Republic of China (PRC) towards the end of the first decade of the new millennium. The first digital humanities research center in China was set up at Wuhan University in 2011, and several other universities have since set up similar institutes, including Fudan University's Institute of Humanities and Social Science Data, Nanjing University's Innovation and Research Center for Digital Humanities, and Peking University's Digital Humanities Lab. Some universities are now offering courses in digital humanities, and a few have started undergraduate majors, although digital humanities education is still in the exploratory stage. Several digital humanities conferences have been organized by Chinese universities, such as the Peking University Digital Humanities Forum, which has been held annually since 2016, when it was co-organized by Peking University Library and the Harvard University Chinese Biographical Database Project. In 2019, China held its inaugural National Digital Humanities Conference in Dunhuang (DH2019), and the second annual Conference (DH2020) took place in Shanghai in November 2020, despite the disruptions caused by the COVID-19 pandemic. Digital humanities projects funded by the National Social Science Fund and the Ministry of Education nearly doubled in the four years between 2014 and 2018 (Wang, Tan, & Li, 2020: 13). Within the same four years, publications in digital humanities in the CNKI (China National Knowledge Infrastructure) database increased from a mere eight to a hundred and sixty (Wang, Tan, & Li, 2020: 11). Digital humanities was identified as one of the top ten academic "hotspots" in 2018 by Renmin University and *Guangming Daily* ("Top ten academic hotspots"). Tsinghua university founded the first Chinese digital humanities journal in the PRC in 2019. While resistance to its development continues as some humanities scholars still cling stubbornly to old ways, others see the emerging field bridging the humanities and the sciences to offer answers to the challenge of "posthumanism," as scientific and technological developments undermine the sense of uniqueness and superiority of humans over other species and raise questions about human beings' ability to control their inventions (Wang, 2018).[16]

From Dewey's perspective, the development of digital humanities as a discipline is both good news and bad news. It is good news as the growth and maturation of the use of digital technology enhances our understanding of the fruits of human civilization with implications for contemporary problems and enables new questions to be asked in new ways to address new audiences, and hopefully also enhance our ability to solve problems. However, with the assertion of disciplinary identity comes the perils of rigid policing of boundaries, abstraction of subject matter, and technical sophistication overshadowing the humanistic value of research. This does not mean we should suppress the growth of digital humanities even if that were possible. On the contrary, the perils the new discipline faces have analogues in all disciplines as long as the prevailing disciplinary structures of knowledge production and dissemination continues to divide what should be united. To counter them, disciplinary boundaries need to be continuously challenged if not completely dissolved, and neither methods nor subject matter should be treated as exclusive properties of disciplines. Instead, the related methods of applying digital technology to the studies of human civilizational records should be a common resource of all humanities, and indeed of all research. Such application should be meaningful for human concerns, and not merely showcase the technical capabilities of the tools.

According to the *Digital Humanities Manifesto 2.0*, "Digital Humanities is not a unified field but an array of convergent practices" (Schnapp & Presner, 2009: 2).

> The Digital Humanities seeks to play an inaugural role with respect to a world in which, no longer the sole producers, stewards, and disseminators of knowledge or culture, universities are called upon to shape natively digital models of scholarly discourse for the newly emergent public spheres of the present era (the www, the blogosphere, digital libraries, etc.), to model excellence and innovation in these domains, and to facilitate the formation of networks of knowledge production, exchange, and dissemination that are, at once, global and local. ... it affirms the value of the open, the infinite, the expansive, the university/museum/archive/library *without walls*, the democratization of culture and scholarship, even as it affirms the value of large-scale statistically grounded methods (such as cultural analytics) that collapse the boundaries between the humanities and the social and natural sciences. (Schnapp & Presner, 2009: 2–3; see also Davidson, 2012)

This is a vision of the digital humanities that would appeal to Deweyans, not only for its rejection of the disciplinary barriers between the humanities and the sciences, but also for its democratic objective of empowering various publics to be producers as well as consumers of knowledge.

In the age of AI, not only must humanities education, in both research and teaching, be united with available technology to transform itself both in subject matter and methods, it must also be united with other sciences in our inquiries into the problems raised by new forms and pervasive use of technology, including those that threaten to blur the boundaries between man and machine. Moreover, we should remain open to the opportunities and not only the risks of that blurring; and understanding and evaluating both will require the knowledge and skills of both the humanities and the sciences. Without the humanities, we risk losing the knowledge and appreciation of what has made us human, so that, even if we survive the existential threat of the competition with machine, we may do so only by becoming a superior form of machine ourselves. Without the sciences, we lose the ability to transform our environment and find the material and practical means to solve our problems and realize our ideals. Instead of coexisting as separate disciplines students must choose one at the expense of the other, the humanities and the sciences need to be integrated in education so that students will learn to approach the problems of their age as simultaneously human and scientific.

4   Conclusion

Dewey's visit to China was a momentous event marking the encounter of American Pragmatism with the Chinese civilization. This encounter has borne many fruits. In the area of education, the above discussion shows the resonances between Dewey's philosophy of education and a Confucian (including both Confucius's own and a modernized Confucianism's) understanding of education with regard to the purpose of education, and its implications for the challenges posed by AI to humanities education today. Rather than rendering the latter obsolete, the age of AI has ever greater need for the humanities as human interactions with AI, and the new possibilities being ushered in by new technologies, raise existential questions that require serious reflection on what it means to be human and how human beings could live meaningful lives. Such reflection is the domain of the humanities.

Both Dewey's growth as the only moral end and Confucius's ideal of personal cultivation to become an exemplary person, as the respective purposes of education in their philosophies of education, require the knowledge of human relationships and experiences, the products of human civilizations which comprise the subject matter of the literature, philosophy, and history, among other humanities subject. Their philosophies of education do not merely provide support for humanities education and defend its continued relevance in the age of AI; they also provide critical perspectives for evaluating how humanities education has been carried out in recent times and provide guidance of what is needed for humanities education to meet the challenges of the age of AI. Most important is the need to overcome the dichotomy between the humanities and the sciences to ensure that education in the age of AI will integrate humanistic purposes to guide our scientific-technological endeavors with the knowledge of the material world and practical means provided by science and technology that challenge and test the viability of the ideas and ideals the humanities produce.

Notes

1   Frey and Osborne's (2013) study of 702 detailed occupations in the US labour market predicted that 47% of them are at risk of computerization over the next two decades.

2 Of the responses received, 52% expect AI and related technologies to have neutral to positive impact on employment (Pew Research Center, 2014). James Bessen (2016) also argues that the foreseeable effect of computerization on employment is marginally positive, even though he admits that new AI technologies might cause job losses in future. Cf. Ford (2015); Avent (2016); and Susskind (2020).

3 While not evident in humanities research and teaching before the advent of digitization, framing qualitative ideas as quantitative problems is very much part of the growing field of digital humanities, which I shall discuss at the end of this chapter.

4 Other similar opinions from within the technological sector can be found in Faisal Hoque's (2018) and Luying Pan's (2019) blogs.

5 https://computing.mit.edu/

6 In-text citations from the Analects give traditional numbering of passages in the transition by Ames and Rosemont (1998).

7 *Junzi* has been translated as "gentleman" or "noble man" and Confucianism has often been charged with Sexism. Adopting the gender neutral "exemplary person" and using the female pronoun when discussing contemporary interpretation and application of Confucianism is not a casual act of "political correctness" but based on arguments regarding the compatibility between Confucius's teachings and gender equality offered elsewhere. For contributions to this discussion, see Chenyang Li (2000); Foust and Tan (2016); and Tan (2006, 2021).

8 In his lectures in China, Dewey also maintained that "education means growth" (Clopton & Ou, 1973: 185). Scholarship bringing together Dewey and Confucianism on issues in education includes Leonard Waks' chapter in this volume, drawing on Confucian personal cultivation to strengthen Dewey's democratic education project. Charlene Tan (2016) discusses the parallels between Dewey and Confucius on the importance of both learner and subject-matter. See also Leonard Tan's discussion of music education (2018).

9 See Su Zhixin's chapter in this volume.

10 Dewey criticized these motives in the application of science (LW 8: 60).

11 Besides the chapter on "Vocational Aspects of Education" in *Democracy and Education* (MW 9: 316–330); other examples include "Some Dangers in the Present Movement for Industrial Education" (MW 7: 98–103), "Industrial Education and Democracy" (MW 7: 104–105), "Education through Industry" in *Schools of Tomorrow* (MW 8: 365–387), "The Need for an Industrial Education in an Industrial Democracy" (MW 10: 137–143), "Learning to Earn: the Place of Vocational Education in a Comprehensive Scheme of Public Education" (MW 10: 144–150), "The Modern Trend Toward Vocational Education in Its Effect Upon the Professional and Non-Professional Studies of the University" (MW 10: 151–157), "Vocational Education in the Light of the World War" (MW 11: 58–69), and "Culture and Professionalism in Education" (MW 15: 193–197).

12 Cf. discussion of the historical evolution of the relation between work and meaning in Susskind (2020: 203–210).

13 See Tan's *Confucian Democracy* (2003: 25–29) for a more detailed discussion of Dewey's "social self-in-the-making."

14 Susskind (2020) also notes that the aim of producing "a people of outstanding character," mentioned in the United Kingdom's Education Act of 1944 introducing free secondary education for all in the country, mostly ignored in the decades that followed, has made a comeback with increasing talk of teaching "character" and "life skills."

15 For more detailed discussions of Deweyan responses to the contemporary revival of Confucianism in China, see Tan (2010, 2012).

16 Wang's conception and analysis of posthumanism are underpinned by apparently dualistic assumptions that are incompatible with both Confucius' philosophy and Dewey's Pragmatism, even though AI does pose challenges discussed earlier.

HUMANITIES EDUCATION IN THE AGE OF AI   251

References

Ames, R. T. (2020). *Confucianism common sense meets the AI revolution* [Online lecture]. Bing Song, Berggruen Institute. https://www.berggruen.org/activity/confucianism-commonsense-meets-the-ai-revolution/

Ames, R. T. (2021). *Human becomings: Theorizing person for Confucian role ethics.* State University of New York Press.

Ames, R. T., & Rosemont, H. Jr. (1998). *The Analects of Confucius: A philosophical translation.* Ballantine.

Auon, J. E. (2017). *Robot-proof: Higher education in the age of artificial intelligence.* MIT Press.

Avent, R. (2016). *Wealth of humans: Work, power, and status in the twenty-first century.* St. Martin's Press.

Bessen, J. (2016). *How computer automation affects occupations: Technology, jobs and skills.* Law and Economics Working Paper. Boston University School of Law. https://scholarship.law.bu.edu/cgi/viewcontent.cgi?article=1811&context=faculty_scholarship

Clopton, R. W., & Ou, T.-c. (Eds.). (1973). *John Dewey: Lectures in China, 1919–1920.* University of Hawaii Press.

Davidson, C. N. (2012). Humanities 2.0: Promise, perils, and predictions. In M. K. Gold (Ed.), *Debates in the digital humanities.* University of Minnesota Press.

Dewey, J. References are to the critical edition published by Southern Illinois University Press. Volume and page numbers follow the initials of the series. Abbreviations for the volumes cited are: EW *The Early Works* (1882–1898); MW *The Middle Works* (1899–1924); LW *The Later Works* (1925–1953).

Dixon, R. (2018, July 6). China plans to dominate AI, with a vanguard of robotic doctors like 'Biomind'. *Los Angeles Times.*

Edwards, C. (2019). *Technology and liberal arts in the age of AI discussed in lecture translated* (SUSTech Newshub, translated and adapted). https://newshub.sustech.edu.cn/html/201904/12787.html

Ford, M. (2015). *Rise of the robots: Technology and threat of a jobless future.* Basic Books.

Foust, M., & Tan, S.-h. (Eds.). (2016). *Feminist encounters with Confucius.* Brill.

Frey, C. B., & Osborne, M. (2013). *The future of employment: How susceptible are jobs to computerisation?* Oxford Martin School, University of Oxford.

Gkritsi, E. (2019). Confucius in Shenzhen: A classical view of AI. *Technode.* http://technode.com/2019/06/11/confucius-in-shenzhen-a-classical-view-of-ai/

Hao, K. (2019). There's no such thing as a 'tech person' in the age of AI. *MIT Technology Review.* https://www.technologyreview.com/2019/03/02/65994/ai-ethics-mit-college-of-computing-tech-humanities/

Hoque, F. (2018, September 18). The case for humanities in the era of AI, automation, and technology. *Fast Company.* https://www.fastcompany.com/90236240/the-case-for-humanities-in-the-era-of-ai-automation-and-technology

Huang, S., Yang, J., Fong, S., & Zhao, Q. (2020). Artificial intelligence in cancer diagnosis and prognosis: Opportunities and challenges. *Cancer Letters, 471,* 61–71.

Hume, K. (2017a). Education in the age of AI. *Quam Proxime/As Near as May Be.* https://quamproxime.com/2017/04/08/educating-for-the-ai-enabled-economy/

Hume, K. (2017b). The utilities of the humanities in the 21st century. *Quam Proxime/As Near as May Be.* https://quamproxime.com/2017/02/20/the-utility-of-the-humanities-in-the-21st-century/

Levy, F., & Murnane, R. J. (2004). *The new division of labor: How computers are creating the next job market.* Princeton University Press.

Li, C. (Ed.). (2000). *The sage and the second sex.* Open Court.

Liberal arts, humanities shine in the age of AI. (2019, March 28). *Times of India.*

Morris, F. (2020, December 28), 'Toxic Individualism': Pandemic politics driving healthcare workers from small towns. *National Public Radio.* https://www.npr.org/2020/12/28/950861977/toxic-individualism-pandemic-politics-driving-health-care-workers-from-small-tow

NACE. (2020). *Job outlook 2020: Key attributes employers seek on students' resumes.* National Association of Colleges and Employers. https://www.naceweb.org/about-us/press/2020/the-top-attributes-employers-want-to-see-on-resumes/

Pan, L. (2019). A case for the humanities [Blog]. *LinkedIn.* https://www.linkedin.com/pulse/case-humanities-liberal-arts-luying-pan?trk=related_artice_A%20Casefor%20Humanities%20in%20the%20Age%20of%20AI_article-card_title

Pew Research Center. (2014). *AI, robotics, and the future of jobs.* http://www.pewinternet.org/2014/08/06/future-of-jobs/

Popper, N. (2016, February 25). The robots are coming for Wall Street. *New York Times.*

Rosemont, Jr. H. (2015). *Against individualism: A Confucian rethinking of the foundations of morality, politics, family, and religion.* Lexington Books.

Schnapp, J., Presner, T., et al. (2009). *Digital humanities manifesto 2.0.* https://www.humanitiesblast.com/manifesto/Manifesto_V2.pdf

Schreibman, S., Siemens, R., & Unsworth, J. (Eds.). (2004). *A companion to digital humanities.* Blackwell.

Schreibman, S., Siemens, R., & Unsworth, J. (Eds.). (2016). *A new companion to digital humanities.* Wiley Blackwell.

Schwab, K. (2016). *The Fourth Industrial Revolution.* World Economic Forum.

Snow, C. P. (1959). *The two cultures and the scientific revolution.* Oxford University Press.

Susskind, D. (2020). *A world without work: Technology, automation, and how we should respond.* Metropolitan Books.

Tan, C. (2016). Beyond 'either-or' thinking: John Dewey and Confucius on subject matter and learner. *Pedagogy, Culture, and Society, 24*(1), 55–74.

Tan, L. (2018). On Confucian metaphysics, the pragmatist revolution, and philosophy of music education. *Philosophy of Music Education Review, 26*(1), 63–81.

Tan, S.-h. (2003). *Confucian democracy: A Deweyan reconstruction.* State University of New York Press.

Tan, S.-h. (2006). Women's virtues and the Analects. In K.-c. Chong & L. Yuli (Eds.), *Conceptions of virtue east and west* (pp. 255–279). Marshall Cavendish.

Tan, S.-h. (2010). Our country right or wrong: A pragmatic response to anti-democratic cultural nationalism in China. *Contemporary Pragmatism, 7*(2), 45–69.

Tan, S.-h. (2012). The pragmatic Confucian approach to tradition in modernizing China. *History and Theory, 51*(4), 23–44.

Tan, S.-h. (2021). From women's learning (*Fuxue*) to gender studies: Feminist challenges to modern Confucianism. In P. D. Hershock & R. T. Ames (Eds.), *Human beings or human becomings? A conversation with Confucianism on the concept of person.* State University of New York Press.

Tonar, R. (2018). Humanity's search for meaning in the age of AI and automation. *Medium.* https://medium.com/@AItheist/humanitys-search-for-meaning-in-the-age-of-ai-and-automation-18c850544502

Top ten academic hotspots in 2018. (2018, January 11). *Guangming Daily.* http://news.gmw.cn/2019-01/11/content_32334118.htm

Wang, N. (2018). Humanities encounters science: Confronting the challenge of post-humanism. *European Review, 26*(2), 344–353.

Wang, X., Tan, X., & Li, H. (2020). The evolution of digital humanities in China. *Library Trends, 69*(1), 7–29.

CHAPTER 13

Education and the Reconstruction of a Democratic Society

Two Main Themes in Dewey's Philosophy of Education

WANG Chengbing and DONG Ming

Abstract

Education and the reconstruction of a democratic society are two themes about which Dewey was especially concerned throughout his life. On the one hand, Dewey regarded education as growth, emphasizing that the end of education is nothing but itself. Dewey received a barrage of criticism for this, as some people saw it as a theory advocating the aimlessness of education. On the other hand, the growth in Dewey's theory is more than the growth of the individual: it also involves thinking from a social perspective, and thus is democracy-oriented growth. However, Robert B. Westbrook and Aaron Schutz point out that Dewey's method of starting with local communities to develop a Great Community has its problems, and his proposal to transform society through schools also faces enormous difficulties. This chapter firstly clarifies Dewey's concept of growth. Then, it discusses the relationships among growth, education, and democracy in Dewey's thoughts. Finally, it analyzes the problems that existed during the development of a democratic society and argues for Dewey's ideal of a Great Community, which has been questioned.

Keywords

John Dewey – growth – experience – community – democracy

∙ ∙ ∙

Education and the reconstruction of a democratic society are two key themes on which John Dewey focused. On the one hand, Dewey equated education with growth, believing that education is aimed at pursuing continuous growth. He defined the concept of growth by analyzing both the conditions that growth should meet and the relationship between experience and growth. For Dewey, growth was merely the reorganization and transformation of educational

© KONINKLIJKE BRILL NV, LEIDEN, 2019 | DOI:10.1163/9789004511477_014

EDUCATION AND THE RECONSTRUCTION OF A DEMOCRATIC SOCIETY   255

experience. On the other hand, Dewey proposed a unique perspective on democracy, that is, democracy as a way of life, and thus as a means of unifying communities. As Dewey's views of democracy and its relationship with growth and education revealed, growth is democracy-oriented, and education aims to imbue citizens with democratic ideals. The realization of democratic ideals is inseparable from the improvement of the citizens' intelligence, which entails education. As Robert B. Westbrook and Aaron Schutz (2001) point out, Dewey's method of developing a Great Community from local communities is problematic, and his social transformation by means of education also faces huge difficulties. In his later years, Dewey abandoned his effort to transform society through schools alone, and was more inclined to pursue his democratic ideal through social activities. By emphasizing the importance of "home education," this chapter provides better connections between Dewey's school education and the transformation of democratic society, and between his local communities and the Great Community, in an attempt to overcome the difficulties Dewey faced.

1   Growth: The Reorganization and Reconstruction of Experience

Dewey maintained that a living organism obtained energy through its interactions with its surroundings, which constituted the process of life. However, the continuation of a species does not depend on a single organism, but on the reproduction of the species as a whole, one generation after another. During this process, individuals who cannot adapt to their surroundings will gradually decline and eventually become extinct, while new forms of life that can better acclimatize to their surroundings will emerge. Dewey used the word *life* to denote the entire range of experiences, both individual and in groups. Life, or experience, merely means to continue oneself through constant renewal. Therefore, the continuation of humans as a species refers to continuation not only in a biological sense, but also in some cultural sense. Thus, the continuation of humankind depends not only on procreation, but also on the communication and transmission of experiences within a group. The process of this communication and transmission within a group is the process of education. Therefore, education is a necessary outcome of human life.

As Dewey (1980) pointed out, the process of education is the process of the reorganization and reconstruction of experiences, that is, growth. Education is merely life, and the process of education is no more than the process of life. In this sense, there is no end beyond the process of education, and the end of education lies in education itself. Further, we accept education simply to develop the ability to accept further education.

It should be noted that Dewey's above-mentioned philosophy was first recognized by Chinese scholars prior to the 1940s. For example, in 1934, Liang Shuming (2005: 685) pointed out that "Dewey's scholarship is linked up," and believed that the reason why Dewey's scholarship appeared to be so coherent was that although he is talking about "education", "society", "livehood" and so on which in our view irrelevant concepts, but in fact is talking about the same thing: "life".

Dewey believed that growth was primarily based on the immature state of individuals. Immaturity has a positive aspect, in that it endows an individual with capacity and potentiality, "expressing a force positively present – the ability to develop" (1980: 46). For Dewey, immaturity was absolute, that is, both infants and adults were in this state. Meanwhile, in line with the continuous state of immaturity, growth was also seen as endless. Furthermore, the state of immaturity had two characteristics: dependence and plasticity. First, Dewey (1980: 49) pointed out that "From a social standpoint, dependence denotes a power rather than a weakness; it involves interdependence." Man is different from other animals; man's instinct develops slowly, which forces man to make up for the insufficiency of his inborn ability and maintain his own survival through exchanges with his social surroundings. Growth is accompanied by this positive form of dependence. As for plasticity, Dewey (1980: 49) pointed out that "It is essentially the ability to learn from experience; the power to retain from one experience something which is of avail in coping with the difficulties of a later situation." Man can increase the meaning of an experience and fulfill the reorganization and reconstruction of experiences only when he is equipped with plasticity, for "plasticity is the capacity to retain and carry over from prior experience factors which modify subsequent activities. This signifies the capacity to acquire habits, or develop definite dispositions" (Dewey, 1980: 51). The most obvious outcome of the existence of plasticity is the development of various habits, and the subsequent adjustment to and of one's surroundings through these habits.

The next question to be considered is, given that growth is the reorganization and reconstruction of experiences, how do we determine which among the great variety of experiences we are subject to deserve our attention? Dewey believed that education should involve experience or experiments. Experience is closely related to Dewey's philosophy of education. Contrary to modern philosophers, who discuss experience in the domain of epistemology, Dewey viewed experience through the lens of existentialism. He held that the development of biology had changed the philosophy of cognition which dominated

EDUCATION AND THE RECONSTRUCTION OF A DEMOCRATIC SOCIETY 257

by perceptions, to the philosophy of experience emphasizing life and activities, and pointed out that experience is "an affair primarily of doing" (Dewey, 1982: 129). Dewey agreed with William James's interpretation of experience, suggesting that "it recognizes in its primary integrity no division between act and material, subject and object, but contains them both in an unanalyzed totality" (Dewey, 1981: 129). However, Dewey went even further by discriminating between two kinds of experience, that is, primary experience and secondary or reflective experience. The former is both the starting point and the end point of empirical naturalism. The objects of study in both philosophy and the sciences mainly belong to the category of reflective experience, and are full of the sense of experience. In Dewey's view, experience (especially reflective experience) is characterized by interaction and continuance. With respect to interaction, Dewey (1982: 129) explained that "The organism acts in accordance with its own structure, simple or complex, upon its surroundings. As a consequence, the changes produced in the environment react upon the organism and its activities." Thus, experience is an outcome combining positive doing or attempting and passive suffering or undergoing. One can have an experience only by consciously relating an activity to the outcome of that activity. Therefore, "The standard to evaluate the value of experience depends on the relations and continuity caused by the experience" (Li, 2012: 65). Dewey (1988: 19) summarized the concept of continuity, stating that "every experience both takes up something from those which have gone before and modifies in some way the quality of those which come after." Contrary to traditional empiricists, who believed that experience was merely the acceptance and recording of perceptions, Dewey argued that the primary function of experience was its guidance of practice. The primary tendency of an organism is, through activities, to acclimatize to or transform its surroundings so as to enable its own development. Experience is based on the past, represented in the present, and oriented toward future.

Growth is the reorganization and reconstruction of experiences. However, this proposition is obviously not relevant to all experiences. As Hildreth (2011: 34) pointed out, the concept of experience referred to by Dewey can be divided into three types: non-educational experience, mis-educational experience, and educational experience. Specifically, non-educational experience is merely unreflective experience, that is, the primary experience referred to by Dewey. Mis-educational experience can be further subdivided into two kinds: one is practice, which involves little thinking, while the other must be analyzed together with educational experience. First, continuity needs to be further defined. Dewey (1988: 19) stated that "It is when we note the different forms in which continuity of experience operates that we get the basis of discriminating among experiences." In other words, the experience that an infant obtains at a particular point can enable him to gain more experience later, and offers him the opportunity to obtain experience in new directions, for the concept of growth must have universal applicability, rather than targeting a particular domain. Second, Dewey emphatically pointed out that interaction endowed the objective and internal conditions necessary for experience with equal importance. The combination of conditions in these two aspects resulted in a situation whereby experience was enabled. Thus, an educator should, in the light of his or her own experiences, determine the directions in which the present experience of an infant could lead and proactively create an environment that could either accommodate or trigger the curiosity of the child, while enabling the child to gain more valuable experience in the future. Thus, only experience that satisfies the strict rules of continuity can be viewed as educational experience. Interaction provides a guiding principle for the activities of educators, while it also appears as a characteristic of experience. Therefore, growth is the reorganization and reconstruction of educational experiences, that is, an organism enables the benign and continuous development of experience during the process of interaction with its surroundings.

2 Education through the Framework of Democrazy: Maximizing Growth

Many people have misunderstood Dewey's concept of growth, thinking that Dewey only cared about individuals while ignoring groups, and that he advocated an individualist view of education. Dewey did believe that education should devote itself to the reorganization and reconstruction of individual experiences, maintaining that this would enable everyone to attain the capability of studying continuously. However, this does not mean that Dewey did not care about the social dimension of education. As David Cohen (1988: 427) stated, many people thought that Dewey's view of education was "child-centered," but what Dewey aimed to achieve through the education of children was social, political, and cultural renewal. Therefore, Dewey stated emphatically that education should be oriented toward society.

James Campbell (1998: 24) noted that Dewey saw human individuals as inherently social creatures for whom a sense of community was natural. Again, for Dewey, communities were essential: we needed to form groups to become human. In Dewey's view, an individual lived in a relationship with others first: "Apart from associations with one another, individuals are isolated from one another and fade and wither; or are opposed to one another and their conflicts injure individual development" (Dewey, 1982: 187). One individual is connected with another, which constitutes a social group or community. Dewey believed that a good social form certainly pointed toward a democratic society, and proposed a unique way of looking at a democracy: "A democracy is more than a form of government; it is primarily a mode of associated living, of conjoint communicated experience" (Dewey, 1980: 93). Therefore, "Democracy should be a social democracy, it should be integrated into one's personality, and become a way of life. That is to say, the democracy claimed by Dewey is a participatory democracy that is linked with daily life" (Tu & Hu, 2011: 28).

In short, a democratic society has two major characteristics. First, it has internality and homogeneity, that is, it advocates the sharing of common interests and experiences as abundantly and pluralistically as possible, and depends on this to maintain social control. Second, it has externality and heterogeneity, in other words, a member of the community should have as many exchanges as possible with others to enable the community to maintain an open attitude (Dewey, 1980: 89). Dewey maintained that a democratic society was one in which every member participated in activities that benefited others, and that everyone should refer to the activities of other members of the community when acting, aware of the results that his own action might yield, making his action meaningful for the life of the community, and reasonable in the context of the overall direction of the community. "One of the ideals of Dewey's political philosophy is to seek and build the Great Community, and the democratic community is the ideal form of the human community" (Zhang M. & Zhang L., 2011: 72). A point that deserves noting is that a community does not have to adhere to monotonous conformity, even though a democratic community suggests shared interests or common objectives to a certain extent, because such conformity can only be regarded as collectivism. A democratic society allows for the existence of a pluralistic view, and enables people to maintain their individuality. Dewey reminded us of the value of differences, or the other way round it would case continuous losses.

Education is necessary for any community that wants to continue, and therefore it cannot separate from certain processes of society. Dewey reiterated that education, especially school education, could not adopt the position of an onlooker, remaining detached from society and only providing a service in terms of knowledge transfer. Instead, it should apply itself to the development and transmission of a democratic way of life and to the rediscovery of democratic forms. Education should be oriented toward democracy and guided by the democratic way of life to produce democratic citizens. As Dewey clearly asserted, "unless education has some frame of reference it is bound to be aimless, lacking a unified objective. The necessity for a frame of reference must be admitted. There exists in this country such a unified frame. It is called democracy" (Dewey, 1987: 415). A democratic society can stimulate everyone in an open and pluralistic way to maximize their capabilities, extending their experience as many directions as possible. Directing education through the framework of democracy can help to fulfill the purpose of education, that is, to maximize growth. As Dewey pointed out, it is necessary for each participant in democratic life to constantly rediscover what democracy as a way of life is like: "The trouble, at least one great trouble, is that we have taken democracy for granted: we have thought and acted as if our forefathers had founded it once and for all. We have forgotten that it has to be enacted anew in every generation, every year and day, in the living relations of person to person in all social forms and institutions" (Dewey, 1987: 416). We often claim that "The devotion of democracy to education is a familiar fact" (Dewey, 1980: 93). That is because the constant discovery of the particular meaning and form of a democratic way of life requires the participation of every individual in the educational process.

In his work *The Public and Its Problems*, Dewey pointed out that given the great volume and complexity of social affairs, the public[1] gradually come to be ignored, remaining in a state of obfuscation and unconsciousness. In brief, formerly small communities have turned into a great society, and previous patterns of association between individuals have been dismantled, but no new form has yet come into being, and the Great Community that Dewey envisaged is still not evident. In Dewey's philosophy, a Great Community is a democratic community consisting of local communities of varying sizes and shapes. Dewey believed that the construction of the Great Community entailed the transmission of knowledge about the social sciences, and required the improvement of the intellectual level of the citizens. In Dewey's view, each member of a community should participate in democratic activities by means of intellectual (scientific) exploration to guarantee the development of democracy in a favorable direction.

Dewey (1984: 116) stressed that intellectual inquiries are scientific inquiries, and that such a form of inquiry requires trust in the process of experience, the "faithfulness to whatever is discovered and steadfastness in adhering to new truth." This methodology reminds us that although the world is constantly changing, we still need to believe that the experience gained in the process of our interactions with the world is full of connections, and can be used to direct practical activities. In Dewey's opinion, the method of intellectual inquiry had been fully utilized in the field of sciences and obtained good results, and the social conditions necessary for intellectual inquiry to be universally applied in the social domain had been achieved.

EDUCATION AND THE RECONSTRUCTION OF A DEMOCRATIC SOCIETY   261

With the abovementioned philosophy as a prerequisite, Dewey redefined the meaning of intellectual inquiry, holding that it was an experimental method that considered social issues in terms of both means and results. It was also a method of cooperation and communication that aimed to publicize various views and interests, and solve problems through mutual understanding and discussion. Democracy implies a way of life within a community, as well as an intellectual approach to inquiry. Therefore, to enhance each person's capacity for intellectual inquiry through education is simply to develop democratic citizens.

3   From Local Communities to a Great Community: An Ideal with Problems

Dewey argued that democracy as a community lifestyle had no unchangeable forms or essential meanings. Democracy has a variety of forms, which vary in accordance with specific situations and historical stages. Therefore, Dewey did not predict an ideal form of democracy, discuss specific issues in relation to democratic practice, or propose any particular method for the realization of the Great Community. Rather, he simply described some vague characteristics, for example, the Great Community had a variety of free forms, was vigorous, flexible, and stable, local communities were no longer isolated, and the community would provide endless and constantly changing meaning (Dewey, 1984: 370).[2]

In this regard, Robert B. Westbrook maintains that Dewey deviated from his own principles, failing to turn the fulfillment of the Great Community into a "working end." The so-called working end is not just imagination or ideal; instead allows actors to study the conditions of action and to give the ideal something that is fulfilled by reality. In Westbrook's view, Dewey's ideal of the Great Community is similar to the too distant end that he himself had criticized for being unable to guide our actions. Dewey did not describe what the Great Community would be like once it was achieved, nor did he specify how the Great Community was to be achieved. Therefore, Westbrook (1980: 239) argued that Dewey's theory of democracy was problematic in that it separated democratic ends from democratic means. Meanwhile, Dewey opposed the faith of a transcendent ideal in the religious sense, but claimed that the faith should be a revisable tendency to action. The latter is the faith in experience itself. In Dewey's theoretical framework, democracy is based on experience, and he embraced the conviction in experience, therefore, democracy gained its legitimacy. However, the theory of democracy needs to be tested in practice to verify whether it is leading us in the right direction. At this point, Westbrook holds that Dewey's conviction in democracy is merely the transcendent faith in the religious sense that he had rejected because he ignored the various historical failures in the practice of his theory of democracy (for example, the Port Huron Statement and the New Left movement), as well as the failures of his own practices (for instance, the League for Independent Political Action and the founding of a Third Party), but persisted with his belief in the form of democracy that he had advocated. Thus, Westbrook came to believe that Dewey's work on democracy did not rely on the positive existence and growth of a democratic community.

In this regard, we propose a different view. As Michael Eldridge has pointed out, Westbrook's opinion regarding Dewey's theory of democracy is tilted too far toward the political realm, possibly because of Dewey's political activities. However, the political dimension was not central to Dewey's view of democracy. Moreover, Eldridge argues that if the concept of a democratic community includes elements such as society, the church, and the neighborhood, Westbrook went too far in asserting that the community was near death. Eldridge (1996: 20) points out that Dewey's faith is the action depending a modifiable tendency. This refers to his belief in experience, that is, that all theories, views, and convictions need to be put into practice through actions and tested in the world of experience, and then revised to guide the activities that follow. The so-called truth or falsity, the good or bad of democracy, depends upon the outcomes of social actions. Dewey (1987: 61) was not an absolutist in political terms; he did not oppose particular forms of representative government, and even admitted that under certain conditions, the force can be intelligently employed. Dewey believed that in the practice of democracy, one must follow a scientific pattern of inquiry and make corresponding decisions during different stages, but the most important thing was that the decision had to be based on the interests of the community and on open communication (Eldridge, 1996: 22–27). Therefore, as Campbell pointed out, Dewey's theory is *"melioristic*, not *optimistic* ... His assumption is not a belief in the eventual triumph of reason in history, but in the worthwhileness of efforts to try to advance the common good" (Campbell, 1995: 261). Therefore, democracy is a way "which believes wholeheartedly in the process of experience as end and as means; ... which is capable of generating the science which is the sole dependable authority for the direction of further experience and which releases emotions, needs and desires so as to call into being the things that have not existed in the past ... the task of democracy is forever that of creation of a freer and more humane experience in which all share and to which all contribute" (Dewey, 1988: 229–230).

Here, we return to the issue of democratic practices. In his work *The Public and Its Problems*, Dewey identified two prerequisites for the fulfillment of the

Great Community, that is, the popularization of social inquiry and local communities. Regarding the former, Dewey pointed out that research should not be confined within academic institutions, but instead should be combined with popular media, turning the results of the specialist academic researchers into tools for each actor's intellectual inquiry. However, as Westbrook (1980: 301) pointed out, and Dewey also admitted, there were significant difficulties in disseminating professional knowledge through the popular media. Westbrook (1980: 510) noted that Dewey set rigorous conditions for the public's process of discovering themselves, and thus shaping the Great Community: "in laying out the 'infinitely difficult' conditions for the emergence of the Great Community and offering little guidance for overcoming them, he [Dewey] inadvertently and ironically made almost as good a case as Lippmann had that the phantom public would not materialize."

The second prerequisite that Dewey advanced was the construction of the Great Community by starting with local communities. However, Aaron Schutz (2001: 302) holds that "the most fundamental problem with Dewey's idea of the Great Community is that it was essentially derived from experiences of interaction in small, face-to-face, local communities." Within a local community, everyone is acquainted with each other, and the experience is so lively that it provides the best environment for intellectual inquiry and democratic life. However, when life extends from a local community to the Great Community, things change. It is not so much a problem of how to improve the accuracy of communication and the speed of transmission, but one of the extent of communication. In this case, more communication may make things worse.

In relation to education, a school is also a local community, and some educators who have been deeply influenced by Dewey still follow the path he advocated for teaching in schools by encouraging students to acquire the habits of communication and collaboration. However, as Schutz (2001: 312) pointed out, this form of cooperation is not popular in society today, and society does not operate in this way. Therefore, Dewey came to be aware in his later years that "the defects of schools mirrored and sustained the defects of the larger society and these defects could not be remedied apart from a struggle for democracy throughout that larger society" (Westbrook, 1980: 510). This also led him to expend considerable energy participating in a range of social activities with a view to disseminating the democratic spirit throughout society.

It is difficult to solve the problem of the relationship between local communities and the Great Community, and this issue is itself a part of the process of democracy. The solution to this problem requires not only the efforts of scholars and governments, but also those of each individual, and thus the improvement of their inquiry capability and democratic spirit. Even more importantly, it is necessary to create the cultural circumstances with which most people identify and that entice them to act. As for whether this problem can be solved, and if so when, we have no idea. Here, we are merely trying to understand this issue by emphasizing the importance of family education.

Local communities are still a key starting point, because as Dewey pointed out, only through face-to-face local communication can dialogue be held between individuals. Dewey (1984: 368) also noted the importance of families, stating that "Democracy must begin at home, and its home is the neighborly community." We all live within families from birth, and thus families have a primariness that other community groups lack. Meanwhile, the family is also a bridge connecting individuals and the Greater Community. The surroundings created by communities indirectly foster our habits. Moreover, Dewey (1983: 88) notes that a habit that has been established has inertia: "No matter how accidental and irrational the circumstances of its origin, no matter how different the conditions which now exist to those under which the habit was formed, the latter persists until the environment obstinately rejects it." Therefore, it is very important for the family to foster good habits among children in their early days through family education. The training of democratic citizens should start with families, and the everyday activities of parents and children. There are still difficulties, of course, because not all parents are aware of the importance of family education. We have the necessary mechanisms to evaluate the capabilities of each staff member in the work situation, but have no way of determining whether a parent is suitably qualified. However, this does not mean that the situation is beyond our control, and we cannot simply sit back and wait until all of these problems have been solved. The spirit of pragmatism tells us that taking action is the top priority, because we can only solve these problems through action and participation.

Acknowledgment

This chapter is a reprint from: WANG, Chengbing, & DONG, Ming. (2019). Education and the reconstruction of a democratic society: Two main themes in Dewey's philosophy of education. *Beijing International Review of Education*, *1*(4), 645–657.

Notes

1 People indirectly influenced by personal activities result in the public. When they realize the indirect influence that they receive and thus consciously unite themselves, the found the State, which is just the politically organized public.

EDUCATION AND THE RECONSTRUCTION OF A DEMOCRATIC SOCIETY 265

2 Generally speaking, philosophers in China have discussed in detail the philosophical significance of John Dewey's idea of community and its role in the revival of Dewey's thoughts
since the end of the twentieth century. See Yang and Wang (2014) and Wang (2002, 2010).

References

Campbell, James. (1995). *Understanding John Dewey: Nature and cooperative intelligence*. Open Court.

Campbell, James. (1998). *Dewey's conception of community*. In Larry A. Hickman (Ed.),
(pp. 23–42). Indiana University Press.

Cohen, David. (1988). Dewey's problem. *The Elementary School Journal, 98*(5), 427–446.

Dewey, John. (1980). Democracy and education. In Jo Ann Boydston (Ed.), *John Dewey,
the middle works, 1899–1924, Vol 9: 1916*. Southern Illinois University Press.

Dewey, John. (1981). Experience and nature. In Jo Ann Boydston (Ed.), *John Dewey, the
later works, 1925–1953, Vol 1: 1925*. Southern Illinois University Press.

Dewey, John. (1982). Reconstruction in philosophy. In Jo Ann Boydston (Ed.), *John
Dewey, the middle works, 1899–1924, Vol 12: 1920* (pp. 77–202). Southern Illinois
University Press.

Dewey, John. (1983). Human nature and conduct. In Jo Ann Boydston (Ed.), *John Dewey,
the middle works, 1899–1924, Vol 14: 1922*. Southern Illinois University Press.

Dewey, John. (1984). The public and its problems. In Jo Ann Boydston (Ed.), *John Dewey,
the later works, 1925–1953, Vol 2: 1925–1927* (pp. 235–372). Southern Illinois University
Press.

Dewey, John. (1984). Individualism, old and new. In Jo Ann Boydston (Ed.), *John Dewey,
the later works, 1925–1953, Vol 5: 1929–1930* (pp. 41–144). Southern Illinois University
Press.

Dewey, John. (1987). Education and social change. In Jo Ann Boydston (Ed.), *John
Dewey, the later works, 1925–1953, Vol 11: 1935–1937* (pp. 408–420). Southern Illinois
University Press.

Dewey, John. (1987). Liberalism and social action. In Jo Ann Boydston (Ed.), *John Dewey,
the later works, 1925–1953, Vol. 11: 1935–1937* (pp. 1–61). Southern Illinois University
Press.

Dewey, John. (1988). Experience and education. In Jo Ann Boydston (Ed.), *John Dewey,
the later works, 1925–1953, Vol 13: 1938–1939* (pp. 1–188). Southern Illinois University
Press.

Dewey, John. (1988). Creative democracy – The task before us. In Jo Ann Boydston
(Ed.), *John Dewey, the later works, 1925–1953, Vol 14: 1939–1941* (pp. 224–230). Southern
Illinois University Press.

Eldridge, Michael. (1996). Dewey' faith in democracy as shared experience. *Transactions
of The Charles S. Peirce Society, 32*(1), 11–30.

Hildreth, R. W. (2011). What good is growth? Reconsidering Dewey on the ends of education. *Education & Culture, 27*(2), 28–47.

Li, Qiang. (2012). Discrimination on the premise of Dewey's idea of educational growth. *Educational Research and Experiment, 30*(4), 63–66 [李强：“杜威教育生长观的前提辨析”，《教育研究与实验》，2012 年，第4期，第63–66页。].

Liang, Shuming. (2005). *Collected works of Liang Shuming* (Vol. 7). Shandong People's Publishing House [梁漱溟：《梁漱溟全集》第七卷，中国文化书院学术委员会编，济南：山东人民出版社，2005 年。].

Schutz, Aaron. (2001). John Dewey and "a paradox of size": Democratic faith at the limits of experience. *American Journal of Education, 109*(3), 287–319.

Tu, Shiwan, & Hu, Zhongping. (2011). Transcending Dualism of knowledge and activity – A restatement of Dewey's teaching theory. *Journal of Higher Education, 32*(7), 24–31 [涂诗万，扈中平：“超越知识与活动的二元对立——杜威教学思想再认识”，《高等教育研究》，2011 年7月，第32卷，第7期，第24–31页。].

Wang, Chengbing. (2002). How to understand the revival of John Dewey's pragmatism. *Academic Forum, 25*(12), 23–27.

Wang, Chengbing. (2010). On John Dewey's view of community and the contemporary significance of Dewey's philosophy. *Man and Ideas, 22*(12), 111–129.

Westbrook, Robert. (2010). *John Dewey and American democracy.* Stanford University, 1980.

Yang, Shoukan, & Wang, Chengbing. (2014). *Pragmatism's trip in China.* China Social Sciences Press [杨寿堪，王成兵：《实用主义的中国之旅》，北京：中国社会科学出版社，2014 年。].

Zhang, Mei, & Zhang, Licheng. (2011). On Dewey's philosophy and contemporary value of democratic community. *Journal of University of Jinan, 21*(6), 72–75 [张梅，张立成：“论杜威的民主共同体理念及其当代价值”，《济南大学学报（社会科学版）》，2011 年，卷21，第6期，第72–75页。].

Index

aesthetics   79, 81, 83, 119, 141, 215

Alexander, Thomas M.   155, 160, 215

Analects   1, 171, 177, 180, 181, 185, 186, 195, 196, 198, 208, 213, 222–224, 227, 228, 230, 250

Artificial Intelligence (AI)   X, 5, 237

associated life   57, 62, 215, 222

becoming   100, 108, 141, 159, 172–175, 177–181, 198, 230, 248

person(s)   1–5, 226

Beijing Normal University   X, 4, 30, 42, 114, 115, 126, 214

Bergson, Henri   72, 100–102, 104

Buddhism   IX, 2–4, 95, 111, 132, 151–153, 155, 162, 163

Nichiren Buddhism   X, 152, 153, 155

Cai, Yuanpei   29, 43, 96, 131, 136

causation   152, 160–164

Chang, Daozhi   119, 121–123, 125, 127, 128

Chen, Baoquan   117, 118

Chen, Duxiu   96

Chen, Heqin   13, 16–17, 19, 29, 63, 68, 94

child-centered   3, 13, 16, 22, 30, 33, 62–64, 71, 258

Chinese education   X, 2, 3, 5, 9, 10, 12–16, 18, 20, 23–26, 28–33, 46, 47, 51, 68, 80, 94, 104–106, 114, 125, 128, 230

classical study   5, 195, 197, 198, 203

classics   IX, 27, 88 195, 197, 203–205, 208

Columbia University   11, 17, 29, 30, 43, 44, 46, 51, 94, 116, 127, 137, 138

community   X, 5, 41, 87, 93, 96, 97, 101, 108, 109, 165, 169–171, 173–175, 177–179, 182–186, 188–190, 207, 223, 225, 228, 238, 243, 255, 258–265

comparative   2, 10, 23, 99, 128, 189, 214, 236

education   26

method   195

perspectives   2, 3, 9

Comparative Education Institute   251

Confucian   IX, 2, 4, 5, 11, 14, 27, 59, 88, 93–111, 138, 141, 169–171, 177, 179–181, 183–188, 194, 195, 197, 199, 203–205, 213, 214, 222–224, 228, 229, 238–240, 243, 244, 246, 249, 250

Confucian Democracy   138, 171, 194, 250

Confucianism

early   5, 212, 213, 215, 222–224, 226, 229

neo-   IX, 85, 88, 99, 111

new   IX, 96, 97, 106, 111

Confucius   1, 12, 23, 27, 43, 94, 97, 100–102, 104, 107, 108, 136, 140, 171, 177, 178, 179, 183, 185, 187, 189, 191, 195–198, 209, 213, 222–224, 226, 227, 230, 238–240, 244, 249, 250

conservative   4, 32, 97, 98, 100, 101, 121, 140

creative/creativity   X, 5, 16, 26, 30, 33, 45, 46, 62, 65, 154, 174, 178–180, 183, 185, 191, 205, 208, 213, 218, 219–221, 226, 228, 229, 242, 246

culture/cultural   IX–XI, 10, 11, 14, 15, 18, 20, 21, 27, 42–44, 46, 52, 53, 55, 58, 62, 65, 67, 69, 80, 85–87, 90, 93, 94, 96–101, 104–107, 109–111, 121, 123, 124, 132, 135–137, 139, 143–145, 155–157, 164, 168–170, 172, 176, 178–180, 186, 188–191, 194–196, 200, 204, 225, 226, 241, 242, 244–246, 248, 250, 255, 258

curriculum   13, 19, 21–26, 63, 64, 68, 105, 109, 115, 116, 119, 121, 123, 163, 197, 201, 203, 205, 206, 208, 236

customs/customary   5, 57, 59, 61, 62, 107, 109, 140, 178, 184, 195, 203, 207

Dao (道)   169, 179, 187, 196, 197, 228

democracy   2, 5, 12–14, 17, 21, 25–28, 30, 32–34, 43, 45, 53, 54, 57, 58, 62, 68, 69, 71–73, 86, 93, 96, 99, 100, 103–105, 107, 108, 110, 115, 117, 119–128, 132–134, 136–138, 142, 143, 146, 170, 171, 176, 187, 189, 190, 193, 194, 199–201, 204, 205, 208, 214, 229, 230, 250, 255, 259–264

Deng, Xiaoping   20, 80

Dewey, John

Confucius 12, 27, 43, 94, 102, 108, 136, 171, 187, 189, 191, 195, 213, 238–241, 244, 249, 250

experience 2–5, 15, 16, 21, 23–25, 27, 33, 53–57, 61, 62, 64–66, 70, 82–86, 117, 123, 155, 156, 171, 172, 175, 176, 182, 183, 186–188, 205, 213, 215–224

habits 55, 57, 59, 61, 62, 140, 157, 170, 171, 190, 201, 204, 221, 222, 244, 256, 263, 264

Hu Shi 3, 42–44, 51–55, 58–60, 65–67, 70, 72, 78, 90, 94, 116, 124, 128, 132, 136, 137, 139, 213, 214

individuality 3–5, 13, 26, 28–31, 57–62, 67–69, 80, 170–174, 182, 187, 190, 191, 213, 215–229, 240–244, 258–260

individuals 2, 14, 18, 19, 24, 58–62, 67–69, 104, 120, 154, 156, 160, 165, 177, 183, 200, 215–222, 229, 243, 255, 256, 258–260, 264

inquiry 3, 26, 52–57, 62, 65, 66, 70, 80, 82, 83, 86, 87, 136, 140, 155, 157, 158, 161, 164, 165, 188, 194, 207, 245, 260–263

Liang Shuming 4, 81, 93–112, 214, 229, 256

misinterpretation 3, 52–54, 58, 62, 65, 69, 70, 143

narrative IX, 114, 115, 169, 191

reconstruction 12, 61, 62, 65, 68, 87, 242, 254–258

science 27, 43, 79, 89, 93, 105, 132, 139, 140, 142, 154, 158, 176, 187, 202, 203, 245, 260, 262

society/social 16, 31, 58–61, 87, 142, 143, 176, 199, 200, 255, 259, 260

Dewey Center, the 23–25, 31

Dewey's lectures 12, 17, 21, 30–32, 52, 67, 72, 81, 118, 119, 138, 145

Dewey's visit of China X, 1, 3, 4, 10, 12, 13, 15, 16, 28, 31, 34, 41–46, 78, 114, 125, 136, 249

dialogue 1–4, 27, 30, 32, 43, 94, 102, 111, 138, 151, 152, 157, 161, 163, 168, 171, 189, 190, 195, 213, 264

Ding, Wenjiang 97, 98

experience 2–5, 14–16, 21, 23–25, 27, 33, 53–57, 61, 62, 64–66, 70, 82–86, 94, 117, 123, 125, 126, 141, 145, 155, 145, 162, 171, 172, 175, 178, 180, 182, 183, 186–188, 205, 213, 215–224

experimentalism 13, 14, 16–18, 29, 47, 55, 78–80

growth XI, 5, 15, 21, 69, 103, 105, 106, 108, 120, 135, 146, 155, 160, 171, 173–175, 186, 189, 200, 202, 215, 218, 222, 240–244, 247, 249, 250, 254–256, 258, 262

Guo, Bingwen 29, 42, 43, 47, 51, 94, 116

habit(s) 55, 57, 59, 61, 62, 140, 145, 157, 170, 171, 190, 194, 201, 204, 221, 222, 244, 256, 263, 264

Hickman, Larry 10, 15, 25, 152, 157, 161, 163

Hu, Shi 3, 4, 6, 11, 13, 14, 17, 26, 29, 42–44, 47, 51–55, 58–60, 65–67, 70, 72, 78–90, 94, 116, 124, 128, 132, 136, 137, 139, 213, 214

humanism/humaneness 2, 4, 30, 152, 156, 157, 181–183, 196, 239, 243

humanities X, 34, 214, 234–237, 241, 243–250

digital 246–248, 250

education 5, 234, 235, 237, 244, 248, 249

ideology/ideological 11, 16, 18, 54, 67, 70, 81, 97, 107, 102, 169, 188, 214

Ikeda, Daisaku X, 152, 156, 157, 161, 163

immediate/immediacy 158, 219, 220

experience 216, 220, 221

sensibility 213, 224, 229

imperial examination 11, 116

individual/individuality/individualism IX, XI, 2–4, 5, 13, 14, 18, 19, 21, 24, 26, 28–31, 54, 57–62, 67–69, 71, 80, 95, 99, 100, 103, 104, 108, 111, 120, 122, 137, 142, 154–156, 160, 170–173, 176, 177, 183, 184, 191, 201, 208, 213, 215–229, 240–244, 255, 256, 258–260, 263, 264

inquiry 3, 26, 52–57, 62, 65, 66, 70, 80, 82, 83, 86, 87, 140, 136, 140, 155, 157, 158, 161, 164, 165, 188, 194, 207, 208, 245, 260–263

intelligence X, 5, 56, 57, 61, 62, 71, 106, 111, 139, 143, 154, 166, 175, 176, 193, 205, 215, 216, 227, 237, 239, 241, 255

inter-action 56, 84, 161, 174, 255

Jiang, Menglin 26, 29, 42, 43, 47, 51, 53, 59, 66–68, 94, 132

Jiangxue (讲学) 107, 109

Junzi (君子) 196, 197, 223–225, 228, 230, 238, 240, 250

INDEX 269

Kaojuxue (考据学) 87, 89
Kilpatrick, William Heard 46
knowledge 4, 19, 21, 22, 29, 42, 46, 54–57, 65, 66, 79, 81, 82, 84, 85, 87, 95, 97–99, 105, 106, 115, 122, 126, 127, 137, 143, 153–155, 160, 166, 196, 198, 202, 204–207, 209, 217, 220, 236, 237, 239, 247–249, 259, 260, 263

Lao Zi 85
learning (by doing) 13, 15–17, 21–23, 125, 128
li (礼) 178, 179, 181, 184, 186, 187, 196, 197, 224–228
Liang, Qichao 59, 60, 67, 98, 124
Liang, Shuming 4, 81, 93–112, 214, 228, 229, 256
life (as education) 16, 17, 43
literary canon 205, 206
Lu, Xun 96

Mahayana 4, 151, 152, 155
mainland 1, 3, 6, 12, 17, 41, 45, 214
Mao, Zedong 17, 18, 21, 135, 136, 188
Marxism 1, 14, 132, 136, 137, 214
May Fourth Movement IX, 1, 3, 11, 17, 43, 93, 104, 105, 117, 118, 126, 132, 134, 194, 226, 245
meliorism/melioristic/ameliorate X, 2, 154, 155, 165, 187, 262
metaphysics 79, 81, 82–84, 86, 90, 154, 157–161
method of intelligence 5
mind-heart, the 226
misinterpretation 3, 52–54, 58, 62, 65, 69, 70, 143
modernization 4, 10, 20, 25, 30–32, 43, 45, 46, 55, 68, 96, 105, 137, 212, 213
Modern Education 4, 11, 24, 46, 47, 105, 107, 117, 119, 124
Monroe, Paul 26, 29, 46, 120, 206
Morning Village of Normal School, the 16, 28
Mr. Democracy/Mr. Science 43, 187

Nagarjuna 152, 157, 159, 160, 163
narrative(s) IX, 96, 114, 115, 169, 186, 191
naturalism 4, 82–86, 88, 90, 145, 156, 159, 191, 257
New Cultural Movement 44, 86

Peasant School, the 109, 110
Peking University 41–43, 72, 96, 116, 131, 138, 139, 156, 256, 247
person(s)/personality 13, 58, 59, 62, 176, 177, 187, 191, 199, 201, 205, 259
philosophy/philosophies IX, X, 1–5, 10, 13, 17–20, 23, 24, 28, 31, 34, 51, 55, 69, 79–81, 83, 84, 86, 89, 90, 93, 108, 110, 111, 136, 151, 156, 213–219, 221, 222, 228, 230, 240, 243, 244, 249, 254, 256, 260
philosophy of education/philosophy of life 5, 11, 13, 44, 54, 72, 79–81, 84, 86, 98, 102, 104, 105, 107, 116, 118, 119, 122, 126, 132, 146, 215, 235, 238, 241, 244, 249, 254, 256
positivism 86
potentiality 4, 215, 217, 218, 221, 222, 226–229, 256
pragmatism IX, 2–5, 13, 14, 16, 17, 20, 23, 25, 31, 45, 52, 66, 70, 72, 78–90, 93, 94, 102, 104, 107, 110, 111, 132, 138, 140, 145, 152, 168–171, 183, 189, 214, 249, 250, 264
progress 42, 46, 60, 61, 68, 69, 71, 89, 100, 105, 107, 117, 144, 154, 200, 218, 219, 221
purpose 5, 19, 21, 58, 60, 94, 106, 107, 154, 156, 160, 235, 237, 238, 240, 249, 260

Qianjia School of Textology (乾嘉学派) 88

radical empiricism 4, 160
realism 83, 85, 90, 161, 162
reception IX, 1, 3, 16, 20, 21, 31, 43, 51–53, 70, 79, 89, 90, 111, 137, 213, 214
religion/religiousness X, 4, 65, 83, 97, 156, 160, 171, 181–183, 186–188, 191, 220
Ren (仁) 177, 178
Renxu Education Program (壬戌学制) 63
Republic of China, the 12, 17, 45, 47, 90, 126, 246
revolution 12, 14, 20, 53, 54, 57, 58, 63, 66, 72, 86, 87, 94, 133–135, 137, 138, 170, 188, 235
    Chinese 12
    cultural 20, 188
    industrial 235
    literary 94
ritual IX, 5, 100, 107, 109, 170–172, 178, 179, 181, 184–186, 195–199, 207, 208, 225, 240, 243
rural education 4, 16, 73, 93, 109

science/scientific method   54, 55, 78, 79, 81, 86, 88, 89, 98, 204, 213, 215
science-metaphysics debate   84
self-action   161, 163
  personal   163
self-cultivation   IX, 2, 4, 5, 27, 171, 193, 195, 197, 198, 203–206, 212, 213, 215, 216, 221–229
social Darwinism   61, 67, 70, 137
society   3–5, 9, 12, 13, 16–21, 24, 25, 28–33, 42–45, 53, 57–63, 66–73, 86, 87, 95–97, 103, 105–108, 110, 111, 115, 118, 123, 126, 141–143, 152, 176, 177, 183, 194, 200, 241, 242, 244, 245, 254, 255, 258–263
Spencer, Herbert   59, 61, 67, 85
spiritual renewal   55, 57
Sun, Yat-sen   12, 53, 54, 57, 66, 67, 70, 72

Tang, Junyi   199
Tao, Xingzhi   6, 13, 16, 17, 26–31, 34, 42, 44–47, 51, 53, 66, 68, 73, 94, 132, 137, 213
Taoism/Daoism   IX, 85, 111
Teachers College, Columbia   30, 44, 46, 116, 127
teaching/teacher(s)   10, 12, 13, 16, 17, 19, 21–23, 27, 28, 30, 33, 44, 46, 64, 65, 100, 107, 115, 116, 118, 124–128, 152, 162–166,

186, 197–199, 202, 204, 207, 229, 230, 238, 245, 248, 250, 263
technology   11, 27, 30, 109, 156, 188, 236, 237, 239, 241, 242, 244, 246–249
traditionalism   94, 98
transaction   5, 82, 90, 158, 161–163, 165, 180, 187, 221, 226

US-China relations   10, 27, 33

vitalism   100–102, 104

wisdom   45, 141, 155, 166, 182, 196, 197, 243, 244

Xiangyue (乡约)   109
Xiao (孝)   109, 196
Xinhai Revolution, the (辛亥革命)   53, 58, 72
Xueheng (学衡)   44

Yan, Fu   59

Zhang, Dongsun   98
Zhang, Junmai   98
Zhongyong (中庸)   180, 181, 185, 186, 213, 222, 224, 225, 230
Zhu, Xi   88, 209

Printed in the United States
by Baker & Taylor Publisher Services